Managing U.S.-Soviet Rivalry

Also of Interest

† *Presidential Decisionmaking in Foreign Policy: The Effective Use of Information and Advice,* Alexander L. George

† *Change in the International System,* edited by Ole R. Holsti, Randolph M. Siverson, and Alexander L. George

† *Studies on a Just World Order, Volume 1: Toward a Just World Order,* edited by Richard Falk, Samuel S. Kim, and Saul H. Mendlovitz

† *Studies on a Just World Order, Volume 2: International Law and a Just World Order,* edited by Richard Falk, Friedrich V. Kratochwil, and Saul H. Mendlovitz

† *Globalism vs. Realism: International Relations' Third Debate,* edited by Ray Maghroori and Bennett Ramberg

U.S. Policy in International Institutions: Defining Reasonable Options in an Unreasonable World, Special Student Edition, Updated and Revised, edited by Seymour Maxwell Finger and Joseph R. Harbert

Nuclear Deterrence in U.S.-Soviet Relations, Keith B. Payne, with a Foreword by Colin S. Gray

Arms Control and Defense Postures in the 1980s, edited by Richard Burt, with a Foreword by Robert E. Osgood

§ *Arms and Politics, 1958–1978,* Robin Ranger

† *China, the Soviet Union, and the West: Strategic and Political Dimensions for the 1980s,* edited by Douglas T. Stuart and William T. Tow.

† *NATO—The Next Thirty Years: The Changing Political, Economic, and Military Setting,* edited by Kenneth A. Myers

† *The War System: An Interdisciplinary Approach,* edited by Richard Falk and Samuel S. Kim

† *The Domestic Context of Soviet Foreign Policy,* edited by Seweryn Bialer

† *The Soviet Union in the Third World: Successes and Failures,* edited by Robert H. Donaldson

† *U.S.-Soviet Relations in the Era of Détente,* Richard Pipes

† *The Soviet Union in World Politics,* edited by Kurt London

The Angolan War: A Study in Soviet Policy in the Third World, Arthur Jay Klinghoffer

† Available in hardcover and paperback.
§ Available in paperback only.

Westview Special Studies
in International Relations

Managing U.S.-Soviet Rivalry:
Problems of Crisis Prevention

Alexander L. George, with contributions by
Coit D. Blacker, Barry M. Blechman, George W. Breslauer,
Gloria Duffy, Paul Gordon Lauren, Larry C. Napper,
Janne E. Nolan, Alan Platt, and I. William Zartman

This book examines the lessons of the U.S.-Soviet experiment with détente in the 1970s, with particular attention to the effort to develop a basis for cooperating in crisis prevention. The authors, less concerned with who was to blame for the failure of détente than with understanding the flaws in its conceptualization and implementation, have joined efforts to analyze the difficulties the two superpowers experienced in their attempt to avoid dangerous confrontations and crises that would damage the overall détente relationship.

The book includes case studies of several Middle East conflicts, the Angolan crisis of 1975, the Rhodesian conflict, the Ogaden war of 1977–1978, the abortive U.S.-Soviet talks on limitation of conventional arms transfers to third areas, and the Soviet combat brigade in Cuba. It also provides an analysis of preventive diplomacy as a strategy for mediating third-area conflicts and avoiding superpower confrontations and offers guidelines for reshaping U.S. relations with the Soviet Union and for moderating competition for influence in the Third World.

Alexander L. George is Graham H. Stuart Professor of International Relations, Stanford University. His first book, *Woodrow Wilson and Colonel House* (1956), written with his wife, Juliette L. George, is widely regarded as a classic study of the role of personality in politics. He is also author of *Deterrence in Foreign Policy* (with Richard Smoke, 1974), which won the 1975 Bancroft Prize, *The Limits of Coercive Diplomacy* (with David K. Hall and William E. Simons, 1971), *Propaganda Analysis* (1959), *The Chinese Communist Army in Action* (1967), and *Presidential Decisionmaking in Foreign Policy* (Westview, 1980). The other contributors to this volume are political scientists, historians, foreign service officers, and members of other government and research institutions. They specialize in affairs relating to the Soviet Union, international security, and arms control.

Managing U.S.-Soviet Rivalry: Problems of Crisis Prevention

by Alexander L. George

with contributions by
Coit D. Blacker
Barry M. Blechman
George W. Breslauer
Gloria Duffy
Paul Gordon Lauren
Larry C. Napper
Janne E. Nolan
Alan Platt
I. William Zartman

Westview Press • Boulder, Colorado

Westview Special Studies in International Relations

Quotations from *White House Years* by Henry Kissinger (Copyright © 1979 by Henry A. Kissinger) are reprinted by permission of Little, Brown & Co.

Copyright © 1983 by Westview Press, Inc.

Published in 1983 in the United States of America by
  Westview Press, Inc.
  5500 Central Avenue
  Boulder, Colorado 80301
  Frederick A. Praeger, President and Publisher

Library of Congress Cataloging in Publication Data
George, Alexander L.
  Managing U.S.-Soviet rivalry.
  Includes bibliographical references and index.
  1. United States—Foreign relations—Soviet Union—Addresses, essays, lectures.
2. Soviet Union—Foreign relations—United States—Addresses, essays, lectures.
I. Title.   II. Title: Managing U.S.-Soviet rivalry.
E183.8.S65G446 1983   327.73047   82-16076
ISBN 0-86531-500-0
ISBN 0-86531-501-9 (pbk.)

Printed and bound in the United States of America

10 9 8 7 6 5

Contents

Preface

In 1978 I was invited to participate in the Pugwash Workshop on "Political and Psychological Aspects of Crisis Management and Prevention" held in Geneva, Switzerland, in December of that year. The invitation provided an opportunity to reflect on the failure of efforts the United States and the Soviet Union had made during the high point of détente to moderate their competition in third areas in the interest of crisis prevention, a failure that had importantly contributed to the erosion of public support for détente in the United States.

The paper ("Towards A Crisis Prevention Regime in U.S.-Soviet Relations") that I presented at the workshop generated unexpectedly lively discussion. The idea that the two superpowers might cooperate more effectively in order to avoid diplomatic confrontations and dangerous crises in third areas drew a variety of critical observations. A number of workshop participants felt that superpower cooperation for crisis prevention might be a good idea in principle but was simply not attainable in practice. Some regarded the idea as overly idealistic and somewhat naive. Others dismissed it on other grounds, saying that given the marked deterioration of the détente relationship in recent years it was now too late to expect cooperation of this kind. These members of the workshop at least agreed that the objective of U.S.-Soviet cooperation to avoid dangerous forms of competition in third areas was desirable, if not feasible. Others, however, were not at all sure that superpower cooperation of this kind was a good idea because it might lead to some kind of U.S.-Soviet condominium that would operate at the expense of weaker states.

Not unexpectedly, Soviet participants in the workshop favored the idea; they regarded the development of a U.S.-Soviet crisis prevention regime as neither impractical to begin with nor a dead issue. The Soviet participants maintained that there had already been instances of cooperation in crisis prevention, and they agreed with my suggestion that it would be useful to study past successes and failures with a view to strengthening cooperative efforts.

With the encouragement of Dr. David Hamburg, M.D., chairman of the workshop conference, and Graham Allison, a participant, I decided to undertake research on the origins, workings, and defects of the two crisis prevention agreements that Nixon and Brezhnev had signed at their summit meetings in 1972 and 1973 and, further, to subject the whole complex problem of crisis prevention to a more searching examination. Research grants in 1979 from the Rockefeller and Ford foundations, which I acknowledge with pleasure, enabled me to pursue the project and to draw others into it as well.

In 1980 I wrote a preliminary report on the project that was published as a working paper by the Center for International and Strategic Affairs, U.C.L.A.[1] This proved to be a fortunate development in that it brought the project to the attention of other scholars and made it possible to interest a number of them in participating as contributors to the present volume.

In the meanwhile I have had opportunities to present preliminary findings and have benefited from incisive discussion at several meetings: at the World Congress of the International Political Science Association held in Moscow in August 1979, at a conference at Brown University in April 1981 organized by Mark Garrison, director of the Center for Foreign Policy Development, and at a conference on "Dealing with International Conflicts in the 1980s" held in Oslo in July 1981 under the auspices of the Norwegian Institute of International Affairs and organized by its acting director, Dr. Daniel Heradstveit.

So many persons have offered useful suggestions and comments as the project developed that it is impossible to list them here in expressing my warm appreciation. Special thanks are extended to John Marcum for helpful comments on my case study of Angola that appears in Chapter 9. I am especially grateful to a number of former government officials—William Hyland, Mark Garrison, Winston Lord, William Quandt, Joseph Sisco, and Helmut Sonnenfeldt—who provided background information for the chapters I have contributed to the book.

For their confidence in the importance of the project and their encouragement to proceed with it I am indebted to Alex Dallin, Robert Legvold, Murray Marder, Enid C. B. Schoettle, John Steinbrunner, John Stremlau, and Samuel Wells, Jr. The Wilson Center of the Smithsonian Institution kindly provided me with visiting scholar privileges in the autumn of 1979. As on many previous occasions David Hamburg has provided the most helpful kind of intellectual stimulation and encouragement for my research.

For unfailing cheerful administrative support, I am indebted, as always, to Mrs. Arlee Ellis and for remarkably efficient secretarial help to Mrs. Alyce Adams and Mrs. Willa Leonard.

Finally, I want to convey a deeply held appreciation to my collaborators in this volume for their willingness to draw on their special knowledge to undertake original research for this project and to express my admiration for the quality of the chapters they have contributed.

It will become quickly evident to the discerning reader that we have not dealt with all aspects of the global competition of the two superpowers. A number of case studies are presented in this book but many other instances of U.S.-Soviet rivalry—some successfully managed, others not—remain to be examined from the standpoint of their implications for crisis prevention. Nonetheless, because the problem is an urgent one, we have not hesitated to formulate theories and to draw lessons from the historical experience that we have examined. Especially at a time when détente has collapsed and the two superpowers are drifting into a confrontational relationship once again, it is possible to become overly pessimistic regarding the likelihood that U.S. and Soviet leaders can find ways of moderating their global rivalry. Certainly the United States and the Soviet Union will continue to pursue divergent foreign policy interests and compete for influence in the third areas. But they also continue to have a common interest in managing their rivalry in order to avoid war-threatening crises and also less dangerous confrontations that further damage their overall relationship. In the pages that follow we have examined a number of strategies, modalities, and requirements for crisis prevention, not all of which depend upon U.S.-Soviet cooperation. We offer these as guidelines for foreign policy planners and as working hypotheses to stimulate reflection and additional research by specialists on international conflict.

Alexander L. George

Notes

1. The paper was initially presented as one of four invited lectures delivered at a conference held at the U.C.L.A. Center in honor of Bernard

Brodie. Titled "Towards a Soviet-American Crisis Prevention Regime: History and Prospects," it was issued as ACIS Working Paper No. 28 and will appear in a forthcoming volume, *National Security and International Stability,* edited by Bernard Brodie, Michael Intriligator, and Roman Kolkowicz.

Managing U.S.-Soviet Rivalry

1
Introduction

Alexander L. George

The current crisis in U.S.-Soviet relations is less immediately threatening of thermonuclear disaster than was the Cuban missile crisis. But, paradoxically, precisely for this reason the current situation offers a more complex challenge to U.S. and Soviet leaders. Crises such as the one that emerged from Soviet deployment of medium-range missiles into Cuba in 1962 often have an unexpected catalytic effect in facilitating an improvement in relationships between the two parties in the dispute. The shared experience of being on the brink of a possibly disastrous war aroused strong incentives to reexamine the past attitudes and policies that had led to the dangerous crisis. Thus, even before the missile crisis was settled, it had triggered a new determination on the part of both Kennedy and Khrushchev to concert efforts, once the crisis was behind them, to develop a more constructive relationship between their countries. It is often remarked in this connection that the character for "crisis" in the Chinese language has a dual connotation: "threat" and "opportunity." Certainly both of these dimensions of crisis were experienced by U.S. and Soviet leaders during the Cuban missile case. As a result, Kennedy and Khrushchev moved expeditiously to relax tensions and, beginning with the partial test ban treaty of 1963, to create the building blocks of a less volatile and more constructive relationship.

The present crisis in U.S.-Soviet relations is of a different order. It poses dangers that are less urgent and opportunities that are more ambiguous and more difficult to grasp than those of the missile crisis. But although the deterioration of U.S.-Soviet relations has not yet led to a new war-threatening confrontation, it has created dangerous instability and uncertainty in the relationship of the two nations.

Because the present crisis creates no sense of urgency and poses no deadlines for remedial measures, each side has shifted to the other side the burden of responsibility for taking corrective action to restore, or at least to prevent further damage to, the relationship.

Since the Soviet invasion of Afghanistan doomed whatever possibility that had still remained for Senate ratification of SALT II, each side has succumbed to the temptation of developing its own self-serving account—all the more dangerous because sincerely believed—of why the détente relationship has eroded. As a result, U.S. and Soviet leaders are now operating with sharply conflicting explanations for what went wrong and who is to blame. Neither side displays much willingness to examine critically those of its policy premises and policies that contributed during the decade of the seventies to the development of the present impasse. Instruments of self-justification and assertions of blame are steadily hardening, fueled by new developments such as those in Poland. This inflexibility is leading inexorably to a new group of rigid mind-sets and mutually hostile images that will severely constrain efforts to halt the drift into a new version of the cold war.

At some point in the future, perhaps to bring to a halt the costly and dangerous new arms race that is underway or perhaps as a result of a confrontation in some part of the world that poses the danger of war, the two sides may agree to a new relaxation of tensions. They may then commit themselves to the goal of defusing Cold War II and to the task of developing a more constructive relationship. But will there be a sufficiently clear understanding of what will then be required to place Soviet-U.S. relations on a more stable footing? Unless the time that is now available is utilized by the two sides to develop an informed, balanced, sufficiently shared understanding of what went awry in the détente of the seventies, an improvement in the tone of U.S.-Soviet relations is likely to result in no more than temporary palliatives that will give way to a new round of disillusionment and hostility.

This book provides an analytical appraisal of the "lessons" of the experiment in détente of the seventies. It is concerned less with assessing blame for the erosion of détente than with understanding flaws in détente's conceptualization and implementation. Accordingly, the chapters that follow seek to identify those constraints that made Soviet and U.S. leaders unwilling or unable to limit their striving for influence and advantage in third areas. The chapters that follow will also analyze various types of difficulties that complicated whatever efforts the two superpowers did make—or might have made—during this period to cooperate in one way or another to avoid confrontations and to prevent their global rivalry from damaging their overall détente relationship.

"Crisis prevention," as it was called, was one of the important objectives of the détente process that Nixon and Brezhnev set into motion in 1972. This objective, however, was not clearly defined. Soviet leaders were interested primarily in avoiding crises that raised the danger of war between the two superpowers. Nixon and Kissinger shared this hope, but, increasingly over time, they emphasized that crisis prevention should include the avoidance of crises in third areas resulting from or exacerbated by assertive Soviet behavior that damaged Western interests *even though* these crises did not create the danger of a U.S.-Soviet military clash. The conception of détente held by U.S. leaders and, indeed, by many congressional leaders and much of the interested public, therefore, included a belief that Soviet adherence to the goal of "crisis prevention" implied a willingness on Moscow's part generally to moderate its foreign policy behavior in third areas. The failure of the two sides to agree on what the goal of crisis prevention was to mean in practice was obscured in the Basic Principles Agreement (BPA) that Nixon and Brezhnev signed at their first summit in Moscow in May 1972. This critical ambiguity was the source of much later difficulty in the seventies.

If the objective of crisis prevention was left ambiguous, the means for achieving the objective articulated by Nixon and Brezhnev only compounded the likelihood of failure and discord. Thus the Basic Principles Agreement was described as providing "rules" of conduct by means of which the global competition of the two superpowers would be somehow moderated and regulated. Subsequently, as we shall see, assertive Soviet foreign policy actions in third areas were regarded as in violation of the rules or code of conduct embodied in the BPA. In turn, the Soviets could and did denounce the unilateral policy pursued by the Nixon administration in the Middle East as contrary to their understanding of détente.

One of the purposes of this study, therefore, is to evaluate the crisis-prevention regime the two sides created in 1972 to serve as part of the détente process. A few preliminary remarks regarding the primitive state of crisis-prevention theory in the burgeoning field of strategic studies will serve to introduce the subject and to indicate its relevance to the development of U.S.-Soviet relations in the post–World War II era.

Contributors to strategic studies have given a great deal of attention to a variety of urgent problems that the two superpowers have had to cope with since World War II—problems of deterrence, crisis management, escalation, coercive diplomacy, arms control, war termination, and avoidance of misperceptions and miscalculations. The equally important problem of how the United States and the Soviet

Union might moderate their global rivalry in order to avoid dangerous confrontations has received much less attention. Crisis prevention may well be considered the orphan of strategic studies.

Part of the explanation for the relative neglect of crisis prevention in strategic studies is that during the cold war the highest priority had to be given to deterrence and crisis management. The great gulf that divided the United States and the Soviet Union appeared to make futile the utilization of diplomacy and negotiation to resolve or moderate the conflicts of interest between the two superpowers. This is not to say that preventing crises was not an important objective during the cold war, but policymakers relied largely on deterrence for that purpose. Deterrence was supposed to discourage encroachments on the free world that might result in crises or war. Even during the cold war, however, the two superpowers found other ways to limit their competition and rivalry in third areas to avoid potential conflict. A notable instance of cooperation in crisis prevention was the Austrian State Treaty of 1955 that created a neutral buffer state and removed it from the ongoing competition between the two superpowers in Europe. To be sure, use of the term "cooperation" in this instance should not obscure the fact that Soviet leaders were willing to accept a unified, neutralized Austrian state to replace the division of that country into occupied zones because they hoped that this concession would further their objective of encouraging neutralism in West Germany.[1] Nonetheless, the Austrian case is instructive and encouraging in calling attention to the fact that possibilities for U.S.-Soviet cooperation in crisis prevention may emerge simply from mutual selfish interest, even in the absence of détente. Admittedly, the creation of neutral buffer states can take place only under special conditions that may or may not emerge again in the future, as, for example, in Afghanistan.

Another instance of U.S.-Soviet cooperation in the interest of crisis prevention occurred during 1961–1962 when President Kennedy, determined to decommit the United States from its involvement in Laos, induced Premier Khrushchev to help bring about a cease-fire there as a prerequisite to American participation in a reconvened Geneva Conference on Laos. At their Vienna summit talks in June 1961 the two leaders agreed that what was at stake in Laos was not worth the risk of a superpower confrontation. In a joint communiqué Kennedy and Khrushchev pledged "their support for a neutral and independent Laos under a government chosen by the Laotians themselves, and of international agreements for insuring that neutrality and independence...."[2] The two sides recognized that achievement of the objective would require cooperation by other states, and they agreed to act in order to ensure the compliance of members of their political blocs. Eventually, in July 1962, a cease-fire was established, and fourteen nations signed the Declaration on the Neutrality of Laos. Although these arrangements were short-lived, they did enable Kennedy to achieve his overriding objective of conducting "an honorable retreat from a strategically weak position."[3]

Although deterrence was an essential part of U.S. containment policy, it soon became evident that it was an unreliable, imperfect strategy at middle and lower levels of conflict. Because deterrence did not prevent dangerous crises from erupting during the cold war, the United States and the Soviet Union were forced to develop an understanding of the requirements and modalities of crisis management. Fortunately the two superpowers have been remarkably successful in cooperating during crises to avoid military clashes between their armed forces. But both sides recognized that skill in crisis management could not be counted upon to prevent war in the future; especially after the Cuban missile crisis, both sides saw the need to move beyond reliance on deterrence and beyond cooperation in managing crises to deal more directly with conflicts of interest that pose the danger of war. The onset of détente following the Cuban missile crisis brought new opportunities and new modalities for crisis prevention, for now there was a shared disposition to utilize negotiation and accommodation to settle some of the long-standing conflicts of interest that had been bones of contention during the cold war.

In the era of détente, U.S. and Soviet leaders rediscovered and applied some diplomatic practices for moderating conflicts that had been a standard feature of classical diplomacy. They negotiated settlements of many unresolved issues of the cold war, stabilizing the status of Berlin and recognizing the existence of the two German states and the division of Europe.

However, the problem of regulating U.S.-Soviet rivalry and competition in the Third World—the Middle East, Africa, Asia, and the Caribbean—still remained. U.S.-Soviet competition in these areas was and continues to be a matter of concern for several reasons. It frequently adds to regional or local instability, even when one or the other side does not intend to exploit such instability for immediate gains. It increases the likelihood of dangerous crises, such as the Middle East war of October 1973, into which the two superpowers may be drawn. And last but not least, during the 1970s the inability of the two sides to moderate their global competition steadily undermined U.S. support for the entire policy of détente with the USSR and, in particular, for the ratification of SALT II.

The objective of crisis prevention and, related to it, the task of managing U.S.-Soviet rivalry in third areas takes on special urgency, to be sure, in the modern era of thermonuclear weapons. But the problem is not a novel one in the history of international relations, and, despite the special complexities crisis prevention has acquired in the modern era, it has not become so different and so idiosyncratic that we can afford to neglect giving some attention to how great powers have gone about it in the past. Accordingly, this study includes a detailed review of the means utilized by the great powers that made up the European balance-of-power system to regulate and manage their rivalry in order to avoid unwanted crises. In Chapter 3 Paul Gordon Lauren identifies and illustrates nine diplomatic options that the European powers utilized from time to time to regulate their rivalries and to reduce the likelihood of crises: (1) arrangements for mutual and collective decisionmaking; (2) the creation of buffer states; (3) establishment of neutral states, zones, and demilitarized areas; (4) arrangements for localizing and restricting regional conflicts; (5) agreements to limit the flow of weapons and other resources to third areas; (6) careful delineation and definition of interests and/or areas of involvement in third areas; (7) agreements to avoid unilateral action in third areas and, if necessary, to intervene only via multilateral action; (8) arrangements for the pacific settlement of disputes; (9) agreements for communication and advance notification of unilateral actions to be taken in third areas.

The various modalities employed by European statesmen in the nineteenth century were imbedded, to be sure, in a relatively well-defined and well-structured international system, and the leaders of the great powers were generally committed to this system's preservation and maintenance. The European balance-of-power system was shattered by World War I and has not since been replaced by a well-defined or well-organized global international system. The modalities of crisis prevention and the experience gained during the nineteenth century, of course, can only be selectively adapted for possible use by the United States and the Soviet Union in the contemporary era. Explicit spheres-of-influence arrangements that played an important role in regulating the rivalry of the great imperial powers in the nineteenth century are much less acceptable in the modern era. Similarly, collective decisionmaking by the superpowers to settle regional conflicts, even when it is undertaken in order to reduce the likelihood of possibly dangerous U.S.-Soviet confrontations, is likely to trigger fears of a superpower condominium that will harm the interests of other states. Notwithstanding these and other constraints, familiarity with the experience of and modalities for crisis prevention in the nineteenth century should be at least suggestive, and some of these modalities may be adaptable and usable in the contemporary situation. Particularly useful for this purpose are some of the general issues and "lessons" derived by Lauren from his examination of the nineteenth century experience.

The experiment in devising a U.S.-Soviet crisis-prevention regime was an integral part of a broader, complex set of understandings, hopes, and expectations associated with the détente process that Nixon and Brezhnev set into motion. The mutual desire to manage U.S.-Soviet global competition was one of several objectives that together composed the long-range goal of détente. The workings and the fate of the quite imperfect crisis-prevention regime were expected even at the time to be inextricably related to the development of the détente process as a whole. It is neither desirable nor possible, therefore, to separate a study of the experiment in crisis prevention from an analysis of the whole détente arrangement entered into by Nixon and Brezhnev in 1972. Chapter 2 examines the objectives and strategy of the Nixon-Kissinger approach to détente and notes the extent to which the Soviet and U.S. conceptions of détente overlapped and diverged. The new relationship that the two super-powers set out to create to replace the confrontation-prone relationship of the cold war was burdened from the start by critical ambiguities and latent disagreements on important issues that created mutually inconsistent hopes and expectations regarding the benefits to be realized from that new détente relationship.

Particularly important were the divergent understandings regarding the countries' respective roles in the Middle East that the two sides brought back from the Moscow summit. The importance of these misperceptions can be fully appreciated only if U.S.-Soviet rivalry in the Middle East prior to the signing of the Basic Principles Agreement is taken into account. From this earlier experience Kissinger had concluded that the Soviets were bent on perpetuating a "no war, no peace" situation in the Middle East. He advocated and finally persuaded Nixon to pursue a policy aimed at rolling back Soviet influence in the Middle East. Far from modifying this policy objective after détente was formalized in the Basic Principles Agreement, Kissinger, as he makes clear in his memoirs, used détente to further his efforts to reduce or eliminate Soviet influence in the Middle East. Because of its critical importance, the subject of Soviet policy in the Middle East from 1967 to 1972 is analyzed by George Breslauer in Chapter 4, which reexamines the thesis that the Soviets wished to maintain a state of hostility, without an actual war, in the Middle East.

Chapter 5 traces the origins of the Basic Principles Agreement and explains how and why it came to contain important ambiguities regarding the objectives and modalities of crisis prevention. Chapter 5 also traces the origins of a second crisis-prevention agreement, the Agreement on Prevention of Nuclear War, signed by Nixon and Brezhnev at their second summit in June 1973, and calls attention to obscurities and loopholes in its provisions for U.S.-Soviet consultation to head off dangerous crises. This chapter also notes the absence of any policy planning in the Nixon administration either before or after the signing of these agreements to address the problems and procedures for implementing them.

In Chapter 6 Coit Blacker describes the Soviet conception of détente and the Soviet leaders' motivation in seeking to formalize it in the Basic Principles document. Blacker also infers from statements by Soviet leaders at the time the considerable hopes and expectations they attached to the BPA, a highly important document in their view.

The first test of the U.S.-Soviet crisis-prevention regime was a particularly severe one. Chapter 7 traces developments leading to the Egyptian-Syrian attack on Israel of October 6, 1973. Were the policies and actions of the USSR and the United States in the Middle East in the sixteen months since the signing of the Basic Principles Agreement and the three months since the Agreement on Prevention of Nuclear War (APNW) consistent with the obligations both countries had assumed to moderate their rivalry and to cooperate in crisis prevention? Had the two sides operated with restraint since then and avoided seeking unilateral advantages in the Middle East, as the BPA seemed to require? Did the Soviet leaders consult those of the United States, as the APNW seemed to require, in order to work together to head off the war Moscow knew the Egyptians and Syrians were planning to initiate? After the war was over did U.S. and Soviet leaders conduct a postmortem on its outbreak in order to clarify and strengthen their crisis-prevention regime?

For Soviet and U.S. leaders to avoid damaging and dangerous confrontations, they must be willing, in the first instance, to moderate their competition. If their striving for advantage at each other's expense in a particular situation proceeds beyond a certain point, they may have great difficulty controlling further escalation of the conflict before it results in a crisis. This excessive competition is essentially what has led to a number of third-area conflicts since the high point of détente in 1972. The Angolan crisis of 1975 is a case in point. Following the Portuguese government's decision to grant independence to its Angolan colony, the United States and the Soviet

Union entered into a low-level, covert competition to enhance the capability of the rival Angolan liberation movements that were jockeying for power within the framework of the provisional government created by the Portuguese authorities. As Larry C. Napper notes in Chapter 8, the balance of forces that existed between the weak Angolan movements was extremely unstable and sensitive to even relatively minor increments of assistance from outside the country. As a result, the battlefield situation was highly volatile and could not be stabilized sufficiently to permit a political solution.

If U.S. policy in Angola suffered because it lacked sensitivity to the local and regional political terrain, the United States learned its lesson there and was able to deal much more effectively with the situation in Rhodesia in the next few years during the transition from white rule to the creation of Zimbabwe under the control of the black liberation movements. This point emerges with great clarity in Napper's comparison of the Angolan and Rhodesian cases.

Even when one or both superpowers are inclined to limit competitive involvement in a particular area, other factors, some not clearly recognized, may operate to draw them in further. Analysis of two strikingly different cases in Chapter 9 shows how the dynamics of escalation can operate to create confrontations that were unexpected and unwanted by one or both superpowers. The inability or unwillingness of the United States or the USSR to control a local ally at an early stage in a regional conflict is a persistent problem and one that can be seen at work, for example, in the War of Attrition between Egypt and Israel in 1970. This case and the Angolan crisis of 1975 offer striking evidence of the difficulty the two superpowers experience in improvising ad hoc ground rules to limit their competition to acceptably low levels. Our analysis of these two cases reveals how easy it is for the United States and the USSR to stumble into confrontations as a result of misperceptions, miscalculations, poor intelligence and analysis, faulty signaling, and bad judgment. There were, as a result of all these factors, missed opportunities for avoiding escalation of superpower involvement in both the War of Attrition and the Angolan case.

The Angolan case is of particular importance in our study because the setback suffered there by the United States badly eroded domestic support for détente and deepened political controversy over policy toward the USSR. Accordingly, Chapter 9 provides a detailed reconstruction and critique of the development of Kissinger's Angolan policy during 1975.

The Ogaden War of 1977–1978 between Somalia and Ethiopia, in which a large-scale Soviet-assisted intervention by Cuban forces once again proved decisive, was another signpost on the road to the collapse of U.S.-Soviet détente. In his detailed study of this case in Chapter 10, Larry C. Napper demonstrates how the intricate political-military terrain of the region influenced superpower policies in ways the powers had not foreseen and identifies factors that inhibited serious U.S.-Soviet crisis-prevention efforts. Despite the Carter administration's often-declared intention not to link Soviet behavior in third areas with other aspects of U.S.-Soviet relations, the U.S. government began to make such linkages after the Ogaden War. Negotiations with the USSR for a limitation of military deployments in the Indian Ocean were suspended, and National Security Advisor Zbigniew Brzezinski warned that Soviet aggressiveness in the Third World could have an adverse effect on a SALT II agreement.

The shelving of the Indian Ocean talks was soon followed by the collapse of another crisis-prevention initiative the Carter administration had undertaken. During Secretary of State Cyrus Vance's trip to Moscow in March 1977 the United States and the USSR had agreed to establish working groups on eight subjects: conventional arms transfers, chemical weapons, antisatellite weapons, limitations on military forces in the Indian Ocean, civil defense, radiological weapons, prior notification of missile test firings, and comprehensive nuclear test ban negotiations. Preliminary consultations on limitation of conventional arms transfers (CAT) were held with the Soviets in Washington in December 1977. A second round of talks was held in May 1978 and a third round in July 1978. During the course of these talks progress was made with the Soviets, but at the same time important differences developed within the Carter administration, and the talks foundered after the fourth round in December 1978 over the issue of whether to discuss constraints on arms transfers to Asia. Discussion of this issue was opposed by a number of senior officials in the administration on the ground that even pro forma discussions with the Soviets on the matter could create problems in U.S. relations with key nations in Asia and damage U.S. security interests.

Because arms transfers are an integral element in the superpowers' competition for influence in third areas, the CAT talks are of particular interest for the present study. In Chapter 11 Barry M. Blechman, Janne E. Nolan, and Alan Platt present a detailed analysis of the Carter administration's effort to develop, together with the Soviets, a framework within which multilateral agreements for limiting arms transfers might be worked out. These authors discuss the disagreements that developed at high levels within the Carter administration; they explain some of the reasons for the collapse of the CAT talks and assess the prospects for future negotiations of this kind.

From the very beginning, strategic arms limitation had been the centerpiece of détente, and the mutual U.S.-Soviet interest in it had provided impetus for the process of détente as a whole. As U.S.-Soviet relations worsened during the Carter administration, President Carter and Secretary of State Vance tried to shield SALT II from the growing disillusionment with détente by attempting to decouple it from other aspects of U.S.-Soviet relations. By the time negotiation of SALT II was finally completed in mid-1979, very little was left on the agenda of the détente process other than the new arms control treaty. Indeed, the staging of the summit meeting in Vienna in June 1979, at which Carter and Brezhnev affixed their signatures to the SALT II treaty, struck many observers as something of a historical anomaly because it was out of phase with the sour relationship that had developed between the two countries. There was, in fact, little else on the summit agenda for the two leaders to discuss; the momentum of détente was virtually stopped, and the problem Carter and Brezhnev now faced was to prevent, if possible, a retrograde movement in their countries' relationship. Nonetheless, the two leaders did reaffirm their adherence to the Basic Principles Agreement of 1972, though without any fanfare, for so much of promise contained in the so-called "charter" of détente had failed of accomplishment. By 1979 the Basic Principles Agreement had become an unpleasant reminder of past failures rather than the road map to a more promising future.

One of the interesting anomalies of crisis prevention is that when the United States and the Soviet Union do not succeed in avoiding a confrontation, they may still be able to terminate it with a crisis-prevention agreement for the future. The terms on which the two sides conclude a crisis may provide the basis or starting point for such an agreement. Despite certain ambiguities in the quid pro quo between Kennedy and Khrushchev that ended the Cuban missile crisis—the United States' agreeing not to invade Cuba in the future in return for Soviet removal of all "offensive" weapons from the island—and the uncertain status of their agreement, the quid pro quo was to provide a useful basis for avoiding crises over Cuba in the future. As Gloria Duffy shows in Chapter 12, the Kennedy-Khrushchev agreement of 1962 constituted a valuable reference point that was effectively utilized by Nixon and Kissinger in 1970 to avoid a potential confrontation over apparent Soviet efforts to build a nuclear submarine base in Cuba. A second potential superpower crisis was averted in April-May 1978. This time the issue was whether

the shipment of a small number of Soviet MIG-23 aircraft to Cuba
violated the 1962 agreement prohibiting deployment of offensive
weapons to the island. For a while the matter of the MIG-23s
threatened to become embroiled in domestic controversy over the
larger issue of U.S.-Soviet relations, but this question was quickly
clarified and settled through diplomatic channels with little, if any,
harm to the overall relationship of the two powers.

Such was not to be the case a year later, however, when U.S.
intelligence discovered a Soviet combat brigade in Cuba. Duffy traces
in detail the developments associated with this discovery that soon
plunged the Carter administration into a major diplomatic confrontation with the Soviet Union. Her case study richly documents
various difficulties that crisis prevention can encounter, all of which
seem to have occurred in this instance of what former CIA Deputy
Director Ray Cline aptly labeled an exercise in crisis "mangling"
rather than crisis management. Indeed, the ineptness of administration
leaders in this case, their poor management of the emerging intelligence
on the brigade, their failure to define for the public its limited
significance for U.S. security, their committing themselves publicly
to removing the brigade before adequate thought had been given to
whether and how this objective could be accomplished—these and
other mistakes paralyzed the ability of diplomacy to find a cooperative
solution to the problem comparable to those that the two sides had
been able to achieve in 1970 and 1978.

The Soviet combat brigade crisis, although it was indeed a "tempest
in a teacup," as it was called, had important political-diplomatic
consequences. As Duffy notes, it contributed greatly to the erosion
of support for Senate ratification of SALT II. In addition, Carter's
belated decision to take an aggressive diplomatic stance on the brigade
issue to compensate for his inability to induce the Soviets to comply
with his earlier demand for a change in the brigade's status marked
a transition for the United States from cooperative back to confrontational methods of dealing with the USSR.

The disposition to return to a confrontational posture received
new impetus with the Soviet invasion of Afghanistan at the end of
1979. President Carter's response to Afghanistan and, more recently,
President Reagan's response to developments in Poland and other
policies undertaken by Reagan's administration have reinforced the
drift to a confrontational relationship.

The Soviet policies and behavior that many American observers
regard as having been responsible for the unraveling of détente are
familiar and do not need recapitulation. Soviet accounts, of course,
give an entirely different picture of what went awry and why. It is

not easy to deduce from these public statements how Soviet leaders privately explain the undoing of détente. In Moscow's view, the unraveling of détente and the subsequent adoption by Washington of confrontational policies indicate that influence over U.S. policy has shifted to groups that have not reconciled themselves to "objective" changes in the world situation and in the balance of forces that place the USSR in a position of "equality" with the United States.

In Chapter 13 George Breslauer addresses the question of why détente failed and evaluates four explanations that have been advanced. He finds insufficiently persuasive the argument that the embryonic collaborative relationship between the superpowers was critically undermined by either Soviet or U.S. bad faith. Each of these two explanations is one-sided and oversimplified; each fails to take into account that no clear definition of obligations existed against which validly to measure bad faith or good faith. A third explanation is that détente collapsed due to mutual misperceptions, missed signals, and misunderstandings. Although there is more to this thesis, it places too much emphasis on accidental factors and downplays the fact that misperceptions and misunderstandings often emerge from more fundamental differences in perspective. A fourth thesis regards the failure of détente as inevitable, given the structure of the international system and differences between the ideologies and foreign policy interests of the United States and the Soviet Union, the different assets and needs that shaped their foreign policies, and the different stages in their involvement in the global arena. This latter explanation, Breslauer argues, has considerable merit, though it is too quick to conclude that the experiment of détente could have ended only as it did.

Briefly summarized, Breslauer's own explanation is that notwithstanding a mutual U.S.-Soviet interest in developing a mixed competitive-collaborative relationship, détente failed "because each side tried to define the terms of competition and the terms of collaboration in ways more geared to maximizing unilateral advantage than to expanding the mutual interest in institutionalizing the relationship." Breslauer provides an analytic framework for and observations that are highly relevant to efforts to reconceptualize détente on a more realistic basis and to understand better the requirements for maintaining a mixed competitive-collaborative relationship.

Crisis prevention, particularly as regards confrontations that pose the danger of war, is a continuing objective of the foreign policy of both superpowers. Nonetheless, there have been and will continue to be many situations in which the United States and the Soviet

Union do not wish to moderate competition for influence or are unable to control the dynamics of escalation. It is fortunate, therefore, that cooperative U.S.-Soviet strategies do not exhaust the means available for crisis prevention in their relationship. Each side can and does pursue unilateral policies to this end that do not require the cooperation or active participation of the other side. The various instruments of containment—including deterrence, alliance arrangements, and economic assistance to strengthen allies and neutrals—are unilateral policies that, skillfully and realistically employed, can contribute to the moderation of superpower rivalry and reduce the likelihood of confrontations.

In addition, a variety of other diplomatic modalities and other international actors can contribute to reducing the occasions for the competitive involvement of great powers in third areas. Insofar as possible, "preventive diplomacy" of this kind should be encouraged, because it reduces the burden on the ability of the superpowers to cooperate effectively to limit the crisis potential of their competition. In Chapter 14, I. William Zartman analyzes the successes and failures of many past efforts at preventive diplomacy in order to develop a better understanding of how it can be utilized more effectively in the interest of avoiding or curtailing superpower competition.

Finally, Chapter 15 evaluates the poorly conceptualized efforts of the two superpowers to develop a crisis-prevention regime and discusses the problems encountered in their attempts to implement this regime within the framework of the evolving détente process. It identifies alternative models of a crisis-prevention regime and assesses their requirements and practicality. Chapter 15 emphasizes that crisis prevention is best viewed not as a strategy but as an objective of foreign policy for which various strategies may be appropriate and effective in different types of contexts. Crisis-prevention strategies may be cooperative enterprises involving both superpowers; indeed, certain types of confrontations are unavoidable unless the two sides find the motivation and modalities for moderating and regulating their competition. But other types of confrontations can be avoided via unilateral policies undertaken by one or the other power or with the assistance of third parties and do not require U.S.-Soviet cooperation.

Notes

1. These brief observations draw upon a case study of the Austrian State Treaty prepared for this study by Casey Gwinn.

2. *Department of State Bulletin* 44 (June 26, 1961), p. 999.

3. This discussion of the Laos crisis of 1961–1962 draws directly from David K. Hall, "The Laotian War of 1962 and the Indo-Pakistan War of 1971," in *Force Without War: U.S. Armed Forces as a Political Instrument,* ed. Barry M. Blechman and Stephen S. Kaplan (Washington, D.C.: Brookings Institution, 1978), pp. 135–221.

Détente: The Search for a "Constructive" Relationship

Alexander L. George

The emergence and development of détente between the United States and the Soviet Union after the Cuban missile crisis of October 1962 reflected a mutual desire to move away from the dangerous confrontational policies of the cold war. For détente to go beyond a mere relaxation of tensions, however, a new relationship between the two superpowers would have to be forged that would moderate the conflictive elements of their earlier relationship. But what kind of nonconfrontational competition would be considered desirable and feasible by each side? Could Soviet and U.S. leaders agree on what form the new relationship should take? Could they find a way to coordinate their policies and behavior to bring about and stabilize a more satisfactory relationship? Could each government cultivate and ensure sufficient domestic support for the new relationship it sought to develop with its adversary?

The Framework of Foreign Policy

We can understand better the challenging task undertaken by Soviet and U.S. leaders and the vicissitudes the détente process was to encounter if we place our discussion within a general foreign policy framework. The essential task of foreign policy is to develop and manage relationships with other states in ways that will contribute to the protection and enhancement of one's own security and welfare. This objective requires that policymakers clearly define their state's interests, differentiate these interests in terms of their relative importance, and prudently weigh the costs and risks of pursuing them. In doing so the policymakers must recognize, analyze, and deal with conflicts of interest with other states. When a mutually acceptable accommodation of conflicting interests with another state is not possible, policymakers must narrow and manage the issues at dispute in ways that reduce these issues' potential for generating destructive conflicts or for contaminating the entire relationship with the other state. The development and management of relationships with other states also requires makers of foreign policy to recognize common interests and to develop policies for promoting them.

So conceived, foreign policy requires that those responsible for conducting it in Washington and Moscow address several interrelated questions. So far as U.S. policy toward the Soviet Union is concerned, the first task is to determine the type of international order and superpower relationship to be created. This definition is necessarily a long-term objective with which more immediate actions and short-term policies must be consistent. Moreover, the relationship sought with the Soviet Union must be judged to be not merely desirable but also feasible. That is, U.S. leaders must have reason to believe that the Soviet Union is capable of and willing to enter into—or accept—such a relationship with the United States. In addition, they must have sufficient resources and appropriate skills for bringing about that kind of relationship.

Second, U.S. policy toward the Soviet Union requires a conception of "grand strategy" for utilizing available resources and employing various policy initiatives and instrumentalities for moving toward the achievement of the preferred U.S.-Soviet relationship. Strategy is not a detailed blueprint or a single scenario for moving from the present starting point to the desired end point; it should be conceived in more flexible terms. A good strategic sense indeed requires judgments as to why certain policy initiatives and options are likely to be effective. But in choosing and implementing a strategy, policymakers must be sensitive to how things are working out and must remain alert to unexpected developments that require adjustments of policy along the way.

Finally, an adequately conceptualized foreign policy will address the question of choosing appropriate tactics and specific means for implementing the grand strategy. Tactics, so conceived, refer to those day-to-day actions of a more specific kind that are initiated by one or the other of the superpowers or taken by a superpower in response to developments that directly or indirectly affect in some way the evolving U.S.-Soviet relationship.

These three components of a well-conceptualized U.S. policy toward the Soviet Union are, of course, interrelated. Whether the long-range U.S.-Soviet relationship aimed at will prove to be feasible depends on whether policymakers can formulate an appropriate strategy. Successful implementation of a sound strategy, in turn, requires that policymakers use available resources and options skillfully, improvise effectively along the way, and avoid allowing the choice of day-to-day tactics to dominate and displace a sense of strategy. An element of improvisation and adaptation is always necessary in foreign policy, but it should exist within the framework of a well-thought-out basic strategy that is designed to further the type of relationship desired with the other state in question. Tactics will not long substitute for such a strategy, and strategy in turn cannot be articulated without being linked to a longer-range goal that is considered desirable or at least acceptable. All this is not to say that foreign policy must be staked on achieving one and only one particular outcome. If alternative outcomes to the development of U.S.-Soviet relations are acceptable, U.S. policy can pose these alternatives to the Soviet Union and attempt to devise strategy and tactics accordingly.

The Origins and Rationale of Détente

These general observations about foreign policy serve as background for understanding the emergence of the détente relationship between the two superpowers in the early 1970s. This relationship did not occur accidentally; it was the result of developments in world politics that U.S. and Soviet leaders recognized and to which they attempted to adapt. Détente—whatever it was intended to be—emerged as a result of policy choices made by the two leaderships, and it was shaped by the way in which they concerted efforts in an attempt to define a new relationship that would replace the acute hostility of the cold war, moderate the conflict potential inherent in their competition, and strengthen cooperation in issue areas in which they believed their interests converged. A mutual desire to move in the direction of détente had been powerfully stimulated by the brush with thermonuclear disaster during the Cuban missile crisis in 1962. Important steps to develop a new relationship were taken during the remainder of the decade of the sixties, but détente was given stronger impetus and moved more steadily in the early seventies during President Nixon's first administration.

It is important to recognize that while both Nixon and Brezhnev wanted to develop a more constructive relationship between their countries, they came to the task from different starting points and with expectations that differed in important respects. As is noted in Chapter 5, Soviet leaders wanted to formalize their relationship with the United States in such a way as to encourage that country to accept the emergence of the Soviet Union as a coequal, with all that they hoped this status would imply for the future. Nixon and Kissinger, on the other hand, wanted to draw the Soviet Union into a new relationship that would enable the United States to maintain as much of its declining world position as possible. They were very much aware of changes in the arena of world politics that were eroding the predominant position that the United States had enjoyed during the cold war. As Nixon put it in his annual foreign policy report to Congress of February 25, 1971: "The postwar order in international relations—the configuration of power that emerged from the Second World War—is gone. With it are gone the conditions which have determined the assumptions and practices of United States foreign policy since 1945."[1]

Nixon had in mind the many important changes that had taken place in the international and domestic environments in which U.S. foreign policy had to operate—and to which it had to adjust. Many of the nations that had suffered severe losses and dislocation from World War II had now substantially recovered. New nations had emerged as the major European powers divested themselves of or were deprived of their colonies. Many of these new states displayed an increasing ability to maintain their independence and to avoid becoming battlegrounds for the cold war. U.S. leaders were experiencing increasing limits on the ability of their policies to influence world developments unilaterally (of this limitation, the Vietnam War was only the most obvious and tragic example). U.S. strategic military superiority was giving way to the achievement of strategic parity by the Soviet Union. But, at the same time, the nature of the Communist challenge to the free world had changed with the passing of Moscow's near-monolithic control of the international communist movement and the emergence of competing centers of communist doctrine, power, and practice. In this regard, particularly, the Sino-Soviet split seemed to offer new opportunities for the United States to benefit from the possible emergence of a tripolar balance of power. Finally, U.S. foreign policy had to adjust to the growing constraints on resources available to support the ambitious global role the United States had assumed during the cold war and to the increasing domestic unwillingness in the United States to continue support of costly commitments abroad.

Accordingly, Nixon and Kissinger sought to introduce a web of incentives into the relationship with the Soviet Union that would give the USSR a stake in a more stable world order and induce it to operate with greater restraint. Thereby, a measure of *self*-containment on the part of Soviet leaders would be introduced that would reduce the need for the United States to rely exclusively on deterrence, as it had in the cold war, to contain the Soviet Union. In time, it was hoped, the new positive relationship with the Soviet Union would become part of a new, more stable international system.

Nixon and Kissinger were intrigued by the possibility of establishing a tripolar balance of power among the United States, the Soviet Union, and the People's Republic of China (PRC). By developing a measure of friendly relations with both of these archrivals, the United States could hope to reduce potential threats to its interests from either side and to induce each to a greater measure of cooperation with U.S. policy. By using its unique middle position in such a triangular relationship, Washington could tilt or threaten to tilt in favor of one or the other of the two Communist rivals, as the situation required, to promote its own interests. Thus, Nixon and Kissinger believed the United States could compensate for the decline of U.S. power by presiding over a tripolar system that, if delicately managed by Washington, would give the United States additional leverage with which to protect and enhance its interests. The immediate, indeed urgent, U.S. objective to be realized by employing this neo-Bismarckian strategy was, of course, to induce both the PRC and the Soviet Union to influence North Vietnam to end the war in Southeast Asia on terms acceptable to the United States.

This is not to say that Nixon and Kissinger viewed the PRC in the same terms as they did the Soviet Union. The major potential threat to U.S. security and worldwide interests was perceived to emanate from the growing power of the USSR. The People's Republic was not a superpower and would not become one for many years. And so the major incentive behind Nixon's improving relations with the PRC was to obtain leverage for developing a more satisfactory relationship with the Soviet Union. The threat of a positive development of U.S. relations with the PRC was supposed to be part of the "stick" that, coupled with the "carrot" of various positive inducements held out to Soviet leaders, would draw the USSR into a more constructive relationship with the United States, one in which the Soviets would restrain themselves from employing the growing power and new global reach of their military forces to make advances at the expense of U.S. interests and the interests of its allies. In seeking an improved relationship with the Soviet Union Nixon and Kissinger did not expect to eliminate competition but merely to moderate it in order to reduce its dangerous potential. What, then, was the grand strategy for achieving the important long-range objective? It had a least four major components.

First, there was Nixon's willingness to acknowledge that the Soviet

Union was entitled to the same status of superpower that the United States enjoyed. Aware of the importance that Soviet leaders attached to achieving equality of status, Nixon was willing to recognize this equality symbolically in various ways, via summit meetings and in rhetorical statements. What "equality" was to mean in practice, however, was left undefined and, as is noted in chapters 5 and 6, was soon to become a source of fundamental friction in the détente relationship.

A second element in the strategy was Nixon's conditional willingness to recognize and legitimize, as it were, the changes in Eastern Europe that had taken place following World War II. Nixon agreed to go along with the long-standing Soviet desire for a formal document, signed by all European countries as well as by the United States, that would recognize existing borders in Europe and thereby tacitly confirm the dominant role of the Soviet Union in Eastern Europe. This recognition of borders was part of the Helsinki Declaration that finally emerged in 1975 from the Conference on Security and Co-operation in Europe. Nixon agreed to move in this direction at the first summit meeting held in Moscow in May 1972, coupling his acquiescence with a Soviet agreement to regularize the status of West Berlin and to engage in discussions for mutual and balanced force reductions in Europe.

A third element of the strategy called for a variety of formal agreements with the Soviet Union to further mutual cooperation and interdependence. Most important in this connection were to be agreements for limiting the strategic arms race. In this respect the two sides were initially successful, and SALT I was signed at the Moscow summit in May 1972. In addition, Nixon offered the prospect of important, continuing economic and technical assistance to the Soviet Union as a major inducement for giving Soviet leaders a strong stake in the evolving constructive relationship. Nixon's willingness to move in this direction was part of the set of understandings developed at the Moscow summit. The trade agreement signed in October, however, was to encounter unexpected difficulties in the Senate and was never carried out, a failure that dealt a major blow to the further development of détente.

The fourth element of their strategy was particularly important to Nixon and Kissinger, even though they recognized its difficulty and elusive character. They hoped that the momentum of détente would lead in time to the development of a new set of norms and rules for regulating and moderating the global competition and rivalry between the two superpowers. A start was made in this direction with some of the provisions of the Basic Principles Agreement (BPA) that Nixon and Brezhnev signed at the Moscow summit. These provisions were characterized as an agreement by the United States and the Soviet Union to cooperate in "crisis prevention," as compared to "crisis management." But neither the objective of crisis prevention nor the means for attempting to achieve it were conceptualized in any useful detail. In fact, the agreement to cooperate in order to prevent dangerous crises contained important ambiguities and unresolved disagreements that were to become a major source of friction.

The Basic Principles Agreement included much more than a vague commitment to crisis prevention. It was described by U.S. and Soviet leaders as a sort of charter for détente. In the document the two sides agreed to adopt the practice of periodical high-level meetings, to continue efforts to limit armaments, and to develop economic, scientific, and cultural ties between their two countries on a long-term basis in order to strengthen their relationship. Nixon tried to clarify the nature of the Basic Principles Agreement for the U.S. public by referring to it as a road map. But terms such as "charter" and "road map" were inadequate designations for what had been accomplished and agreed to in Moscow. So far as the analogy of a road map is concerned, the Basic Principles Agreement was certainly not a Cooks Tour itinerary for a voyage that the two parties had decided to embark upon together; it was more in the nature of Lewis and Clark's rough description of uncharted territory. Perhaps a more apt way of characterizing the Basic Principles Agreement would be to explain it as a contractual arrangement of a very loose and general character, the specifics of which remained to be filled in over time. In the parlance of nineteenth-century European diplomacy, the BPA (together with associated agreements and understandings arrived at in the Moscow summit) was in the nature of a rapprochement (i.e., an arrangement in which both sides express a desire to search for agreements on various issues) but went beyond that to an entente (in which the two sides recognize a similarity of views and interests that, however, are limited to certain issues). In other words, as George Breslauer puts it, U.S. and Soviet leaders set out to develop a new relationship of restrained "collaborative competition" to replace the "confrontational competition" of the cold war. However, important aspects of the collaborative competition, including what has been called the "rules" of détente, remained to be worked out.

Ambiguities and Latent Disagreements

As will be noted in later chapters the BPA itself left ambiguous the operational meaning of the "equality" that Nixon seemed willing to accord the Soviet Union. The available historical record does not indicate that the two sides discussed what their interests were in different parts of the world or that they attempted to assess how seriously their conflicting interests might clash and set into motion efforts to determine how these interests might possibly be accommodated in due course. It is possible, of course, that Nixon and Brezhnev shied away from a fuller discussion of their latent disagreements and accepted the ambiguities of the BPA, hoping for the best. Whatever the explanation, the absence of clarification and assessment of conflicting interests left the leaders' mutual desire for a relationship of collaborative competition highly vulnerable to future developments. Mutually inconsistent hopes and expectations emerged regarding the benefits to be realized from the new détente relationship.

Two issues were particularly important areas of misunderstanding. One concerned the respective interests of the two superpowers in the Middle East and the role the two sides would play in the search for a solution of the Arab-Israeli conflict; the other issue had to do with the limits the United States would observe in developing closer ties with the People's Republic of China (PRC).

With respect to the Middle East, as subsequent chapters will trace in detail, Soviet leaders hoped that Nixon's recognition of the Soviet Union's "equality" and the fact that they were cooperating to further the détente process implied a willingness on the president's part to recognize Moscow's interests in the Middle East and to continue efforts to develop a joint U.S.-Soviet approach to a settlement of the Arab-Israeli dispute. But, without disabusing the Soviets of this notion, Nixon and Kissinger planned to continue the concealed policy they had been pursuing, which was aimed at reducing Soviet influence in the Middle East as much as possible. Thus, as Kissinger reveals in his memoirs, "To some extent my interest in détente was tactical, as a device to maximize Soviet dilemmas and reduce Soviet influence as in the Middle East."[2] It was not long after the high point of détente at the Moscow summit that the divergence of the two superpowers' expectations and policies regarding the Middle East began to manifest itself. The divergence was heightened by circumstances surrounding the outbreak of the Arab-Israeli war of October 1973. Nonetheless, the war ended, seemingly with provisions for joint U.S.-Soviet sponsorship of negotiations for carrying out the cease-fire provisions. But Kissinger soon placed himself in control, edging the Soviets out of the process, and thereafter engaged in "exclusionary diplomacy" in the Middle East conflict in face of repeated Soviet protests.

Washington's relations with Beijing was another issue with respect to which Soviet hopes and expectations were to be disappointed. Nixon's trip to the PRC preceded by several months the first summit meeting with Brezhnev in Moscow. The Soviet leader could barely conceal his anxiety over the further development of the U.S.-PRC relationship and attempted to entice the United States into a common front against Beijing. This attempt was turned aside by Nixon and Kissinger, who were intent on developing détente with Beijing precisely so as to obtain leverage against Moscow. Brezhnev pursued the subject on a number of subsequent occasions. "No occasion," remarked Kissinger, "was too unpromising for him to pursue his obsession with China."[3] In a retrospective analysis of the deterioration of U.S.-Soviet relations, William Hyland, Kissinger's close associate during the Nixon-Ford administration, attributes considerable importance to the China factor in the erosion of U.S.-Soviet détente: "The Soviets gradually came to make a U.S. willingness to drop the China option and take up a semi-alliance with Moscow a critical test of detente." Hyland summarizes Brezhnev's efforts in 1972 and 1973 to draw Nixon in this direction, and, continuing, he notes that it was Nixon's rejection of Moscow's desire for "a semi-alliance" against the PRC and Ford's rejection of a similar probe by the Soviet leader at the Vladivostok meeting later "that became one of the decisive factors in the waning of detente."[4] Ironically, therefore, Nixon's and Kissinger's hope of utilizing their détente with Beijing to induce Moscow to behave with restraint in its relations with the United States foundered in the end because it clashed with Brezhnev's own hope that he could exploit détente with Washington in order to isolate the PRC.

Domestic Constraints on Foreign Policy: The Need for Policy Legitimacy

As was already noted, a well-conceptualized policy toward the Soviet Union integrates three elements: a long-range objective with respect to the type of relationship that is desired or considered acceptable; the outlines of a grand strategy for using available resources and policy means for accomplishing that objective; and a sense of appropriate tactics for implementing the strategy. To conduct a long-range foreign policy of this kind, a president must find ways of dealing with the special requirements for democratic control of foreign policy. Public opinion, Congress, the media, and powerful interest groups often assert themselves in ways that seriously complicate and jeopardize the ability of an administration to pursue long-range foreign policy objectives in a coherent, consistent manner. This is a fundamental problem that every president, beginning with Franklin Roosevelt, has encountered in attempting to develop and pursue long-range policy toward the Soviet Union. To cope with the many-faceted domestic constraints on his Soviet policy, the president must achieve a fundamental and stable national consensus, one that encompasses enough of the key members of his own administration, of Congress, and of the interested public. Such a consensus cannot be achieved and maintained by the president simply by his adhering scrupulously to constitutional-legal requirements for the conduct of foreign policy or by his following the customary norms for consultation of Congress or by conducting an "open" foreign policy that avoids undue secrecy and deceptive practices or by attempting to play the role of broker, mediating and balancing competing demands and claims on foreign policy advanced by numerous interest groups.

Neither can a president develop the required consensus merely by invoking the symbols of "national interest" or "national security" on behalf of his policy. Both of these concepts have become so ambiguous and elastic, so shopworn through overuse in the past as political rhetoric for justifying controversial and questionable decisions, that large elements of the public and of Congress are no longer persuaded that an administration's foreign policy actions are appropriate and should be supported merely because a president considers them necessary for national interest or national security.

A president can obtain legitimacy and support for his foreign policy only if he succeeds in convincing the right members of his administration, Congress, and the public that his policy is soundly conceived. "Policy legitimacy," as this critical requirement for effective conduct of foreign policy may be referred to, requires two things: First, a president must convince others that the objectives of his foreign policy are desirable or necessary and therefore worth pursuing—in other words, that his policy is consistent with fundamental national values and will contribute to the enhancement of these values. This is the normative or moral component of policy legitimacy. Second, a president must convince others that he and his advisers know how to achieve the desirable long-range objectives of his policy. In other words, he must convince others that he understands the Soviet Union and the world situation well enough to influence the course of events in the desired direction with the means and resources at his disposal. This is the cognitive component of foreign policy; it must be adequately understood and accepted by Congress and the interested public.

Thus, policy legitimacy has both a normative dimension and a cognitive basis. The normative component of a policy establishes its *desirability* or necessity; the cognitive component establishes its *feasibility.* Policy legitimacy is invaluable, indeed necessary, for the conduct of a long-range policy such as the détente policy pursued by President Nixon. If the president gains this kind of understanding and acceptance of his policy, then and only then does a bipartisan foreign policy become possible. When a president's foreign policy enjoys sufficient legitimacy, the day-to-day actions he takes to implement it become less vulnerable to the many pressures and constraints a democratic political system otherwise imposes on the conduct of foreign policy that jeopardize the chief executive's ability to pursue his goals in a coherent, consistent manner.[5]

Policy legitimacy for détente was necessary also in the Soviet Union but, of course, the problem of domestic constraints on the conduct of a long-range foreign policy of this kind arises in a less acute form in a nondemocratic political system. Nixon and Kissinger were acutely aware of the dimensions of the challenge they faced in obtaining and maintaining sufficient domestic support for their détente policy. In his earlier scholarly study of the Concert of Europe system, Kissinger noted the failure of statesmen of that era to maintain domestic support for their policies. "The acid test of a policy," Kissinger emphasized, ". . . is its ability to obtain domestic support. This has two aspects: the problem of legitimizing a policy within the governmental apparatus . . . and that of harmonizing it with the national experience."[6]

Ironically, in the end Kissinger and the two presidents he served also failed to meet the "acid test" of their policy of détente. The problems they encountered in this respect are sobering and have been discussed elsewhere.[7] Suffice it to say that the erosion of domestic support for their complex détente policy increasingly burdened and eventually crippled the effort to develop détente with the Soviet Union. Critical in this respect was the perception that détente was not effective in dissuading Soviet leaders from embarking on an increasingly assertive policy in third areas. In response to this turn of events, President Ford and Kissinger were forced into making a belated effort to define the rules of détente in such a way as to label assertive Soviet actions as violations or, at least, as contrary to the spirit of détente. As one observer noted, Kissinger's denunciations of Soviet policy in Angola in late 1975 seemed to indicate that he had changed his mind or come to a new awareness as to what détente required: "He did so after he saw that political support for détente in the United States would be difficult to maintain if Moscow did not restrain itself."[8]

Gradually, as the initial promise of détente proved elusive and

concern with Soviet policy in third areas mounted, Kissinger began
to redefine détente's objectives. In his major defense of détente in
September 1974 he had emphasized, still hopefully, that it entailed
"the search for a more *constructive relationship* with the Soviet
Union. . . ." Almost a year later, in July 1975, as William Hyland
notes, Kissinger's emphasis was shifting: "We consider detente a
means to regulate a *competitive relationship. . . .*"⁹ With a further
erosion of domestic support for détente that extended to important
elements of the Ford administration and the Republican party, the
themes of balance of power and containment began to reappear and
to assume new prominence in Kissinger's statements regarding the
objectives of the administration's foreign policy. While it would be
too much to say that détente foundered on the inability of the two
superpowers to manage their rivalry in third areas, the increasingly
assertive character of Soviet foreign policy in the mid-seventies
contributed to erosion of the legitimacy of the détente policy and
became a major issue in the presidential election of 1976, first in
the contest for the Republican nomination, in which Reagan mounted
a strong challenge to President Ford, and then in the presidential
contest between Ford and Carter.

President Carter attempted to retain and strengthen what remained
of the détente relationship, but the efforts of his administration in
this direction were handicapped by inadequate conceptualization of
a comprehensive policy toward the Soviet Union, poor policy implementation, and divided counsels at the highest policymaking level.
If Carter had a clear notion of the type of relationship with the
Soviet Union that U.S. policy should seek to bring about, that
conception was not accompanied by a well-developed idea of grand
strategy or consistently implemented with appropriate tactics. Carter
never succeeded in gaining policy legitimacy and stable domestic
support for his policy toward the Soviet Union. Soviet activities in
third areas continued to be of concern in Washington and further
eroded domestic support for what remained of détente, a trend that
developments in Poland accentuated at the beginning of President
Reagan's administration.

Notes

1. Richard M. Nixon, *U.S. Foreign Policy for the 1970's: Building for
Peace* (Washington, D.C.: Government Printing Office, February 25, 1971),
p. 3.

2. Henry Kissinger, *White House Years* (Boston: Little, Brown & Co.,
1979), p. 1255.

3. Henry Kissinger, *Years of Upheaval* (Boston: Little, Brown & Co., 1982), p. 1173. The various efforts made by Brezhnev in conversations with Nixon and Kissinger to lure the United States into understandings and agreements that would serve to isolate the People's Republic of China or to obtain their acquiescence to possible Soviet moves against the PRC are summarized by Kissinger. (See also pp. 233, 274–286, 294–295; and *White House Years,* pp. 1146, 1251–1252.)

4. William G. Hyland, *Soviet-American Relations: A New Cold War?* (Santa Monica, Calif.: RAND Corp., May 1981), p. 25.

5. For a more detailed discussion of policy legitimacy and its relationship to the long-range objectives of foreign policy, and to the grand strategy and tactics employed, see Alexander L. George, "Domestic Constraints on Regime Change in U.S. Foreign Policy: The Need for Policy Legitimacy," in *Change in the International System,* ed. Ole R. Holsti, Randolph M. Siverson, and Alexander L. George (Boulder, Colo.: Westview Press, 1980), pp. 233–262.

6. Henry Kissinger, *A World Restored* (New York: Houghton Mifflin, 1957), p. 327.

7. George, "Domestic Constraints."

8. Leslie Gelb, *New York Times,* 14 December 1975.

9. Henry Kissinger, "Detente with the Soviet Union," address given September 19, 1974 (*Department of State Bulletin,* October 14, 1974); Kissinger, "The Moral Foundations of Foreign Policy," address given July 15, 1975 (*Department of State Bulletin,* August 4, 1975), as quoted in Hyland, *Soviet-American Relations,* pp. 31–32. (Italics added.)

3
Crisis Prevention in Nineteenth-Century Diplomacy

Paul Gordon Lauren

The many sources of tension and discord in the world make international stability both precious and precarious. Clashes of national interest and ambition combine with competition for power and influence. Conflicts between change and continuity intertwine with claims of sovereignty and exclusive privilege. Images and misperceptions complicate facts, emotions imperil reason, and the presence of armed force, either used or threatened, hovers over all. It is the volatile mixture created by these forces and others that makes the outbreak of a serious crisis so dangerous. Crises can burst out suddenly, threaten vital interests, demand quick decisions, place leaders under severe stress, and raise enormous risks by rapidly approaching the critical threshold between peace and war. Any international crisis has the potential for exploding into violence and endangering the entire diplomatic system. To avoid war by preventing crises in advance thus has been a fundamental preoccupation of statesmen for ages.

Crisis prevention, due to its importance, has attracted the attention of some of the best theoreticians and practitioners in the realm of diplomacy. The distinguished and perceptive French diplomat of the eighteenth century, François de Callières, for example, devoted considerable effort to attempting to understand the subject. His interest and concern centered not so much on managing crises once they had broken out and keeping them within certain bounds as on averting crises in the first place by foresight, restraint, and skillful diplomacy. Mindful of how crises were prevented in the past and deeply worried about the future, he advised his sovereign to realize that a statesman

> must labor to remove misunderstandings, to prevent subjects of dispute
> from arising. . . . He must always assume that there is no prince nor
> state in the world which does not desire to avoid a condition of crisis,
> and that those princes who love to fish in troubled waters will never
> lack the means to stir them up, but that the storms which such men
> conjure up are apt to overwhelm them so that the wise negotiator will
> do all he can to avoid giving provocation. . . .[1]

Crisis Prevention and the
Classical System of Diplomacy

Although the sagacious counsel of de Callières remains as valid
today as when it was written, historical experience reveals that leaders
are more successful in practicing crisis prevention during some periods
than in others. Statecraft in de Callières's own eighteenth century,
for example, generally confirmed his fears instead of his hopes. Nearly
continuous intrigue, conflict, and war characterized the times. "It
was generally accepted throughout the century," writes one authority,
"that relations between the states of Europe were dominated by
greed, fear, and envy."[2] Diplomats thought about the idea of a system
of states and recognized that a balance of power might serve as a
limitation upon aggression[3] but rarely took action to enhance harmony
or to maintain the peace by preventing crises. They largely based
their calculations on narrow self-interest and seldom considered
collective needs of the whole. As historian Friedrich Meinecke commented, "never was the isolation of the power-state carried so
far . . . never, either before or since, did universally European ideas
and interests form such a small part, as they did then, in European
policy of the first rank."[4]

In light of this record from the eighteenth century—and particularly
from the perspective of our own twentieth—the nineteenth-century
practice of crisis prevention appears especially impressive. The statesmen of 1815 and those who followed possessed frightful memories
of the failures bequeathed by previous power plays and of the recent
trauma of revolutionary upheaval and Napoleonic domination. In
the aftermath of disaster they determined that only collective action
designed to forestall cataclysmic war would guarantee future survival.
The chief architects of the new order therefore began to speak explicitly
of the need for a "system" and for considerations based upon what
was "best for the general interest."[5] They understood that in order
to steer between the Scylla of anarchy and the Charybdis of hegemony
by one power, they would have to learn how to prevent crises and
regulate their heretofore dramatically violent competition. The results

of their efforts eventually produced, in the words of scholar Hajo Holborn,

> a European political system whose foundations lasted for a full century. For a hundred years there occurred no wars of world-wide scope like those of the twenty-odd years after 1792. Europe experienced frightful wars, particularly between 1854 and 1878, but none of them was a war in which all the European states or even all the great European powers participated. The European wars of the nineteenth century produced shifts of power, but they were shifts within the European political system and did not upset that system as such.[6]

The remarkable successes of the Great Powers created an epoch of "unprecedented peace" and one that, despite its many problems and imperfections, is still described as the golden age of the "classical system" of diplomacy.[7]

This diplomatic system of the nineteenth century consisted of three major, and interrelated, components. One of these was *structure.* The skilled negotiators who assembled at the Congress of Vienna in 1815 convinced themselves that only a balance of power would be able to preserve the peace so recently won at such great price. They considered that an equilibrium of forces among several states would provide the most critical and realistic structural factor for deterring unilateral attempts at domination. Moreover, they recognized the importance of power rather than ignoring or deploring it and therefore included those capable of affecting the system in their arrangements. Thus they deliberately and wisely refused to let their greed and passion for revenge cripple France and prevent that country from assuming an appropriate role as one of the five Great Powers. Among this select group, the diplomats created a rough parity of power with territory, resources, and population distributed as equitably as possible, adjusting Russian acquisitions in Poland, Austrian gains in Italy, Prussian holdings in the Rhineland and Saxony, and British spoils in the Mediterranean. The statesmen believed that such a structure not only would provide their countries with compensation for their war efforts but would balance strengths against each other, deter aggression, and thereby afford the best guarantee of stability.

The classical system of diplomacy also possessed the element of *shared goals and objectives.* Leaders understood perfectly well that the maintenance of any system required agreement upon fundamental aims by all the major participants. There could be no power so dissatisfied that it questioned the legitimacy of the entire international order and sought the overthrow of the system through revolutionary foreign policy.[8] The assurance of shared goals was the other reason for including France as an integral part of the new framework. Together the Great Powers could agree upon a common purpose: to create a collective security arrangement designed to maintain the peace internally and externally throughout Europe. They sought to insure the survival and independence of themselves by insuring the same for each other. A realistic assessment of security requirements and a remarkable degree of cultural homogeneity convinced them that they all possessed a vested interest in the system. Their goal of preservation could not be achieved unless they accepted the existence of the others and defined their own individual interest in terms of a larger common good. Therefore, they had to strike a difficult balance between the desire to improve, secure, or retain purely selfish objectives on the one hand and the need to maintain the system as a whole on the other. Under this arrangement, armed force could be a permissible or legitimate instrument of policy if it were employed for limited ends. Any war that seriously threatened the existence of another member, however, and thus jeopardized the entire system, had to be prevented.

The third feature of this system took the form of *means* designed to achieve the goals and objectives. Statesmen at Vienna and their successors were not so naive as to think that they had created a utopia or even had protected themselves against future crises simply by redrawing the map or by joining hands for common aims. They recognized that conflict and competition among themselves could not easily be prohibited or eliminated in the real world of international politics. Yet they did believe that such competitive behavior need not be totally arbitrary, haphazard, or unrestrained. By means of certain rules, norms, agreements, understandings, and procedures, such behavior possibly could be regulated and constrained to remain within mutually accepted boundaries. Any changes or adjustments that occurred, therefore, would be *within* the system rather than *of* the system itself. Such means could guide the direction of competition and promote cooperation in the interest of system maintenance, preferably by averting serious and destabilizing conflicts before they even started. To accomplish this end the diplomats created the means of crisis prevention.

Crisis-Prevention Regimes

To maintain and protect this diplomatic system, the Great Powers of Europe deliberately created a wide variety of crisis-prevention regimes. Throughout the nineteenth century, diplomats continually expressed the need to forestall crises "by seeking to introduce into international relations fixed principles," "bounds of legitimate competition," "rules," "regulations," and "limits."[9] They recognized that it would be in "the common interest of the nations . . . to draw up, in a spirit of mutual good will, such conditions as would . . . prevent disputes and misunderstandings."[10] Toward this end, they expended a great deal of effort in developing various "rules of the game" to regulate their competition and thereby prevent crises.[11] These rules sought to coordinate relations, minimize friction, avoid misperceptions and miscalculations, clarify respective interests, establish restraints, and make clear distinctions between legitimate and illegitimate ends and means in the pursuit of policy. The diplomats created some of these rules of accommodation as binding obligations in explicit treaty form with the force of international law. Other rules were more implicit in nature, taking the form of tacit understandings or gentleman's agreements to be honored as moral commitments of customary practice.[12] Together, these various kinds of rules, regulations, norms, agreements, understandings, and procedures established a sophisticated and highly differentiated array of regimes designed to prevent the outbreak of serious crises.

Mutual Consultation and Collective Decisionmaking

Those leaders who gathered at the Congress of Vienna faced the formidable tasks of redrawing the map of Europe, adjusting competing claims for territory and influence, restoring the balance of power and legitimate rulers, and establishing peace on an enduring foundation. They realized all too well that their repeated failure to submerge their individual differences during the Napoleonic wars had nearly cost them the Continent. Pursuit of narrow, selfish interests by separate states in the past had resulted only in disaster. Men like Austrian foreign minister Clemens Prince Metternich, British foreign secretary Robert Stewart Viscount Castlereagh, and their colleagues realized that they could maintain the peace won at such cost on the battlefield only by working together, regulating their competition, establishing collective security, and attempting to achieve common policies. Toward these ends, they believed that mutual consultation and collective decisions would be one of the best means of preventing crises. Precisely for this reason of wanting "to prevent the general Tranquillity . . . from being again disturbed," they signed the Quadruple Alliance, pledging themselves to hold periodic meetings "for the purpose of consulting upon their common interests, and for the consideration of the measures which at each of these periods shall be considered the most salutary for the repose and prosperity of Nations, and for the maintenance of the Peace of Europe."[13]

Ideas for a federation or concert to avert upheavals, of course, had been discussed among publicists back in the eighteenth century. At that time, however, the concept progressed little further than words; no steps were taken to make it operational. Now, with the signing of the Quadruple Alliance, the signatories established themselves as a continuing European directorate, or as what was at first called the Concert of Europe. Due to their political, military, economic, and other powerful resources, the Great Powers considered that they possessed the means and the ability to govern. Without qualms or apologies they arrogated to themselves the right of, and assumed the responsibility for, maintaining peace and stability. Although the arrangement was far from perfect,[14] the Powers impressively overcame many of their serious differences in interpretation of what constituted a danger to their system or in political philosophy and met together in numerous congresses and conferences "to procure some orderly regulation of the competition of interests."[15] Over the period of a century,[16] representatives of these states met with each other on a timely basis at the highest levels when problems emerged. They sought to develop specific understandings when threats to the peace engaged mutual interests and when it became necessary for adjustments in policy to be conducted in concert. Indeed, it was this practice of mutual consultation and collective decisionmaking that produced the wide variety of other crisis-prevention regimes discussed below.

Under the Concert of Europe, leaders frequently sought joint meetings. The following proposal from Napoleon III to Queen Victoria was not at all unusual: "This is a matter for serious reflection. Let us not delay taking a decision until sudden and irresistible events disturb our judgment, and draw us, in spite of ourselves, in opposite directions. I now therefore propose to your Majesty to regulate the present, and secure the future, by means of a Congress."[17]

Mutual consultations and collective decisions could involve all of the Powers, as did creating Belgium in 1831, regulating the straits of the Dardanelles and the Bosphorus in 1841, preserving the Danish crown in 1952, protecting Luxembourg in 1867, resolving several Balkan issues in 1878, and settling African matters in 1885. Or these meetings could require participation of only those states immediately concerned with a particular problem or geographical area,[18] as in the instances of Austria and Prussia dealing with Holstein and Hesse in 1850; Britain and France with Spain evolving a crisis-prevention regime for the western Mediterranean in 1907; and Germany, Britain, and France with Denmark, Sweden, and the Netherlands attempting to avert crises in the North Sea in 1908. In all of these cases, statesmen explained the rationale for their collective actions as being "to obviate the misunderstandings and disputes which might in future arise,"[19] "for diminishing occasions of conflict,"[20] "to remove any suspicion,"[21] and to create "a means adapted for the prevention of conflicts."[22]

Creating Buffer States

Beyond the promise and practice of general consultation, the Great Powers took definite measures to avert the occurrence of crises. They understood, for example, that the presence of powerful neighbors on contiguous territory can readily breed border incidents, misunderstandings, and confrontations. To prevent these dangers, the diplomats of the classical period occasionally created buffer states that physically separated their countries or their respective areas of interest. As described by one statesman, buffers were "constructed in order to keep apart the frontiers of converging Powers."[23] Diplomats declared these states to possess a national existence of their own and to be outside the arena of legitimate international competition. Buffers were endowed with the normal attributes of sovereignty. They generally could conduct their own foreign policies, control their own domestic affairs, and maintain their own armed forces and fortifications. Moreover, to make these states effective as cushions between rivals, buffers were guaranteed their independence by treaty. This feature was an attempt to render aggression less likely by automatically making it an international issue and thereby increasing the potential costs and risks of extending a frontier by violating the independence of a buffer.

One of the most complicated and difficult problems facing statesmen at the Congress of Vienna, for example, concerned the fate of Germany. In the almost complete absence of natural barriers for protection, the intense competition that had led to many wars in the past could easily erupt into crises in the future. To forestall this possibility, the Powers decided to counterbalance their rival claims by keeping the German lands divided into more than thirty separate states. They believed that such an arrangement in central Europe would provide an effective shock absorber or buffer against crises resulting from competition. The arrangement would prevent France from launching an attack to the east, Austria from moving north, and Prussia from expanding to the west. This design was, in fact, what Wilhelm von Humboldt of the Prussian delegation meant when he said that Germany's "true and actual purpose [was] to secure peace, and its whole existence [was] therefore based upon a preservation of balance through an inherent force of gravity."[24]

Many years later, in 1907, the same motivation led the British and the Russians to take similar steps. As each country expanded its influence in Asia, they increasingly began to run into each other, causing considerable friction. The competition became particularly intense in territory contiguous to India, where the rivalries of Britain and Russia clashed directly. In an effort to avert catastrophe in the future, the British sent their able negotiator, Sir Arthur Nicolson, to Saint Petersburg to arrange a settlement in which "the guiding principle was that of the erection of a barrier of buffer regions."[25] The result for the northeast frontier was in the form of the buffer state of Tibet, which physically separated the interests of the two states. According to the official communication stating the rationale for this measure among others, the negotiators "determined to conclude Agreements destined to prevent all cause of misunderstanding between Great Britain and Russia" and to avoid "all cause of conflict between their respective interests" in this area of potential confrontation.[26]

Establishing Neutral States,
Zones, and Demilitarized Areas

The Powers similarly sought to prevent the outbreak of crises by deliberately creating neutral states and zones in areas of potential friction. Toward this end they mutually identified territories lying directly in the geographical path of possible expansion or conflict and assigned to them a special status, more distinguished than that of a mere buffer: neutrality. Collective guarantees declared the area to be inviolable and announced that here only a hands-off policy would be viewed as acceptable. Neutralized territory—*terra nullius*—could not be employed as an alliance partner in peace or as a military ally in war. In making these commitments states thus denied themselves the opportunity to gain political objectives and to station or send armed forces through the area. Self-restraint was evident in both ends and means. Neutrality attempted to protect the weak from the strong but especially to protect the strong from themselves. The purpose of all such arrangements, said Lord Curzon after leaving the Foreign Office, was simple and direct: "to keep apart two Powers whose contact might provoke collision."[27]

During the nineteenth century European diplomats created three neutral states on the Continent. At the Congress of Vienna eight Powers guaranteed the neutrality of Switzerland, located in an area of potential competition among France, Prussia, and Austria. The recognition of conflicting interests among these same states, with the addition of Britain, resulted in the famous establishment of neutral Belgium in 1831. As the six signatories to the treaty declared, the object of their action was "to prevent events from disturbing the general peace."[28] Statesmen made similar expressions with the neutralization of Luxembourg in 1867, committing themselves to "the withdrawal of the artillery, munitions, and every object which forms part of the equipment of the [Luxembourg] Fortress" and promising "that no Military Establishment shall be there maintained or created." They pledged to respect the neutrality of Luxembourg and simultaneously required that Luxembourg "be bound to observe the same neutrality towards all other States."[29]

When the difficulties of neutralizing an entire state became too great, the Powers focused their attention upon a more restricted zone or a very specific area. Upon redrawing borders after the Napoleonic upheavals, for example, they realized that rival claims would bring Russia, Prussia, and Austria physically into direct contact with each other at the precise location of Cracow in eastern Europe. With this defenseless city wedged precariously at the intersection of its gigantic neighbors, the possibilities for future tension and crises appeared overwhelming. To prevent such events, the Powers mutually agreed to exercise self-restraint by pledging "to respect and to cause always to be respected, the Neutrality of the Free Town of Cracow and its Territory. No armed force shall be introduced upon any pretense whatever."[30]

The unique status of neutrality thus involved both political and military dimensions, and the intertwined complexities of these two features made mutual agreement difficult to obtain. The Great Powers impressively overcame their differences and achieved neutralization in the cases just cited. But on other occasions, they decided that partial accord was better than none and therefore attempted to find consensus on only the military aspects of self-restraint. They described such agreements as crisis-prevention regimes for demilitarization or nonfortification, and believed that they could avert problems by limiting the means available to themselves in particular areas. Lengthy negotiations, for example, resulted in several agreements closing the critical straits of the Dardanelles and the Bosphorus to ships of war during times of peace[31] or in demilitarizing the Black Sea.[32] The same considerations of forestalling crises by restricting means in the Mediterranean found form in the 1863 agreement on the Ionian Islands of Greece, in which the Powers pledged that "no armed force, either naval or military, shall at any time be assembled or stationed upon the territory or in the waters of those Islands."[33]

One of the most interesting cases of demilitarization limited to a very precise area is that of the Åland Islands. Situated between Sweden and Finland, and astride both the Baltic Sea and the Gulf of Bothnia, this group of small islands occupies a critical location. Ownership of this archipelago and use of its excellent anchorages as a naval base affords any country a great deal of strategic strength. Although several Powers greedily sought control of the Ålands, statesmen finally recognized by the middle of the nineteenth century that possession by any one nation would be regarded as a grave threat by all others in the area. Consequently, numerous efforts[34] successfully prohibited weapons and armed force from the islands in order "to remove distrust and avoid conflict by means of international agreement rather than have recourse to the sword."[35] An official assessment by a participant in one of these negotiations spoke clearly to the point of crisis prevention:

> Our natural instinct is to ignore the significance of these, in themselves unimportant, little islands, like many other inconvenient areas in the world, but it is by no means impossible that in the distant future they may generate a spark that will light a big conflagration. As a bone of contention between two Powers . . . they are capable of starting a struggle that may easily extend in scope; and as a strategic key to the Baltic, their possession may exercise an unwholesome attraction to more powerful and more predatory neighbors, the consequence of which, as in other historical precedents, may well be incalculable. The negotiations, therefore, had for their object a convention which would diminish, if it cannot obviate for all time, the chances of either of these two contingencies.[36]

Localizing and Restricting Regional Conflicts

During the nineteenth century the Great Powers also made deliberate efforts to contain regional conflicts as a means of preventing larger confrontations among themselves. They feared that a minor dispute or clash might easily escalate out of control into something much more serious. Such a dispute could provide an example for others who wanted to challenge the status quo, a pretext for outside involvement or unilateral intervention, or a spark to ignite more extensive tensions. For this reason, diplomats attempted to localize or confine a number of confrontations to areas of limited geographical scope and to restrict or restrain the parties of a small dispute that threatened to disrupt or explode the larger peace.

One of these important and successful attempts to localize a regional conflict occurred in the case of the revolution in Belgium. During the late summer of 1830, the long-smoldering discontent of

Belgian subjects placed under the control of the Dutch exploded in open rioting. The Danish king, William I, rushed troops into Brussels to crush the rebellion, but these were soon repulsed. Encouraged by their victory, the Belgians escalated the struggle. Continued fighting became serious and soon threatened to spill over the boundaries of Belgium and Holland. There was fear that France might attempt to annex part of the territory in dispute, that Prussia and Russia might send in armed forces, and that the local conflict thus would quickly expand into a major European crisis. To forestall this possibility, representatives of the Powers met together and decided upon collective action in imposing a settlement upon the immediate disputants, dissolving the union of the Low Countries, and pledging self-restraint among themselves. They explained their motivation for this action in terms of containing the conflict and thereby preventing a larger crisis. The official protocol stated their "firm determination to oppose, by all means in their power, any renewal of the struggle" that "would be the source of great misery to both countries, and would threaten Europe with a general war, the prevention of which is the first duty of the five Powers."[37]

Efforts made to localize conflicts were not simply restricted to those involving only small states, although such problems obviously could be handled with much greater ease. On many occasions one or another of the Great Powers themselves was party to a controversy that prompted collective action by the others. One of the major sources of this kind of situation occurred in the ever-troublesome and complicated area of the Balkans, where Austria and Russia continually vied for advantage. In 1875 an insurrection broke out against Turkish rule in Bosnia and Herzegovina. The national self-consciousness of these provinces had been enflamed by propaganda from Serbia and Montenegro, areas that now dreamed of acquiring the territory in question for their own. This hope of annexation, when mixed with the Austrian and Russian rivalries in the region, greatly increased the chances of a major explosion. In order to avert such a calamity, Austria, Russia, and Germany concluded an agreement that was soon accepted by Britain and France as well. The wording of the arrangement provides an explicit statement of an attempt at crisis prevention:

> The Powers have come to an agreement to make use of all the influence at their disposal in order to localize the conflict, and diminish its dangers and calamities by preventing Serbia and Montenegro from participating in the movement.
> Their language has been the more effectual from being identic, and

has, consequently, testified the firm determination of Europe not to permit the general peace to be imperilled by rash impulses.[38]

Limiting Means in Third Areas

The Powers of Europe similarly attempted to avert major crises by deliberately limiting the resources available to various actors and thereby restraining them. On various occasions the Powers agreed not to provide certain states or actors with military supplies, financial aid, logistical assistance, political or diplomatic support, or any other means that would increase the likelihood of confrontations into which they might be drawn. A deliberate restriction of arms was, of course, an integral part of any demilitarization, nonfortification, or neutralization process. Diplomats negotiated the Ålands settlement, for example, "in order to guarantee that these islands shall never become a source of danger from the military point of view," and did so by strictly prohibiting any "installation utilized for war purposes" and "the manufacture, import, transport, and re-export of arms and war material."[39] At other times they established self-imposed ground rules between themselves regarding their supply and use of weapons in particular areas of the world. The Brussels Act of 1890, signed by seventeen nations, provides one of the best known of these agreements. Detailed provisions of this convention instituted controls over the importing, transporting, and supplying of "fire-arms, and especially of rifles and improved weapons, as well as of powder, balls, and cartridges" in order to prevent any serious crisis emerging from "the pernicious and preponderating part played by fire-arms" in large portions of Africa.[40]

In some cases these agreements made a careful distinction between the types of means considered to be legitimate in a given context, prohibiting military resources but allowing competition to proceed in other ways. Mutual restraint could be applied to the use of armed force or to political influence while at the same time permitting rivals to employ economic means. Such a situation emerged, in fact, between Britain and Germany after they signed an agreement designed to prevent crises between themselves or their clients in East Africa. Responding to an inquiry from Berlin, Lord Salisbury said that, in his opinion, "it was not the intention of either Government to restrict the subjects of the other from *bona fide* trading operations within the sphere assigned to it." He continued,

> Her Majesty's Government will therefore be prepared to admit the principle that German subjects may establish trading stations within the British sphere and acquire land necessary for the purposes of such

stations, on the understanding that claims to political, sovereign, or exclusive rights ... are inadmissible, and provided that the Imperial Government admit the same principle as regards British subjects in the German sphere.[41]

The Great Powers also reached agreements that limited nonmilitary resources in third areas. In addition to restraints on weapons and ammunition, they committed themselves either explicitly or tacitly not to employ political, economic, or even diplomatic means in particular places. At times such arrangements related to the carving out of spheres of influence.[42] Yet, on other occasions, agreements concerned a mutual restraint on all sides rather than simply a division of interests or areas. In their central Asian competition, for instance, the British and Russians reached several agreements of this nature. During the early 1870s, they both agreed not to lend any kind of assistance or encouragement to various local factions fighting for control of Afghanistan, despite the efforts of clients or potential clients to make them do so.[43] Later they pledged to abstain from the use of any political or economic means to seek special privileges or concessions and even committed themselves to refrain from sending diplomatic representatives to Afghanistan at all.[44]

Delineating Interests and Areas of Involvement

Diplomats of the nineteenth century also sought to prevent crises by delineating and defining interests and/or areas of involvement. They believed that their competition could be more easily regulated by recognizing, insofar as possible, each other's interests and prerogatives. Negotiators therefore attempted to identify the nature of these interests and the location of these areas, variously described as "paramount interests," "special concerns," "spheres of interest," "spheres of influence," and "spheres of action." The Powers drew demarcation lines, set limits, and established ground rules for their competition in order to avoid misunderstandings and disputes. They hoped that by such means, all parties would know what was—and, just as important, what was not—legitimate in pursuing objectives. This clarification was the motivation behind the 1884–1885 Conference of Berlin, which, in the words of one authority, "had not been called as the result of a crisis, but rather in an attempt to forestall the possibility of one arising."[45]

At times, these arrangements regarding special interests and areas resulted from informal, tacit understandings that had evolved through time. The Powers understood from long, and sometimes painful, experience that the straits of the Dardanelles and the Bosphorus always concerned Russia, that North Africa continually interested France, and that the Balkans never failed to attract the attention of Austria. They recognized that military questions on the Continent always alerted the Germans, and that naval matters could be counted upon to raise the sensitivities of the British. During 1877, for instance, Britain believed that a local confrontation in Turkey might "unfortunately spread" if confusion arose as to "what the most prominent of [our] interests are." For this reason, the Earl of Derby as foreign secretary clearly identified matters of British concern as being the area near the Suez Canal, Constantinople, the status of the Bosphorus and Dardanelles, and the Persian Gulf.[46] Much later, in 1907, Sir Edward Grey expressed the same idea when he said in concluding an agreement with Russia that "it has not therefore been considered appropriate to introduce into the Convention a positive declaration respecting special interests" of his country in the Persian Gulf, "the result of British action in those waters for more than one hundred years." "His Majesty's Government," he wrote,

> have reason to believe that this question will not give rise to difficulties between the two Governments should developments arise which make further discussion affecting British interests in the Gulf necessary. For the Russian Government have in the course of the negotiations leading up to the conclusion of this Arrangement explicitly stated that they do not deny the special interests of Great Britain in the Persian Gulf— a statement of which His Majesty's Government have formally taken note.[47]

These particular expressions of interest, like others, did not necessarily entail or even imply ownership or control. Indeed, some claims were strongly disputed. Such statements did, however, serve to identify a country's respective interests and areas to all others and thereby "to introduce Formality and decorum into proceedings which, unless thus regulated and diffused, might endanger the peace of nations."[48]

The most explicit and formal of these kinds of agreements were those delineating and defining particular spheres of influence. Although the marking off of specific regions within which each of the contracting parties could pursue its activities without competition from the other was instituted by the crowns of Castile and Portugal in the fifteenth century, the practice did not become common until the nineteenth century. At that time it became quite acceptable for two or more states to agree mutually upon their respective areas of interest, the proper rules to be observed, the means to be employed, and their reciprocal obligations not to create interference in the sphere reserved for the other. These agreements almost always included explicit statements indicating the desire to minimize friction by differentiating interests or areas and thus to prevent crises. They expressed the hope of "fixing the limits of [the countries'] respective spheres of influence, so that in the future there may be no difference of opinion between the allied Governments" and of removing "as far as possible all causes of doubt and misunderstanding."[49] This was the purpose of the 1824 Anglo-Dutch treaty regarding respective rights and obligations in the Malacca Peninsula, Sumatra, and the Straits of Singapore.[50] The Germans negotiated similar agreements in 1885 with the French regarding the west coast of Africa and Oceania and then with the British "for separating and defining the spheres of action of Great Britain and Germany in parts of Africa" where the interests "of the two countries might conflict."[51] Here they established a dividing line and pledged not to make territorial acquisition, accept protectorates, or interfere in any way within the area reserved for the other.

Among the most interesting and detailed of all the spheres-of-influence agreements are those created by the British, Russians, Persians, and Afghans in central Asia. The competition between empires, feuds among local rivals and factions, and fluidity of ill-defined borders continually threatened the area with major crises. To prevent such an occurrence, statesmen attempted to establish definite ground rules and limits over a period of many years, beginning with Count Nesselrode's 1844 memorandum "to preserve them from dangerous contact."[52] In 1869 Count Gortchakoff assured Lord Clarendon that Afghanistan at least lay "completely outside the sphere within which Russia might be called upon to exercise her influence,"[53] and subsequent understandings confirmed this arrangement. Imprecision, however, bred confusion and distrust, and even in private correspondence leaders expressed the feeling that "as long as the boundary remains undefined, we are of the opinion that there will be more or less risk of misunderstanding and anxiety."[54] Finally, in 1907, after persistent efforts, an elaborate and comprehensive agreement formally created well-defined demarcations, recognized the independence and integrity of the area, and established Afghanistan and the southern portion of Persia to be in the British sphere of influence, the northern portion of Persia to be in the Russian sphere, and a neutral zone lying between them to separate each one.[55] The purpose of the entire arrangement, the two powers announced shortly thereafter, could be found in the desire "to avoid any cause of conflict between their respective interests" and "to prevent misunderstandings in the future."[56]

In some of these agreements delineating and defining of spheres, as in the case of Afghanistan and Persia, the wishes of local rulers were consulted, taken into account, and confirmed by international accords. In other situations, particularly those in Africa, the interests of the inhabitants were ignored completely and crushed during the heyday of imperialism. At times the creation of spheres of influence by the Europeans led to protectorates, brutal suppression, or direct conquest. On other occasions the process resulted in a certain degree of stability and protection. From the perspective of native populations, therefore, spheres of influence brought mixed results, both curses and blessings. From the perspective of the Great Powers who originated the practice, however, such arrangements accomplished to a surprising degree what they were designed to do: namely, to prevent crises by regulating competition among nations. "Difficulties were anticipated and avoided," as one noted authority observes, "by the exercise of an accommodating spirit on both sides; and force, which loomed so largely in the colonial settlements of the eighteenth century, gave place to agreement."[57] The controversy surrounding assessments of spheres of influence will undoubtedly continue, but as Lord Curzon—who himself participated in many of these negotiations—concluded, these arrangements made "on the whole for peace rather than for war—which is perhaps a sufficient vindication of them."[58]

Intervening by Multilateral Action

The possibility that conflicts in third areas might escalate into major confrontations was a problem that continually haunted the Great Powers. Their many crisis-prevention regimes for localizing regional conflicts, limiting means available to actors, and delineating specific interests or areas of involvement provide ample testimony to this concern. In the event that these particular solutions proved inadequate and it appeared that the general peace might be threatened, however, statesmen believed that prevention required the more serious and active measure of intervention. Although careful distinctions could be made in this regard among the types of means to be employed for economic or for political coercion, the use of armed force for military action remained an ever-present threat. In cases where force was employed, few diplomats suffered under any illusions about the potential dangers. As Castlereagh observed early in the nineteenth century: "The principle of one State interfering by force in the internal affairs of another . . . is always a question of the greatest possible moral, as well as political, delicacy." Nevertheless, even he recognized that at times "when actual danger menaces the system of Europe," such intervention may be necessary to restrain local actors and thus keep the peace.⁵⁹ To regulate those occasions and therefore prevent crises between themselves, the Great Powers established by both explicit and implicit agreements that intervention, if any, must be a collective enterprise rather than a unilateral action by a single state seeking exclusive advantage.

The several cases of multilateral intervention during the nineteenth century demonstrate the determination of the Powers to practice crisis prevention by joint action. With the outbreak of revolution in Naples during the summer of 1820, for instance, equilibrium throughout the Italian peninsula was seriously jeopardized. Sensitive to Austrian interests in particular and to the stability of the status quo in general, Metternich immediately wanted to send troops across the border to crush the insurrection. He clearly understood, however, that such blatant unilateral intervention would be completely unacceptable to the other Powers. Consequently, representatives met in concert at Troppau and then Laibach to decide upon a mutual policy. In the end, and despite many differences, Austria, Russia, and Prussia authorized Austrian troops to intervene in Italy as agents of collective European action.⁶⁰ The British and the French, who abstained in this case, had no hesitation about intervening a short time later during the Greek revolt when Great Power rivalries in the eastern Mediterranean came into play. Here, Britain, France, and Russia announced that peace had to be protected "by preventing, as far as possible, all collision between the Contending Parties." Toward this end, they agreed upon multilateral intervention in which they would all take part. Moreover, they inserted a significant clause that would thereafter become customary in such mutual action: a pledge that they would "not seek . . . any augmentation of territory, any exclusive influence, or any commercial advantage for their subjects, which those of every other Nation may not equally obtain."⁶¹

Intervention in Greece, of course, marked just the beginning of many involvements in the affairs of the Ottoman Empire. The long-festering problem of the "sick man of Europe" resulted from internal decay and corruption, Balkan nationalism, religious passions, Egyptian ambitions, and Great Power jealousies, all of which contributed their share to the difficulties that plagued European diplomacy for decades. To prevent any or all of these potentially destructive forces from upsetting the general peace and balance of power, the Powers frequently intervened on a multilateral basis in the territory of the Turks. They selected this course in 1839–1840 to check the threat posed to the sultan by Mehemet Ali, whose forces from Egypt stood at the gates of Constantinople. In this situation, Britain, Austria, Prussia, and Russia together signed a convention "to prevent the effusion of blood which would be occasioned by a continuance of the hostilities" by "maintaining the integrity and independence of the Ottoman Empire as a security for the peace of Europe"[62] and actively intervened to defeat the Egyptians and thus enforce their decision. Much later, in 1897, when Crete arose in revolt against Turkish rule, the Powers sent naval forces and landed troops on the island to prevent the disturbance from expanding, and they did so under the collective auspices of Britain, Austria-Hungary, France, Germany, Italy, and Russia.[63] When the rule against exclusive advantage and aggrandizement was ignored, as in 1853 and 1877, when Russia unilaterally intervened to make gains at the expense of everyone else, the result could be war or serious confrontation. As long as it was practiced, however, multilateral intervention could be very successful in preventing crises.

Practicing the Pacific Settlement of Disputes

At times the efforts of the Powers to regulate their competition by creating rules and procedures took a more structured form than those discussed thus far. In another attempt to forestall major confrontations, statesmen sought to adjust and resolve differences at low levels by means of what they described as the pacific settlement of international disputes. Either by refining long-standing diplomatic practices or by creating new techniques, they worked to bring contending parties together and then to give advice or render decisions that would facilitate the removal of the initial cause of controversy. Toward this end, diplomats employed the means of "good offices," mediation, commissions of inquiry, and conciliation based upon compromise and the resolution of political differences. In addition, they utilized arbitration, adjudication, and other forms of judicial settlement based upon provisions of international law. All these means were designed in one way or another to allow disputants to come to an understanding by exchanging views, utilizing the services of a neutral third party, elucidating the facts underlying a difference by the use of impartial investigators, submitting to the decisions of arbitrators, or reconciling opposing claims, and thereby prevent serious crises.

The practice of pacific settlement of disputes had a well-established tradition in diplomacy. It was not at all uncommon for one state or another to either offer its services or be requested to do so. Britain proffered its good offices and mediation in the 1826 dispute between Greece and the Ottoman Empire, and in 1842 Prussia served as the arbiter in a controversy between France and Britain. There were many other examples. As the nineteenth century progressed, however, statesmen desired in certain cases to make the practice more formal and obligatory than in the past. Consequently, in the 1856 Peace of Paris, Austria, France, Britain, Prussia, Russia, Sardinia, and Turkey stipulated that in case a difference that threatened peace should arise between the Ottoman Empire and one or more of the signatory Powers, the parties would be obliged, before having recourse to the use of force, to afford "the opportunity of preventing such an extremity by means of their Mediation."[64] The fourteen signatories of the General Act of the 1884–1885 Conference of Berlin similarly pledged that to avert crises due to disputes in parts of Africa, they would "bind themselves, before appealing to arms, to have recourse to the mediation of one or more of the friendly Powers."[65] The Hague peace conferences of 1899 and 1907 carried this process even further by creating the Permanent Court of Arbitration and signing the Convention for the Pacific Settlement of International Disputes.[66]

Although these elaborate mechanisms and promises suffered from such qualifying phrases as "as far as circumstances may allow,"[67] and even though offers of mediation sometimes were rebuffed,[68] the practice of pacific settlement of disputes increasingly played a role in preventing crises.[69] Even cautious observers like international legal expert L. F. Oppenheim maintained that the value of these means "cannot be over-estimated" and that hostilities "have been frequently prevented" due to their use.[70] In the last two decades of the nineteenth century, for example, there were no fewer than ninety international arbitrations between various states, not including other forms of settlement.[71] Obviously, the easiest ones to settle were those that did not threaten vital interests and in which both sides desired amicable resolution. Nevertheless, any number of these cases involved significant issues, such as the *Alabama* claims arbitration in 1871–1872 between Britain and the United States regarding the obligations of neutrality and the 1902 *Sergent Malamine* settlement between France and Britain concerning commitments to rules prohibiting the shipment of arms into third areas.[72]

One of the most successful cases of pacific settlement occurred in the 1904 Dogger Bank incident. At the beginning of its voyage to the Far East, the Baltic fleet of Russia encountered a group of harmless British fishing vessels in the North Sea. Incredibly, the Russian admiral mistook the trawlers for Japanese torpedo boats and opened fire. The damage and death caused by this unprovoked attack caused a storm of indignation and anger in Britain. Highly volatile emotions and the desire for revenge created a situation where "the betting was about even between peace and war."[73] Any escalation would create a crisis in Anglo-French-Russian relations, encourage

Germany to exploit the tsar's predicament, and push the two sides closer to armed conflict, which neither wanted. To avert these dangers, Britain and Russia, exercising remarkable restraint, agreed through the mediation of France to establish an international commission and accepted an award of indemnity to the victims of the incident—all by peaceful means. According to historian A.J.P. Taylor, this pacific settlement prevented a major crisis, if not war itself. The Dogger Bank resolution, he writes, marked "the end of an epoch in European history—the epoch in which an Anglo-Russian conflict seemed the most likely outcome of international relations. This conflict had been expected in the Near East for fifty years, in central Asia for twenty, and in the Far East, with the greatest likelihood of all, for ten. After November 1904 the conflict was indefinitely postponed."[74]

Communicating and Providing Advance Notification

Statesmen also attempted to avert the outbreak of crises by developing any number of procedures for communication that demonstrated mutual respect, built confidence, avoided surprises, and generated good will. One of the major reasons for practicing collective decisionmaking was that the technique afforded the statesmen the opportunity to inform, consult, solicit opinion, and discuss important problems with each other in advance of any change in position. This accomplishment is clearly evident in one ambassador's assessment of the Berlin Conference of 1884–1885:

> When the Conference assembled there was much confusion of thought, leading to distrust among the different nations as to territorial and commercial rivalries; but there was imperfect knowledge of facts, and a danger of friction lay in that ignorance. Study of the past and a temperate discussion of the future have had a marked effect in allaying in most quarters mutual suspicions, and if distrust has not been altogether removed it can hardly fail to be so sooner or later by the general understanding which has been arrived at on questions hitherto subjected to independent and more or less irresponsible treatment.[75]

Believing that this result could occur even when there was no formal meeting in concert, the Powers frequently provided advance notification and explanations of initiatives or intended actions in order to discover whether, why, and to what extent others might object.

Sometimes this "rule" of communication and advance notification was implicit in nature and simply part of customary diplomatic practice designed to enhance mutual understanding. Upon concluding their agreement for demolishing the Dutch fortresses in 1831, for instance, Britain, Austria, Prussia, and Russia believed it to be important for the future that they send a copy of the protocol to France. The signatories therefore collectively stated that "being desirous to give a further proof of the reliance they place on the disposition shown by the Government of His Majesty the King of the French for the maintenance of the general Peace," they thought it "their duty to communicate" the text of their decision.[76] During 1877 the British similarly calculated that explicit and unambiguous communication assured the best means of practicing crisis prevention with Russia. For this reason, the Earl of Derby sent a dispatch to the Russian court to "make it clear" as to precisely what position Her Majesty's government would take in order "that there should be no misunderstanding as to their positions and intentions."[77] When this practice of providing advance notification was not honored, as in the several cases of Kaiser Wilhelm II with his diplomatic leaps, serious crises resulted. Indeed, the Kaiser's tendency to create fait accomplis and to score quick, cheap victories in this manner contributed to the collapse of the nineteenth-century system of diplomacy itself.

On other occasions, the Great Powers sought to make advance communication an explicit and legally binding rule, in every sense of the word. The 1885 General Act of the Berlin Conference stipulated that to prevent conflicts from arising, any state extending its influence in designated parts of Africa "shall accompany the respective act with a notification thereof, addressed to the other Signatory Powers of the present Act in order to enable them, if need be, to make good any claims of their own."[78] The Brussels Act of 1890 establishing a crisis-prevention regime for limiting means to third areas similarly required that states communicate information to each other regarding the traffic in firearms and ammunition.[79] When negotiating the 1908 agreement to maintain peace in the North Sea, the signatories also pledged that if events threatened stability in the area, they would "communicate with each other for concerting among themselves" upon ways to take common measures for protecting the status quo.[80] Through such means the Powers attempted to prevent the outbreak of serious crises.

Some Issues and Lessons

These many crisis-prevention regimes created throughout the nineteenth century introduced an imaginative array of diplomatic efforts designed to maintain international stability. By combining the particular structure and conditions of their time with skill, and ingenious means, the Great Powers successfully managed to overcome serious differences and difficult obstacles in order to reach agreement upon ways to regulate competition. Their experience in this endeavor raises a number of interrelated issues and suggests several lessons about the practice of crisis prevention.

Solutions Tailored to Problems

Statesmen of this period possessed an acute appreciation for the realities and complexities of international politics. They knew that dangerous forms of competition and crises can be initiated and perpetuated by a multiplicity of factors in strikingly different contexts, areas, and situations. Devising effective prevention strategies requires accurately anticipating probable developments, diagnosing the characteristics of a given problem, and reaching common agreement upon an appropriate solution. These several tasks cannot be accomplished by simply creating a single, all-purpose rule of behavior designed to treat every contingency. For this reason the diplomats carefully designed many different kinds of regimes to meet many different kinds of problems. The wide variety in this repertoire, ranging from mutual consultation and decisionmaking through delineation of interests to communication and advanced notification, as discussed, provided the opportunity for flexibility in tailoring a solution to the special and specific requirements of the problem at hand. A potential crisis in Europe required different treatment from one in Africa, and a confrontation over vital interests needed a different regime from one involving only minor concerns.

Specificity of Conditions

The careful tailoring of solutions to particular problems is closely related to the feature of specificity in conditions. Most of the crisis-prevention regimes treated in this chapter provided very specific terms and conditions. The agreements limiting means in third areas, for example, went to great lengths in identifying precisely which kinds of weapons, if any, were permissible as instruments of policy. Those conventions establishing neutral or demilitarized zones carefully defined the location and boundaries of such territory. Many accords delineating spheres of interest or influence spelled out in detail the precise lines of demarcation, including latitude and longitude coordinates, river valleys, or other prominent and unmistakable geographical features. Specificity in such cases, particularly when it was made explicit in treaty form, provided little room for variations in interpretation. Diplomats sought to reach agreement on specific conditions for specific problems and, conversely, to avoid nebulous, abstract, and grandiose schemes. As the British Foreign Office stated in responding to Napoleon III's proposal for a vague and all-encompassing conference without a clear agenda or precise terms for crisis prevention, there would be "more apprehension than confidence from the meeting of a congress of sovereigns and ministers without fixed objects, ranging over the map of Europe, and exciting hopes and aspirations which they might find themselves unable either to gratify or to quiet."[81] Experience demonstrated that those regimes not containing precise conditions could provoke disputes, as in those cases early in the nineteenth century involving intervention in the affairs of another state.

Understanding on Substance and Procedure

This specificity of crisis-prevention regimes, in turn, is intimately connected with the degree of mutual understanding among the actors over conditions for compliance. Statesmen of the period believed that clarity and precision minimize confusion, disagreement, and subsequent dispute. They recognized the advantages of insuring that "conditions are laid down so clearly that they cannot be subject to diverse interpretations."[82] For this reason, much care was taken in negotiating precise terms designed to be applicable to specific situations. This feature, enormously enhanced by the cultural homogeneity among the diplomats themselves in speaking a common language and sharing common values, resulted in a relatively clear understanding—in both letter and spirit—among the Great Powers on matters of substance and procedure in their crisis-prevention regimes.[83] In fact, at times their agreements even explicitly stated that the objectives and means were "well understood" by all parties and not subject to misinterpretation.[84]

Change and the Need for Adjustment

Prevention, by its very nature, is concerned with anticipated change in the future. Those diplomats of the nineteenth century who practiced crisis prevention clearly recognized that change would occur. This awareness was what prompted them in the first place to direct that change in desired ways within the mutually accepted structure, goals, and means of the international system itself. Yet they also understood that change would continue, even after they had reached some agreement upon basic norms and created specific crisis-prevention regimes. They possessed few illusions that such rules would usher in permanent peace or solve all problems in the future. The statesmen at Vienna certainly did not expect their settlement to last as long as it did, for they already had seen many treaties come and go, and the experience of the Hundred Days after Napoleon's escape did little to increase their faith in future stability.[85] Instead, they and their successors accomplished what they could in the hope of creating "a ground of confidence" and "stepping stones" toward future agreements.[86] The resulting regimes evolved over the lengthy period of a century, as the diplomats realized by learning from successes and failures that adjustment would constantly be necessary as changed circumstances and conditions required.

One newspaper gave precise expression to this point of change and the need for adjustment in praising the crisis-prevention accord on the Baltic Sea by observing that "it may rightly be held to contribute to the interests of peace" but warning that "no one will naturally lose sight of the fact that [the accord] does not exclude the possibility of risk in the future." Too great a reliance, argued the paper in a statement only partially cited before, "must not be placed in the treaties—they have been concluded before now and broken before now, and thus it will ever be as long as men are men. But here is a praiseworthy desire to remove distrust and avoid conflict by means of international agreement rather than have recourse to the sword."[87]

Differentiated Assessment of Interests

When creating their crisis-prevention regimes, the Great Powers also made efforts to differentiate their respective interests. Wanting to avoid the serious dangers that await those who fail to distinguish between the important and the unimportant or those who maintain that each issue is as critical as all others, they sought to assess the relative weight of matters or areas capable of provoking confrontation. This was the purpose behind their negotiations to draw demarcation lines, set limits, and identify "paramount interests" and "special concerns." In terms of issues, leaders came to understand that naval and trade matters invariably interested the British while military questions concerned the Germans. In terms of geographical location, physical proximity frequently provided the most crucial element, leading the English Channel and Iberian peninsula to be of the greatest importance for Britain and France, the Balkans for Austria and Russia, and so on. For third areas around the globe, the diplomats established more explicit agreements on areas of interest and spheres of influence, as was described above. Here, they delineated and differentiated respective interests and prerogatives. The recognition of these various asymmetries of interest, they believed, would help regulate their competition and thereby prevent dangerous crises.

Reciprocal Advantage

Diplomacy is often defined as a "commerce in mutual benefits," for only as long as reciprocal advantages accrue or harmony prevails can there be any assurance that agreements will be fulfilled.[88] Statesmen of the classical system understood this principle very well, and they realized that the creation of crisis-prevention regimes had to provide mutual benefits in order to be effective. The general avoidance of conflict involving the risk of war among the Great Powers, of course, was to the advantage of all. Above and beyond that general proposition, however, the specific regimes had to provide specific benefits. As Chancellor Otto von Bismarck stated in his introductory speech before delegates to the Conference of Berlin, the best way "to forestall disputes which might result" from the pursuit of policy was to "regulate" competition by an accord based upon an "equality of rights and uniformity of interests" to insure reciprocal advantage.[89] This dimension of mutual benefit is particularly evident in those regimes for mutual consultation, collective decisionmaking, spheres of influence and interest, and multilateral intervention. In each instance, the relative advantages accruing to one of the Powers accrued to the others as well.

Mutual Restraints

Reciprocal advantages of crisis-prevention regimes cannot be considered in isolation, however, for they represent only one side of the coin. The other side is that of mutual restraints, or, at least to some degree, reciprocal disadvantages. Diplomats of this period recognized that benefits seldom are achieved in the world without costs. Rules of the game can be effective only if they are observed and respected by *all* sides party to an agreement. This necessity requires actors deliberately to deny themselves certain objectives and the use of certain means and thus to tie their hands and place restrictions upon their own freedom of action. Similarly, the actors must be prepared in advance to accept the possibility of unfavorable consequences and situations that might develop as a result of observing the established rules. These obligations evenly applied to all signatories of any agreement, as was indicated in the protocol between the Germans and the British regarding Africa that stipulated a "reciprocal undertaking" to honor pledges and a recognition that "the engagement to carry out these rules was made on the understanding that assurances of a similar nature would be given" by each government to the other.[90] The regimes for buffer states, neutral zones, and demilitarized areas, and the limitation of means within third areas in particular demonstrate this element of self-denial and mutual restraint necessary for the prevention of crises. In signing the Belgian agreement, for example, the Powers denied themselves the opportunity to seek exclusive or unilateral benefits and pledged their "firm determination not to seek in the arrangements relative to Belgium, under whatever circumstances that may present themselves, any augmentation of territory, any exclusive influence,—any isolated advantages."[91]

Rights and Responsibilities

The combination of both advantages and restraints in any effective crisis-prevention regime is part and parcel of the larger issue of rights and responsibilities. Diplomats of the nineteenth century believed that one could not obtain or enjoy privileges without incurring concomitant duties. The right to demilitarize an area, to intervene in the affairs of another state, or to be invited as a participant in collective decisionmaking, in the minds of these statesmen, came only with the accompanying acceptance of responsibility for preserving the stability and integrity of the system, honoring commitments, and taking action to enforce the rules if necessary. At times this attitude found expression in terms of pragmatic self-interest with the calculated knowledge that "no Power can free itself from . . . treaties without at the same time freeing others."[92] Yet on many other occasions this sense of duty was expressed in terms of moral responsibility and obligation.[93] As Castlereagh observed, "the Great Powers feel that they have not only a common interest, but a common duty to attend to."[94] It may be difficult for us, living as we do in a more cynical and lawless century, to believe that statesmen were sincere in such statements or in the respect that they paid to responsibilities. But the Powers did not lightly violate their pledged word during this period, and even as late as 1914 the world was shocked when one leader shamelessly referred to a particular treaty for crisis prevention as "a scrap of paper."[95]

Serious and Responsible Communication

"If the peace of Europe is to be maintained," observed Lord Clarendon in a letter to his ambassador in Paris, "it will not do to shrink from examining . . . questions with a firm intention of solving them."[96] This direct and realistic approach, he and his contemporaries believed, depended first and foremost upon serious and responsible communication among themselves. They understood that effective coordination of policies and regulation of competition requires continuous and forthright dealings among the participants to engender confidence. For this reason, as was previously indicated, several crisis-prevention regimes specifically made provision for communication, consultation, and advance notification to demonstrate mutual respect, avoid surprises, and generate good will. The diplomats knew, however, that procedure alone does not guarantee substance or quality. Communication must also be both serious and responsible. A sense of common interest and purpose can hardly be enhanced by deliberately deceiving others, blatantly lying, grossly distorting facts, engaging in propaganda, or avoiding substantive issues by trying to make gains in what scholar and negotiator Fred Iklé calls certain kinds of "side effects."[97] Indeed, as Bismarck painfully discovered after unifying the German Reich by less than honest means, a reputation for trust and credibility once lost is not easily regained, and its loss can seriously impair the ability to create or enforce viable crisis-prevention regimes.

The Spirit of Compromise

Statesmen who practiced crisis prevention during this period also strongly appreciated the fundamental fact that diplomacy entails compromise. A balance between advantages and restraints, between rights and responsibilities, and between selfish national interests and the larger common interests in the system can only be achieved by making concessions and adjustments. Absolute security for one country, by definition, means absolute insecurity for all others.[98] An international system composed of several states thus requires a spirit of accommodation among all of its members that can be made operational and applied to specific situations and problems. This requirement explains the constant reference throughout negotiations to the need for a "spirit of moderation" and for making "reasonably advantageous compromises" and "indispensable concessions."[99] Crisis-prevention regimes succeeded when all sides believed that they shared equally in both the costs and the benefits of compromise.

$$*\quad*\quad*\quad*$$

The unprecedented peace and stability during the classical system of diplomacy makes the nineteenth century a particularly fruitful field for study and reflection. Success in avoiding a war that ensnared all of the Great Powers at the same time was the result of many factors, a number of which will probably never exist again. The structure of the balance of power and the agreement upon objectives for the system, enhanced by a cultural homogeneity comprising common traits, ideology, and values, contributed their part. Overseas expansion, limited means of destruction in warfare, and a small number of actors promoted stability in Europe. Attention to domestic problems and industrial development, fear of revolution, and other factors encouraged peace as well. Due credit must also be given, however, to the remarkable skill of the diplomats themselves in taking measures and inventing means designed to avert the explosion of crises. Their sophisticated practices left an impressive legacy, one that can be judged on its own merits and one that can provide valuable historical perspective for those more recent efforts at crisis prevention discussed in the following chapters.

Acknowledgments

The author gratefully acknowledges permission granted by the Controller of Her Majesty's Stationery Office to cite unpublished, Crown-copyright materials in the Public Record Office.

Notes

1. François de Callières, *On the Manner of Negotiating with Princes* (Notre Dame, Ind.: University of Notre Dame Press, 1963), pp. 111–112. (Translation of *De la Manière de négocier avec les Souverains,* 1716.)

2. M. S. Anderson, *Eighteenth Century Europe, 1713–1789* (London: Oxford University Press, 1968), p. 47.

3. For this point of view, see A.H.L. Heeren, *Handbuch der Geschichte des europäischen Staatensystems und seiner Kolonien* (Göttingen: Röwer, 1811 ed.), and the discussion in Gordon A. Craig, "On the Nature of Diplomatic History," in *Diplomacy: New Approaches in History, Theory and Policy,* ed. Paul Gordon Lauren (New York: Free Press, 1979), pp. 28–30.

4. Friedrich Meinecke, *Machiavellism: The Doctrine of Raison d'État* (New Haven: Yale University Press, 1957), pp. 321–322. For similar expressions, see Albert Sorel, *L'Europe et La Révolution française,* 8 vols. (Paris: Plon, Nourrit, 1885–1904), especially vol. 1, and F. H. Hinsley, *Power and the Pursuit of Peace* (London: Cambridge University Press, 1967), pp. 187–188.

5. See Great Britain, Public Record Office, Foreign Office, 92/30, Letter No. 1, Secret and Confidential, from Castlereagh (Paris) to Clancarty (Frankfort), 5 November 1815 (hereafter cited as PRO/FO).

6. Hajo Holborn, *The Political Collapse of Europe* (New York: Knopf, 1966), p. 27.

7. See F. S. Northedge and M. J. Grieve, *A Hundred Years of International Relations* (New York: Praeger, 1971), p. 1; Heinz Sasse, "Von Equipage and Automobilen des Auswärtigen Amts," *Nachrichtenblatt der Vereinigung Deutscher Auslandsbeamten* 10 (October 1957):145; Charles Burton Marshall, "The Golden Age in Perspective," *Journal of International Affairs* 17 (1963):9–17; and Paul Gordon Lauren, *Diplomats and Bureaucrats* (Stanford, Calif.: Hoover Institution Press, 1976), pp. 1, 23–33, and 222–228.

8. See Henry Kissinger, *A World Restored* (New York: Grosset & Dunlap, 1964 ed.), pp. 1–2.

9. Among many examples, see "Declaration Signed by Great Britain, Austria, France, Prussia, Russia, Sardinia, and Turkey Respecting Maritime Law, 16 April 1856," in Edward Hertslet, ed., *The Map of Europe by Treaty*, 4 vols. (London: Butterworth, 1875–1891), 2:1282–1283; "Protocols and General Act of the West African Conference, Meeting of 15 November 1884," in Great Britain, Parliament, *Parliamentary Papers, 1884–1885*, 55:143–144; and "Agreement Between Great Britain and the Ameer of Afghanistan, 12 November 1893," in Great Britain, Foreign Office, *British and Foreign State Papers, 1901–1902*, 95:1049.

10. Letter from Baron Plessen (London) to Earl Granville, 8 October 1884, in Great Britain, Parliament, *Parliamentary Papers, 1884–1885*, 55:456, may be taken as typical of many such expressions.

11. For general discussions of "rules of the game," see Hedley Bull, *The Anarchical Society: A Study of Order in World Politics* (London: Macmillan, 1977), pp. 54–57, 117, 208–209, and 219–221; Raymond Cohen, "Rules of the Game in International Politics," *International Studies Quarterly* 24 (March 1980):129–150; Stephen A. Garrett, "Nixonian Foreign Policy: A New Balance of Power—or a Revised Concert?," *Polity* 8 (Spring 1976):389–421; and Richard Elrod, "The Concert of Europe," *World Politics* 28 (January 1976):159–174.

12. Those of us living in a more lawless age must remember that treaty commitments and moral obligations were taken very seriously in the nineteenth century, and promises made were not lightly broken. It is for this reason that the specific words of the texts that follow in this chapter are so significant.

13. "Treaty of Alliance and Friendship Between Great Britain, Austria, (Prussia, and Russia), 20 November 1815," in Hertslet, *Map of Europe*, 1:374–375.

14. For an expression of this opinion, see W. N. Medlicott, *Bismarck, Gladstone, and the Concert of Europe* (London: Athlone, 1956), especially p. 18; and Alan Sked, ed., *Europe's Balance of Power, 1815–1848* (London: Macmillan, 1979).

15. The words are those of René Albrecht-Carrié, *The Concert of Europe, 1815–1914* (New York: Harper & Row, 1968), p. 31.

16. Considerable historical dispute exists over the precise duration of the Concert of Europe. Some scholars, like Albrecht-Carrié *(The Concert of Europe)* and Carsten Holbraad *(The Concert of Europe: A Study in German and British International Theory, 1815–1914* [London: Longman, 1970]), maintain that it lasted an entire century. Others, like Elrod ("The Concert of Europe," pp. 160–163) and Paul W. Schroeder *(Austria, Great Britain and the Crimean War* [Ithaca, N.Y.: Cornell University Press, 1972]), argue that it ended in 1848 or 1854 or 1856. The only point presented here is that regardless of whether the label of "concert" is applied or not, the Great Powers met for mutual consultation and collective decisionmaking throughout the century, as the various treaties and agreements discussed below testify.

17. "Letter from Napoleon III to Queen Victoria, 4 November 1863," in Hertslet, *Map of Europe,* 2:1576. In this particular case, the proposal failed to materialize due to its overgeneral nature.

18. It is important to recognize in this regard that there never was a rule requiring complete unanimity of all the Powers on all questions.

19. "General Act of the Berlin Congress, 1885," in Great Britain, Parliament, *Parliamentary Papers, 1884–1885,* 55:438.

20. PRO/FO, 371/527, Despatch No. 7, Confidential, from R. Rodd (Stockholm) to Grey, 14 January 1908.

21. PRO/FO, 371/528, Despatch No. 190 from F. Lascelles (Berlin) to Grey, 27 April 1908.

22. "Agreement Between the Austrian and Prussian Ministers, 29 November 1850," in Hertslet, *Map of Europe,* 2:1143. These several quotations may be taken as representative of many others.

23. George Curzon, *Frontiers* (Oxford: Clarendon Press, 1907), p. 32.

24. As cited in Gordon A. Craig, *Europe Since 1815* (New York: Holt, Rinehart, & Winston, 1971 ed.), p. 18.

25. The words are those of Albrecht-Carrié (*The Concert of Europe,* p. 256).

26. "Convention . . . Between Great Britain and Russia, Containing Arrangements on the Subject of Persia, Afghanistan, and Tibet," in Great Britain, Parliament, *Parliamentary Papers, 1908,* Cmnd. 3750, 125:482–483.

27. Curzon, *Frontiers,* p. 28. Interestingly enough, another British statesman, Lord Carrington, recently has proposed neutrality as a possible means of preventing a major confrontation between the Americans and the Soviets in Afghanistan.

28. "Traité conclu à Londres, le 15 novembre 1831 . . . pour la constitution du royaume de Belgique et de son indépendance et de sa neutralité," A. de Clercq, *Recueil des Traités de la France,* 23 vols. (Paris: Amyot, 1861–1919), 4:146.

29. "Treaty . . . Relative to the Grand Duchy of Luxembourg and the Duchy of Limburg," in Hertslet, *Map of Europe,* 3:1804.

30. "General Treaty Between Great Britain, Austria, France, Portugal, Prussia, Russia, Spain, and Sweden, 9 June 1815," in ibid., 1:219.

31. "Convention Between Great Britain, Austria, France, Prussia, Russia, and Turkey Respecting the Straits of the Dardanelles and Bosphorus, 13 July 1841," and "Convention . . . Respecting the Straits of the Dardenelles and Bosphorus, 30 March 1856," in ibid., 2:1024–1026 and 1266–1269.

32. "General Treaty of Peace Between Great Britain, Austria, France, Prussia, Russia, Sardinia, and Turkey, 30 March 1856," in ibid., pp. 1256–1257.

33. "Treaty Between Great Britain, Austria, France, Prussia, and Russia, for the Annexation of the Ionian Islands to Greece, 14 November 1863," in ibid., pp. 1569–1574.

34. These agreements began in 1856 with the "Convention Between Great Britain, France, and Russia, Respecting the Åland Islands, 30 March 1856," in ibid., pp. 1272–1273; continued with the 1908 North Sea agreement; and

then were again reconfirmed with the 1921 "Convention relative à la Non-Fortification et à la Neutralisation des Iles d'Åland," in PRO/FO, 371/6774.

35. *Svenska Dagblad,* as cited in PRO/FO, 371/529, Despatch No. 71 from R. Rodd (Stockholm) to Edward Grey, 28 April 1908.

36. PRO/FO, 371/6774, Despatch No. 1, Confidential, from J. D. Gregory (Geneva) to Curzon, 20 October 1921.

37. Annexe E [Protocole no. 49] "Note adressée le 15 Octobre 1831 par la Conférence de Londres," in de Clercq, *Recueil des Traités,* 4:143–145.

38. The "Andrassy Note" of 1875, in Adolphe d'Avril, *Négociations relatives au Traité de Berlin et aux arrangements qui ont suivi* (Paris: Leroux, 1886), pp. 101–102. In this particular case, the subsequent "rash impulses" of the local actors frustrated the efforts of the Powers, who were able to prevent a major European war but not one between Russia and Turkey.

39. PRO/FO, 371/6774, "Convention relative à la Non-Fortification et à la Neutralisation des Iles d'Åland," in Despatch No. 1 from J. D. Gregory (Geneva) to Curzon, 20 October 1921.

40. "General Act of the Brussels Conference, 2 July 1890," in Great Britain, Parliament, *Parliamentary Papers, 1892,* 95:49. Also see "Protocol Between Great Britain, the Independent State of the Congo, France, Germany, Portugal, and Spain, Prohibiting the Importation of Fire-arms, Ammunition, etc., Within a Certain Zone in Western Equatorial Africa, 22 July 1908," in Great Britain, Foreign Office, *British and Foreign State Papers, 1907–08,* 101:176–177.

41. Enclosure to Despatch from E. Malet (Berlin) to Salisbury, 19 March 1887, in Great Britain, Foreign Office, *British and Foreign State Papers, 1886–87,* 78:1051–1052.

42. See below for further discussion.

43. "Correspondence Respecting Central Asia," in Great Britain, Parliament, *Parliamentary Papers, 1878,* Cmnd. 2169, 80:633 ff.

44. "Convention . . . Between Great Britain and Russia, Containing Arrangements on the Subject of Persia, Afghanistan, and Tibet, 31 August 1907," in Great Britain, Parliament, *Parliamentary Papers, 1908,* Cmnd. 3750, 125:485.

45. Albrecht-Carrié, *The Concert of Europe,* p. 310.

46. "Despatch from the Earl of Derby to Count Shuvaloff, Defining British Interests in the East, 6 May 1877," in Hertslet, *Map of Europe,* 4:2615.

47. "Despatch from Sir Edward Grey to Sir A. Nicolson (St. Petersburg), 29 August 1907," in Great Britain, Parliament, *Parliamentary Papers, 1908,* Cmnd. 3750, 125:478.

48. The words are those of Curzon, *Frontiers,* p. 47.

49. These words of the Anglo-Afghan agreement of 12 November 1893 in Great Britain, Parliament, *Parliamentary Papers, 1905,* Cmnd. 2534, 57:457–459, may be taken as typical of many others.

50. See M. F. Lindley, *The Acquisition and Government of Backward Territory in International Law* (London: Longmans, Green, & Co., 1926), p. 209.

51. "Arrangement Between Great Britain and Germany Relative to Their

Respective Spheres of Action," in Great Britain, Parliament, *Parliamentary Papers, 1884–1885,* Cmnd. 4442, 55:553.

52. "Un ancien diplomate," *Etude diplomatique sur la guerre de Crimée,* 2 vols. (St. Petersburg: Librarie de la cour imperiale, 1878), 1:15n.

53. Gortchakoff, as cited in Curzon, *Frontiers,* p. 42.

54. "Letter, Secret, from Northbrook to Duke of Argyll, 9 September 1872," in Great Britain, Parliament, *Parliamentary Papers, 1878,* Cmnd. 2169, 80:650–651.

55. "Convention . . . . Between Great Britain and Russia, Containing Arrangements on the Subject of Persia, Afghanistan, and Tibet, 31 August 1907," in Great Britain, Parliament, *Parliamentary Papers, 1908,* Cmnd. 3750, 125:482–485.

56. "Anglo-Russian Note . . . for Safeguarding the Interests of the Two Governments in Persia, and for Preserving the Independence of That Country, 11 September 1907," in Great Britain, Foreign Office, *British and Foreign State Papers, 1908–1909,* 102:906–907.

57. Lindley, *Acquisition and Government,* pp. 210–211.

58. Curzon, *Frontiers,* p. 48.

59. The "Castlereagh Memorandum," in Sir Charles Webster, *The Foreign Policy of Castlereagh, 1815–1822,* 2 vols. (London: Bell & Sons, 1963 ed.), 2:239–240.

60. "Declaration of the Allied Sovereigns of Austria, Prussia, and Russia . . . 12 May 1821," in Hertslet, *Map of Europe,* 1:667–669. See also Hans Schmalz, *Versuche einer Gesamteuropäischen Organisation, 1815–1820* (Bern: Sauerländer, 1940). The Austrian forces put down the uprising with little difficulty and then quickly withdrew. In 1823 France acted in the same manner for Europe in Spain.

61. "Treaty Between Great Britain, France, and Russia for the Pacification of Greece, 6 July 1827, and Additional Article," in Hertslet, *Map of Europe,* 1:769–773.

62. "Convention Conclue entre les Cours de la Grande Bretagne, d'Autriche, de Prusse, et de Russie . . . pour la Pacification du Levant, 15 July 1840," in Great Britain, *Parliamentary Papers, 1841,* 24:721–723.

63. "Collective Note Presented to the Porte by . . . Great Britain, Austria-Hungary, France, Germany, Italy, and Russia, 2 March 1897," in Great Britain, Parliament, *Parliamentary Papers, 1897,* 102, 1:116–118.

64. "General Treaty of Peace Between Great Britain, Austria, France, Prussia, Russia, Sardinia, and Turkey, 30 March 1856," in Hertslet, *Map of Europe,* 2:1255. See also "Protocol of Conference . . . Suggesting the Reference of Disputes Between Foreign Powers to the Mediation of a Third Power, Previous to Hostilities, 14 April 1856," in ibid., p. 1277.

65. "Protocols and General Act of the West African Conference," in Great Britain, Parliament, *Parliamentary Papers, 1884–1885,* 55:441.

66. James Brown Scott, *Les Conventions et déclarations de la Haye de 1899 et 1907* (New York: Oxford University Press, 1918).

67. Ibid., p. 43.

68. The 1856 agreement was invoked, for example, in 1864 with reference

to Danish affairs and again in 1866 concerning Austro-Prussian disputes without success.

69. Among many who hold this view, see the contemporary Charles Calvo, *Le Droit international théorique et pratique, précedé d'un exposé historique des progrès de la science du droit des gens,* 5th ed., 6 vols. (Paris: A. Rousseau, 1896), especially vol. 3; Raoul Genet, *Traité de diplomatie et de droit diplomatique,* 3 vols. (Paris: Pedone, 1931–1932), especially vol. 3; and J. L. Simpson and H. Fox, *International Arbitration: Law and Practice* (New York: Praeger, 1959), p. 12.

70. L. Oppenheim, *International Law, a Treatise,* 3rd ed., ed. R. Roxburgh, 2 vols. (London: Longmans, Green, & Co., 1921), p. 15.

71. H. La Fontaine, *Pasicrisie internationale, histoire documentaire des arbitrages internationaux* (Berne: Stämpfli, 1902), p. viii.

72. See John Bassett Moore, *History and Digest of International Arbitrations,* 6 vols. (Washington, D.C.: Government Printing Office, 1898), 1:495–682; and "Sentence arbitrale pronouncée par le Baron Lambermont dans l'Affaire du 'Sergent Malamine,'" in Great Britain, Foreign Office, *British and Foreign State Papers, 1901–1902,* 95:141–142.

73. Raymond Sontag, *European Diplomatic History, 1871–1932* (New York: Century, 1933), p. 102. See also Richard Ned Lebow, "Accidents and Crises: The Dogger Bank Affair," *Naval War College Review* 31 (Summer 1978):66–75.

74. A.J.P. Taylor, *The Struggle for Mastery in Europe, 1848–1918* (Oxford: Clarendon Press, 1954), p. 425. See also the similar opinion of Oppenheim, *International Law,* 2:15.

75. "Despatch from Sir E. Malet (Berlin) to Granville, 21 February 1885," in Great Britain, Parliament, *Parliamentary Papers, 1884–1885,* Cmnd. 4284, 55:123.

76. "Note Addressed by the Plenipotentiaries of Great Britain, Austria, Prussia, and Russia to the Plenipotentiary of France Communicating the Protocol, 14 July 1831," in Hertslet, *Map of Europe,* 2:857.

77. "Despatch from the Earl of Derby to Count Shuvaloff, Defining British Interests in the East, 6 May 1877," in ibid., 4:2615.

78. "General Act of the Berlin Conference, 26 February 1885," in Great Britain, Parliament, *Parliamentary Papers, 1884–1885,* 55:312.

79. "General Act of the Brussels Conference, 2 July 1890," in Great Britain, Parliament, *Parliamentary Papers, 1890,* 95:51.

80. See "Declaration and Memorandum Communicated by Herr von Stumm," 15 April 1908, in PRO/FO, 371/529.

81. "Letter from Earl Russell (London) to Earl Cowley (Paris), 12 November 1863," in Hertslet, *Map of Europe,* 2:1579.

82. The words are those of de Calliéres, *On the Manner of Negotiating,* p. 135.

83. For more discussion on this matter, see François Guizot, *Mémoires,* 2 vols. (Paris: Michel Lévy Frères, 1859), 2:266; and Gabriel Hanotaux, "L'Europe qui naît," *La Revue hebdomadaire* 48 (30 November 1907):563,

a copy of which is also on file in Germany, Politisches Archiv des Auswärtiqes Amt, Abteilung IA, Frankreich 105, no. 1, vol. 26.

84. "Protocol No. 11 of a Conference Held at the Foreign Office, 20 January 1831," in Great Britain, Parliament, *Parliamentary Papers, 1833,* 42:299.

85. Sked, *Europe's Balance of Power,* pp. 2–3.

86. Among many expressions of this nature, see "Correspondence Respecting Central Asia," in Great Britain, Parliament, *Parliamentary Papers, 1878,* Cmnd. 2164, 80:639; and Letter, Confidential, from C. Thomas of the Admiralty to the Foreign Office, 8 January 1908, in PRO/FO, 371/527.

87. *Svenska Dagblad,* as cited in PRO/FO, 371/529, Despatch No. 71 from R. Rodd (Stockholm) to Edward Grey, 28 April 1908.

88. Charles Thayer, *Diplomat* (New York: Harper & Brothers, 1959), p. 253.

89. "Protocol No. 1, Meeting of 15 November 1884," in Great Britain, Parliament, *Parliamentary Papers, 1884–1885,* Cmnd. 4442, 55:143–144.

90. See letter from Earl Granville to Count Münster (London), 16 May 1885, and letter of response from Count Münster to Earl Granville, 2 June 1885, in ibid., p. 555.

91. "Protocol No. 11 of a Conference Held at the Foreign Office, 20 January 1831," in Great Britain, Parliament, *Parliamentary Papers, 1833,* 42:299.

92. Circular note from François Guizot, 3 December 1846, in Hertslet, *Map of Europe,* 2:1076.

93. See, among many examples, letter from Sir E. Malet (Berlin) to Earl Granville, 21 February 1885, in Great Britain, Parliament, *Parliamentary Papers, 1884–1885,* Cmnd. 4284, 55:123; and Charles Depuis, *Le Principe d'équilibre et le concert européen* (Paris: Perrin, 1909).

94. Webster, *Foreign Policy of Castlereagh,* 2:160.

95. This point is made particularly in Craig, *Europe Since 1815,* p. 35.

96. Letter from Clarendon to Cowley (Paris), 17 May 1866, in Hertslet, *Map of Europe,* 3:1666.

97. Fred C. Iklé, *How Nations Negotiate* (New York: Praeger, 1964), pp. 50–58.

98. See Kissinger, *A World Restored,* p. 2.

99. See, among many examples, PRO/FO, 92/30, Letter No. 1, Secret and Confidential, from Castlereagh (Paris) to Clancarty (Frankfort), 5 November 1815; and Depuis, *Le Principe d'équilibre,* p. 230.

4
Soviet Policy in the Middle East, 1967–1972: Unalterable Antagonism or Collaborative Competition?

George W. Breslauer

Western literature on Soviet policy in the Middle East during 1967–1972 is largely in agreement that the Soviet leadership did not want another Middle East war to break out during these years. But that same body of literature is divided over whether the Soviets genuinely wanted a peace settlement in the area. Some authors conclude that Soviet leaders favored the perpetuation of a condition of "no war, no peace."[1] In contrast, other authors contend that Soviet diplomats sought to forge a superpower collaborative relationship that might bring about a settlement of the Arab-Israeli confrontation.[2] Similarly, some authors contend that the Soviet Union had an "objective" strategic, political, or economic interest in maintaining a condition of "controlled tension" (i.e., no war, no peace) in the region.[3] Other authors claim that the advancement of Soviet objective interests was better served by the negotiation of a peace settlement and the stabilization of conditions in the region.[4]

These bodies of literature do not address each other. For the most part, the authors make their arguments without rejecting or even examining the premises and methodologies of those with whom they disagree. Accordingly, the purpose of this chapter will be to reconstruct Soviet behavior in the region and in superpower diplomatic forums as a means of testing these alternative hypotheses. I will do this by reshuffling the evidence currently available in English-language memoirs and secondary literature.[5] The burden of my argument will be that Soviet behavior during 1967–1972 indicated intense Soviet interest in a political settlement of the conflict based on superpower collaboration—but not at any price; and neither the United States nor Israel was willing to pay the Soviet price.

I will be arguing that the "no war, no peace" hypothesis is unconvincing, but let us first be clear as to what that hypothesis means. For one thing, the claim is that the perpetuation of conflict was a conscious Soviet strategy, not simply an incidental product of the interaction of Soviet, U.S., Egyptian, and Israeli policies. That is, the argument is not that, *given* the existing U.S., Egyptian, and Israeli policies, Soviet policy *in effect* perpetuated a condition of no war, no peace. Rather, the hypothesis claims that such perpetuation was a conscious goal.

For another thing, the claim is that Soviet policies were relatively coherent and consistent (as strategies are supposed to be). They were the work of a rather unified, consensual, and clearly calculating decisionmaking elite. The "no war, no peace" viewpoint does not deny that Soviet decisionmaking entails bargaining among competitive elites; nor does it preclude uncertainty and occasional confusion as the explanation for given actions. However, the hypothesis presumes that bargaining, uncertainty, and confusion come into play only in the determination of *tactics.* The elite is assumed to be unified in its commitment to a *strategy* of "no war, no peace."

The hypothesis can be restated in terms of its view of Soviet preference ordering among the goals being pursued by the USSR's Middle East policy. Let us assume that Soviet policy in the region, during 1967–1972, was driven by the following goals (listed in random order): (1) maintenance, consolidation, and expansion of influence in the Arab world, with influence building being an end in itself, for political, ideological, and prestige reasons; (2) geostrategic rivalry with the United States, leading the Soviets to use influence to gain strategic assets (e.g., military bases, port facilities, anti-Western allies); (3) economic advantages, such as hard currency from arms sales; (4) avoidance of superpower confrontation, both because of its intrinsic dangers and because (after 1969) of the damage it might do to détente; and (5) maintenance of a dialogue with the United States regarding terms for a peace settlement between the Arabs and the Israelis.

The "no war, no peace" hypothesis views Soviet maintenance of a dialogue with the United States as a purely tactical consideration, geared toward limiting damage to détente, avoiding superpower confrontation, and inducing the United States to pressure Israel to withdraw from occupied territories without an equivalent Arab concession. Furthermore, the hypothesis views influence building and geostrategic rivalry as Soviet leaders' primary goals in the region, goals for which they were willing to sacrifice economic benefits (if necessary) and risk superpower confrontation. Finally, a central claim of this perspective is that Soviet leaders believed that a peace settlement in the Middle East would endanger their other goals; a settlement would reduce their opportunities for influence building, for gaining strategic assets, and for earning hard currency from arms sales.

The hypothesis may not be entirely convincing, but it is certainly compelling. First, it is consistent with Soviet behavior before 1967, when first Khrushchev and then Brezhnev and Kosygin indicated little interest in superpower collaboration and very great interest in high-risk superpower competition in the Middle East. Indeed, Soviet behavior in the months preceding the Six-Day War (June 1967) was almost reckless. A second reason the hypothesis compels attention is that it is consistent with a very broad consensus among analysts of Soviet behavior (both moderates and "hard-liners") about the depth of Soviet commitment under Brezhnev to influence building, geostrategic rivalry, and confrontation avoidance. A third reason for the attractiveness of the hypothesis is that it is consistent with Soviet risk-taking inclinations in the Middle East during 1967–1972. Thus, those who argue that Soviet behavior was "irresponsible," insincere, or the like can point to: (1) Soviet failure to prevent or halt Nasser's War of Attrition (1969–1970); (2) Soviet assumption of the air defense of Egypt (1970–1972); (3) Soviet collusion with Egypt in violating the cease-fire of the summer of 1970; and (4) Soviet abetting of the Syrian invasion of Jordan in the fall of 1970. Finally, the "no war, no peace" hypothesis is consistent with significant retrogressions in the Soviet bargaining position during the nation's dialogue with the United States. Thus, those who argue that Soviet negotiating concessions were insincere and merely tactical can point, in particular, to the retrogression of June 1969 and to the December 1969 Soviet rejection of the Rogers Plan.

These qualities of the hypothesis have encouraged most U.S. policymakers, and many U.S. academics, to embrace it. Yet the interpretation is also vulnerable, and therefore it is more compelling than conclusive. Taking stock of its vulnerabilities will help us to build an alternative characterization of Soviet strategy. First, the fact that the Soviets were following such a strategy before 1967 does not mean that they were necessarily following the same strategy between 1967 and 1972. For one thing, the shock of the Six-Day War could well have impressed on Soviet leaders the extent of Arab military weakness and the willingness of Israel to engage in preemptive warfare in the face of provocation. Soviet confidence in the USSR's ability to prevent war without permitting peace could well have been shaken, inducing a reevaluation of strategy. For another thing, the rise of détente during 1968–1970 raised the costs to the Soviets of attempting to pursue a tenuous strategy of "no war, no peace." There was a constant threat that, if the Middle East situation got out of hand, the ensuing crisis could set back negotiations toward Soviet higher-priority goals: arms control, European security, and trade.

A second vulnerability of the hypothesis is the tendency of analysts to take Soviet actions (from risk-taking on the ground to retrogressions on the U.S.-Soviet diplomatic track) out of context. This approach makes little sense from a scholarly standpoint. Soviet actions, as indicators of Soviet strategy, can only be interpreted in the context of the definitions of restraint and reciprocity that the superpower patrons brought to the conflict. Moreover, no single relationship can be examined in isolation. How we interpret an escalation of Soviet military commitment to Egypt, for example, depends in part on the Israeli-Egyptian and U.S.-Israeli military relationships at the time. Thus, the Soviets took over the air defense of Egypt only after Israeli deep penetration bombing of that country was aimed at toppling the Nasser regime, thereby possibly violating a tacit understanding between the superpowers that allegedly grew out of the 1967 war. Similarly, Soviet diplomatic retrogressions cannot be evaluated without reference to what was happening on the ground at the time. Soviet willingness to collude with the United States at the expense of the superpowers' respective allies apparently varied, being in part a function of the varying military relationship between Egypt and Israel.

A third vulnerability of the hypothesis is that no analyst, to my knowledge, has grappled with the methodological dilemmas involved in testing the "no war, no peace" claim. How would one convince a skeptical, objective observer of its truth? As things stand, I suspect that a Soviet analyst, using the same methodology, could as easily make the case that the United States was following a strategy of "no war, no peace" and that the United States did not engage in "responsible" behavior.[6]

Fourth, and finally, the hypothesis is vulnerable in its imputing to the Soviets an objective interest in avoiding peace. Just as many arguments could be made on behalf of the opposite proposition. Thus, one could argue that the Soviets' experience in the Middle East from 1955 to 1967 had taught them that instability and conflict (both inter-Arab and Arab-Israeli) are endemic to the region and would not be eliminated by an armed peace reached between Israel and her neighbors.[7] Hence, even a peace settlement would not markedly reduce Soviet opportunities for competitive influence building. Or one could argue that only some sort of peace settlement would allow the Soviets to garner the prestige and international legitimacy they covet from acting as the recognized partner of the United States in regional conflict amelioration.[8] Then, too, one could argue that an armed peace guaranteed by the superpowers "would make the Soviet Union less dependent on unstable regimes in the Arab world by providing it with an additional, more solid and secure means of participating in the politics of the region."[9]

In contrast to the "no war, no peace" hypothesis, this perspective imputes greater Soviet interest in superpower collusion as an end in itself. It also imputes to the Soviets interest in a particular *type* of peace settlement in the region—one that amounted to an armed peace within secure and recognized borders, but not one that attempted to eliminate all sources of conflict in the region.

Although the "no war, no peace" hypothesis is vulnerable and unconvincing, one would be mistaken to go too far in the opposite direction—to view the Soviets' commitment to a peace settlement as a priority for which they were willing to sacrifice a great deal. Some synthesis of these two positions would better qualify as the alternative hypothesis to be tested. Such an interpretation would acknowledge the depth of the Soviet commitment to influence building and geostrategic rivalry in the region but would not write off Soviet diplomatic concessions and collaborative offerings as tactical ploys. Rather, it would view the Soviets as driven by mixed motives (neither totally benevolent nor totally duplicitous), seeking to play the competitive game in the Middle East while simultaneously attempting to collaborate with the United States in ways that would nudge the local actors toward an armed peace. Such a settlement would defuse the Arab-Israeli conflict as a source of potential superpower confrontation while establishing a great power collaborative presence in the region to guarantee the peace. Viewed from the Soviet perspective, peace was neither a condition to avoid at all costs nor an end in itself. The Soviets were not interested in a peace settlement that would reduce their influence in the region. Hence, they were less likely to be cooperative when they perceived that the United States was trying to drive a wedge between the USSR and Egypt. In contrast to the "no war, no peace" interpretation, which views the Soviets as a *mitigable, but essentially unalterable, antagonist* in the Middle East at the time, this interpretation views them as a *collaborative competitor.*[10]

Before beginning our examination of Soviet policy, let me say a few words about the limitations of the available evidence. Although an enormous amount of evidence is available,[11] vital information about the extent to which the Soviets pressured their Arab allies either is missing or is based frequently (but not always) on possibly biased testimony by Anwar Sadat and Mohamed Heikal. Lawrence Whetten appears to have studied or been exposed to diplomatic correspondence and interviews, but on the matter of Soviet pressure, all too often his study leaves us without a footnote.[12] Obviously, we also lack testimony about Soviet Politburo deliberations. More inside information is available on Soviet-U.S. negotiations, but the content or minutes of private, informal conversations (if they took place) have not come to light, and our knowledge of the content and clarity of Soviet-U.S. understandings regarding restraint and reciprocity remains skimpy. All these limitations notwithstanding, we have a great deal to go on.

From the Six-Day War to the War of Attrition (June 1967–April 1969)

After the Six-Day War, the Soviet Union massively resupplied its clients in the Middle East, indicating its continued determination to serve as their military and political patrons in the international arena. But patronage is not necessarily warmongering; U.S.-Soviet negotiations began almost immediately to defuse the situation and to prevent another outbreak of hostilities that might have resulted in a superpower confrontation. But the positions of Egypt and Israel were miles apart. Egypt demanded total and unconditional Israeli withdrawal from the occupied territories and compensation to the Arab states for the damage inflicted on them by the war. But Egypt offered nothing in the way of peace, freedom of navigation, or recognition in return. Israel demanded direct negotiations between the local belligerents, looking toward a final peace agreement that would accord recognition and full rights in the region to the state of Israel, coupled with the possibility of some border adjustments. Israel offered no withdrawal from the occupied territories until such terms were worked out.

Both the Soviet and U.S. governments saw danger in this situation. The result of months of Soviet-U.S. negotiation after the war was United Nations Resolution 242, which avoided the issue of whether Israel would have to withdraw from *all* the land it occupied but basically called for Israeli withdrawal in exchange for Arab negotiations with Israel through a UN mediator, looking toward a final peace agreement that would ensure the sovereignty, independence, security, and regional navigation rights of all states in the area. Thus, the resolution called, in effect, for Arab recognition of Israel and an end to the Arab-Israeli state of war in exchange for total, or substantial,

Israeli withdrawal from occupied lands. The details could be hammered out once the basic principles were accepted.

Beyond this resolution, in the course of bargaining with the United States, Soviet negotiators made several other concessions: they agreed to drop their condemnations of Israel and their demands for refugee compensation from drafts put forward at the United Nations. And they agreed with the United States that a peace agreement should result in a superpower arms embargo of the region.[13] Soviet leaders, as a result, had a selling job to do among their Arab allies, for UN Resolution 242, and the additional Soviet concessions, diverged sharply from the maximal Arab position. When Soviet leaders tried to justify their program to Arab officials, the result was allegedly "stormy" sessions.[14] Indeed, the Soviet effort was unsuccessful. At the Khartoum Conference of August 1967, Arab heads of state lined up behind an intransigent posture of "no concessions."[15]

During 1968, Egypt's Nasser was getting impatient to recover the occupied territories. In the course of the year, he reached the conclusion that, if the territories were not recoverable by purely military means, they would have to be recovered by a combination of military and political pressure on Israel. Egyptian artillery barrages across the Suez Canal would keep the pressure on Israel while simultaneously keeping the conflict on a high flame, thereby inducing the United States and the USSR to collude at Israeli expense in order to avoid another war. Great power pressure on Israel would then force that country out of the occupied territories, even without a peace settlement.[16]

If this was Nasser's plan, he received little encouragement from the United States. The Johnson administration had decided to keep supplying Israel's military needs and to wait out the Arabs until they were ready to negotiate with Israel on moderate terms. Moreover, although there was sentiment welling up within the U.S. State Department for pressuring Israel to make concessions, the Johnson administration would not consider such a step in an election year.[17]

The Soviets did not give blanket endorsement to Nasser's change in tactics. In July 1968, Nasser visited Moscow for what the Soviet press referred to as "frank" discussions. According to insiders, Soviet leaders were unambiguous in conveying to Nasser the following points: (1) that the USSR placed highest priority on avoiding a direct clash with the United States in the Middle East; (2) that Nasser was engaging in "daydreams" if he thought that a military solution was possible in the foreseeable future; (3) that the Soviet Union would not meet Nasser's request for a long list of the most advanced, offensive military weaponry; and (4) that Nasser would be better advised to moderate his demands and seek a political solution to the conflict.[18] The Soviets did sweeten the pill by increasing military assistance to Egypt. But the nature of that assistance, and the nature of these "frank" discussions, suggest that Soviet leaders neither endorsed nor encouraged Nasser's argument that direct military pressure on Israel was a necessary supplement to the diplomatic bargaining process.[19] Soviet fears of uncontrolled escalation won out in Moscow's calculations.

On the diplomatic track during 1968, neither Nasser nor the government of Israel moderated their demands. Both UN mediator Gunnar Jarring's mission and the deliberations during the fall 1968 General Assembly meetings failed to make substantive progress toward reducing the gap. According to Heikal, Moscow did not conceal its disappointment, communicating to Nasser that it had hoped Johnson would be more willing to pressure Israel during his lame duck period (April–December 1968). At the same time, the Soviets tried to placate Nasser with predictions that the Nixon administration would be more forthcoming.[20]

After the election, however, Soviet leaders got to work immediately to influence the incoming Nixon administration in the direction of a superpower collaborative relationship in the Middle East. Both insiders' accounts and the evolution of formal Soviet negotiating positions indicate seriousness of intent. Thus, in December 1968, Soviet Foreign Minister Andrei Gromyko visited Cairo, where he asked Egyptian Foreign Minister Riad what Riad would think of formal U.S.-Soviet negotiations as a substitute for the UN-sponsored Jarring mission. Riad inquired as to what was wrong with Jarring. Gromyko replied: "He has no navies in the sea and no missiles in the air."[21] Apparently, Gromyko believed that only superpower collusion of some sort could generate enough pressure on local actors to make progress.

In order to interest the United States in such collaboration, the Soviet government came forth in the same month, December 1968, with its "first comprehensive plan for a peace settlement,"[22] which incorporated a number of additional divergences from the maximal Arab position, on both substantive and procedural matters. The Soviet plan echoed the letter of the Arab demand for total withdrawal, but with enough ambiguities and new wrinkles to violate the spirit of that demand, as well as the spirit and letter of other Arab demands. The plan has been summarized as follows:

> The plan envisioned the full implementation of 242 according to a prescribed timetable, beginning with formal confirmation by the belligerent states that they intended to carry out the provisions of the

resolution. This would have been followed with proclamations by all belligerents that they were prepared to reach a peaceful settlement and by Israel that it was prepared to withdraw from the occupied Arab territories before a fixed date. Negotiations or "contacts" between the belligerents would then be used to reach an agreement on secure and recognized borders, freedom of navigation in international waterways, a just solution of the refugee problem, and the territorial integrity and political independence of each state. Following an initial, partial Israeli withdrawal, Egypt would begin to clear the Suez Canal. At a later date to be agreed upon, Israel would complete its withdrawal to the pre–June 1967 borders, and Arab military and political control would be re-established over the occupied territories. At the same time, UN forces might return to the Sinai Peninsula and the situation of May 1967 might be restored. . . . The Security Council would guarantee freedom of passage through the Tiran Straits and the Gulf of Aqaba. Agreed-upon borders would be guaranteed by the four big powers and might include demilitarized zones between Israel and its neighbors.[23]

That Soviet leaders considered this a serious proposal (though perhaps only an initial bargaining position) was further indicated by the fact that they did not advertise its contents. They conveyed the plan to the U.S. government in a formal diplomatic note.

Nixon's national security adviser, Henry Kissinger, was apparently not impressed. Immersed in the details of learning his new job, preoccupied with Vietnam and preparations for SALT negotiations, convinced that there had been no change in the pre-1967 Soviet strategy of "no war, no peace" in the Middle East, adhering to a global strategy of containing the expansion of Soviet influence, and believing that, at the time, a Middle East stalemate served U.S. interests, Kissinger dismissed the Soviet proposal out of hand.[24] Israel also denounced the plan. The United States then countered with a twelve-point plan of its own, which Egypt promptly denounced.

But there were forces within the U.S. government that did not share Kissinger's burdens, beliefs, or perspectives. Secretary of State William Rogers and Assistant Secretary Joseph Sisco sought to begin serious discussions with Soviet diplomats to explore areas of possible compromise. Their interest was fueled further by Soviet Ambassador Anatolyi Dobrynin's approach to Kissinger on March 3, 1969, in which the ambassador further moderated the Soviet provision about the timing of Israeli withdrawal—now allowing for such withdrawal after other features of the settlement were executed. Moreover, Dobrynin indicated "a preference to discuss some of the more delicate subjects, such as frontiers, in the White House Channel," rather than in more public forums—an additional indication of Soviet willingness

to consider *territorial* compromise that might come under attack
from the USSR's allies.[25] From the Soviet standpoint, one might
surmise, prior publicity about such discussions would incur the wrath
of the USSR's allies before the Soviet negotiators could be sure that
the United States would make analogous concessions.

Rogers and Sisco, though not Kissinger, were eager to follow up
on Dobrynin's offer. Talks between Sisco and Dobrynin took place
frequently during March and April 1969. Sisco was offering near-
total Israeli withdrawal in exchange for a peace agreement that would
accord Israel full diplomatic recognition and guaranteed, secure
borders. Dobrynin was interested, wanting to explore and specify
further the terms of such a deal. On April 14, Dobrynin approached
Kissinger about the possibility of a joint U.S.-Soviet proposal that
would specify in more detail the final borders to which Israel might
eventually withdraw. And on April 11, Nasser's aide, M. Fawzi,
informed Kissinger that the Soviet Union was "pressing" Egypt "in
the direction of peace."[26]

During March and April 1969, however, events on the ground
were beginning to outpace diplomatic movement behind closed doors.
Fighting escalated between Egypt and Israel, between Israel and the
fedayeen (guerrillas), and among forces within Lebanon. Perhaps in
response to this escalation, or possibly because of fears of superpower
collusion at his expense, Nasser launched his War of Attrition along
the Suez Canal in early April 1969.

Before turning to the War of Attrition, let us review the period
since the Six-Day War (June 1967) for lessons that might bear on
the alternative hypotheses being tested in this chapter. Both hypotheses
accept the notion that the Soviets were in favor of no war at this
time. The important question is whether the Soviets were also in
favor of no peace (in line with the theory that they were unalterable
antagonists) or were now in favor of pushing local actors toward a
peace settlement (in accordance with the image of them as collaborative competitors). And if they favored the latter policy, what kind
of peace settlement did they want?

Three indicators have emerged from our analysis to suggest that
the Soviets were pushing for a peace settlement during these years.
The first such indicator was the extent of the Soviets' willingness to
dissociate themselves from maximal Arab demands. The most important of their concessions related to issues of frontier adjustment,
the negotiating process, and the timing of Israeli withdrawal from
occupied territories. The Soviets repeatedly indicated their willingness
to sanction border adjustments and demilitarized zones, and their
interest in great power guarantees of border security after a settlement

had been implemented. The Soviets also supported *indirect* Arab-Israeli negotiations. And the Soviets conceded that Israeli withdrawal could be postponed until other components of the peace settlement had been executed.

A second indicator of Soviet seriousness about the peacemaking process was the USSR's eagerness to collude with the United States behind closed doors. Such collusion was to specify border adjustments out of the view of Soviet Arab allies and to help mobilize U.S. pressure on Israel to withdraw to those borders.

A third indicator of Soviet intentions was insider testimony about Soviet efforts to convince the Arabs in general, and Nasser in particular, of the need to seek a political solution to the problem. Mohamed Heikal's testimony about the content of Soviet statements during Nasser's July 1968 trip to Moscow squared with the tone of the communiqué issued after that visit. These indicators in turn squared with Fawzi's remark to Kissinger as well as with the nature of the allegedly tempestuous sessions between Soviet and Arab officials in the summer of 1967.

Yet there were definite limits to the willingness of the Soviets to pressure their allies. Soviet behavior was that of a collaborative *competitor* of the United States in the Middle East, not that of a benevolent partner. Soviet military resupply of the Arabs after the Six-Day War implied a commitment not to force the Arabs to negotiate with Israel from a position of military prostration. Moreover, the Soviet pledge to use superpower collaboration to get the occupied territories returned to Arab sovereignty also indicated limits on Soviet dissociation from the Arab position. What these factors added up to was a Soviet effort to work with the United States to forge a peace settlement that would maintain or expand Soviet influence in the region—a settlement that would basically trade peace for territory, with the "armed peace" guaranteed by the Great Powers. Toward this end, the Soviets were willing to diverge from the Arab position and to apply limited forms of pressure on Nasser to be accommodative. But they were not willing to push so strongly as to *force* their allies to comply—partly because such action might induce a backlash against them in the Arab world, and partly because there was no evidence at the time that the United States was twisting the arms of the Israelis to induce the Israeli government to moderate its position. Indeed, these two motivations reinforced each other. Soviet eagerness to collude with the United States in private indicates a fear that significant Soviet pressure on the Arabs, in the absence of simultaneous and equivalent U.S. pressure on Israel, might be interpreted as betrayal in the Arab world. The Soviets were interested in a peace settlement, but not at the price of their influence in the Arab world. Thus, they behaved like collaborative competitors, not consensual partners or unalterable antagonists.

The War of Attrition (April 1969–August 1970)

From a military standpoint, Nasser's War of Attrition initially had considerable success. During the spring and early summer of 1969, Israel suffered casualties along the Suez Canal greater than the nation could afford to bear over an extended period. Israeli policymakers concluded that decisive action was needed to reverse the tide, and on July 20, 1969, the Israeli air force (IAF) began heavy bombing and strafing of Egyptian positions along the canal. By the end of the summer, Israel was inflicting disproportionate casualties and damage on the Egyptians. By September–October 1969, the Egyptian SAM-2 antiaircraft defense system along the canal had been destroyed, a development that gave Israel uncontested dominance of the air space over the canal zone. The IAF was able to pound Egyptian positions almost at will.

Beginning in the end of July (that is, after the IAF entered the War of Attrition), Soviet military assistance to Eygpt grew rapidly. Expanded arms deliveries, and an influx of Soviet military advisers, have been traced back to this period.[27] Sometime in the fall of 1969, when Egyptian defenses collapsed, the Soviet leadership made another decision. They apparently decided *in principle* that *direct* Soviet military intervention would be required to reestablish Egyptian defenses and to prevent another humiliating military defeat. However, the decision was not implemented until several months later—perhaps because the Soviets wanted first to see whether the United States would restrain Israel from pushing the Israeli military advantage still further.[28]

No such restraint was forthcoming. In January 1970, Israel extended its bombing campaign inland to urban areas of the Nile Valley and Nile Delta. The announced goal of such bombing was to force Nasser to call off the War of Attrition (Egyptian artillery fire across the canal intensified in December 1969), but Israeli politicians also spoke of their intention to bring Egypt to its knees and to topple the Nasser regime.[29] Egypt was helpless to stop the raids, short of giving in to Israeli terms for a settlement. And this Nasser was not willing to do.

Nor were the Soviets willing to force him to do so. The Israeli bombing campaign instead triggered execution of the earlier Soviet decision to defend Egypt against Israeli saturation bombing.[30] The consequence was an incremental but steady expansion of the Soviet military commitment to Egypt from February to July 1970.[31] First, SAM-3 antiaircraft missiles, run by Soviet personnel, were supplied to defend Egyptian urban centers and the Aswan Dam. Then Soviet planes and pilots were deployed over the inland areas to challenge Israeli jets. Once these missions were accomplished, the observable Soviet military commitment deepened still further. From May 1970 onward, the number of Soviet pilots, missile personnel, SAM-3s, airplanes, and air bases rose sharply. In addition, during the night of June 29, SAM-3 batteries were advanced to within thirty kilometers of the Suez Canal. This movement indicated that the Soviets had enlarged their goals from stopping Israeli deep penetration raids to neutralizing Israeli air superiority in the canal zone, broadly defined. Soviet pilots also extended their air cover to include the canal zone itself, thus neutralizing the advanced technology that the United States had given to Israel to knock out the SAM-3s. By the summer of 1970, there were ten to twenty thousand Soviet military personnel in Egypt.

The escalation did not end at this point. Soviet and Israeli pilots engaged each other at several points during the summer of 1970. And after the cease-fire went into effect on August 8, the Soviets and Egyptians decided to defy international opinion and to ignore possible costs to the negotiating process, by using the cover of the Egyptian-Israeli cease-fire to construct a massive, and nearly impregnable, air defense system along the Suez Canal.

This pattern of steadily increasing Soviet military involvement in the War of Attrition provides considerable evidence for the view of Soviet behavior as duplicitous or even reckless. Yet there were real limits to Soviet involvement that must be recorded if we are to arrive at an accurate characterization of Soviet strategy during this period. For one thing, the Soviets neither instigated nor encouraged Nasser's launching of the War of Attrition. According to Heikal, in May 1969, Soviet leaders "begged Nasser to use every effort to halt the 'war of attrition' across the Suez Canal." Reportedly, Soviet leaders conjured up dire images of what might happen if Egypt miscalculated or if things escalated beyond Egyptian control. Moreover, "they suggested a whole series of ingenious formulas, worked out by them, which they thought might succeed in stopping the fighting."[32] Heikal does not reveal whether the Soviets made any concrete threats to punish Egypt if that nation refused to heed Soviet urgings. But Jon Glassman does note that Soviet arms shipments were *not* such as to "assure [the] success" of the war of attrition.[33]

Even after Israel had turned the tide in the War of Attrition, the

Soviet government placed real limits on the depth of its military commitment to Egypt. On December 9, 1969, Anwar Sadat led a delegation to Moscow, where he requested Soviet delivery of improved MIG-21s capable of challenging Israeli air superiority over the canal zone. The Soviets refused.[34] On January 22, 1970, some two weeks after the start of Israeli deep penetration raids on Egypt, President Nasser journeyed to Moscow to request a Soviet air defense system, as well as a long list of advanced offensive weaponry capable of taking the war to Israeli urban centers. The Soviets met the first request, as we have seen, but with hesitation, and only after Nasser threatened to resign in favor of a pro-United States government. But the Soviets categorically refused to entertain the request for advanced offensive weaponry.[35]

These limits remained in place even after May 1970, when the Soviets expanded their defense of Egyptian airspace and their overall military involvement in Egypt. Thus, in June 1970, the Soviets refused Nasser's request for air cover over the canal zone. Egyptian goals had escalated as the defense of Egypt became more secure; Nasser was eager to take the offensive against Israel, hoping to cross the canal. From all accounts, the Soviets wanted no part of such an adventure. Indeed, in late June 1970, Nasser traveled again to the Soviet Union, where Soviet leaders persuaded him to postpone indefinitely his goal of crossing the canal in favor of consolidating military parity in the canal zone, under the cover of which operation the Soviet Union would press the United States to force greater Israeli flexibility on withdrawal terms.[36]

This evidence supports the notion that the Soviets wanted no war in the region at the time. They were willing to deepen their military commitment, but they sought to prevent it from resulting in an expanded war. If anything, they sought to force the war back to the canal zone rather than let it spread—either eastward (toward the Sinai and Tel Aviv) or westward (toward Cairo). In itself, however, this evidence does not controvert the "no war, no peace" hypothesis, which also presumes a Soviet strategy of preventing the situation from getting out of control. That hypothesis claims that the Soviets seek to keep the pot boiling but also seek to prevent it from boiling over. Furthermore, that hypothesis has the virtue of highlighting the fact that, in restricting the War of Attrition to the canal zone, the Soviets were compressing it into the one area in which the Egyptians had tactical superiority in artillery exchanges, once Israeli air superiority had been neutralized by their Soviet patrons.

Yet, on balance, the "no war, no peace" characterization of Soviet strategy at this time is a weak one. We will have occasion to examine

Soviet peace proposals later in this chapter. For the moment, however, we can look at two other indicators of Soviet intentions that bear on the hypothesis. For one thing, the hypothesis presumes Soviet self-confidence about Moscow's ability to control escalation and manage a duplicitous strategy. The evidence (cited above) from Heikal instead portrays a Soviet leadership that was intensely nervous about the War of Attrition and that "begged" Nasser to call it off. For another thing, the hypothesis presumes a lack in the Soviets of a genuine sense of *aggrievement* in making decisions to escalate their involvement.

Yet there is plentiful evidence to suggest that the Soviets felt aggrieved by U.S. and Israeli policies and that they viewed Soviet involvement as a response to actions that violated the USSR's conception of the superpowers' responsibility for reciprocity and restraint in their relationship. Of course, each superpower accepted the legitimacy of its client's basic grievances; and it is worth bearing in mind that Egypt started the War of Attrition. We are not seeking morally to evaluate each side's position in the escalating conflict. But if we wish to define the Soviets' strategy during these years, we need to understand their conceptions of restraint and reciprocity between the superpowers, as those powers interacted in the Middle East.

Once the Israelis had turned the tide in the War of Attrition (late summer 1969), they pressed their advantage, destroyed the Egyptian air defense system along the canal, and, throughout fall 1969, pounded Egyptian positions at will. The Egyptian military position had virtually collapsed. These successes were facilitated (if not condoned) by U.S. delivery to Israel in September 1969 of Phantom jets that would ensure long-term, total Israeli air superiority. In light of the timing, delivery of those jets sent the Arab diplomatic world into a furor.[37] Egyptian leaders sensed a U.S.-Israeli conspiracy to pound Egypt into submission. There is also substantial, though indirect, evidence to suggest that the Soviets reached a similar conclusion. Many analysts, focusing on different indicators of Soviet perspectives, identify a fundamental change in Soviet definitions of the situation during the fall of 1969—after delivery of the Phantoms, and after Israel had destroyed Egyptian air defenses.[38]

It was at this time (fall 1969) that the Soviets seem to have made the decision in principle to restore Egyptian defenses, with their own personnel if need be. But they were apparently not anxious to act on that commitment. Instead, they looked for signs of U.S. pressure on Israel to exercise restraint. No such signs of real pressure were forthcoming. Israeli officials consulted with U.S. officials during

December 1969, probably in evasive terms, and drew the conclusion that the United States would condone a further escalation of Israeli bombing.[39] Though there is no direct evidence, it is unlikely that the Soviets were unaware of such consultations; and it is likely that, when deep penetration raids began on January 7, 1970, the Soviets, prone to accept conspiracy theories anyway, sensed U.S.-Israeli collusion. Even after Nasser's visit to Moscow in late January 1970, the Soviets apparently stalled for a month before acting on their specific commitment to take over Egyptian air defense. During that interval, Soviet Prime Minister Kosygin sent a letter to Nixon (with similar communications to U.K. Prime Minister Harold Wilson and French President Georges Pompidou) in which Kosygin warned that if Israeli air attacks continued, "the Soviet Union will be forced to see to it that the Arab states have the means at their disposal, with the help of which a due rebuff to the arrogant aggressors could be made."[40]

It is unclear whether this note was a cover for an irreversible decision already made, or whether Soviet leaders would have been willing to reverse their decision had the United States induced Israel to call off their deep penetration raids. The historical sequence does not allow us to test Soviet intentions, for Nixon rejected the Soviet grievance as illegitimate, and Israel further escalated the bombing in February.

Kissinger was incensed by the steadily deepening Soviet military commitment to Egypt.[41] He viewed it as a geopolitical challenge that could not go unanswered. It was not, in his eyes, a logical Soviet response to Israeli escalation (though others in the U.S. government, less influential than Kissinger, viewed it as such).[42] Kissinger saw Israeli escalation as a reasonable and legitimate response to Nasser's War of Attrition; therefore, Soviet behavior had now taken the escalation one step further and had additionally introduced a superpower military presence that was unacceptable. Hence, in Kissinger's opinion, the Soviet Union had changed the name of the game and it needed to be faced down.

Moscow worked with a different definition of geopolitics. After the Israelis took the war to the Egyptian heartland and threatened to topple the Nasser regime, the Soviet leadership defined the game as a geopolitical challenge to which *they* had to respond if they were to maintain their credibility as patrons in the international system. When Kissinger criticized Soviet involvement at a press conference, defining the proper military balance in the region as a condition of Israeli military superiority, one frustrated Soviet diplomat exclaimed, "Doesn't he realize that our commitment to Egyptian defense is every bit as firm as the American commitment to Israeli security?"[43] The Soviets had been denying Nasser the means to take the war into the Sinai or into the heart of Israel. The United States, the Soviets thought, was not preventing the Israelis from broadening the war. The argument that the Soviets genuinely felt aggrieved is not all that implausible.[44]

Within this context of escalation and counterescalation, still another source of Soviet aggrievement arose. U.S. toleration of Israeli actions from the fall of 1969 onward looked to the Soviets like an effort to pound Nasser into submitting to Israeli settlement terms. Such a development called into question the credibility of the Soviet commitment to Egypt. But beyond matters of credibility, it also had implications for the future of superpower collaboration in the Middle East and the Soviet role in forging and enforcing a settlement in the region. For, to the Soviets, it has been argued, Israeli bombing looked like an effort, encouraged by the U.S. government, to convince Nasser that he no longer had a military option, that his hope of keeping military pressure on Israel, while the United States and the USSR colluded at Israel's expense, was a dream.[45] By logical extension, the suspicious Soviets would conclude that the United States was trying to drive a wedge between Egypt and the USSR by convincing Nasser that the road to realization of any of his goals lay through Washington, and Washington alone.

The Soviets did not base this conclusion solely on conjecture. Since coming into office in January 1969, Kissinger had been much cooler to the idea of superpower collaboration in the Middle East than had William Rogers or Joseph Sisco.[46] As a result, exploratory initiatives by Rogers and Sisco rarely had the full backing of the White House. And while Rogers and Sisco indicated sympathy for the Soviet dilemma in response to Israeli deep penetration raids, Kissinger did not, and Israel showed no signs of being under real, severe pressure to exercise restraint. As a result, Nasser's threat of late January 1970 to resign in favor of a pro-United States government struck a sensitive chord in Soviet leaders.

Soviet fears that the United States had turned from superpower collaboration to unilateralism were heightened during the spring and summer of 1970. From April 10 to April 14, Joseph Sisco was in Cairo, where part of his mission was to persuade Nasser to turn toward Washington for peace. Nasser was receptive, as he indicated publicly in a speech on May 1.[47] American commitment to unilateralism was deepened thereafter. From April 29 through early June 1970, Kissinger and the National Security Council undertook a reappraisal of U.S. policy in the Middle East, concluding that the direction of Middle East policy should be transferred from the State Department to the White House and that the basic mission of that policy should be an end to the War of Attrition under unilateral U.S. auspices, geared ultimately toward undermining Soviet influence in the region.[48] On June 19, 1970, the United States offered a cease-fire plan and a proposal for the renewal of peace talks through UN mediator Gunnar Jarring. In an unprecedented move, the United States chose not to seek prior Soviet agreement to the initiative.[49] Credit for a cease-fire, if one materialized, would be granted entirely to the United States.

The Soviets were aware of what was happening, though they could not be certain of its consequences. We may assume that their emotional reactions ranged from apprehension to hostility. More concretely, though, it is quite plausible to interpret the escalation of Soviet commitment to Egyptian defense as partially a reaction to fears of exclusion. The main source of Soviet influence in Egypt, and in the rest of the Arab world, was military assistance. The Soviets could provide economic aid for industrial development and political patronage in international forums. But what counted most to the Arabs was military assistance to recover from the 1967 debacle and to create a military instrument sufficiently credible to prevent Israel from dictating terms. The Israeli military escalation, coupled with the U.S. turn toward unilateralism, looked to the Soviets like a calculated effort to convince the Arabs that the Arab world did not have a military instrument and that their only hope for a settlement on tolerable terms lay through Washington, which, of the two superpowers, was the only one capable of pressuring Israel. In short, these developments looked like an effort to convince the Arabs (Egypt in particular) that the Soviets had little to offer.[50]

There is more than simply insiders' descriptions available to suggest that a sense of aggrievement on this score contributed to the pattern of Soviet involvement. The timing of Soviet counterescalations also frequently coincided with an enhanced perception of political exclusion. For instance, in November 1969, Nasser floated a trial balloon to encourage the U.S. unilateral initiatives.[51] Several weeks later, the Soviets indicated to Sadat their willingness in principle to restore the Egyptian defense system. In January 1970, when Nasser threatened the Soviets that he would resign in favor of a pro–United States government, the Soviet leadership discarded previous hesitations and agreed to let the Soviet armed forces take over Egyptian air defenses. Soviet military involvement increased sharply once again in May 1970, shortly after Sisco's visit to Cairo and Nasser's expressed receptivity to U.S. feelers. Finally, after the U.S.-sponsored cease-fire-and-negotiation plan went into effect, the Soviets willingly conspired with the Egyptians to violate the cease-fire by surreptitiously moving a wall of SAM-3s up to the canal.[52] It is as if the Soviets, in response to the drift of events (both military and diplomatic), sought ways to demonstrate to the Egyptians that the Soviets still had a great deal to offer—specifically, control of the military option, without which the Israelis and the U.S. leaders would seek to impose their terms on an isolated and/or militarily vulnerable Egypt.

In sum, it is too simplistic to point to Soviet military involvement in Egypt as proof that the USSR was following a strategy of keeping the pot boiling during the War of Attrition. Considering Soviet definitions of reciprocity and restraint on the part of the superpower patrons of the conflict, escalated Soviet military involvement need not be interpreted as incompatible with a peace-seeking strategy. To explore this point further, we need to turn our attention to the diplomatic track.

After Nasser launched the War of Attrition, the "pace of diplomacy quickened."[53] During May and June 1969, according to most sources, discussions between Sisco or Rogers on the U.S. side and Dobrynin or Gromyko on the Soviet side made progress in narrowing the gap between the formal diplomatic positions of the superpowers. Specifically, in exchange for a tacit U.S. commitment to pressure Israel to withdraw from occupied territories (with the issue of the extent of withdrawal remaining unsettled), the Soviet Union accepted the idea of a package settlement of the conflict, including a lasting peace agreement, Arab recognition of Israel, and a negotiating process based on indirect talks between the belligerents through a UN mediator.[54] This acceptance represented an unprecedented degree of Soviet dissociation from the maximal Arab position.

There is considerable, and mutually reinforcing, evidence that Soviet leaders tried to sell this new formula to their Arab allies. First, Mohamed Heikal reports that, at the June 1969 Moscow conference of world communist parties, Gromyko approached Arab delegations with "yet another proposal for a Middle East settlement which bore remarkable similarities to the American proposal for a settlement. . . . They both seemed to commit the Arabs to such things as direct negotiations with Israel, joint Arab-Israeli patrolling of the frontier areas, and so on, all of which were quite unacceptable at that time."[55] Second, before the end of that conference, Gromyko flew to Cairo for reportedly "frank" (i.e., blunt and conflictual) talks, in which the Soviet foreign minister tried to convince Nasser to accept the new formula. But Nasser was intransigent, apparently angered that the Soviets would embrace a forthcoming negotiating position at a time when Egypt was doing so well on the military front. The result of these talks was that the Soviets backed down, as was reflected in a Soviet-Egyptian communiqué that acceded to the Egyptian position and a Soviet note to the U.S. government that withdrew previous Soviet concessions. The Soviets had given "grudging support" to the intransigence of their client.[56]

Kissinger's claim that the Soviets were not really interested in peace in the Middle East had apparently been vindicated by the Soviet retrogression. But Sisco and Rogers were prepared to persevere. Sisco went to Moscow in July with a new U.S. proposal that built upon and subsumed earlier Soviet concessions.[57] He was to be disappointed, for the Soviets were no longer in a bargaining mood.

By late summer 1969, however, the Soviet bargaining position began to soften, though it is unclear whether this change was first cleared with Egypt.[58] Intense negotiations began shortly thereafter between U.S. and Soviet diplomats, resulting in a brief of October 28, 1969. The brief called for indirect Israeli-Egyptian negotiations through Gunnar Jarring, attempting to establish peace and normalization of relations in exchange for the occupied territories, with the timing of Israeli withdrawal left unspecified and the possibility of minor border adjustments left open.[59] In its general contours, then, the brief restored the progress that had been made during May 1969, before the Soviet retrogression.

This brief became known as the first Rogers Plan. Although the Soviets helped to negotiate its terms, they declined to cosponsor it. Instead, they let Rogers offer it to the local actors as a U.S. initiative. Nasser rejected it emphatically on November 6; Israel denounced it on December 21. On December 23, 1969, the Soviet government followed suit, delivering to the United States a formal rejection of the Rogers Plan.

Because of Soviet diplomatic backtracking and the subsequent escalation of Soviet military involvement in Egypt, U.S. leaders turned away from the superpower collaborative approach and explored ways of striking a deal with Cairo independently of the Soviet Union.[60] Little progress was made, and Soviet military involvement grew.

Diplomatic efforts got back on track, however, in June 1970, as a result of initiatives by Secretary of State Rogers. As a sign of goodwill, Rogers gained substantive concessions from the U.S.-Israeli side, which he expected to be reciprocated: the United States had, since March 1970, been holding up Israel's arms package for the year. Moreover, Israel reaffirmed its commitment to UN Resolution

242 as a basis for negotiations and agreed to indirect talks rather than direct ones.[61]

The Soviet Union was receptive. On June 2, Dobrynin informed Sisco that his government had secured two important concessions from Nasser: a commitment to restrain the fedayeen in territories under Egyptian control during a cease-fire, and a promise that, with the signing of a peace agreement with Israel, the state of war would come immediately to an end, even if the agreement was to be implemented in stages.[62] At a meeting on June 24, the Soviets went still further, calling for "an indefinite extension of a ceasefire into a 'formalized state of peace,' similar to the arrangement that existed between the Soviet Union and Japan."[63] Moreover, a week later, Soviet leaders met with Nasser in Moscow and pressured him to accept a negotiation process geared toward "a settlement based on Resolution 242 'with due account for the legitimate rights and interests of all peoples in the area,' including Israel." This proposal was interpreted in an authoritative Soviet periodical several days later to mean that the pace of Israeli withdrawals would be commensurate with the pace of negotiations, that once Israel went back to the borders of pre-June 1967 those borders would be demilitarized and patrolled, and that all states would have to recognize the sovereignty, independence, and legitimacy of Israel.[64]

This set of concessions was the most forthcoming Soviet position in a year. Nasser was ostensibly forced to accept them as preconditions for Soviet defense of his airspace, despite the threat that accepting them would alienate him from most radical Arab forces.[65]

The diplomatic momentum did not stop there. In mid-July 1970, Sisco brought forth another peace bid that further dissociated the U.S. position from Israeli demands. That bid implied a U.S. commitment to the pre-June 1967 borders of Israel, allowing for only the most minimal border adjustments, if any, and sought to include concern for the "rights and claims" of the Palestinians in peace negotiations. Within two weeks, the Soviet Union, Egypt, and Jordan accepted the offering, whereas Syria, Iraq, and the Palestinians rejected it. The Soviets reciprocated with further negotiating concessions of their own, conceding that (1) no Israeli withdrawal would be required before a detailed package was signed, (2) the package would include the provisions outlined in the first days of July (discussed in the preceding paragraphs), and would be jointly guaranteed by the superpowers, and (3) a peace settlement would not require refugee resettlement in Israel. The Soviets then pressured their Arab clients to line up behind this plan, though they did not succeed in breaking the intransigence of Algeria, Iraq, and the Palestinians.[66]

The United States was not forthcoming in response to these latest collaborative offerings. According to William Quandt, Nixon was by this time more intrigued by the prospect of a separate deal with Nasser: "The American response was to ignore the Soviet bid for a joint initiative and to press forward instead with its own unilateral call for a ceasefire and renewed talks."[67]

Soviet-Egyptian cease-fire violations incensed both Israeli and U.S. leaders. Israel refused thereafter to participate in the indirect talks being mediated by Gunnar Jarring. The superpower ("two-power") talks were formally suspended. And the United States delivered to Israel substantially more than the arms package that had been held up since March in the interest of negotiations.[68] Kissinger's skepticism about Soviet intentions appeared to have been vindicated once again— at least in the eyes of U.S. governmental leaders, Rogers and Sisco among them.

Were the Soviets following a "no war, no peace" strategy during the War of Attrition? The diplomatic track provides some strong support for an affirmative answer. The Soviet retrogression of June 1969 and rejection of the Rogers Plan in December 1969 are properly cited as indications that the Soviets backed off when real progress toward a settlement formula was being made. Hence, the argument goes, they could not really have been interested in a settlement.

Yet there are other ways of reading the evidence. These interpretations require that one view Soviet actions, not in a vacuum, but relative to the military situation on the ground and relative to the state of U.S.-Israeli relations. For the Soviets were hardly interested in peace at any price: they would not pressure their clients more than the United States was visibly inclined to pressure Israel; they would not support a settlement for which they and the United States would not receive equal credit, and in which the two superpowers would not have an equal enforcement role; and they would not force their clients to negotiate from a position of military prostration.

During 1969–1970, Soviet willingness to collaborate meaningfully was greatest under conditions of rough parity or stalemate on the military front. Such was the case during the first five months of 1969; it was again the case during the spring and summer of 1970. U.S. and Soviet negotiating positions converged to the greatest extent at those times. Soviet rejection of the Rogers Plan in December 1969 was galling to U.S. policymakers. But that action may well be explicable in terms of the military situation at the time. Israel was scoring tremendous successes in the war along the canal. Nothing in Israeli military behavior, in the Israeli diplomatic position, or in the pace of U.S. arms deliveries to Israel gave hope of Israeli flexibility or signaled U.S. willingness to pressure Israel sufficiently to force such flexibility, Nasser was desperate. The Soviets accepted his insistence that Egypt not be asked to negotiate from a prone position.[69]

Would the Soviets have accepted the Rogers Plan if Nasser had been willing to accept it? Probably they would have. The issue for the Soviets was not the justice or injustice of the substantive terms. They themselves had espoused much the same terms earlier that year and had helped to negotiate the Rogers Plan itself. The issue for them was *both* the intransigence of their client *and* the fact that Nasser's intransigence was a product of military desperation. The USSR had regularly demonstrated that it was unwilling to risk its influence in the Arab world by being the only superpower to coerce its clients. In contrast, during the spring and summer of 1970, when the U.S. was holding up Israel's arms package, the Soviets threatened to withdraw their defense of Egyptian airspace if Nasser did not accept the converging U.S.-Soviet terms for a settlement.

Indeed, after the Soviets rejected the Rogers Plan, they continued diplomatic efforts to sell it to Nasser. The selling point they brought to those efforts was their willingness to restore Egyptian defenses so that Egypt would not be negotiating from a position of abject weakness. Thus, at the January 1970 meeting in Moscow, according to Nadav Safran, "In exchange for their support the Soviets demanded from Nasser that once Egypt's bargaining position was sufficiently restored, he would make an earnest effort to seek a political solution on terms akin to those of the Rogers Plan."[70] Similarly, according to Quandt, "In a secret meeting with Rogers on May 11, Ambassador Dobrynin stated that the Soviet Union had managed to obtain political concessions from Nasser in return for the new arms shipments that were just beginning to Egypt."[71] In light of Soviet pressure on Nasser that summer, it seems plausible to conclude that the Soviet strategy during 1970 involved a commitment to achieving military stalemate in the War of Attrition as a precondition for negotiations based on some variant of the Rogers Plan of October 1969. That plan would accord the Soviets a coequal sponsoring and enforcement role while delivering on the Soviet commitment to the Arabs to secure return of occupied territories through superpower collaboration.

However, one major event during the War of Attrition is not so easily explained in these terms: the June 1969 diplomatic retrogression. This development took place at a time when Egypt was *not* prostrate militarily; on the contrary, the Arab side was doing very well in the war. If the Soviets had colluded with the United States at this time, putting forth a joint program for cease-fire and settlement (as Rogers and Sisco were suggesting), the Egyptian bargaining position would not have been a weak one. Yet the Soviets backed off. Why?

As we have seen, the Soviet retrogression was not self-initiated; the Soviets were not uncomfortable with the substance of the terms being offered by Sisco. Gromyko tried to sell the proposal at the meeting of world communist parties in Moscow in June 1969. Brezhnev and Gromyko both urged Nasser to accept it. What was at issue once again was Soviet unwillingness to twist arms very hard to bring their client into line. Nasser was emotional about the issue. He had long been trying to convince the Soviets to accept and support his tactic of combining military with political pressure on Israel. The Soviets had balked. He initiated the War of Attrition on his own, and at some risk. Now that the effort was paying dividends, he was not about to let the Soviets prevent him from pressing his advantage and securing the best possible bargaining position. In light of the depth of Nasser's feelings, the Soviets grudgingly chose not to bully him.[72]

Why did they make that choice? There are several possibilities, and more research on the events of this month is needed. One possibility, of course, is that the Soviet commitment to a peace settlement was very low or nonexistent. The June 1969 retrogression is perhaps the single most compelling bit of diplomatic evidence in support of the "no war, no peace" hypothesis. But the very fact that events of this month stand alone in not being easily explained in other terms undermines the hypothesis. For if the Soviets were following such a strategy, we would expect a series of such anomalies.

A second possibility is that a hard-line coalition suddenly emerged ascendant in Moscow's Middle East policy in June 1969. We know that 1969 was a year of change in Soviet foreign and domestic policy more generally.[73] We also know that 1969 was the year in which Brezhnev pushed to the fore, forging a dominant coalition based on his priorities in budgetary, administrative, and participatory policy, as well as on Soviet policy toward arms control, West Germany, and Eastern Europe.[74] Still, the problems with this hypothesis prevent us from readily accepting it. Analysts who identify a hard-line turn in Soviet *published* definitions of the Middle East situation trace its onset to the period of September to November 1969—three to five months after the diplomatic retrogression of June. The evidence of Gromyko's efforts to persuade Nasser in June further erodes the argument. Finally, the coalition-shift theory—ostensibly a shift away from collaboration toward intransigence—cannot explain the resurgence of the Soviet collaborative urge, and of Soviet willingness to pressure Nasser, some nine to twelve months later.

A third possibility, which I find most plausible, is that the Soviets were simply not willing to bully Nasser when things were finally going well for him and when he, along with other Arab leaders, was adamant about pressing his advantage. Since the 1967 war, Soviet leaders had been rather consistent on this score. They had dealt with Arab leaders most coercively (by withholding the most advanced weaponry) when attempting to prevent them from going to war. Little coercion appears to have been used (until the summer of 1970) in pressing Nasser, or other Arab leaders, to be forthcoming about settlement terms. This tendency reflected more than just Soviet identification with the Arab cause. It also reflected (1) the severe limits on the USSR's ability to control its clients (who were neither satellites nor choiceless dependents), (2) the asymmetry of patron-client relationships in the Middle East—the Egyptians could turn to the United States if frustrated by Soviet pressure, whereas Israel would not turn to Moscow, (3) the intense Soviet desire to maintain and consolidate the USSR's influence in Egypt, and (4) the fact that Israel was not under obvious pressure to be publicly forthcoming about settlement terms. All four of these considerations bore on the Soviet commitment to competitive influence building, a commitment that was always higher in the Soviet scale of preferences than the search for a peace settlement. Thus, the June 1969 retrogression, although deserving of more research, appears explicable in terms of an image of the Soviets as collaborative competitors rather than unalterable antagonists.

From the Death of Nasser to the Expulsion of Soviet Military Personnel from Egypt (September 1970–July 1972)

During this period from the death of Nasser through the expulsion of Soviet military personnel from Egypt, the general Soviet vision of combining collaboration and competition did not change. What did change was Soviet estimation of U.S. sincerity about superpower collaboration and of Egyptian reliability as an ally. The consequence was a change in Soviet tactics in the Arab world, but within the context of a continuing Soviet commitment both to prevent war and to advance the prospects for a peace settlement, based upon an armed peace guaranteed by the great powers.

There is plenty of evidence during these years to support an image of the Soviets as unalterable antagonists. Most of the evidence concerns patterns of Soviet military assistance to the Arab world.[75] Thus, after the Jordanian crisis (fall 1970), Soviet arms deliveries to Egypt increased suddenly and markedly. From January to March 1971, the Soviets extended their air defense of Egypt to cover the entire country, delivered large inventories of MIG-21s, and sent to Egypt highly advanced defensive weaponry that had never before been deployed outside the Soviet Union. Moreover, throughout 1971, there took place a marked escalation of Soviet *promises* about arms deliveries: in May, July, and October 1971, Soviet leaders promised Sadat the MIG-23s and SCUD missiles (weaponry that could allow Egypt to extend a war to the Israeli heartland) that he and Nasser had long been unsuccessfully demanding.

During this period, the Soviets also undertook a major effort to diversify and solidify their bases of influence in the region as a whole.[76] After the Jordanian crisis, the Soviets sealed a large arms deal with Syria. During 1971, they used a variety of means to upgrade their ties with South Yemen, Morocco, and Algeria, while simultaneously offering economic assistance to the conservative monarchies in the region. During the first half of 1972, the Soviets stepped up arms deliveries to Syria (now including SAM-3 antiaircraft missiles in the package), strengthened their ties with Libya and Algeria, and signed a Treaty of Friendship and Cooperation with Iraq. Moreover, they encouraged Iraq to nationalize Western oil interests and accorded Baghdad large sums of money to develop, refine, and transport oil in place of relying on Western multinationals. In sum, the trend is unambiguous. Throughout this period, Moscow escalated military and political competition in the region.

Although the Soviets stepped up their military stake, it would be a mistake to confuse this escalation with an intent to encourage Arab belief in a military solution to the conflict with Israel. The available evidence regarding diplomatic interactions and arms transfers suggests that the Soviets remained consistent in their "no war" stance. After the Jordanian crisis, Marshal Zakharov, Premier Kosygin, and President Podgorny all urged Sadat to extend the ceasefire, to exercise caution, and to refrain from resuming the War of Attrition. They urged him to agree in principle to put off plans for going to war with Israel until all Soviet military personnel had been replaced by properly trained Egyptian personnel (a distant goal at the time).[77] Indeed, the Soviets were so insistent on caution that they reportedly "shocked" their Egyptian hosts.[78] The same persuasive efforts characterized the consistent Soviet opposition to Sadat's "year of decision" announcement—that 1971 would be marked either by a peace settlement or by renewed warfare. And lest these urgings be written off as a subterfuge, we are also privy to the transcript of secret discussions between Soviet Politburo members and a delegation of Syrian Communists in May 1971. The Soviets insisted that a military solution to the Arab-Israeli conflict was not "realistic," for the Arabs would surely lose.[79]

Beyond persuasion and urgings, the Soviets also used coercion—specifically, denial of matériel—to communicate the same point. According to Whetten, Podgorny informed Sadat in January 1971 that he would not receive Soviet support for a resumption of the War of Attrition.[80] In March 1971, Brezhnev informed Sadat that the Soviets would deliver missile-launching Ilyushin bombers only on the conditions that they be manned by Soviet crews and that the decision to use them be made in Moscow: "If we don't give you all the arms you ask for," Brezhnev explained, "it's not because we're afraid but because we think that each armament should be related to the appropriate stage of the struggle."[81] And the Soviets were determined to maintain control over the definition of just what "stage of the struggle" the Egyptians had reached. Similarly, in December 1971 (the last month of Sadat's year of decision), the Soviets suddenly removed their "missile crews, aircraft, and air defense equipment from the Aswan Dam area."[82] This action may have been prompted by the Soviet decision to assist India in its war with Pakistan. Or it may have been part of an effort to prevent Sadat from taking rash action against Israel.

Still another indication that the Soviets were attempting to combine political-military competition with the avoidance of confrontation was the fact that, during the entire period, they never delivered the oft-promised advanced weaponry (MIG-23s, TU-22 fighter-bombers, and surface-to-surface SCUD missiles) that might embolden Sadat to launch an all-out war on Israel.[83] The gap between Soviet pledges and Soviet deliveries actually widened during this period. That gap cannot be attributed to specific intervening conditions at a point or two in time, for the Soviets repeatedly promised and repeatedly reneged.[84] The most likely explanation is that the Soviets were hoping, through their pledges, both to stall Sadat and to pressure the United States and Israel to moderate their bargaining positions.

Advocates of the "no war, no peace" interpretation need not disagree with this view of Soviet intentions, for such theorists concede a Soviet commitment to confrontation avoidance. They can point, however, to expanded Soviet military and political competition during this period as evidence that the Soviets were trying to prevent peace by keeping the pot boiling. But there are several problems with this conclusion. First, the Soviet commitment to competitive influence building was an end in itself; it need not be interpreted as an instrumental means toward frustrating progress on the diplomatic track. Second, Soviet actions were not taking place in a vacuum; rather, they were taking place in a context of military escalation on both sides. After the cease-fire of August 1970, the Nixon administration rewarded Israel with accelerated delivery of A-4s and F-4s, as well as an unusually large arms package. In December 1971, the United States released for delivery to Israel still more F-4 fighter planes that had been held up since March at the insistence of William Rogers.[85] And in February 1972, the United States agreed to a long-term arms deal for Israel that would deliver forty-two F-4s and eighty-two A-4s,[86] an unprecedented deal that prompted Sadat to complain to Soviet leaders that the United States had bought Israel a new air force.[87] One cannot say that Soviet arms deliveries to Egypt and Syria were simply reactive to U.S. arms transfers to Israel. The sequencing of decisions is too irregular to support such a conclusion. But U.S. arms transfers were not simply reactive either. Governmental decisions on both sides appear to have been decisively influenced by an effort to keep pace with the escalating demands of both nations' unmanageable clients.

Yet the expansion and deepening of Soviet commitments *was* reactive in one very important sense. Given the unruliness of the USSR's clients, and given the U.S. effort to drive a wedge between the Soviet Union and Egypt, Soviet commitments frequently deepened precisely in order to increase Arab dependence on the Soviets.

Throughout the first year of Sadat's rule in Egypt, Soviet leaders received unambiguous signs and signals that the new Egyptian leader distrusted them more than Nasser had. Direct comments by Sadat or his aides communicated the message that he was using the Soviet connection for tactical and temporary purposes.[88] Sadat was also highly receptive to unilateral U.S. diplomatic efforts to arrange an interim settlement along the Suez Canal.[89] He purged the allegedly pro-Soviet "Sabry group" from the Egyptian leadership and reversed Nasser's socializing drift by wooing both domestic and foreign capitalists to improve the performance of the Egyptian economy. He initiated an entente with Saudi Arabia and sought Saudi financial assistance in diversifying his sources of arms. When President Jaafar Numeiri slaughtered most of the Communist party membership in the Sudan (after an abortive coup attempt in which the Soviet Union had a hand), Sadat praised and assisted Numeiri, even as the Soviet Union was denouncing and seeking to isolate him.

The Soviet government was also receiving clear signs and signals that the United States had abandoned superpower collaboration in favor of the Kissingerian strategy of going it alone in the Middle East, driving a wedge between the Soviet Union and Egypt, and securing a settlement only when Egypt, and the moderate Arab regimes, accepted U.S. premises about the shape of a settlement and the importance of excluding and reducing Soviet presence in the region. Top Soviet leaders were informed directly of the new U.S. strategy by Egyptian and Saudi leaders.[90] Moreover, U.S. behavior seemed to confirm the truth of the warnings. Not only were Rogers and Sisco seeking to negotiate such a unilateral interim settlement, but Kissinger was simultaneously communicating to Sadat that expulsion of the Soviet military presence was a prerequisite for Israeli flexibility.[91] And through it all, the U.S. government refrained from routine consultations with Soviet leaders that had previously accompanied most U.S. diplomatic efforts.[92]

Soviet leaders were deeply worried about Sadat's shows of independence and about U.S. efforts to exploit and extend them. In private conversations, they warned Sadat of U.S. motives and Israeli intransigence, urging him not to forget that the road to realization of his goals (i.e., return of the occupied territories) lay through Moscow, not Washington. When Sadat ignored such warnings, Soviet leaders criticized him for perfidy and warned him that the Soviet Union might have to reevaluate its support for Egypt.[93] But rather than withdraw support, the Soviets deepened it.

The escalation of Soviet competition for influence in the region does not follow exactly the escalation of U.S. military support for Israel. But it does correlate rather strikingly with the growing perception of Sadat's unreliability as an ally and of U.S. eagerness to exploit that unreliability to Soviet disadvantage. The Syrians' backing down in Jordan (fall 1970) was followed by a surge of arms deliveries to Egypt and a large arms deal with Syria—as if to demonstrate that the Syrian actions should not cast doubt on Soviet dependability as a patron. The Soviet escalation of arms deliveries, and of promises, during 1971 proceeded apace with Sadat's growing signs of independence. The upgrading of ties with South Yemen, Morocco, and Algeria during 1971 also appears to have been insurance against Egyptian unreliability. Finally, after Sadat gave still greater signs of independence in early 1972, the Soviets increased arms deliveries to Syria and deepened ties with Libya, Algeria, and Iraq.[94]

Thus, it would be more than dubious to argue that the escalation of Soviet competition in the region proves Soviet insincerity about furthering the prospects for peace. The escalation only supports the conclusion that the Soviets were not interested in a peace that would diminish their influence in the region.

Indeed, when we turn to the diplomatic track, we find that the Soviets apparently perceived no fundamental incompatibility between

their commitments to superpower competition and superpower collaboration. During this period, they continued earlier efforts to induce
the United States to pressure Israel, to restore the collusive approach
to a peace settlement, and to moderate Arab demands in order to
facilitate the search for an armed peace. In the fall of 1970, they
reiterated their flexible negotiating position of July 1970 while urging
Sadat to pay more attention to a diplomatic solution to the conflict.[95]
    But the U.S. government was not of a mind to listen to Soviet
signals or to interpret Soviet motives generously. After the Jordanian
crisis, U.S. leaders made up their minds to proceed alone. The months
of February to August 1971 were dominated by a unilateral effort
to pry Sadat away from the Soviet Union and to negotiate an interim
accord between him and the Israelis. The Soviets complained frequently about U.S. unilateralism, and they rejected the idea of an
interim agreement unlinked to a comprehensive settlement plan.[96]
They viewed this rejection as the only way to ensure that an interim
agreement not be used as a lever to drive a wedge between the USSR
and Egypt.
    As it was, the U.S. unilateral effort failed.[97] At that point (August
5, 1971), Nixon sent a letter to Brezhnev, suggesting a return to
superpower collaboration. According to Kissinger, the letter was a
smoke screen, calculated to make the Soviets believe that the United
States was sincere about collaboration so Moscow would continue
to pressure its allies to refrain from going back to war. The assumption
was that, with time, Soviet allies would become so disenchanted
with Moscow's caution that they would forsake the USSR and turn
westward once again.[98]
    The strategy worked in that Brezhnev's reply reaffirmed Soviet
interest in collaboration and Soviet dismay with earlier U.S. efforts
to work unilaterally.[99] At the end of September 1971, Gromyko spoke
at length with Kissinger and Nixon about the furtherance of the
peace process in language that indicated Soviet flexibility on the
terms of final settlement but Soviet insistence that negotiations look
toward a final settlement, not interim accords. Gromyko suggested
that Middle East discussions be put into the special White House
channel, that interim agreement "be linked specifically and in detail
to a final settlement," and that, after Israeli withdrawal and the
implementation of a peace settlement, the Soviet Union would
withdraw all its forces from the Middle East, join in an arms embargo
of the area, and participate in the process of guaranteeing the
settlement.[100] These proposals were essentially the terms that Soviet
leaders urged their allies to accept during visits to Moscow by various
Arab leaders.[101]

Yet there were few signs that the United States was willing or able to pressure Israel. In response to the War of Attrition, Israeli demands had escalated to include substantial border modifications.[102] In addition, the ascendancy of the Nixon-Kissinger team over the Rogers-Sisco team in Middle East policymaking ushered in a sharp reduction in U.S. willingness to dissociate the United States from Israeli maximal demands.[103] Soviet-Egyptian military actions during June–July 1970 also led Nixon to assure Israel that the United States would never pressure the Israelis to return all the occupied territories.[104] And in February 1972, talks between Joseph Sisco and Israeli ambassador Yitzhak Rabin, the results of which were reported in the *New York Times,* wedded the United States to the Israeli position in negotiations on all procedural and substantive matters.[105]

Despite this evidence, the Soviets made further concessions on the diplomatic track—though it is unclear whether they still entertained hopes of furthering a peace formula in the Middle East or were largely seeking to further the cause of détente in general. In April 1972, Gromyko conceded the possibility of decoupling an interim agreement from a final settlement, as long as he and Kissinger "simultaneously reached a secret understanding on the terms of a comprehensive settlement, which would be surfaced and implemented immediately after [the] Presidential election."[106]

The most far-reaching concession, however, came at the May 1972 summit. There, Kissinger and Gromyko worked out and signed a set of "general working principles" for an overall Middle East settlement. Those principles were weaker and vaguer than UN Resolution 242, were ambiguous about the extent of Israeli withdrawal, and allowed for substantial border modifications by leaving out the usual caveat that only "minor" border rectifications could be considered.[107] In other words, the Soviets were now willing, to an unprecedented extent, to hedge their long-standing promise to their Arab allies. And Kissinger was genuinely surprised that the Soviets were dissociating themselves from what *he* had always defined as the "maximum Arab program." "I have never understood why Gromyko accepted them," he notes.[108] But it was too late for him to reevaluate his beliefs about Soviet intentions in the Middle East, Soviet interest in a settlement, or the Soviet role in his geopolitical vision. He simply wrote Gromyko's acceptance off as either a fluke or a sign that Israeli intransigence had paid off (i.e., as showing that the Soviets were either overtired or desperate).[109] Either way, he could deny the implications for possible resurrection of superpower collaboration in the region.

Sadat did not deny those implications, however. He added the

May summit to his list of grievances against the USSR and decided that it was time for a bold stroke. In July 1972, he demanded the immediate withdrawal of Soviet military personnel from his country.

Conclusion

The argument that Soviet leaders were involved in a calculated effort to maintain a condition of "no war, no peace" in the Middle East during 1967–1972 is difficult to sustain in light of the evidence presented in this chapter. It is true that certain ambiguities have not been resolved by reshuffling the available evidence; but that is the case with almost any historical study. The crucial consideration is *not* whether the "no war, no peace" hypothesis has been definitely disproved; such a conclusion would be almost impossible in the absence of candid memoirs by Soviet leaders. The more important consideration is whether Soviet behavior along various military and political tracks is *more plausibly* explained by an alternative characterization of Soviet strategy. Characterization of the Soviet Union as a collaborative competitor, driven by mixed motives (neither completely benevolent nor completely duplicitous), appears to do a better job of explaining the evolution of Soviet behavior during the years in question.

My argument can be summarized as follows. From mid-1967 through mid-1972, the Soviet leadership sought a peace settlement, based on superpower collaboration, that would simultaneously reduce the probability of military confrontation with the United States in the Middle East, advance the cause of détente, and create a more stable base of influence for the USSR in Middle Eastern affairs. The Soviets sought to bring about an armed peace based upon Israeli withdrawal from occupied territories, Arab recognition of and normalization of formal relations with Israel, and a coequal superpower role in enforcing the peace. Soviet behavior during these years indicates a belief that such settlement terms would work to the advantage of Soviet interests—both regional and global.

But Soviet behavior also indicates a determination that the peacemaking *process* must not threaten Soviet influence in the region by forcing the USSR to pressure the Arabs significantly more than the United States was pressuring Israel. To some extent, this belief left the USSR hostage to the emotionalism of Arab leaders, to the escalating military conflict on the ground, and to the U.S. commitment to maintaining Israeli military superiority. For under these conditions, it became very difficult to specify what constituted equivalent pressure by the superpowers on their clients. The tension between Soviet commitment to a peace settlement and Soviet fear of overpressuring the Arabs appears to have shaped Moscow's approach to U.S.-Soviet collaboration. The Soviets appear to have concluded that some form of undercover U.S.-Soviet collusion was desirable and necessary. This decision would appear to explain their occasional willingness to make concessions on Arab territorial demands and their repeated efforts to put U.S.-Soviet negotiations into a secret forum—the White House channel. This method of negotiating would allow them to make verbal concessions that would not become public until it was clear that the United States was willing to reciprocate with equivalent pressure on Israel. *Joint* U.S.-Soviet pressure on local actors would remove the possibility that Egypt would turn westward if alienated by unilateral Soviet pressure. Lack of prior publicity was crucial. The maintenance of Soviet regional influence was the highest Soviet priority, but the commitment to a peace settlement of the kind just outlined was real nonetheless.

Many of the zigs and zags of Soviet policy—and many of the apparent contradictions between Soviet behaviors on different tracks—can be explained in terms of this mixed goal structure. For the Soviets were caught up in what game theorists might call "a multiple actor game of approach-avoidance." They sought genuinely to collaborate with the United States but simultaneously to compete with Washington for influence in the region. Hence, they would approach the United States to further the cause of collaboration, while avoiding taking positions that would give the appearance of selling out their clients. Similarly, they would support Egypt in order to consolidate their influence and advance their competitive standing but try not to change conditions enough to provoke an Israeli preemptive strike or an Egyptian military offensive. They would urge the Egyptians to moderate their military and political behavior, but they would shy away from coercing too severely for fear of compromising their influence in Egypt and in the Arab world in general.

Soviet calculations regarding the tactics most likely to advance the USSR's goals were complicated by the uncertainties inherent in this game of approach-avoidance. The boundaries between effective pressure and excessive pressure, between competition and possible confrontation, or between collaboration with the United States and the appearance of selling out the Arabs were never clear and were constantly shifting. The Soviets were often feeling their way.[110]

Calculation was complicated further by the fact that they were trying to collaborate with a U.S. government that was divided internally with respect to both strategy and tactics, that was frequently hostage to Israeli actions, and that was also engaged in a game of approach-avoidance toward the Soviets, the Israelis, and the Egyptians. William Rogers and Joseph Sisco often advanced negotiating positions that received little support from the White House. U.S. denial of Israeli demands never matched Soviet denial of Egyptian demands. Kissinger and Nixon adhered to a strategic conception that was incompatible with the Soviet image of a settlement and a peacemaking process. Specifically, (1) they rejected any approach that required substantial and sustained U.S. pressure on Israel; (2) they accepted the notion that Israeli military superiority was a necessary condition for avoiding another war and for convincing the Arabs to accept Israeli conditions for peace; (3) they rejected as illegitimate Soviet efforts to use the peacemaking process as a means of consolidating or expanding the USSR's influence with Arab clients; and (4) they viewed as both desirable and possible a separate peace, mediated by the United States, that would result in a significant *reduction* of Soviet influence in the region.

Given the very different priorities and perspectives of the Kremlin and the White House, it was most probable that each side would embrace a very different definition of superpower restraint and reciprocity in their relationship. The incompatibility of their respective definitions was constantly demonstrated by their responses to the escalating military conflict in the region during the War of Attrition. Under these conditions, it would have been remarkable had the collaborative relationship succeeded in advancing the cause of peace.

Before closing, let me emphasize the limits of the claims I am making. Even if the result of our analysis is to discredit the "no war, no peace" hypothesis in favor of the "collaborative competitor" interpretation, it would *not* necessarily follow that: (1) greater U.S. receptivity to Soviet collaborative offerings would have headed off the 1973 war; (2) U.S. interests (however these might be defined) would have been better served by drawing the Soviet Union into a collaborative relationship; (3) the U.S. ought to abandon Camp David in favor of U.S.-Soviet collaboration to settle the Palestinian problem; or (4) the Soviet collaborative streak is necessarily as strong today as it was in 1967–1972. Any of these propositions may be correct, but none of them can be resolved through the evidence presented in this chapter. The purpose of this study has been more limited: to advance a reasonably persuasive explanation of Soviet behavior during 1967–1972. Yet surely, that is a necessary component of any effort responsibly to address the broader questions.

Acknowledgments

I wish to thank the following individuals for their useful comments on an earlier version of this paper: Robert O. Freedman, Alexander

George, Galia Golan, Robert Legvold, James Noyes, Alvin Rubinstein, and Stephen Walt. I alone am responsible for the final product.

Notes

1. This position is argued, in varied forms, in the following works: Robert O. Freedman, "Detente and US-Soviet Relations in the Middle East During the Nixon Years (1969–1974)," in *Dimensions of Detente* ed. Della W. Sheldon (New York: Praeger, 1978), p. 116; Abraham S. Becker, Bent Hansen, and Malcolm H. Kerr, *The Economics and Politics of the Middle East* (New York: American Elsevier Publishing Co., 1975), pp. 112–113; Alvin Z. Rubinstein, *Red Star on the Nile* (Princeton, N.J.: Princeton University Press, 1977), p. 340; John C. Campbell, "The Communist Powers and the Middle East: Moscow's Purposes," *Problems of Communism* 21, no. 5 (September-October 1972): 51; Henry Kissinger, *White House Years* (Boston: Little, Brown & Co., 1979), chaps. 10, 14, 15, and 30; and Pedro Ramet, *Sadat and the Kremlin,* Student Paper no. 85 (Santa Monica, Calif.: California Seminar on Arms Control and Foreign Policy, February 1980), p. 31.

2. See Lawrence L. Whetten, *The Canal War: Four-Power Conflict in the Middle East* (Cambridge, Mass.: MIT Press, 1974); Jon D. Glassman, *Arms for the Arabs* (Baltimore: Johns Hopkins University Press, 1975); Karen Dawisha, *Soviet Foreign Policy Towards Egypt* (London: Macmillan Press Ltd., 1979); O. M. Smolansky, "The United States and the Soviet Union in the Middle East," in *The Soviet Threat: Myths and Realities,* ed. Grayson Kirk and Nils H. Wessell (New York: Academy of Political Science, 1978), pp. 99–109; Oded Eran, "Soviet Policy Between the 1967 and 1973 Wars," in *From June to October: The Middle East Between 1967 and 1973,* ed. Itamar Rabinovich and Haim Shaked (New Brunswick, N.J.: Transaction Books, 1978), pp. 25–52.

3. For example, Rubinstein, *Red Star.* Indeed, this position has become conventional wisdom among politicians in Washington. In the wake of the decline of détente, it has also been generalized as a characterization of Soviet "interests" in the Third World (see, for example, Seweryn Bialer, *Stalin's Successors* [Cambridge and New York: Cambridge University Press, 1980], p. 265).

4. For example, Dawisha, *Soviet Foreign Policy,* pp. 212–213; Eran, "Soviet Policy Between the Wars," p. 47.

5. In addition to the literature cited in notes 1–4, I have drawn on evidence presented in: Yaacov Bar-Siman-Tov, *The Israeli-Egyptian War of Attrition, 1969–1970* (New York: Columbia University Press, 1980); Bradford Dismukes, "Large-Scale Intervention Ashore: Soviet Air Defense Forces in Egypt," in Bradford Dismukes and James McConnell, eds., *Soviet Naval Diplomacy* (New York: Pergamon Press, 1979), pp. 221–239; Saad El Shazly, *The Crossing of the Suez* (San Francisco: American Mideast Research, 1980); Galia Golan, *The Soviet Union and the Palestine Liberation Organization* (New York: Praeger, 1980); Robert O. Freedman, *Soviet Policy Toward the*

Middle East Since 1970, rev. ed. (New York: Praeger Special Studies, 1978); Mohamed Heikal, *The Road to Ramadan* (New York: Quadrangle, 1975); Mohamed Heikal, *The Sphinx and the Commissar* (New York: Harper & Row, 1978); Ilana Kass, *Soviet Involvement in the Middle East: Policy Formulation, 1966–1973* (Boulder, Colo.: Westview Press, 1978); William B. Quandt, *Decade of Decisions: American Policy Toward the Arab-Israeli Conflict, 1967–1976* (Berkeley: University of California Press, 1977); Yaacov Ro'i, *From Encroachment to Involvement* (New York: John Wiley & Sons, 1974); Anwar el-Sadat, *In Search of Identity* (New York: Harper & Row, 1977); Lawrence L. Whetten, *The Arab-Israeli Dispute: Great Power Behaviour,* Adelphi Paper no. 128 (London: International Institute for Strategic Studies, 1977).

6. Indeed, one proponent of the hypothesis admits the shaky ground on which it stands by adding: "Needless to say, some might likewise charge the United States with not really wanting a settlement because of its partiality to Israel" (Campbell, "The Communist Powers and the Middle East," p. 51).

7. See Eran, "Soviet Policy Between the Wars," p. 47; the term "armed peace" is Eran's.

8. This is the main thrust of Smolansky, "The United States and the Soviet Union in the Middle East."

9. Eran, "Soviet Policy Between the Wars," p. 47.

10. See Dina Rome Spechler, *Domestic Influences on Soviet Foreign Policy* (Washington, D.C.: University Press of America, 1978), pp. 64–68, for alternative Soviet views of the United States as "adverse partner," "realistic competitor," "unalterable antagonist," and "mitigable opponent." For the concept "collaborative competition," see Chapter 13 of this book.

11. In addition to the prodigious research in Soviet published sources that went into many of the books used here, the works by Kissinger, El Shazly, Heikal, and Sadat are memoirs by insiders who interacted with the Soviets; the book by Bar-Siman-Tov taps memoirs by Israeli leaders and interviews with Israeli officials; and the book by Quandt is based in part on personal experience within the U.S. government.

12. In response to my query about the sources for certain claims, Whetten assured me that "in most of the cases, [my statements] came from my personal knowledge while I served as the senior political analyst for Head-quarters USAFE [United States Air Force in Europe]. To my knowledge, all the points were unclassified at the time I wrote the book" (personal communication, June 19, 1981).

13. Whetten, *The Canal War,* pp. 47, 54.

14. Ibid., p. 46.

15. Ibid., p. 50; Rubinstein, *Red Star,* p. 38; see also Dawisha, *Soviet Foreign Policy,* pp. 49–50, for a slightly different interpretation.

16. Bar-Siman-Tov, *The War of Attrition,* pp. 43–45, 50–52; also, Rubinstein, *Red Star,* pp. 66–67.

17. Quandt, *Decade of Decisions,* pp. 66–68.

18. Whetten, *The Canal War,* pp. 67–68 (based on reports by Heikal); Bar-Siman-Tov, *The War of Attrition,* pp. 46–47; Rubinstein, *Red Star,* pp. 59–63.

19. In contrast, Eran ("Soviet Policy Between the Wars," p. 33) claims that the Soviets did indeed accept Nasser's premise in spring-summer 1968. He bases that conclusion largely on changes in Soviet published commentary about guerrilla operations at the time. But Eran's interpretation receives little support elsewhere. Golan (*The Soviet Union and the PLO,* pp. 44–46) uses the same sources but emphasizes the limits of the Soviet change in doctrine, concluding that it was simply a sop to Nasser, who had undertaken a rapprochement with Fatah, rather than a change in Soviet perspectives on the role of military pressure in the search for a settlement formula. Bar-Siman-Tov (*The War of Attrition,* pp. 56–57) uses Heikal and Sadat to argue the opposite of Eran's interpretation. Other viewpoints opposed to Eran's thesis can be found in: Rubinstein, *Red Star,* pp. 59–65; Kass, *Soviet Involvement,* pp. 65–66; or Ro'i, *From Encroachment to Involvement,* p. 484.

20. Heikal, *Sphinx and Commissar,* p. 193.

21. Heikal, *Road to Ramadan,* pp. 56–57.

22. Whetten, *The Canal War,* p. 68.

23. Ibid., pp. 68–69.

24. Kissinger, *White House Years,* pp. 347, 349.

25. Ibid., pp. 354–355.

26. Ibid., pp. 355–363.

27. Bar-Siman-Tov, *The War of Attrition,* pp. 146, 233, nn. 3–4.

28. Ibid., pp. 145–147.

29. Ibid., pp. 104–105, 121–125; Quandt, *Decade of Decisions,* p. 95; Rubinstein, *Red Star,* p. 108.

30. Bar-Siman-Tov, *The War of Attrition,* pp. 147–151.

31. Ibid., pp. 159–160; Dismukes, "Large-Scale Intervention"; Glassman, *Arms for the Arabs,* pp. 70–78.

32. Heikal, *Sphinx and Commissar,* p. 193; for corroboration see Sadat, *In Search of Identity,* p. 196; Kass, *Soviet Involvement,* pp. 81–82; and Rubinstein, *Red Star,* pp. 80–85.

33. Glassman, *Arms for the Arabs,* p. 72. Indeed, Sadat claims (*In Search of Identity,* p. 196) that the Soviets punished Nasser by "never ma[king] good our loss in ammunition."

34. Bar-Siman-Tov, *The War of Attrition,* pp. 114, 137.

35. Glassman, *Arms for the Arabs,* pp. 75, 109; Whetten, *The Canal War,* pp. 90–91; Bar-Siman-Tov, *The War of Attrition,* p. 138; Rubinstein, *Red Star,* pp. 107 ff. Bar-Siman-Tov uses Heikal as his source but claims that Heikal "largely confirms what was already known."

36. Glassman, *Arms for the Arabs,* p. 80; Whetten, *The Canal War,* p. 103; Bar-Siman-Tov, *The War of Attrition,* pp. 164–165; Sadat, *In Search of Identity,* p. 198.

37. Quandt, *Decade of Decisions,* p. 88.

38. Kass, *Soviet Involvement,* pp. 89 ff.; Rubinstein, *Red Star,* pp. 103–105; Becker, *Economics and Politics,* pp. 86–87; Ro'i, *From Encroachment to Involvement,* pp. 514–515.

39. Bar-Siman-Tov, *The War of Attrition,* pp. 130–131; Whetten, *The Arab-Israeli Dispute,* pp. 17–18.

40. This passage from Kosygin's letter to Nixon is quoted in Kissinger, *White House Years,* p. 560. Citing the same passage, Quandt notes that the full text of Kosygin's note was published in *Arab Report and Record,* March 1–15, 1970; p. 167. For additional accounts and interpretations of Kosygin's letter see Glassman, *Arms for the Arabs,* p. 75; Whetten, *The Canal War,* pp. 91–92; Rubinstein, *Red Star,* pp. 110–112; Bar-Siman-Tov, *The War of Attrition,* pp. 147–148.

41. Kissinger, *White House Years,* pp. 569–573.

42. Bar-Siman-Tov, *The War of Attrition,* pp. 157, 236, nn. 44–46.

43. Whetten, *The Canal War,* p. 114; see also the sources cited in note 40.

44. Indeed, Heikal (*Sphinx and Commissar,* p. 197) argues that, by the end of 1969, "the Russians were beginning to appreciate . . . the unrewarding nature of negotiating for a Middle East settlement with the Americans." The published Soviet hard-line turn of fall 1969 often stressed disillusion with U.S. intentions and with U.S. sincerity regarding the search for peace. See Rubinstein, *Red Star,* pp. 103–105, and Kass, *Soviet Involvement,* pp. 89 ff.

45. Eran, "Soviet Policy Between the Wars," pp. 35–36; circumstantial support for this argument can be found in Rubinstein, *Red Star,* p. 101.

46. Quandt, *Decade of Decisions,* chap. 3; Kissinger, *White House Years,* chap. 10.

47. Bar-Siman-Tov, *The War of Attrition,* pp. 165–166.

48. Ibid., pp. 172, 239, nn. 97–98.

49. Ibid., p. 172.

50. See Heikal, *Road to Ramadan,* p. 95; Heikal, *Sphinx and Commissar,* p. 202; Kissinger, *White House Years,* p. 579; Sadat, *In Search of Identity,* p. 198.

51. Rubinstein, *Red Star,* pp. 99, 101.

52. Both Whetten (*The Canal War,* p. 136; *The Arab-Israeli Dispute,* pp. 19–20) and Eran ("Soviet Policy Between the Wars," pp. 37–38) stress Soviet aggrievement as a backdrop to the cease-fire violations. Rubinstein (*Red Star,* pp. 124, n. 96; 125), in contrast, does not see aggrievement in the Soviet calculations. But Rubinstein's conclusion is based in part on his interpretation of a quote from Heikal about Brezhnev's statements (ibid., p. 124, n. 96). Rubinstein imputes a rather benign tone to Brezhnev's statement. Yet Sadat's autobiography, published after Rubinstein's book went to press, reports that Brezhnev's statement was made in a state of rage (*In Search of Identity,* p. 198).

53. Quandt, *Decade of Decisions,* p. 85.

54. Whetten, *The Canal War,* pp. 71–75; Kissinger, *White House Years,* pp. 366–367; Quandt, *Decade of Decisions,* pp. 86–87.

55. Heikal, *Sphinx and Commissar,* p. 195.

56. Rubinstein, *Red Star,* pp. 85–86 and p. 85, n. 62. Whetten, *The Canal War,* p. 73. The term "grudging support" is Rubinstein's. He cites British journalists in Cairo at the time as his source regarding a clash between Nasser and Gromyko. Rubinstein feels these journalists exaggerate the intensity of the clash, but he does not deny its existence.

57. Quandt, *Decade of Decisions,* p. 88.

58. Whetten, *The Canal War,* pp. 74–75.

59. Ibid., pp. 75–76.

60. Ibid., p. 91; Quandt, *Decade of Decisions,* pp. 96 ff; Kissinger, *White House Years,* pp. 560 ff.

61. Quandt, *Decade of Decisions,* p. 99.

62. Ibid.

63. Whetten, *The Canal War,* p. 104.

64. Ibid., pp. 103–107.

65. Ibid., pp. 106–107; Bar-Siman-Tov, *The War of Attrition,* pp. 164–165; 237, n. 74; 238, n. 76.

66. Whetten, *The Canal War,* pp. 112–117.

67. Quandt, *Decade of Decisions,* p. 99.

68. Kissinger, *White House Years,* pp. 586 ff; Whetten, *The Canal War,* pp. 128–129.

69. This is the position argued in Whetten, *The Canal War,* p. 82.

70. Bar-Siman-Tov, *The War of Attrition,* p. 232, n. 55, paraphrasing Nadav Safran, *Israel—The Embattled Ally* (Cambridge, Mass.: Harvard University Press, 1978), p. 437. Although I have not seen this claim explicitly contradicted elsewhere in the literature, I have also not seen it advanced or substantiated elsewhere. Safran's book contains no footnotes.

71. Quandt, *Decade of Decisions,* p. 79.

72. Sadat (*In Search of Identity,* pp. 187, 198) provides useful examples of how Nasser used his emotionalism to manipulate the Soviets.

73. Robert C. Horn, "1969: Year of Change in Soviet Foreign Policy," paper presented at meetings of the Western Slavic Association, San Diego, February 1976; George W. Breslauer, *Khrushchev and Brezhnev as Leaders: Building Authority in Soviet Politics* (London: Allen & Unwin, 1982), chaps. 11 and 15.

74. Breslauer, *Khrushchev and Brezhnev,* chap. 11; Peter M. E. Volten, *The Soviet "Peace Program" and Its Implementation Towards the West* (Amsterdam: Foundation for the Promotion of East-West Contacts, Free University, 1977).

75. This paragraph is based on Glassman, *Arms for the Arabs,* pp. 83–87, 90; Heikal, *Sphinx and Commissar,* p. 224; and Whetten, *The Canal War,* pp. 162–166, 188.

76. This paragraph is based on Glassman, *Arms for the Arabs,* pp. 83, 96; Whetten, *The Canal War,* pp. 215–216; Freedman, *Soviet Policy Since 1970,* pp. 47–95.

77. Heikal, *Road to Ramadan,* pp. 112, 117; Heikal, *Sphinx and Commissar,* p. 217; Whetten, *The Canal War,* p. 154.

78. Freedman, *Soviet Policy Since 1970,* p. 49.

79. The transcript was published in a Lebanese journal and is discussed in most secondary literature on the period (for example, Glassman, *Arms for the Arabs,* p. 88).

80. Whetten, *The Canal War,* p. 154; unfortunately, Whetten supplies no documentation for this claim.

81. Heikal, *Sphinx and Commissar,* p. 224.

82. Rubinstein, *Red Star,* p. 163.

83. On the fact of Soviet unwillingness to deliver these advanced weapons, the secondary literature is in agreement. Even political adversaries such as Sadat and El Shazly are in agreement on these facts, despite their different evaluations of Soviet commitment to the Egyptian cause (see Sadat, *In Search of Identity,* pp. 185–187, 198, 212, 219, 220–221, 225–228; and El Shazly, *Crossing the Suez,* pp. 28, 29, 102, 106, 141, 157–158, 160, 161–162). The Western literature, however, is split over how much importance to attach to these facts as signs of Soviet "moderation" (see, for example, Rubinstein, *Red Star,* pp. 192 ff.).

84. For example, the Indo-Pakistani war of November-December 1971 is occasionally cited to explain the USSR's failure to deliver on its promises of October 1971.

85. Quandt, *Decade of Decisions,* p. 147.

86. Ibid.

87. Heikal, *Sphinx and Commissar,* p. 252.

88. For compelling inside testimony, see Heikal, *Road to Ramadan,* pp. 120, 173; and Heikal, *Sphinx and Commissar,* p. 226.

89. Rubinstein, *Red Star,* pp. 135, 137, 140–144, 148.

90. Heikal, *Road to Ramadan,* p. 146; Heikal, *Sphinx and Commissar,* p. 235.

91. Quandt, *Decade of Decisions,* pp. 138–145.

92. Whetten, *The Canal War,* p. 194.

93. That Soviet leaders were getting visibly nervous about the situation is evident from Heikal, *Road to Ramadan,* p. 173; Heikal, *Sphinx and Commissar,* pp. 219, 237; Sadat, *In Search of Identity,* p. 222; Rubinstein, *Red Star,* p. 158; and Whetten, *The Canal War,* pp. 198–199.

94. See sources in note 76.

95. Heikal, *Sphinx and Commissar,* p. 217; Whetten, *The Canal War,* p. 136.

96. Kissinger, *White House Years,* pp. 1285–1288.

97. Quandt, *Decade of Decisions,* pp. 138–143.

98. Kissinger, *White House Years,* pp. 1285–1286, 1288–1289.

99. Ibid., p. 1286.

100. Ibid., pp. 1286–1288.

101. Rubinstein, *Red Star,* pp. 157–159; Whetten, *The Canal War,* pp. 210–211.

102. Rubinstein, *Red Star,* p. 137.

103. Kissinger, *White House Years,* chaps. 14 and 30; Rubinstein, *Red Star,* p. 138.

104. Bar-Siman-Tov, *The War of Attrition,* p. 182.

105. Quandt, *Decade of Decisions,* p. 147; Whetten, *The Canal War,* p. 204.

106. Kissinger, *White House Years,* p. 1292.

107. Ibid., pp. 1293–1294; Quandt, *Decade of Decisions,* pp. 150–151.

108. Kissinger, *White House Years,* p. 1294.

109. Ibid., pp. 1294, 1297.

110. The reader will note that this characterization treats the Soviet leadership as a relatively unified actor with respect to overall strategy, though with a mixed goal structure. I find this a more persuasive approach than that used by Kass (*Soviet Involvement*), who ascribes changes in Soviet behavior to coalition shifts within the leadership. The striking continuity in Soviet priorities and settlement terms across the three subperiods investigated in this study undermines the coalition-shift theory.

5
The Basic Principles Agreement of 1972: Origins and Expectations

Alexander L. George

At their first summit meeting in Moscow, in late May 1972, Nixon and Brezhnev signed a number of agreements and communiqúes. The most important of these, achieved after last-minute negotiations at the summit itself, was the SALT treaty limiting strategic arms. The two leaders also signed a more general document, the Basic Principles Agreement (BPA), that constituted a sort of charter defining the basis for the further development of détente. In this document the two sides agreed to hold periodic high-level meetings, to continue efforts to limit armaments, and to develop economic, scientific, and cultural ties between their two countries on a long-term basis in order to strengthen their relationship.

Of particular interest here are several other articles in the document that constituted, as it were, an agreement to cooperate in crisis prevention. These were, interestingly, placed at the beginning of the document and were couched in the following terms:

First. They [the United States and the Soviet Union] will proceed from the common determination that in the nuclear age there is no alternative to conducting their mutual relations on the basis of peaceful coexistence. Differences in ideology and in the social systems of the U.S.A. and the U.S.S.R. are not obstacles to the bilateral development of normal relations based on the principles of sovereignty, equality, noninterference in internal affairs and mutual advantage.

Second. The U.S.A. and the U.S.S.R. attach major importance to preventing the development of situations capable of causing a dangerous exacerbation of their relations. Therefore, they will do their utmost to avoid military confrontations and to prevent the outbreak of nuclear war. They will always exercise restraint in their mutual relations, and will be prepared to negotiate and settle differences by peaceful means. Discussions and negotiations on outstanding issues will be conducted in a spirit of reciprocity, mutual accommodation and mutual benefit.

Both sides recognize that efforts to obtain unilateral advantages at the expense of the other, directly or indirectly, are inconsistent with these objectives.

The prerequisites for maintaining and strengthening peaceful relations between the U.S.A. and the U.S.S.R. are the recognition of the security interests of the parties based on the principle of equality and the renunciation of the use or threat of force.

Third. The U.S.A. and the U.S.S.R. have a special responsibility, as do other countries which are permanent members of the United Nations Security Council, to do everything in their power so that conflicts or situations will not arise which would serve to increase international tensions. Accordingly they will seek to promote conditions in which all countries will live in peace and security and will not be subject to outside interference in their internal affairs.[1]

Considerable information is available on the origins of the Basic Principles Agreement, particularly in Henry Kissinger's *White House Years*. I have supplemented this information by interviewing a number of high-level foreign policy specialists in the Nixon administration. At the outset of preparations for the summit, five months before it took place, the Soviet ambassador to Washington, Anatolyi Dobrynin, raised with Kissinger the possibility of including a declaration of principles on the agenda of the summit meeting. This suggestion was not unexpected; U.S. policymakers were aware of the predilection of the Soviet leaders for formalizing the basis of their relations with other states and of their success in obtaining French and Turkish leaders' approval for such declarations. They anticipated that Brezhnev would attempt to obtain Nixon's formal acceptance of peaceful coexistence as a basis for U.S.-Soviet détente.

It is interesting, therefore, that Nixon instructed Kissinger to take a tough stand on the ground rules for détente in discussions with Soviet leaders during Kissinger's secret trip to Moscow in April 1972 at which final preparations for the summit meeting in May were to be made. Nixon wanted Kissinger to state the U.S. disagreement with the Soviet definition of peaceful coexistence sharply and explicitly. In his memoirs, Kissinger reports that Nixon told him "to emphasize the need for a single standard: we could not accept the proposition that the Soviet Union had the right to support liberation movements all over the world" or the right to insist on applying "the Brezhnev Doctrine inside the satellite orbit."[2]

Kissinger, however, chose not to follow Nixon's instructions fully.

As he admits in his memoirs,[3] Kissinger softened the hard position the president had wished him to take on this and on matters having to do with Vietnam. Evidently, with linkage in mind, Kissinger did not want to push the Soviets too hard lest he lose the possibility, to which he gave higher priority, of encouraging Brezhnev to induce Hanoi to take a more accommodating posture in the Vietnam negotiations. Shortly before Kissinger's secret trip to Moscow in April the United States, in response to a major North Vietnamese offensive in South Vietnam, had begun heavy air attacks on Hanoi and Haiphong. Later, after an intensification of the North Vietnamese offensive, Nixon ordered the mining of the Haiphong harbor. The president was so concerned that Soviet leaders might respond by canceling the summit that he seriously considered calling it off himself. By the time he arrived in Moscow in late May, the president seems to have dismissed any thought of thrashing out his disagreement with his hosts' concept of peaceful coexistence. There is no indication in either Kissinger's or Nixon's memoirs that this fundamental disagreement was even discussed, let alone resolved, at the summit. Several of my interviewees confirmed that the matter was not debated at the Moscow preparatory meeting in April or at the summit meeting in May.

As a result, the Basic Principles Agreement signed by Nixon and Brezhnev ignored the long-standing disagreement between the two sides on this important matter. Instead of opposing inclusion of "peaceful coexistence" in the document, Nixon and Kissinger contented themselves with introducing into the same document their own principles of international restraint, such as those that Nixon had enunciated in his address to the United Nations in October 1970 and that Kissinger had preached to the Soviets on various occasions. Thus, the final version of the Basic Principles Agreement included each side's favored phraseology for defining the rules of the game. Article 1 of the agreement (quoted above) contained Brezhnev's formulation that "in the nuclear age there is no alternative to conducting . . . mutual relations on the basis of peaceful coexistence." But Article 2 of the document contained phrases that echoed Nixon's and Kissinger's long-standing exhortation to the Soviets to forego "efforts to obtain unilateral advantage" at the expense of the West and to "exercise restraint" in Soviet foreign policy.[4] It should be noted, however, that this language was considerably more vague (since the precise scope and meaning of "restraint" and "unilateral advantage" had never been specified) than the concept of peaceful coexistence, whose implications for Soviet support of national liberation movements and foreign policy in third areas had been spelled out on many occasions prior to the summit meeting. Despite the U.S. leaders' effort to balance or qualify the language of Article 1 with that of Article 2, the net result was clearly advantageous to the Soviets, for they had secured in a formal document the agreement of the United States that its relations with the Soviet Union would henceforth be conducted on the basis of peaceful coexistence. Thereby, so the Soviets could believe, peaceful coexistence had been legitimized.

In this important respect, then, the Basic Principles document was only a pseudoagreement. It gave an erroneous impression that the United States and the Soviets were in substantial agreement on the rules of the game and the restraints to be observed in their competition in third areas. It would have been far preferable from the U.S. standpoint for the two sides openly to state that they disagreed over peaceful coexistence and that in this important respect the rules for regulating their competition in third areas remained an unresolved issue, just as the leaders of the United States and People's Republic of China had done earlier in that portion of the Shanghai communiqué that dealt with the unresolved problem of the status of Taiwan. As it was worded, the Basic Principles Agreement eventually contributed to what domestic critics of Nixon and Kissinger referred to as the overselling of détente.

Why, then, did Nixon and Kissinger accept so ambiguous a statement on the rules for détente vis-à-vis third areas? Apparently for a combination of reasons: they were eager to get the Soviet leaders to agree to put pressure on Hanoi to moderate its position in the peace negotiations; they recognized and wanted to reciprocate in some way for the fact that Soviet leaders, placing détente with the United States ahead of Soviet support for Hanoi, had not retaliated for the damage to the USSR's interests inflicted by U.S. mining of the Haiphong harbor, through which Soviet assistance flowed to North Vietnam. It is also possible that Nixon and Kissinger believed that by introducing their concepts of "mutual restraint" and "no unilateral advantages" into the document they were somehow delimiting peaceful coexistence and giving it a more acceptable meaning. Perhaps they also believed, as did one of my interviewees, that acceptance of the Soviet concept in the Basic Principles document was not in itself significant or damaging because in actuality whether Soviet behavior in third areas is or is not assertive depends at bottom on whether sufficient constraints and disincentives are brought to bear.

The Agreement on Prevention of Nuclear War (June 1973)

A year later, at their second summit meeting in the United States, Nixon and Brezhnev signed the Agreement on Prevention of Nuclear

War (APNW) in which they reiterated their commitment to cooperate in crisis prevention. Of particular interest is that this second agreement included a much stronger and more explicit obligation that the two powers engage in urgent consultations if situations developed anywhere in the world that raised the risk of nuclear war. It should be noted that the APNW was designed to avert not merely a nuclear war between the two superpowers but also, by clear implication (at the insistence of the U.S. leaders), any nuclear combat that might occur between either of the superpowers and any other country. The relevant portions of the agreement were the following:

> Article 1. The United States and the Soviet Union . . . agree that they will act in such a manner . . . as to exclude the outbreak of nuclear war between them and between either of the parties and other countries.
> Article 4. If at any time relations between the parties or between either party and other countries appear to involve the risk of a nuclear conflict, or if relations between countries not parties to this agreement appear to involve the risk of nuclear war between the United States of America and the Union of Soviet Socialist Republics or between either party and other countries, the United States and the Soviet Union, acting in accordance with the provisions of this agreement, shall immediately enter into urgent consultations with each other and make every effort to avert this risk.[5]

The origins of the APNW are not without interest, for they reveal some of the complexities and risks of attempting to formulate crisis-prevention agreements of a more specific character than general principles of the kind embodied in the BPA. The content of the APNW, Kissinger notes in a detailed account of the bizarre negotiations leading to the agreement, was "about 180 degrees removed" from the original proposal advanced by Brezhnev.[6] In the guise of proposing a specific crisis-prevention agreement that was ostensibly in the mutual interest of the two superpowers, the Soviet leader pressed upon Nixon and Kissinger a proposal that was flagrantly self-serving. This proposal was not abruptly rejected, as it deserved to be, because Nixon and Kissinger thought it prudent, given their hope for Soviet assistance in ending the Vietnam War, to keep the discussion going and to gradually transform the initial Soviet draft into an acceptable elaboration of some of the provisions already set forth in the BPA.

Although Kissinger gave clear indications of the unacceptable character of the initial Soviet proposal in the first volume of his memoirs,[7] he reserved a detailed description for his second volume. Toward the end of the secret trip to Moscow Kissinger undertook in April 1972 to prepare the ground for the first summit, Brezhnev asked to see him in private and "suddenly introduced the idea of an 'understanding' not to use nuclear weapons against each other."[8] Kissinger indicates that he politely turned the idea aside, given its explosive consequences for the NATO Alliance and the People's Republic of China, and suggested that it might be discussed at the Moscow summit the following month. The Soviets pressed their case, however, and prior to the summit meeting Dobrynin presented Kissinger "with a brief draft treaty to be signed as soon as convenient."[9] Not only would the two superpowers renounce the use of nuclear weapons against each other but, according to the draft proposal, they would also "prevent" situations whereby actions by third countries might lead to a nuclear war. As Kissinger notes, "we were being asked to dismantle the military strategy of NATO and at the same time to proclaim a virtual U.S.-Soviet military alliance designed to isolate or impose our will on China or any other country with nuclear aspirations."[10]

At the Moscow summit Brezhnev took up his proposal directly with Nixon, linking it with a delicate but unmistakable suggestion that the United States and the Soviet Union shared a concern over the PRC's nuclear aspirations. Nixon parried the Soviet leader's proposal, diverting it into the special Kissinger-Dobrynin diplomatic back channel.[11] In the following months Kissinger succeeded in gradually transforming the Soviet proposal into a quite different agreement, the APNW, that was then signed by the two leaders at their second summit meeting. At one point in these highly secret and sensitive back channel negotiations the Soviets amended their initial proposal, agreeing that the use of nuclear weapons would not be precluded in a war involving NATO and the Warsaw Pact countries but suggesting that the two superpowers agree to limit use of nuclear weapons in such a conflict to the territory of their European allies, thereby proscribing the employment of such weapons against the territory of the United States and the Soviet Union. At the same time in these negotiations, the Soviets continued efforts to get the United States to agree to formulations that would give Moscow a free hand to deal with the People's Republic of China without fear of becoming embroiled in a nuclear war with the United States.[12]

In the end, resisting additional Soviet negotiating pressures, Kissinger—with important assistance from British specialists—succeeded in transforming the original proposal to renounce use of nuclear weapons against each other into a more innocuous agreement to embrace the objective of avoiding nuclear war, which was made to depend on renouncing the threat of force in diplomacy. Another clause in the agreement that was finally accepted by the two sides provided for consultation when situations arose that posed a risk of nuclear war. "What had started out as a Soviet step toward a [superpower] condominium," Kissinger concludes, "had evolved into an elaboration of the 'Basic Principles of U.S.-Soviet Relations' signed at Moscow the previous year."[13]

The announcement of the signing of the APNW at the end of the second summit came as a surprise to the public and triggered immediate concern as well as curiosity among the media correspondents assembled at Kissinger's press conference. On this occasion, defending the APNW as still another useful contribution to cooperation in crisis prevention, Kissinger did broadly imply that the new agreement stemmed from an earlier Soviet proposal that, he added without revealing its contents, had been "transformed." Kissinger stated, in response to probing questions from the correspondents, that the United States had indeed consulted with and reassured both its NATO allies and the PRC prior to completion and signing of the APNW. He also explicitly rejected the notion that the second summit and, in particular, the APNW was the beginning of some kind of superpower condominium.[14]

U.S. Expectations

In his memoirs Kissinger minimizes the significance of the two agreements and the expectations he attached to them. But in press conferences that he held immediately after each of the two summits Kissinger defended the BPA and the APNW before skeptical journalists and argued that the agreements were not empty declarations. He emphasized that although the two sides had acted to *manage* crises in the past, they had not until now attempted to lay down "general rules of conduct" to *prevent* crises from occurring. Under sharp questioning from some of the journalists, Kissinger readily acknowledged that the agreements were not binding or self-enforcing and that there was no guarantee they would be observed; nonetheless, he stated, the agreements could make a positive contribution. Kissinger expressed the cautious hope that the BPA would mark "the transformation from a period of rather rigid hostility to one in which, without any illusions about the differences in social systems, we (i.e., the Soviets as well as the United States) would try to behave with restraint and with a maximum of creativity in bringing about a greater degree of stability and peace."[15] Interviews with several Nixon administration officials involved in the two summits also established that the crisis-prevention principles imbedded in the two agreements had not been regarded as just window dressing.

How would the provisions of the agreements apply in any particular situation? Kissinger was reluctant, even when pressed by reporters, to address specific questions of this kind. He acknowledged the critical importance of just how the principles would be implemented, but he dealt with this question in a perfunctory way, implying that implementation would depend on "good faith" and the "wisdom" of the two sides.

Failure to Provide and Plan for Implementation of the Crisis-Prevention Agreements

Presently available information (from public sources and interviews) indicates that neither side attempted to engage the other in followup conversations to consider the operational implications of their agreements. Also, the two sides did not attempt to set up institutionalized arrangements for periodic joint discussions about how the general principles would apply to countries and regions that were potential points of dangerous crisis. Kissinger evidently felt that it sufficed to leave each side to adapt the general principles to any particular case. Each side would determine for itself how its behavior in concrete situations should be guided by the principles. No doubt Kissinger counted upon the Soviet leaders' interest in additional benefits from the détente process to restrain Soviet foreign policy.

If the two sides were content to let the prospects for successful cooperation in crisis prevention rest with their agreement on general principles, one may ask whether the U.S. government initiated any policy planning studies to consider the implications of the agreements or to devise procedures for making effective use of them. My inquiries indicate that no such studies were undertaken either in the office of the special assistant for national security affairs or in the State Department.

Implications and Ambiguities of the Crisis-Prevention Agreements

What can be said about these efforts to formulate general principles that would serve to moderate competition between the two superpowers and to articulate their seemingly parallel interest in crisis prevention? In the first place, as subsequent events were to make clear, each side read its own hopes and desires into the language agreed upon in the BPA and APNW. Thus, for example, the two powers had rather different conceptions of the types of "dangerous crises" that these two agreements were supposed to help them avoid. The Soviet leaders were interested primarily in using such agreements to help avoid or control crises carrying the danger of nuclear war with the United States. Nixon and Kissinger, on the other hand, were interested, in addition to this, in using the agreements (together, of course, with positive inducements offered by a continuation of the détente process) to moderate Soviet efforts to make gains in third areas at the expense of the West, whether or not such assertive behavior should lead to dangerous crises of the kind feared by the Soviets. But for the Soviets the virtue of the agreements consisted in making it safer for them to engage in low-level, controlled efforts to advance their influence in third areas. Hence the Soviet leaders attached particular significance to their ability to get U.S. leaders to accept "peaceful coexistence" as the basis for their mutual relations in the nuclear era. We have already noted that in this respect the BPA was a pseudoagreement, given the fact that the two sides shied away from discussing their differences on this important matter.

For the Soviets, this achievement was reinforced and enhanced by what they regarded as a formal acceptance by Nixon of the political equality of the Soviet Union and the United States. The value of Article 1 of the BPA from the Soviet standpoint was that it committed the United States to developing "normal relations" with the Soviet Union on the basis of the principle of "equality." Article 2 further committed the United States to the principle that peaceful relations required recognition of Soviet "security interests . . . based on the principle of equality and the renunciation of the use or threat of force." These articles were phrased as applying equally to both sides, but they can be presumed to have had special significance for Soviet leaders as constituting a formal acknowledgment by Nixon and Kissinger that the Soviet achievement of strategic military parity entitled the USSR to be treated as a political-diplomatic equal as well. Consistent with this acknowledgment, in the Soviet view, was the apparent fact that the Nixon administration was already working together with the Soviet Union to develop general principles for a Middle East settlement. To the Soviets this constituted a practical recognition by the United States of Soviet security interests in the area and U.S. acceptance of the necessity of seeking a basis for joint action with the Soviet Union. As a matter of fact, however, this understanding was a gross misperception of the U.S. attitude and an incorrect appraisal of the Middle East policy Nixon and Kissinger were actually pursuing (see Chapter 7).

As was the case with "peaceful coexistence," the concept of

superpower "equality" and the question of whether the two sides shared a sufficiently common understanding of its practical operational implications were not discussed at either summit. It would appear that Nixon and Kissinger believed that although they were indeed recognizing and accepting Soviet achievement of strategic military parity they were only according the Soviets a symbolic form of political equality. There is no indication that the U.S. leaders were aware of the special significance that their Soviet counterparts attached to the references to "equality" included in the Basic Principles Agreement. This is not to say that Kissinger failed to perceive Brezhnev's sensitivity on the subject of "equality," but he appears to have misinterpreted it as a sign of the Soviet leader's psychological insecurity. Thus, in his account of his secret trip to Moscow in April 1972, Kissinger recalls, not without a trace of disparagement of the Soviet leader: "Equality seemed to mean a great deal to Brezhnev. It would be inconceivable that Chinese leaders would ask for it. . . . To Brezhnev it was central. . . . He expressed his pleasure when in my brief opening remarks I stated the obvious: that we were approaching the summit in a spirit of equality and reciprocity. What a more secure leader might have regarded as a cliché or condescension, he treated as a welcome sign of our seriousness."[16] It is clear from this observation that even at the time he wrote his memoirs Kissinger failed to understand the political significance that the Soviet leaders attached to being accorded the status of equality with the United States and the hopes and expectations this acceptance generated.

In addition to the unresolved disagreements over "peaceful co-existence" and the ambiguities and misunderstandings as to "equality," the inclusion of hedges and escape clauses further limited the utility and prospects of the agreements to cooperate in crisis prevention. Since the Basic Principles Agreement was a public document, it was essential for Nixon and Brezhnev to anticipate and allay, if possible, the suspicion that the agreement of the two superpowers to cooperate to prevent dangerous crises jeopardized the sovereignty or interests of other countries or weakened existing commitments by the United States or Soviet Union to their allies. Thus Article 12, the final article in the BPA, stated that "the basic principles set forth in this document do not affect any obligations with respect to other countries earlier assumed by the USA and the USSR." A similar proviso was included in the APNW. The potential conflict between such provisions and the commitment to act to prevent dangerous crises remained unresolved and, as we shall see in Chapter 7, was to emerge in the Middle East sooner than Nixon and Brezhnev could have expected at the time of the Moscow summit.

Notes

1. The text of the Basic Principles Agreement is reproduced in *Department of State Bulletin* June 26, 1972, pp. 898–899.

2. Henry Kissinger, *White House Years* (Boston: Little, Brown & Co., 1979), p. 1136.

3. Ibid., pp. 1135–1137, 1144–1148, 1150–1151, 1154–1164. Not only did Kissinger moderate the hard position Nixon wished him to take in the negotiations with the Soviets, he put the best light possible on the Basic Principles Agreement draft in his final reporting cable from Moscow, in which he assured Nixon that the agreement "includes most of our proposals and indeed involves a specific renunciation of the Brezhnev doctrine" (p. 1153). As a matter of fact, as Kissinger indicates elsewhere in his memoirs, the draft agreement contained no specific reference to the Brezhnev doctrine, only a phrase to the effect that both sides renounced any special privileges in any part of the world, which, he adds, "we, at least, interpreted as a repudiation of the Brezhnev Doctrine for Eastern Europe" (p. 1151).

4. Ibid., pp. 1131–1132, 1150–1151. Kissinger reports that Brezhnev gave him a Soviet draft of the Basic Principles document and invited him to "improve" it so as to make it acceptable. Kissinger and his aide, Helmut Sonnenfeldt, did redraft the document, which was then accepted by the Soviet leaders.

Curiously, in describing the contents of the agreement, Kissinger mentions the principle of restraint that he included in the document but does not mention that it also contained the Soviet concept of peaceful coexistence.

5. The text of the Agreement on Prevention of Nuclear War is reproduced in Henry Kissinger, *Years of Upheaval* (Boston: Little, Brown & Co., 1982), pp. 1234–1236.

6. Ibid., p. 282.

7. *White House Years,* pp. 1151–1152, 1208, 1251.

8. Ibid., p. 1152.

9. *Years of Upheaval,* p. 275.

10. Ibid.

11. *White House Years,* pp. 1208, 1251.

12. *Years of Upheaval,* p. 277.

13. Ibid., p. 285.

14. See Kissinger's news conferences in Washington, D.C., June 22nd and in San Clemente, June 25th, transcribed in *Department of State Bulletin,* July 23, 1973, 134–150; see especially pp. 141–147, 147–150.

15. For verbatim transcripts of Kissinger's press conferences on these two occasions see *Department of State Bulletin,* June 26, 1972, pp. 883–898, and July 10, 1972, pp. 40–49; and July 23, 1973, pp. 134–150. For a balanced assessment of the uses and limitations of these efforts to develop ground rules to regulate U.S.-Soviet competition, see Helmut Sonnenfeldt, "Russia, America and Detente," *Foreign Affairs* (January 1978) especially pp. 291–294.

16. Kissinger, *White House Years,* p. 1141; see also *Years of Upheaval,* pp. 231, 249.

6

The Kremlin and Détente: Soviet Conceptions, Hopes, and Expectations

Coit D. Blacker

In his opening address to the Twenty-Sixth Congress of the Communist Party of the Soviet Union (CPSU) in February 1981, Soviet President Brezhnev vigorously asserted the Kremlin's undiminished interest in the development of normal relations with the United States. With equal vigor, Brezhnev underscored Moscow's commitment to a "radical improvement" in the international political environment. "In this respect," the Soviet leader pronounced, "the reliable compass has been and remains the Peace Program proclaimed by the Twenty-Fourth [1971] and Twenty-Fifth [1976] CPSU Congresses."[1] Brezhnev's ringing endorsement of détente, in connection with both the superpower relationship and the Kremlin's relations with the capitalist world more generally, struck many in the West as oddly, even inexplicably, out of step with the political realities of the day.

In light of the profound deterioration in relations between Washington and Moscow over the preceding eighteen months, it was difficult for observers in the United States to explain Brezhnev's remarks as anything other than a ritualistic and insincere defense of a failed policy. A second interpretation, that the Soviet president's words merely reflected the inability of a confused and exhausted leadership to fashion an alternative policy course, found a receptive audience in the West, as well. The unwillingness of many analysts of Soviet affairs to take Brezhnev at his word is symptomatic of a larger problem that has plagued the U.S.-Soviet relationship since the initiation of the détente process in the late 1960s. Although American policymakers, beginning with Nixon and Kissinger and continuing through Carter, have gone to considerable lengths to define and characterize the détente relationship with Moscow, they have not, for the most part, absorbed much of what the Soviet leadership has said and written on the subject over the last ten years. As a consequence, U.S. officials do not adequately understand the Soviet conception of détente and the hopes and expectations attached to détente by Moscow. For Washington, the pursuit of a less hostile and more cooperative relationship with Moscow is one policy choice among several; for Brezhnev and his Politburo colleagues, détente represents a fundamentally new departure in superpower relations that has been dictated by revolutionary changes in the international environment. Moreover, the Soviets believe, this historic turn is permanent in character. Simply expressed, there exists no viable alternative. Viewed in this context, what some Western observers saw as an almost pathetic recapitulation of familiar and discredited Soviet themes by Brezhnev at the Twenty-Sixth Congress was, in Moscow's view, a new call for reason and realism.

American frustration with the disinclination of the Soviet Union to abide by the so-called "rules of détente," as these rules were conceived by officials of the Nixon, Ford, and Carter administrations, has been perceived by the Kremlin as contrived and disingenuous, an intentional distortion of reality engineered by the opponents of the policy. In part, this viewpoint reflects the Soviet conviction that powerful and well-placed "cold warriors" in the United States understand both the reasons for and the implications of détente but seek to mislead the U.S. public in order to perpetuate their own political and economic interests. The Soviets respond to the charge of breaking the rules in a number of ways. They regularly recount, for example, their own grievances against Washington's policies, which, they allege, are inconsistent with the "relaxation of international tensions." Unlike the U.S. leaders, however, they have not at any point threatened to jettison the policy in favor of some other construct. The identification of Brezhnev and others in the Politburo with détente does not fully explain their steadfast adherence to it. Two factors, the Soviets allege, make détente a principled and "objectively" determined political course.

First, Kremlin leaders find it difficult to conceive of an alternative policy in an environment dominated by the ever-present risk of strategic nuclear conflict between the two superpowers. They argue that the United States has no option but to moderate its traditional anti-Soviet posture because of the Kremlin's ability to inflict catastrophic destruction on the United States in the event of direct hostilities. When the Soviets allege that détente is the result of certain "profound" changes in the international environment, including a progressive shift in the "correlation of forces" in favor of the socialist countries, they mean above all the dramatic growth in Soviet strategic nuclear capabilities that enables them to confront the United States as a relative equal. The alternative to détente, according to the Kremlin, is an unregulated arms competition between the superpowers and frequent as well as dangerous political-military confrontations in areas of high tensions, such as the Middle East. Soviet military power, they believe, should compel the United States to seek the resolution of its differences with the USSR through a combination of accommodation and negotiation.

Second, the Soviets regard the maintenance of the détente relationship with the United States as a necessary precondition for the successful resolution of many outstanding Soviet security problems. Soviet spokesmen contend that the equality implied in the relationship requires that the United States accept the "legitimacy" of Soviet interests in a number of regions adjacent to the borders of the USSR that, however, fall beyond the reach of the Kremlin's political and military control. U.S. nuclear superiority for much of the post–World War II period effectively prevented the Soviet Union from playing what it would describe as a "constructive" role in the political and economic affairs of such Western-dominated enclaves as Western Europe, the Middle East, the Persian Gulf, and northeast Asia. To express the USSR's position another way, Soviet leaders hope, and would like U.S. policymakers to believe, that Moscow's enhanced military capabilities at the strategic level leave Washington with little real choice but to acknowledge the emerging global character of the Kremlin's political interests.

To understand why Soviet leaders feel as they do, this chapter examines in some detail the origin and early development of the détente process as viewed from the Kremlin, as well as the connection in Soviet thinking between this new relationship and Soviet security interests in other parts of the world. A general characterization of Moscow's views, such as this one, attempts to depict the dominant, operative beliefs and hopes within the Soviet leadership group, thereby foregoing a more detailed analysis of different perspectives on détente within the Soviet establishment.

The Origin and Development of Détente

For the Kremlin, the roots of the détente relationship are to be found in a number of "objective" developments, the most important of which are military in nature. In contrast to many Western analysts, who tend to focus on such "subjective" factors as changes in international political conditions, perceptions, and even personalities, the Soviets attribute the U.S. willingness to embark on a number of high-level negotiations on sensitive political and military issues to the achievement by the Kremlin of equality in the area of strategic nuclear weapons. Conventional wisdom in the West asserts that by concluding the first strategic arms limitation agreements with the United States in 1972 and thereby shedding the stigma of inferiority, Soviet leaders hoped to gain for their country recognition of its status as the "other" superpower. The achievement was held to be important largely for perceptual reasons, as the agreements signaled little more than a confirmation of an existing state of affairs. The Kremlin, however, drew a very different conclusion.

The attainment of equality in strategic nuclear weaponry, and its confirmation in SALT, signaled to Moscow the de facto abandonment by the United States of all claims to military superiority, by reference to which, it was alleged, Washington had sought (sometimes successfully, sometimes not) to determine the outcomes of all major international political conflicts. It was by virtue of superiority in central strategic systems, according to the Kremlin, that the United States was able to maintain order and to prevent unwelcome change throughout much of the imperialist world, and, at the same time, to coerce and intimidate the Soviet Union. Until the development by Moscow of intercontinental capabilities equal to those of the United States, at least in quantitative terms, Washington enjoyed the ability in any serious confrontation with the Soviet Union to threaten escalation to the level of a central strategic exchange. "Escalation dominance" afforded the United States enormous leverage over the Soviet Union, which Kremlin leaders found, for understandable reasons, both unacceptable and dangerous. Parity in strategic forces, the Soviets argued, effectively deprived Washington of this long-held advantage.[2]

The Kremlin hoped that U.S. policymakers would accept these implications of parity. The Soviets believed, for example, that Washington had finally come to grips with the fact that this new, more equal relationship in strategic forces could not be effaced by even a major U.S. increase in military spending because of the demonstrated Soviet willingness and ability to compete successfully with the United States in this field. They even felt that they had secured U.S. consent to the situation in the May 1972 Basic Principles Agreement signed by Brezhnev and Nixon in Moscow. This document, which U.S. policymakers have tended to dismiss as too general to have any practical significance, clearly stated that " . . . in the nuclear age there is no alternative to conducting [U.S.-Soviet] relations on the basis of peaceful coexistence. Differences in ideology and in the social systems of the U.S.S.R. and the U.S.A. are not obstacles to the bilateral development of normal relations based on the principles of sovereignty, equality, noninterference in internal affairs and mutual advantage." The agreement went on to note that "efforts to obtain unilateral advantage at the expense of the other, directly or indirectly," were inconsistent with the objectives of détente and that the prerequisites for the further development of relations between Washington and Moscow were "the recognition of the security interests" of the two parties, "based on the principles of equality and the renunciation of the use or threat of force."[3]

Soviet leaders assumed that the United States' adherence to the Basic Principles Agreement formally marked Washington's renunciation of a policy that, until the late 1960s, had been based upon the existence of superior and more numerous nuclear forces. Expressed in the most succinct form, the success of the Soviet Union in pulling abreast of the United States with regard to long-range nuclear weapons meant that Washington was no longer able to deal with the Kremlin from a "position of strength" or to impose its will by the threat to employ its military power.[4] Moreover, nothing the United States might do could possibly alter the situation in the foreseeable future.

In describing the significance of equality, one senior Soviet analyst, writing shortly after the second Nixon-Brezhnev summit in 1973, was quick to draw the connection between the establishment of parity in the strategic nuclear relationship and the rather abrupt turn toward "realism" in the conduct of U.S. foreign policy. He wrote:

> The growth of the Soviet Union's defensive might dispelled hopes that the U.S.A. would be able to achieve military superiority, which would have enabled it to reach its goals with the help of the use of military force or the threat of its use. . . . these changes proved sufficient for a significant segment of the U.S. ruling circles, not to mention the broad public, to understand that military forces cannot serve, so to speak, as "the heart and soul" of all foreign policy as the logic of the "Cold War" presumed.[5]

The Soviets also attached considerable importance to the formal identification of certain "parallel interests" of the two superpowers, which they felt had emerged as a consequence of Moscow's now-confirmed status as Washington's nuclear equal. The most important of these parallel interests was a commitment on the part of both countries, expressed in the Basic Principles Agreement, to do their utmost to prevent the outbreak of nuclear war through mutual restraint, consultation, and a willingness to negotiate differences.[6]

On one level, the BPA was important to the Soviet leadership because of the lingering Soviet suspicion that the United States might revert, at some point in the future, to its old habits of seeking to impose its will on the Kremlin through "nuclear blackmail"; although such a tactic could not, under contemporary conditions, achieve the desired result, it could bring the world perilously close to the abyss. It was deemed prudent, for this reason, to obtain an explicit U.S. rejection of this technique as a diplomatic tool in advance of the next crisis.

On a second level, however, the Soviets recognized that the inclusion of this provision in the Basic Principles Agreement was in essence the positive expression of what was for the United States a decidedly negative development: the Kremlin's achievement, through the growth of its nuclear arsenal, of the neutralization of U.S. strategic power. This development was, for Soviet leaders, profoundly liberating. It strongly suggested that the Kremlin could no longer be deterred by Washington from playing a more prominent role in the political and military affairs of countries and regions beyond the borders of the socialist community because the basic enforcement mechanism of the U.S. policy of containment—nuclear superiority—had been eliminated.

The Basic Principles Agreement was important, therefore, because in Moscow's eyes it lent a kind of bilateral legal sanction to the Kremlin's new status as Washington's equal. In addition, the Soviets appeared to believe that the document would provide them with an invaluable mechanism by which to influence future U.S. foreign policy and thus regulate to a degree the superpower relationship. For these reasons, the Kremlin's analysis of the Basic Principles Agreement bordered on the euphoric in the first weeks after the Moscow summit. As one Soviet observer declared in a lengthy *Pravda* article on June 15, 1972, "It is difficult to overestimate the importance of the fact that the U.S.S.R. and the U.S.A.—powers with the greatest military potential, powers belonging to different social systems—have agreed, by what is for all practical purposes a treaty, to build their relations on [the basis of peaceful coexistence]."[7] He went on to note, "The provision stating that the 'prerequisites for maintaining and strengthening peaceful relations between the U.S.S.R. and the U.S.A. are the recognition of the security interests of the parties' . . . is also in itself the equivalent of a very important international agreement."[8]

The realization by the Soviet Union of military equality with the United States therefore had much wider and more concrete implications for Kremlin leaders than their U.S. counterparts seemed able to comprehend at the time. In the Soviet view, this equality should facilitate participation by the Kremlin in the search for the resolution of major international disputes (defined as those involving the United States), not because Washington consented to Moscow's involvement, but because the USSR's equality rendered the United States powerless to prevent it. In this regard, Western analysts were somewhat perplexed, given the Kremlin's rather modest international commitments, by Foreign Minister Gromyko's statement at the Twenty-Fourth CPSU Congress in 1971 that "there is no question of any significance which can be decided without the Soviet Union or in opposition to her."[9] Many in the United States interpreted Gromyko's remark as little more than a boast, an expression of wishful thinking. For the Soviet leadership, the foreign minister's observation was a useful assertion of a new reality, based on a dispassionate analysis of objective factors—most importantly, the demonstrable shift of the strategic balance in a direction favorable to Moscow. From the Kremlin's perspective, parity marked the emergence of the Soviet Union as a superpower in *political as well as in military terms.*

What Gromyko and others in the Soviet hierarchy realized at a much earlier stage than their counterparts in Washington was that confirmation of the Kremlin's status as a superpower was the necessary precondition for its assumption of a truly global role. They wished to believe, simultaneously, that whether their country chose to assume such expanded worldwide responsibilities was, for the first time, a decision that was exclusively theirs to make, in no way dependent upon what the U.S. leaders might define as appropriate or legitimate.

That the Soviet leadership was fully prepared—even eager—to shoulder the responsibilities of "globalism" was apparent as early as the first Nixon-Brezhnev summit in May 1972. Moreover, the Soviets thought that they had attained Washington's acquiescence to their doing so. The 1972 Basic Principles Agreement obligated the two sides not only to prevent the development of situations capable of causing a dangerous exacerbation of their relations but also to settle their differences by "peaceful means."[10] Less than a week after Nixon's departure from the Soviet Union, the leadership provided its own, rather more developed interpretation of that provision. The logic of nuclear equality, according to an authoritative statement in *Pravda,* required more than a basic commitment to avoid direct military confrontations between the two superpowers. Nuclear equality also necessitated a willingness on both sides to resolve "disputed international questions" by negotiations based on "observance of the principles of equality and equal security . . . mutual respect of interests

and the universal affirmation in international relations of the principles
of peaceful coexistence of states with different social systems.''[11]

The statement in *Pravda* was significant for at least two reasons.
First, it advanced the thesis that in areas where the interests of the
United States and the Soviet Union were directly engaged, the reality
of strategic equality should dictate that the two countries cooperate
in the search for viable, long-term solutions to their political and
military differences. For Moscow, the principal regions of concern
were Europe, the Middle East, and, to a lesser extent, northeast Asia
because of their geographic proximity to the Soviet Union.

Consistent with this interpretation, Moscow and Washington had
pledged in the communiqué that concluded the 1972 summit to
cooperate in efforts to bring about a peaceful settlement of the conflict
in the Middle East and to take additional steps to ensure a peaceful
future for Europe, "free of tensions, crisis, and conflict."[12] Georgi
Arbatov, director of the Institute of the United States and Canada,
writing in *Pravda* in 1973, went so far as to argue that the further
development of Soviet-U.S. relations required not only "the prevention of new conflicts and crises" in the international area but also
"the creation of a mechanism that would make it possible in good
time to solve emerging problems through negotiation."[13] Whether
and to what extent Arbatov was reflecting the Kremlin's thinking in
this respect is uncertain, but such a nascent interest in a crisis-
prevention regime with Washington had never before been made so
explicit. Second, Arbatov's analysis in *Pravda* conveyed a hopeful
expectation that nuclear parity would have an enormous and, from
the Soviet perspective, positive impact on the competition between
Moscow and Washington for political and military influence in third
areas.

Just as détente symbolized for Moscow the end of Washington's
ability to dominate, without reference to Soviet preferences, political,
military, and economic developments in such Western-oriented environments as the NATO countries and the Middle East, so too did
détente presage a significant setback for the U.S. position in much
of the Third World. According to Soviet analysts, the success of the
United States throughout the entire post–World War II period in
"imposing its will" on many Asian, African, and Latin American
countries had been achieved through frequent recourse to military
force.[14] The suggestion was that prior to the arrival of strategic parity
between the two superpowers, the Kremlin had been deterred in
many instances from challenging U.S. policy or from assisting those
elements opposed to imperialism because of Washington's superior
"power projection capabilities" and ultimately its capacity to engage

in "nuclear blackmail." Equality in nuclear weapons sharply reduced the credibility of the latter threat, thus affording the Kremlin increased opportunities to aid its friends in distress.

For Soviet leaders if not for U.S. policymakers, the logic of the Soviet analysis of competition in third areas was both compelling and self-evident. The Soviets went to considerable lengths from 1972 to 1974 to emphasize that the détente relationship with the United States would "powerfully and materially" assist the cause of national liberation, precisely because it should serve to restrain U.S. power in pursuit of "counterrevolutionary" aims.[15] The Kremlin did not seek to mislead U.S. policymakers on this issue; in fact, it attempted to persuade Washington to accept and adjust to Moscow's view of the realities. Soviet spokesmen repeatedly stressed that the "international class struggle," the historically determined conflict between the forces of socialism and imperialism, would continue unabated, regardless of the status of the bilateral relationship between Washington and Moscow at any given time.[16] Moreover, the Soviet Union would lend whatever help it deemed appropriate (and prudent) to those engaged in this struggle. "We have always regarded, and regard now," Brezhnev declared in 1973, "as our inviolable duty stemming from our Communist convictions, from our Socialist morality, to render the widest possible support to the peoples fighting for the just cause of freedom. This has always been the case, this will be the case in the future as well."[17]

What policymakers in the United States would come to regard as a violation of détente, namely, Soviet assistance to various revolutionary movements in the less developed world, the Kremlin argued was not simply consistent with the policy but a predictable consequence of it. Even in this area, however, the Kremlin seemed eager to avoid excessive friction with the United States. Arbatov, for example, in a *Pravda* article written shortly after the second Nixon-Brezhnev summit of June 1973, indicated a willingness on the part of the Soviet Union to cooperate with the United States in efforts to reduce the incidence of violence in the struggle between socialism and imperialism in third areas, provided Washington exercised a meaningful degree of restraint in its own policies, even arguing that such an agreement would represent "an enormous gain for the cause of peace."[18] Interestingly, Arbatov's offer was not echoed in other Kremlin statements and was never again made in comparable terms. Its disappearance may have been prompted by the October 1973 war in the Middle East, the conduct of which may have convinced Soviet leaders that Arbatov's expectations concerning the prospects for meaningful superpower restraint in third areas during times of acute crisis were unrealistically optimistic.

The Soviets recognized, in something of a paradox, that their now-greater freedom to engage the United States, both politically and militarily, at regional and subregional levels—as a result of their capacity to neutralize U.S. strategic power—might in fact precipitate a dangerous confrontation with Washington. Consequently, they sought and obtained in 1973 a reaffirmation of those provisions of the 1972 Basic Principles Agreement concerning the avoidance of nuclear conflict. In the Agreement on Prevention of Nuclear War, signed in June 1973, the two sides pledged themselves to prevent the development of situations that could precipitate a nuclear exchange and, in the event such a risk were to appear, to enter into "urgent consultations" in order to diffuse the crisis.[19] In other words, the competition, though perhaps intense, must not be allowed to get out of hand. In the view of one Western analyst, the Soviet leadership may well have felt that one of the principal benefits of SALT I and of such attendant documents as the Agreement on Prevention of Nuclear War was that they made the world "safe for conflict," presumably conflict of the nonnuclear variety.[20]

Whatever the Soviets may have sought through détente with the United States (and the evidence suggests that they sought a great deal, especially in the areas of economics and trade), in political-strategic terms their objectives were essentially threefold. Of overarching importance, because without its realization the second two were unattainable, was their goal of official confirmation as Washington's nuclear equal; at the same time, they labored to secure a pledge from the United States not to "upset" this relationship of forces at any point in the future. Soviet leaders hoped they had attained these aims through the signing of the SALT accords and the conclusion of the Basic Principles Agreement.

Second, as a consequence of their equality in the military dimension, they pressed their claims for political equality. They did so by asserting that such status could not be denied them because the United States was no longer in a position militarily to prevent the Kremlin from playing a "legitimate" role in Western European and Middle Eastern affairs. What this role might be, to be sure, was left ambiguous because Soviet leaders did not find it useful to define and delimit their interests or clearly to distinguish interests from aspirations. What was more important for the present was to assert the claim that henceforth they should share with the United States responsibility for charting the political and military development in these areas. This right, too, they argued, was assured in the Basic

Principles Agreement in the form of a mutual commitment to respect the security interests of the two parties and to forego all efforts "to obtain unilateral advantage."

Third, through such mechanisms as the Agreement on Prevention of Nuclear War, they attempted to reduce the risks associated with Soviet-U.S. competition in the Third World. At the same time, they underscored their determination to continue their support for those forces engaged in the national liberation struggle. Much to their later consternation, Soviet authorities were never able to communicate with much clarity to policymakers in the United States their rather complicated position on this sensitive issue.

The Connection of Détente
to Regional Soviet Security Concerns

Of the Kremlin's three principal objectives in détente, U.S. policymakers really understood only the first. The second they regarded as presumptuous, or at least premature; consistent with this view, Philip Windsor, a noted British analyst of Soviet affairs, charged in 1979 that the Kremlin had become a superpower "purely" by virtue of its strategic relationship with the United States and that it had done so before it had acquired "any of the dimensions of a global power."[21] The third objective, the attempt on Moscow's part to moderate through prior agreement the risks associated with superpower competition in the Third World, deepened the level of the USSR's involvement in various national liberation struggles; but this objective struck many U.S. officials as self-serving, deceptive, and insincere, a disturbing example of the Kremlin's penchant for political legerdemain.

There was an awareness among Western political leaders, largely inchoate during the early years of détente, that strategic nuclear equality between Washington and Moscow had undermined to a degree the reliability of U.S. security guarantees to its principal allies in Europe, the Middle East, and the Far East, although the precise implications of this novel situation were less than apparent. The suggestion, however, that an inevitable consequence of this development was permanently greater Soviet access to and influence over noncommunist countries closely tied to the United States was dismissed as the function of the Kremlin's rather bloated self-image, a case of ambition exceeding capabilities. To the West, parity in strategic nuclear terms carried with it few special privileges in the international political domain, beyond the recognition that in those areas where the Soviet Union had long exercised an imperial prerogative, its interests would be respected. But that had been the case, in any event, for virtually the entire post–World War II period.

Obviously, Soviet leaders did not find this Western assessment congenial. They judged their objectives to be both realistic and attainable, based on their analysis of the structure and conduct of modern U.S. foreign policy. The central and enduring feature of that policy, Kremlin spokesmen argued, was the capability of the United States throughout the first two decades following World War II to draw numerous lines in all parts of the world and to declare the areas that fell within those parameters to be of "vital interest."[22] Washington's claims were respected for the most part because of the United States' quantifiable advantage in strategic forces, which more than compensated for any regional military imbalance unfavorable to the West.

Through nuclear superiority, the United States was able, therefore, to provide important and credible assurances to its major partners in Europe and Asia, to maintain its authority within alliance structures, and to coerce into obedience its more reluctant allies and friends around the globe. In areas where the military or strategic interests of the United States and its regional allies were essentially the same, such as Western Europe, the Soviets were able to influence developments only indirectly and in a negative way (perceptions of "the Soviet threat" were useful devices to promote Western unity, for example). Where one or more countries in a region might be opposed to U.S. preeminence, for whatever reason, the Soviets were able to play a more significant role in many cases, by becoming the political and military patron of the state or states hostile to Washington's policies or presence. The Middle East after 1955 is perhaps the most evident illustration of such a situation.

The Kremlin regarded environments such as the Middle East as especially unsatisfactory, insofar as the maintenance of the USSR's position in the area rested upon continuous tension and conflict among regional actors. The need for Soviet support would presumably diminish, as would Soviet influence, were the differences separating the parties to be resolved without Soviet participation in the peace process. Of even greater concern to Moscow, taking sides in regional conflicts involving the United States always carried with it an element of risk; the outbreak of a local war might precipitate a military confrontation between the two superpowers, an unwelcome prospect to Kremlin leaders in an environment characterized by U.S. nuclear dominance.

As was discussed in the preceding section, Soviet authorities gave the impression of being firmly convinced in the early 1970s that the arrival of parity at the strategic level had thoroughly undermined the operative basis of U.S. foreign policy. Equality in nuclear weaponry also signified equality in vulnerability. How credible was it for policymakers in Washington to pledge themselves to the defense of their European and Asian allies in the event of Soviet aggression if, by so doing, they were to place at risk the lives of a hundred million U.S. citizens? How supportive of Israeli interests could the United States afford to be, in the event of a large-scale conflict between Tel Aviv and its neighbors, when any intensification of the conflict might well bring about the direct intervention of the Kremlin on behalf of its regional clients? Without a believable capacity to threaten escalation, how was Washington to deter Soviet action? By attaining strategic equality, the Soviets believed that the United States would be eventually compelled to undertake an "agonizing reappraisal" of its security commitments worldwide; Washington's allies would be forced to do the same. The result of such deliberations could only lead in the long run to one outcome: a self-interested search on the part of the United States' partners and clients for supplementary or perhaps alternative security arrangements, in order to compensate for Washington's now less dependable guarantees. Under such altered conditions, the Soviets anticipated a heightened interest in, and sensitivity to, their own policy preferences on the part of those countries within effective range of Soviet military power.

To ensure such approaches, the Kremlin maintained a gradual, consistent, and comprehensive effort to enlarge and modernize its conventional military capabilities, an effort that actually predated the initiation of détente and that continued unabated throughout détente's tenure.[23] Once again, the logic of such an undertaking seemed, to Soviet officials, unassailable. With a degree of mutual paralysis characterizing the strategic nuclear relationship between the superpowers, which made conflict at that level unlikely, the greatest practical inhibition on the use of nonnuclear Soviet military forces in regions outside Eastern Europe had been removed. This change suggested to Soviet analysts the possibility, if not the likelihood— at any number of geographic points at which the "vital interests" of Washington and Moscow intersected—of a conventional military engagement between Soviet and U.S. forces (or between those of their close allies) that might remain limited in character.[24]

The buildup in Soviet conventional capabilities was clearly directed, in the first instance, to deterring such conflicts; in the event deterrence failed, however, such forces would permit the resolution of conflict on terms advantageous to the Kremlin. By the mid-1970s the Soviets had attained conventional military forces increasingly capable of satisfying both requirements in the areas of greatest concern to the Kremlin, including the European theater, opposite the countries of Southwest Asia and the Persian Gulf, and along the border with China.[25]

Clearly, the Soviets recognized that the loss of U.S. superiority at the strategic level intensified the concern of Washington's allies over the various regional military balances. In this context, the significant growth of Soviet conventional forces served to reawaken latent fears concerning Moscow's intentions. Most importantly, the buildup lent a new sense of urgency and authority to Moscow's repeated calls for the convocation of various international conferences to consider regional security issues, in which the Soviet Union would participate as an equal and thereby enjoy opportunities for enhancing its influence. In reviewing the history of the Conference on Security and Cooperation in Europe, for example, Soviet spokesmen attributed its success to what they termed the spirit of "realism" that emerged on that Continent in the early 1970s—at precisely the time Washington and Moscow were negotiating the first strategic arms limitation agreements.[26] The timing, the Kremlin insisted, was not coincidental. They described their participation in the 1973 Geneva Conference on the Middle East, and specifically their assumption of the chairmanship with the United States of that effort, as a function of similar processes.[27]

For all these reasons, the Soviets discerned a direct connection between the détente relationship with the United States and the possible resolution along favorable lines of many of their regional security problems and aspirations for additional influence. Their hopes have been conveyed, for the most part, unambiguously. In areas proximate to the borders of the socialist community, in which the Soviet Union, like the United States, has historic and "legitimate" interests, the Soviets have sought appropriate and permanent recognition of their concern. They have sought, as well, to displace the United States as the sole external arbiter of each region's development and to influence both the rate and the nature of change therein. They have sought to reduce whatever level of threat they confront in each area through a combination of military strength, seemingly reasonable proposals, and negotiation. Moreover, they have hoped that the confirmation of equality in the strategic nuclear balance, and the implications of that confirmation, as well as the steady expansion of their conventional capabilities, would ensure enhanced political authority. For much of the détente period they also felt that these "objective factors" should encourage a policy of accommodation on the part of the United States and its allies.

The Soviets seemed convinced, as well, that détente was transforming the rules governing the competition between the two super-powers in third areas, giving the USSR, in the words of one Soviet official, "equal right to meddle."[28] As in areas proximate to the Soviet Union, the growth in Moscow's strategic nuclear capabilities would force Washington to adjust to the Kremlin's higher political and military profile in more distant regions. The development of the Soviet Union's conventional military capabilities, which was so useful in shaping the perceptions of Moscow's principal adversaries in Europe and Asia, could now be utilized in more direct ways to assist the cause of revolution and national liberation in countries located hundreds and even thousands of miles from the Soviet homeland.

As a result of this conviction, the Soviets undertook, beginning in the late 1960s, a concerted effort to expand their power projection capabilities, concentrating specifically on the procurement of "blue water" naval forces (largely for the purposes of establishing a visible military presence in distant areas) and long-range transport aircraft (in order to deliver men and matériel in significant numbers in as short a time as possible).[29] Both capabilities had long been central features of the U.S. military posture, enabling the United States, in Moscow's view, to protect its global interests and to limit the involvement of other external actors. The development of such forces by the Kremlin implied, at a minimum, a willingness to employ them, given the opportunity and a conducive environment.

In line with this analysis and with the evolution of its strategic and nonnuclear military capabilities, the Kremlin rejected from the outset the contention that détente between the two superpowers required for its continuation a pause or a cessation in the struggle between the "forces of progress and the forces of reaction." Various Western-formulated "codes of conduct" that suggested such a commitment were dismissed as unrealistic and prejudicial to the interests of the socialist community, as the West would always find ways to circumvent such an agreement through clandestine operations and subversion; a commitment of this nature, therefore, was not simply undesirable but also unenforceable. The only obligation implied under the terms of détente was that Washington and Moscow take steps, either on their own or bilaterally, to make sure that their support of clients in these turbulent areas did not precipitate a superpower confrontation.[30]

The Soviet leadership preferred to believe that Western countries both understood and accepted its position on this issue. When U.S. policymakers began, as early as 1975, to charge Moscow with violating the "code of détente," as Kissinger did in reaction to the Soviet Union's military support for the Marxist factions in the Angolan and Mozambican civil wars, the Kremlin reacted with a combination of surprise and disbelief. From the Soviet perspective, the assistance was both modest in scope and consistent with Moscow's emergence as a global actor. It is unlikely that Soviet leaders viewed their greater involvement in southern African affairs as a particularly high-risk venture. The ability to compete with the United States on more equal terms for political and military influence in countries not aligned with either Washington or Moscow was alleged, after all, to be one of the principal and, indeed, self-evident results of détente. Soviet spokesmen seemed to be arguing and urging that the appropriate Western response to the greater involvement of the Socialist countries in the national liberation struggles of Africa and Asia was not to threaten Moscow with the abandonment of détente but to recognize that such assistance constituted a legitimate exercise of Soviet power and that it was certain to continue, regardless of Washington's protests. That the United States and its allies would lend to their friends and clients whatever level of support they deemed consistent with larger security goals in response to these Soviet activities was fully anticipated.

Conclusion

The purpose of this analysis has been to examine in some detail Soviet conceptions of the USSR's political and military relationship with the United States between 1971 and 1980, the so-called period of détente. Several conclusions flow from this study: that the Kremlin regards "peaceful coexistence" and "relaxation of international tensions" as policies objectively determined by the advent of strategic nuclear parity between the two superpowers, and that this new relationship undermines U.S. "positions of strength," ensures the global political power of the Soviet Union, and enables the socialist countries to compete more effectively with the West for access and influence throughout the less developed world. All these conclusions have important implications for the conduct of U.S. foreign policy in the 1980s. At a minimum, the analysis suggests that policymakers in the United States have had at best a partial or incomplete understanding of the assumptions that guide Soviet conduct in world affairs. It also suggests that to deal creatively and effectively with the political and military challenges posed by Moscow will require of U.S. leaders a much greater awareness of and sensitivity to Soviet security concerns than has been evident in the past.

This is not to argue that any U.S. government should subscribe to the Kremlin's interpretation of international politics. Soviet convictions and perceptions are as ethnocentrically based, as "subjective," as those of any other country. The more profitable course may be to participate in the search for a "common language" as proposed by Brezhnev in an April 1981 speech. Doubtless, such an effort would require a good deal of determination and patience. A more active and sustained superpower dialogue on issues of joint concern would not eliminate the confusion, misunderstanding, and tension that has plagued the relationship since its inception; it could, however, facilitate communication and restore an element of predictability to the interaction between Washington and Moscow.

Notes

1. L. I. Brezhnev, "The Report of the CPSU Central Committee to the 26th Congress of the Communist Party of the Soviet Union and the Party's Tasks in the Fields of Domestic and Foreign Policy," *Pravda,* February 24, 1981, pp. 2–9 (*Current Digest of the Soviet Press* 33, no. 8:13).

2. For a detailed treatment of this issue, see, for example, Henry Trofimenko, *Changing Attitudes Toward Deterrence,* ACIS Working Paper no. 25 (Los Angeles: University of California at Los Angeles, Center for International and Strategic Affairs, July 1980), especially pp. 4–11.

3. "Basic Principles of Relations Between the Union of Soviet Socialist Republics and the United States of America," *Pravda,* May 30, 1972, p. 1 (*Current Digest of the Soviet Press* 24, no. 22:22).

4. Trofimenko, *Changing Attitudes,* pp. 17–18.

5. Georgi Arbatov, "Soviet-American Relations at a New Stage," *Pravda,* July 22, 1973, pp. 4–5 (*Current Digest of the Soviet Press* 25, no. 29:2).

6. Ibid.

7. Yu. Chernov, "Real Force of International Development," *Pravda,* June 15, 1972, pp. 4–5 (*Current Digest of the Soviet Press* 24, no. 24:3).

8. Ibid.

9. As reported in Robert Legvold, "The Concept of Power and Security in Soviet History," *Prospects of Soviet Power in the 1980s, Part I,* Adelphi Paper no. 151 (London: International Institute for Strategic Studies, 1979), p. 6. Legvold also discusses the purpose behind and the significance of this oft-quoted Gromyko statement in the course of his sophisticated and elegant analysis.

10. "Basic Principles of Relations," *Pravda,* May 30, 1972 (*Current Digest of the Soviet Press* 24, no. 22:22).

11. "On the Results of the Soviet-American Talks," *Pravda,* June 2, 1972, p. 1 (*Current Digest of the Soviet Press* 24, no. 22:25).

12. "Joint Soviet-American Communique," *Pravda,* May 31, 1972, p. 1 (*Current Digest of the Soviet Press* 24, no. 22:24).

13. Georgi Arbatov, "Soviet-American Relations," *Pravda,* July 22, 1973 (*Current Digest of the Soviet Press* 25, no. 29:4).

14. See F. Ryzhenko, "Peaceful Coexistence and the Class Struggle," *Pravda,* August 22, 1973, pp. 3–4 (*Current Digest of the Soviet Press* 25, no. 34:5), as well as a more detailed treatment of the same issues in Sh. Sanakoyev, "The World Today: Problem of the Correlation of Forces," *International Affairs* (Moscow), no. 11 (November 1974) especially pp. 44–45.

15. One of the clearest expositions of the relationship between détente and the national liberation struggle is contained in V. Razmerov, "Leninist Foreign Policy: An Important Factor in Contemporary World Development," *International Affairs* (Moscow) (May 1974):7–8.

16. See Brezhnev's address to the 1973 World Congress of Peace Forces, as reported in *Pravda,* October 27, 1973, pp. 1–3 (*Current Digest of the Soviet Press* 25, no. 43:6); for a somewhat less polemical statement, see Henry Trofimenko, "America, Russia and the Third World," *Foreign Affairs* 59, no. 5:1021–1040.

17. As quoted in Razmerov, "Leninist Foreign Policy," p. 8.

18. Arbatov, "Soviet-American Relations."

19. "Agreement Between the Union of Soviet Socialist Republics and the United States of America on the Prevention of Nuclear War," *Pravda,* June 23, 1973, p. 1 (*Current Digest of the Soviet Press* 25, no. 26:13). For a detailed account of the original Soviet proposal for an agreement not to use nuclear weapons against each other, which Kissinger succeeded in transforming into what became the Agreement on Prevention of Nuclear War, see Chapter 5.

20. Philip Windsor, "The Soviet Union in the International Political System of the 1980s," *Prospects of Soviet Power in the 1980s, Part II,* Adelphi Paper no. 152 (London: International Institute for Strategic Studies, 1979), p. 8.

21. Ibid., p. 2.

22. The use of this imagery is of relatively recent origin, although essentially the same message has been communicated by Soviet analysts for decades. See V. Svetlov, "The Duplicity of Imperialist Propaganda," *Pravda,* January 5, 1980, p. 4 (*Current Digest of the Soviet Press* 32, no. 1:3–4); A. A. Gromyko's address to the 35th session of the United Nations General Assembly, September 23, 1980, as reported by TASS (*Foreign Broadcast Information Service Daily Report, Soviet Union,* September 24, 1980, p. CC2); and I. Aleksandrov, "Concerning the Policy of the New U.S. Administration," *Pravda,* March 25, 1981, pp. 4–5 (*Current Digest of the Soviet Press* 33, no. 12:3–4).

23. Western assessments of the expansion of Soviet conventional military capabilities are numerous. The most recent and comprehensive is the study by John M. Collins, *U.S.-Soviet Military Balance: Concepts and Capabilities 1960–1980* (New York: McGraw-Hill, 1980); see pp. 177–237 and 291–394. Also useful are the three *Department of Defense Annual Reports* (*Fiscal Year 1979, Fiscal Year 1980,* and *Fiscal Year 1981;* Washington, D.C.: Government Printing Office, February 2, 1978; January 25, 1979; and January 29, 1980), prepared by the staff of former Secretary of Defense Harold Brown; see also

earlier reports prepared by the staff of former Secretary of Defense Donald Rumsfeld.

24. Official Soviet statements on the possibility of limited, nonnuclear military engagements between Soviet and U.S. (or Warsaw Pact and NATO) forces are all but nonexistent. The judgment can be made, nonetheless, based on an analysis of the number and composition of Soviet conventional forces deployed along critical "theaters of military operations" in the USSR and Eastern Europe. See Collins, *U.S.-Soviet Military Balance,* and the recent writings (1975–1980) of John Erickson in such journals as *Strategic Review.*

25. Not all Western observers of Soviet military developments support this view. Harold Brown, in *Department of Defense Annual Report, Fiscal Year 1982* (Washington, D.C.: Government Printing Office, 1981), pp. 63–91, for example, advances a more optimistic analysis of U.S. and Western abilities to contain even a major conventional Soviet military assault in these areas than do other experts, including Collins and Erickson. The evidence, however, would seem to support the findings of the more pessimistic Western specialists.

26. See "A. A. Gromyko's Speech at the Conference on Security and Cooperation in Europe," *Pravda,* July 4, 1972, p. 5 (*Current Digest of the Soviet Press* 25, no. 27:1–2).

27. See, especially, "Statement by Andrey Gromyko at the Peace Conference to the Middle East," TASS, December 21, 1973 (*Foreign Broadcast Information Service,* "Soviet Union," December 26, 1973, pp. F1–2).

28. Alexander Dallin, "The Road to Kabul: Soviet Perceptions of World Affairs and the Afghan Crisis," in Vernon Aspaturian, Alexander Dallin, and Jiri Valenta, *The Soviet Invasion of Afghanistan: Three Perspectives,* ACIS Working Paper no. 27 (Los Angeles: University of California at Los Angeles, Center for International and Strategic Affairs, September 1980), p. 57.

29. For a sophisticated discussion on the expansion and modernization of the Soviet navy in the 1970s, see the seminal works of Michael McGwire, especially "Naval Power and Soviet Global Strategy," *International Security* 3, no. 4:134–189. See also Michael McGwire, ed., *Soviet Naval Developments: Capability and Context* (New York: Praeger, 1973), as well as the two later companion volumes, *Soviet Naval Power: Objectives and Constraints* (New York: Praeger, 1975), and *Soviet Naval Influence: Domestic and Foreign Dimensions* (New York: Praeger, 1977). One of the most informative works on the development of Soviet long-range airlift capabilities is Robert P. Berman, *Soviet Airpower in Transition* (Washington, D.C.: Brookings Institution, 1977).

30. See Brezhnev's address to the 1973 World Congress of Peace Forces, *Pravda,* October 27, 1973 (*Current Digest of the Soviet Press* 26, no. 43:6), for a representative sampling of Soviet sentiment on this issue. For a more extensive discussion of the same concepts, see Colonel I. Sidelnikov, "Peaceful Coexistence and the Security of the Peoples," *Krasnaya Zvezda,* August 14, 1973, pp. 2–3 (*Current Digest of the Soviet Press* 25, no. 34, pp. 34–35).

7

The Arab-Israeli War of October 1973: Origins and Impact

Alexander L. George

Developments leading to the Arab-Israeli war on October 6, 1973, provided the first test of the new U.S.-Soviet crisis-prevention regime.[1] Unfortunately, this first test was about as severe a one as could have been contrived. It came only a few months after Nixon and Brezhnev signed the Agreement on Prevention of Nuclear War (APNW) at their second summit in Washington. An examination of the origins of the war will reveal the difficulties of implementing the key provisions of this agreement and the earlier one on basic principles.

Divergent U.S. and Soviet Policies in the Middle East

It is true that the Soviets did not go as far as they might have (or as far as they ought to have gone, according to one possible interpretation of their responsibilities under the agreements) to prevent the Arab attack or to consult adequately with the United States to enlist its cooperation to this end. Nonetheless, if one examines the totality of Soviet behavior—not only in the weeks and months immediately preceding the outbreak of the war but also in the several years prior to the war—and if one takes into account the difficult constraints under which the Soviet leaders had to operate, one sees evidence that Soviet leaders did operate with considerable restraint for a while in the Middle East and that they did make some effort to cooperate in crisis prevention. What is more, some aspects of U.S. policy in the Middle East in the years immediately preceding the outbreak of the October War as well as thereafter are difficult to reconcile with the injunction of the Basic Principles Agreement (BPA) that both sides forego efforts to derive "unilateral advantage," an injunction that Nixon and Kissinger had included in that document.

As many specialists on Soviet policy in the Middle East have recognized, Soviet leaders tried for several years to discourage Sadat from resorting to force. Although important facts remain obscure and unverified, it appears that at first the Soviets did withhold military equipment and supplies deemed necessary by Sadat for a major Arab attack.[2] The Soviets also counseled Sadat to seek his objectives through diplomacy rather than force. Kissinger was quite aware of the Soviets' actions at the time. In fact, this pattern of Soviet restraint of Sadat and Kissinger's expectation that the Soviets would continue this policy contributed to the failure of U.S. policymakers later on, in 1973, to become unduly alarmed at the flow of Soviet military supplies to Egypt and Syria or to take the other intelligence warnings of the forthcoming Arab attack seriously.

The Soviet Union's policy of restraining Sadat was not without serious diplomatic and political costs for the USSR's position in the Middle East. At one point, in July 1972, Sadat became so frustrated and furious over the fact that the Soviets were giving priority to détente with the United States over effective assistance to the Arab states that he expelled most of the fifteen thousand Soviet military advisers from Egypt. Other considerations, to be sure, may also have entered into Sadat's decision.[3] Soviet reluctance to facilitate Arab military action against Israel may well have stemmed, as some analysts believe, from a desire not to damage the development of détente with the United States. But Moscow's restraint undoubtedly also reflected its expectation that the Arab states would suffer another quick defeat if they attacked Israel. In that event the Soviet Union would be faced once again, as in 1967 and 1970, with the difficult task of bailing the Arabs out, thereby risking a military confrontation with Israeli forces if not also with the United States.

More generally, perhaps Soviet leaders believed that their position in Egypt rested rather tenuously on the continuation of the Arab security dilemma vis-à-vis the Israelis. It may be, as many observers have suggested, that Moscow believed it could exert maximum influence at minimum cost and risk in a "no war, no peace" situation in the Middle East. (For a critical assessment of this thesis see Chapter 4.) But, if so, the unpredictable factor was Sadat. The Egyptian leader found the "no war, no peace" situation intolerable and maneuvered repeatedly, and eventually with a degree of success, to take advantage of the rivalry and diplomatic disunity of the two superpowers.

Kissinger was well aware that the Soviet Union was experiencing serious dilemmas and difficulties in its relations with Egypt well before Sadat expelled the Soviet military advisers. In fact, while the

Soviets were restraining Sadat, Kissinger was secretly pursuing a Machiavellian strategy to heighten the Soviet Union's diplomatic difficulties with its Arab clients. What Kissinger hoped for and was working toward was a reversal of alliances whereby the United States would replace the Soviet Union as Egypt's ally.[4] Kissinger had come to this view quite early in the Nixon presidency, when the president had given the State Department primary responsibility for dealing with the Arab-Israeli conflict and had permitted Secretary of State William Rogers to take various diplomatic initiatives aimed at bringing about a settlement. As early as the meeting of the National Security Council on December 10, 1969, Kissinger states in his memoirs:

> I challenged the fundamental premise of our diplomacy that the continuing stalemate [in the Arab-Israeli conflict] strengthened the Soviet Union's position. In my view the opposite was the case; the longer the stalemate continued the more obvious would it become that the Soviet Union had failed to deliver what the Arabs wanted. As time went on, its Arab clients were bound to conclude that friendship with the Soviet Union was not the key to realizing their aims. Sooner or later, if we kept our nerve, this would force a reassessment of even radical Arab policy.
>
> This was my strategy, which gradually became our policy from 1969 onward (over the corpses of various State Department peace plans, gunned down by the passions of the partners in the area rather than by me). In 1972 and 1973 the strategy began to succeed.[5]

Again, commenting on the fact that "the various negotiating schemes of 1969 proved stillborn," Kissinger indicates that he regarded this situation as reinforcing the merits of his own strategic conception for the Middle East.

> But through this turmoil the inherent strength of the American position in the Middle East also gradually emerged. Nobody could make peace without us. Only we, not the Soviet Union, could exert influence on Israel. Israel was too strong to succumb to Arab military pressure, and we could block all diplomatic activity until the Arabs showed *their* willingness to reciprocate Israeli concessions.... Nixon equivocated, believing in my strategy but authorizing (and then aborting) State's tactics. In the process, partly by default, we began to follow my preferred course. The bureaucratic stalemate achieved what I favored as a matter of policy: an inconclusive course that over time was bound to induce at least some Arab leaders to reconsider the utility of relying on Soviet arms.... They would, I thought, have to come to us in the end.

So in 1969, not without debate and much hesitation, the basis was laid for the later reversal of alliances in the Middle East. . . .[6]

Writing several years before Kissinger's memoirs were published, Middle East specialist William Quandt, who served on the National Security Council staff from 1972 to 1974, analyzed the period of "Standstill Diplomacy: 1971–73" in the Middle East. He noted that with the restoration of a cease-fire along the Suez Canal, the weathering of the Jordanian crisis of 1970, and the death of Nasser in September 1970, the situation in the Middle East "appeared to American policymakers to be less dangerous and more manageable than at any time since the 1967 war." The White House now exerted more control over Middle East policy and kept a tighter leash on the State Department. By August 1971 the promising possibility of an "interim settlement" between Egypt and Israel had failed, and the U.S.-Israeli relationship passed through a period of unusual warmth. "Even President Sadat's bold move in expelling more than ten thousand Soviet advisers from Egypt in July 1972," the former NSC staff specialist writes, "was not enough to lead to a major reassessment of American policy." Instead, U.S. policy in the Middle East was dominated by Kissinger's strategic conception, with which Nixon was now more fully in agreement. "United States diplomacy continued to aim," Quandt continues, "at what Kissinger was later to term 'the complete frustration' of the Arabs, *a policy which he* [Kissinger] *admitted was short-sighted and may have contributed to the October 1973 War.*"[7] Quandt gives no reference for Kissinger's admission, and one assumes, therefore, that it was not among his public statements. Nor do the two volumes of Kissinger's memoirs contain such an admission.

The conclusion Quandt draws from his retrospective examination of the period of "Standstill Diplomacy" in 1971–1973 may also be noted: "The period from 1971 to 1973 thus seems to have been one of lost opportunities to prevent war and move toward a settlement." Admittedly with the advantage of hindsight, Quandt continues, "it appears that the type of agreement arrived at between Israel and Egypt in January 1974 [i.e., a partial withdrawal of Israel forces from the Suez Canal after the October War] could have been reached three years earlier at much less cost." Quandt qualifies his criticism of this "uninspiring chapter" in U.S. diplomacy by recognizing that during this period the White House was intensely preoccupied with other foreign policy problems and opportunities—the Vietnam War, the cultivation of détente with Beijing, and the SALT negotiations with the Soviets—to which it gave higher priority than to the seemingly stable and satisfactory situation in the Middle East. Each of these issues, if properly handled, could lead—and in fact did lead—in 1972, the presidential election year, to important achievements, whereas "the same election-year imperatives dictated a very low profile in the Middle East," where, "in the absence of any chance for a negotiated agreement . . . Nixon focussed instead on maintaining the military balance in Israel's favor, thereby preventing an unwelcome outbreak of the fighting and no doubt earning the gratitude of Israel's many supporters in the United States."[8]

Kissinger himself indicates that what finally got him directly involved in the execution of Middle East policy was Nixon's desire to keep things quiet in that area during the election year. Responding to a Soviet request to do so, Nixon directed Kissinger to begin exploratory discussions on the Mideast issue in the secret diplomatic back channel with Dobrynin. These discussions became a useful means for furthering the strategy that Kissinger had so long advocated for producing a prolonged stalemate in the Middle East.[9] As part of this strategy, Kissinger found occasion to exploit the Soviet interest in achieving and furthering détente. Both during his secret trip to Moscow in April to prepare for the summit as well as at the summit itself, Kissinger pretended in private discussions with Gromyko to be willing to seek a basis for a joint U.S.-Soviet approach to a Middle East settlement. Kissinger did so, he explains, "to gain time and to use the prospect of future U.S.-Soviet consultations for whatever effect it might have as an incentive for Soviet restraint."[10] During the summit meetings Nixon suggested that Gromyko and Kissinger try to agree on some general principles on the Middle East to guide further negotiations to take place in the fall.[11] In these conversations, Kissinger related, "I conducted what was in effect a delaying tactic. Gromyko was experienced enough to know what I was doing; he put on no real pressure; the Soviets clearly wanted no crisis over the Middle East." Nonetheless, the conversations with Gromyko ended with "a tentative agreement on a number of 'principles,'" which, Kissinger adds, were very vague and did not go beyond existing United Nations resolutions. "Their practical consequence was to confirm the deadlock. Dobrynin and I were supposed to refine them after we were both back in the United States."[12] Making little effort in his memoirs to conceal the tactical use of his diplomatic exchanges with Gromyko, Kissinger notes that "the principles quickly found their way into the overcrowded limbo of aborted Middle East schemes—as I had intended."[13]

In an equally candid and self-congratulatory way, Kissinger explains that he pretended to be seeking a joint U.S.-Soviet approach in order "to give the Soviets an incentive to keep the Middle East calm . . . a strategy that would only magnify Egyptian restlessness with Soviet policy."[14] Kissinger deliberately slowed down diplomatic efforts to deal with the issues dividing the Arabs and the Israelis in order to produce a prolonged stalemate. He hoped thereby to demonstrate to Sadat the Soviet Union's impotence and its inability to render any significant help to the Arab cause. "I calculated," Kissinger reveals in his memoirs, almost as if he were confiding to his diary, "that the longer the process went on, the more likely Sadat would seek to deal with us directly."[15]

At the first summit meeting in Moscow (May 1972) Kissinger managed—somewhat to his own surprise—to get Brezhnev to agree to a very bland communiqué on the Middle East situation that was certain to lead Sadat to feel the Soviets had decided to put détente with the United States above any real assistance to the Arab cause against Israel. The effect on Sadat was predictable. As Sadat records in his memoirs, the U.S.-Soviet communiqué came as a "violent shock" to Egypt.[16]

Less than two months were to pass before Sadat expelled Soviet military advisers from Egypt. In his memoirs Kissinger states that Sadat's action came "as a complete surprise."[17] However, a few months earlier Kissinger had found ways to let Sadat know that the Soviet military presence in Egypt prevented the United States from pressing the Israelis for concessions and, more generally, from playing a more active role in bringing about a settlement.[18]

Sadat's expulsion of the Soviet military advisers gave Kissinger the opportunity he had been waiting for and encouraging through his secret diplomacy. But for various reasons Kissinger moved slowly. To be sure, he was heavily preoccupied with critical phases of the Vietnam negotiations; and he observes with an air of resignation in his memoirs that "the seminal opportunity to bring about a reversal of alliances in the Arab world would have to wait until we had finally put the war in Vietnam behind us."[19] But it is also clear that Kissinger did not feel the situation in the Middle East was yet ripe for a major U.S. diplomatic initiative. His preferred strategy of prolonging the stalemate in the Middle East had now succeeded in its first objective, namely, enhancing the Arab states' disillusionment with their Soviet ally to the point that Egypt would turn to the United States for diplomatic assistance in regaining its lost territory from Israel. But the second objective of Kissinger's stalemate strategy—forcing Egypt to moderate its demands and to indicate a willingness to compromise before the United States would move to press Israel for concessions—remained to be realized. Hence, Sadat's sense of urgency for achieving his objectives, once he expelled Soviet advisers and turned to the United States, was not shared by Kissinger, who hoped and expected that delaying tactics on his part would soften the Egyptian leader's demands. Kissinger's policy was based on the incorrect assumption that Sadat "had no choice but to await the American diplomatic initiative."[20] Failing to take seriously the idea that Sadat did have a military option, Kissinger believed that by stalling and rejecting Egypt's initial proposals for a settlement of the Arab-Israeli conflict he would force Sadat eventually to soften his position.

Thus, when Sadat, shortly after having expelled the Soviet military advisers from Egypt, let it be known through a secret diplomatic back channel to the White House that he was interested in reviving the idea of an interim agreement along the Suez Canal, Kissinger put off consideration of specifics, arguing the necessity for preliminary exploratory discussions leading to a face-to-face meeting. Sadat proposed a secret meeting between Kissinger and Sadat's national security adviser, Hafiz Ismail, to be held in October 1972.[21] Kissinger informed the Egyptian leader that the United States would not be able to take the diplomatic initiative in dealing with the Arab-Israeli dispute until after the U.S. presidential elections in November.

The meeting with Ismail finally took place in Washington in late February 1973. In this and several subsequent meetings with Ismail over the next few months, Kissinger made no progress in getting the Egyptians to soften their demand that an interim agreement for a disengagement along the Suez Canal be part of an agreed-upon plan for an overall settlement to be implemented in stages.[22]

Becoming frustrated and impatient with Nixon and Kissinger, Sadat turned to the Soviets once again for military supplies. The expulsion of their military advisers in July 1972 had faced Soviet leaders with the possibility of a total collapse of their remaining position in the Middle East. Given a chance to recoup its position, the Kremlin was more forthcoming this time. Major Soviet military equipment began to flow into Egypt and Syria. Though Soviet leaders still hoped that Sadat would not plunge into war, this possibility could not be excluded, and at some point they appear to have given reluctant approval for Egypt's use of force, if necessary, to recover its territory.[23]

Soviet Warnings of War

The rapprochement between Egypt and the USSR was well underway when the second summit meeting between Nixon and Brezhnev took place in June 1973, this time in Washington and San Clemente. According to Nixon's own account, Brezhnev hammered at him about the danger of war in the Middle East and the need for U.S. diplomatic pressure on Israel in the interest of a Middle East settlement.[24] After the Arab-Israeli war was brought to a close, Brezhnev and other Soviet spokesmen claimed that the Soviet premier had given Nixon advance warning at the June summit meeting of the danger of war in the Middle East, as was called for by the U.S.-Soviet crisis-prevention agreements.[25] Brezhnev's warnings, however, were of a general character. He did not state that Sadat had definite, firm plans for an attack; nor did he pinpoint the specific dates of a possible attack. So the most that can be said is that Brezhnev's comments to Nixon constituted what intelligence specialists refer to as "political" rather than a "strategic" warning. U.S. officials later acknowledged having received general warnings of the danger of war but denied that these Soviet warnings had suggested that an attack was imminent. "We interpreted the warnings," one U.S. official said, "as efforts to press us to pressure Israel into moving toward a Middle East settlement."[26]

To some extent, therefore, Brezhnev did fulfill his obligation to consult with the United States if a dangerous crisis threatened to erupt. But as so often happens, the recipient of the warning did not regard it as credible. U.S. leaders dismissed Brezhnev's warnings to Nixon as scare tactics to pressure the United States to change its Middle East policy. The administration made little use of the warning. Kissinger might have used it, however equivocal it seemed, to energize his diplomatic activity in the Middle East and to give Sadat more credible assurance of support for reclaiming the Sinai. But Kissinger did nothing, so strong was the belief in Washington that an Arab attack against the much stronger Israeli forces would be irrational and, therefore, would not take place.

One should note the intriguing possibility that Soviet leaders gave the United States another indirect warning of the imminent Arab attack on Israel. Moscow evidently received definite information about the forthcoming Arab attack from Sadat a few days or perhaps a week before it occurred. Three days before the war started the Soviets began to evacuate Soviet civilian personnel from Egypt and Syria. The question arises whether this move was intended by Brezhnev as an indirect signal to the United States of the forthcoming attack. According to presently available information, Soviet officials have never claimed that the pullout of Soviet personnel was intended to warn the United States and that it therefore constituted an additional effort to honor the crisis-prevention agreements.

Whether or not the Soviets intended the evacuation of Soviet civilians from Egypt and Syria as a signal to the United States, such an unusual action might have been taken by U.S. intelligence as a strong indicator of the forthcoming Arab attack. But for various reasons it was not. In his memoirs Kissinger states that "we uncritically accepted the Israeli assessment that the reason [for the evacuation of Soviet dependents] was either a 'crisis in relations with Egypt and Syria or the result of a Soviet assessment that hostilities may break out in the Middle East.' But the only danger of hostilities foreseen lay in the 'action-reaction cycle': each side's fear that its adversary was about to attack." Kissinger adds that if only he and intelligence specialists had asked the right questions about the removal of the Soviet dependents, they "would have rapidly reached the heart of the matter."[27]

Nothing in the available record indicates that Kissinger considered asking the Soviets why they were taking their citizens out of Egypt and Syria and whether they expected war. It is perhaps unlikely that the Soviets would have revealed what they knew. They were caught in a situation in which honoring the crisis-prevention principles conflicted with their responsibilities to their Arab allies. For the Soviet leaders to have given the United States unequivocal warning of the forthcoming attack would have betrayed their Arab allies and deprived those allies' attack of the military surprise on which its success depended. Under the circumstances it is noteworthy that the Soviets went so far as to pull their citizens out of Egypt and Syria.[28]

The preceding account of the origins of the October War has suggested some of the complexities of the Middle East situation that made it a particularly severe first test of the new U.S.-Soviet crisis-prevention agreements. After the failure of initial efforts to find a basis for diplomatic cooperation in dealing with the underlying conflict of interests between the Arab states and Israel, the Nixon administration and the Soviet Union pursued divergent foreign policy objectives and strategies in the Middle East that conflicted at critical junctures with crisis-prevention requirements. Even while pretending to cooperate with each other, each power pursued a covert unilateral policy in the Middle East—the United States in seeking to effect a reversal of alliances that would exclude Soviet influence in the Middle East, the Soviet Union in arming Egypt and Syria for war. The diplomatic disunity of the superpowers gave Egypt, the local actor that was most dissatisfied with the status quo, an opportunity to maneuver and to use force for its own policy objectives.

This case is a reminder, therefore, that crisis prevention is not subject to exclusive control by the two superpowers. Competition between them in third areas may allow a highly motivated local actor to play one power off against the other and to pursue its own interests in ways that generate dangerous crises into which the superpowers are then drawn. This indeed happened during the October War. The breakdown of a cease-fire arranged through Soviet-U.S. cooperation led to a dangerous confrontation between the two superpowers when Washington responded with an alert of its strategic forces to Brezhnev's threat of unilateral intervention.

After the Arab-Israeli war ended, it would have been desirable for Soviet and U.S. leaders to discuss lessons that could be derived from that experience for clarifying and strengthening their crisis-prevention agreements. Presently available information, from public sources and interviews, indicates that no U.S.-Soviet postmortem analysis was undertaken or even suggested by either side. And there is no evidence that such a postmortem was conducted within the U.S. government to understand better the requirements for making more effective use of the crisis-prevention agreements. The general principles agreed to by Nixon and Brezhnev at their two summit meetings played even less of a role in constraining the behavior of the two sides in subsequent crises in Angola and the Horn of Africa.

Impact on Détente

Failure of the Soviets to prevent their Arab allies from starting the war and the support Moscow gave the Arabs during the war called into question within the United States the entire détente relationship. From an early stage in the crisis Nixon and Kissinger attempted to limit the political damage at home to their détente policy. They were not inclined to berate the Soviets for having failed to warn them more explicitly of the forthcoming Arab resort to arms or to initiate urgent consultation with the United States to head off the war. At his press conference on October 12, 1973, Kissinger dealt cautiously with a question as to whether the Soviets had advance knowledge of the Arab attack and should have informed the United States and whether they had encouraged the attack.[29] Both Nixon and Kissinger chose to emphasize, instead, that the close relationship developed between the two sides during the era of détente had proven itself because it had aided them in concerting their policies to avoid war and bring about a cease-fire. "Without detente," Nixon stated in his press conference of October 26, "we might have had a major conflict in the Middle East. With detente, we avoided it."[30] Kissinger echoed this theme in his press conference of November 21: "The relationship that had developed between the two governments and between the two leaders played a role in settling the crisis even though it had not yet been firm enough to prevent the crisis."[31] The president went further, stating that the crisis had in fact improved "the outlook for a permanent peace" in the Middle East because the two superpowers had now agreed that "it is necessary for us to use our influence more than we have in the past to get the negotiating track moving again" and had chosen to use their influence with their allies in the Middle East "to expedite a settlement."[32]

Although the outbreak of the war had caught Washington by surprise, Nixon and Kissinger quickly perceived that the war provided still another opportunity to bring about the reversal of alliances in the Middle East that Kissinger had long sought. With Egypt looking once again to the United States and with Israel as heavily dependent as ever on Washington for military supplies and financial assistance, Kissinger moved as soon as the cease-fire was firmly established to place himself at the hub of diplomatic efforts to bring about a disengagement of the military forces of the combatants.

We need not concern ourselves with the details of the intricate step-by-step diplomatic effort that Kissinger personally orchestrated in the next months. The arrangements to implement UN Resolution 340 included a multilateral conference of all belligerents in Geneva under the auspices of the UN secretary general and cochaired by the United States and the Soviet Union. However, Kissinger succeeded in diverting the negotiation of concrete issues into bilateral channels in which he played the role of go-between and mediator between Israel and Egypt-Syria. In consequence, the Geneva Conference itself became "a forum that would provide the symbolic umbrella" for bilateral negotiations between the combatants under the auspices of Kissinger. The primary value of Geneva was "to legitimize the settlement process" and, the U.S. negotiators hoped, "to give the Soviets enough of a sense of participation to prevent them from disrupting the peace effort. . . . "[33] In this fashion, Kissinger kept the Soviets out of the substance of the negotiations.

However disturbing it was to find themselves excluded from the negotiating process, the Soviets could hardly afford to disrupt the peacemaking efforts or to call attention to their impotence by visible protests or initiatives that were likely to fail. Their role as cochairmen of the conference clearly afforded them only symbolic equality with the United States, thus shattering the hope generated by the 1972 and 1973 summits that the two superpowers would work together as equals in finding a solution to the long-standing Arab-Israeli conflict. It is important to note that this hope had been nourished during the course of the October War by an extraordinary com-

munication Nixon sent to Brezhnev. Shortly after Kissinger arrived
in Moscow on October 21 to work out arrangements for a cease-
fire, Nixon wrote to Brezhnev as follows: "The Israelis and Arabs
will never be able to approach the subject by themselves in a rational
manner. That is why Nixon and Brezhnev, looking at the problem
more dispassionately, must step in, determine the proper course of
action to a just settlement, and then bring the necessary pressure
on our respective friends for a settlement. . . . "[34]

Nixon's startling overture to Brezhnev only recently revealed by
Kissinger in the second volume of his memoirs, throws new light
on Brezhnev's "ultimatum" to Nixon a few days later, in which he
protested the Israeli violation of the cease-fire. In this communication
the Soviet leader proposed joint U.S.-Soviet intervention and threatened unilateral intervention if the United States did not agree to
act jointly. This aspect of Brezhnev's letter, which triggered a U.S.
military alert, has been public knowledge for some time. In the
second volume of his memoirs Kissinger discloses, evidently for the
first time, that Brezhnev's letter proposed not only joint U.S.-Soviet
military intervention to ensure a cease-fire but, in Kissinger's words,
"also the imposition of a comprehensive peace."[35]

Soviet leaders complained repeatedly at being excluded from the
Middle East negotiations. Gromyko took this issue up with Nixon
in early February.[36] When Kissinger visited Moscow in late March
1974 he was charged by Brezhnev with trying to keep the Soviet
Union out of the real negotiations and was strenuously accused of
violating the agreements that the peace talks would be held under
joint U.S.-Soviet auspices. Kissinger, in turn, tried to make the Soviet
leaders content with their lesser role, if only to keep them from
attempting to disrupt his efforts.[37]

The third summit between Nixon and Brezhnev, held in Moscow
in late June 1974, accomplished little in the way of important new
agreements or in the way of recouping the damage to détente
occasioned by the October War and its aftermath. Several months
after Nixon's resignation in August 1974, President Ford traveled to
Vladivostok for a quick meeting with Brezhnev, primarily to discuss
a SALT II agreement but also to review the situation in the Middle
East. The Soviets insisted on returning the negotiations process to
Geneva, while Ford maintained that Egypt and Israel favored continuation of the step-by-step process that was being furthered by
Kissinger.[38]

Although it would be going too far to say that détente was dealt
a mortal blow by the October War, the relationship between the two
sides was never the same thereafter. The war was an ugly reminder

that underlying the mutual desire for enhancing cooperation there remained important conflicting interests and a dynamic of competition that could not easily be restrained or moderated. The war and its aftermath strengthened suspicions on each side that the other side defined détente differently and would ignore or misuse détente when the opportunity arose to advance its own interests. It would become more difficult thereafter to maintain the momentum of détente and to move ahead with the agenda for additional cooperation between the two superpowers.

Notes

1. According to available information, from interviews as well as public sources, neither Soviet nor U.S. leaders invoked the BPA or the APNW for any purpose or with reference to any potentially troublesome situation until *after* the Arab attack on Israel in October 1973.

2. See, for example, Alvin Z. Rubinstein, *Red Star on the Nile* (Princeton, N.J.: Princeton University Press, 1977); Jon D. Glassman, *Arms for the Arabs* (Baltimore: Johns Hopkins University Press, 1975); Galia Golan, *Yom Kippur and After* (Cambridge: Cambridge University Press, 1977); Lawrence L. Whetten, *The Canal War* (Cambridge, Mass.: MIT Press, 1974); Robert O. Freedman, *Soviet Policy Toward the Middle East Since 1970* (New York: Praeger, 1975); William B. Quandt, *Decade of Decisions* (Berkeley: University of California Press, 1977); Nadav Safran, *Israel: The Embattled Ally* (Cambridge, Mass.: Harvard University Press, Belknap Press, 1978). Rubinstein (*Red Star,* pp. 192–197) also considers the alternative hypothesis that Sadat deliberately exaggerated Soviet constraints on his military plans.

In his memoirs Kissinger acknowledges that Soviet leaders did behave with restraint in the Middle East in 1972 and attempted to discourage Sadat from resorting to force, among other reasons, he adds, because they "were willing to pay *some* price for détente." Henry Kissinger, *Years of Upheaval* (Boston: Little, Brown & Co., 1982), p. 204.

3. Sadat may have believed he had to remove most of the Soviet military advisers to gain freedom of action to initiate war. Sadat might well have believed that Soviet opposition to his exercise of the Egyptian military option against Israel would have been much stronger were Soviet military advisers, some of whom were manning operational military systems, to remain, thereby raising the risk of Soviet military involvement as well as diplomatic complications.

4. Kissinger, *White House Years* (Boston: Little, Brown & Co., 1979) pp. 376, 379, 1247–1248, 1279, 1285–1290, 1292–1296, 1300; see also Kissinger, *Years of Upheaval,* pp. 196, 201–202.

5. Kissinger, *White House Years,* p. 376.

6. Ibid., pp. 378–379.

7. Quandt, *Decade of Decisions,* pp. 128–129. (Italics added.)

8. Ibid., pp. 129–130. It should be noted that Quandt, even though he served on the NSC staff under Kissinger, may not have been fully aware of his superior's back-channel discussions with Soviet Ambassador Dobrynin.

9. Kissinger, *White House Years*, pp. 1285–1292; Kissinger, *Years of Upheaval*, pp. 196, 204.

10. Kissinger, *White House Years*, p. 1151.

11. Ibid., p. 1246.

12. Ibid., p. 1247.

13. Ibid., p. 1294; see also pp. 1246–1248, 1297, 1300; and Quandt, *Decade of Decisions*, pp. 149–150, 158.

14. Kissinger, *White House Years*, pp. 1288–1289.

15. Ibid., p. 1290. It is possible, of course, that Kissinger presents himself in his memoirs as being more purposeful and clever in maneuvering to bring about a reversal of alliances than he actually was. But the account Kissinger gives of the unilateral policy and of the stratagems and tactics he employed on its behalf was confirmed in essentials in an interview with a high-ranking official of the Nixon administration.

16. Anwar Sadat, *In Search of Identity* (New York: Harper & Row, 1978), p. 229.

17. Kissinger, *White House Years*, p. 1295.

18. William Quandt, at the time a specialist on the Middle East on the staff of the National Security Council, later reported that "in June [1972] Saudi Arabia's minister of defense, Prince Sultan, reported to [Sadat] on his conversations with Nixon and Kissinger. Until the Soviet presence in Egypt was eliminated, the Americans would not press Israel for concessions" (Quandt, *Decade of Decisions*, p. 151; see also p. 158). See also Mohamed Heikal, *The Road to Ramadan* (New York: Quadrangle, 1975), pp. 170 ff., esp. 174 and 183; and Rubinstein, *Red Star*, p. 197.

19. Kissinger, *White House Years*, p. 1300.

20. Kissinger, *Years of Upheaval*, pp. 205–206.

21. Kissinger, *White House Years*, pp. 1298–1300.

22. Kissinger, *Years of Upheaval*, pp. 205–227. (The Nixon administration's failure to exploit the possibilities created by Sadat's expulsion of the Soviet military advisers is noted and criticized by Rubinstein, *Red Star*, p. 202.)

23. As in the case of Soviet supplies to Egypt prior to Sadat's expulsion of Soviet military advisers, important facts remain obscure or unverified regarding the resumption and increase in Soviet military supplies in 1973 and Soviet acquiescence to and support of Sadat's war plans. See sources cited in note 2; see also Heikal, *Road to Ramadan*, p. 181.

24. Richard M. Nixon, *Memoirs* (New York: Grosset & Dunlap, 1978), p. 885: see also p. 1031. Kissinger, too, recalls that Brezhnev and Gromyko warned of the danger of war both in Moscow in early May and at the summit in June; "but we dismissed this," he adds, "as psychological warfare because we did not see any rational military option that would not worsen the Soviet and Arab positions" (*Years of Upheaval*, p. 461). Kissinger's

account contains important new information about intelligence warnings of the Arab attack and the American response to them (ibid., pp. 461–465).

25. In a speech to the World Peace Congress Brezhnev claimed that the Soviet Union had "numerous times warned that the Middle East situation was explosively dangerous" (*New York Times,* Oct. 27, 1973). Later, in a response to Senator Henry Jackson's charge that Soviet behavior in the recent Middle East war had violated the Nixon-Brezhnev Agreement on Prevention of Nuclear War, a Soviet diplomat was cited in an article by Leslie Gelb as emphasizing that Moscow had repeatedly warned Washington from June to September that war was imminent in the Middle East (*New York Times,* Dec. 21, 1973). A similar account, evidently based on an interview with the same Soviet diplomat, was contained in Murray Marder's account in the *Washington Post,* December 20, 1973.

26. *New York Times,* Dec. 21, 1973.

27. Kissinger, *Years of Upheaval,* pp. 466–467.

28. It should be noted that several reports, as yet unconfirmed, allege that Soviet ambassador Dobrynin advised Kissinger on October 5 that the Arab attack would be launched on the following day. (Tad Szulc, "Seeing and Not Believing," *New Republic* 169, no. 25 (December 22, 1973), pp. 13–14; Galia Golan, "The Soviet Union and the Arab-Israeli War of October 1973," *Jerusalem Papers,* Hebrew University of Jerusalem, June 1974, p. 15.

The possibility that the Soviets may have intended the evacuation of their civilians as a signal to the United States is considered and not rejected by Kissinger, *Years of Upheaval,* p. 469; see also William Quandt, *Soviet Policy in the October 1973 War* (Santa Monica, Calif.: RAND Corp., R-1864-ISA, May 1976), pp. 11–12; Glassman, *Arms for the Arabs,* p. 123; and Rubinstein, *Red Star,* pp. 259–262. A Soviet specialist on U.S. affairs has indicated in a private conversation that the evacuation of Soviet civilians from Cairo was done in a deliberately conspicuous manner to warn the United States of the impending attack (Dan Caldwell, personal communication).

29. "Secretary Kissinger's News Conference of October 12, 1973," *Department of State Bulletin,* October 29, 1973, pp. 532–541.

30. "President Nixon's News Conference of October 26, 1973," *Department of State Bulletin,* November 12, 1973, pp. 581–584.

31. "Secretary Kissinger's News Conference of November 21, 1973," *Department of State Bulletin,* December 10, 1973, pp. 701–710.

32. "President Nixon's New Conference of October 26, 1973."

33. Quandt, *Decade of Decisions,* p. 213. See also Kissinger, *Years of Upheaval,* pp. 747, 755, 794, 815, 843.

34. Ibid., p. 551. Kissinger also reports that prior to Nixon's letter to Brezhnev he himself received a cable in which the president expressed the conviction that the United States and the USSR should jointly impose a

comprehensive peace in the Middle East—a course of action that Kissinger strongly opposed (ibid., p. 550; see also p. 202).

35. Ibid., p. 583.
36. Ibid., pp. 940–943.
37. Ibid., p. 1022.
38. Quandt, *Decade of Decisions,* p. 261.

8
The African Terrain and U.S.-Soviet Conflict in Angola and Rhodesia: Some Implications for Crisis Prevention

Larry C. Napper

One of the important diplomatic objectives of the 1972–1980 détente period was the development of a regime for prevention of U.S.-Soviet crises in the Third World. Among the initiatives taken to achieve this goal was the Basic Principles Agreement, approved by Nixon and Brezhnev at the May 1972 Moscow summit.[1]

Despite the initial optimism generated by this agreement, the two superpowers never seriously attempted to implement the Basic Principles Agreement through development of concrete arrangements and specific mutual obligations governing their relations in the Third World. The gap between the rhetoric of détente and the reality of superpower conflict became painfully apparent during subsequent crises in the Arab-Israeli war of 1973, Angola, the Horn of Africa, and Afghanistan.

Criticism of U.S.-Soviet crisis-prevention efforts has tended to focus primarily on the perceptions, objectives, and policies of the superpowers. However, the history of recent U.S.-Soviet crises in the Third World suggests that conditions and variables beyond the effective control of superpower policymakers have set important parameters for U.S.-Soviet conflict. In some cases, local conditions and the policies of Third World actors have seemed to drive the

Opinions expressed in the article are the author's and do not necessarily reflect those of the U.S. government.

superpowers toward confrontation, and in other cases the local contextual variables have tended to mute U.S.-Soviet conflict. This paper seeks to assess the impact of these contextual variables on U.S.-Soviet conflict in the Angolan and Rhodesian crises. The different outcomes of superpower conflict in Angola and Rhodesia were significantly influenced by at least four African terrain variables: (1) the effectiveness of African regional organizations, (2) the nature of the decolonialization process, (3) the local military balance, and (4) the character and extent of involvement by the Republic of South Africa. Another major variable that influenced U.S.-Soviet conflict was the Sino-Soviet competition for influence with the African liberation movements of Angola and Rhodesia. The case studies that follow focus on the impact of these variables and lead to the conclusion that the "terrain of international politics" in Southern Africa acted as a "third element" shaping the policies of the United States and the USSR and decisively affecting their interactions.[2]

Angola: Competition Becomes a Superpower Crisis

Following the April 1974 Lisbon coup, the initial proposals by the Portuguese Armed Forces Movement for gradual transition to independence in Angola were rejected by all segments of a deeply divided Angolan liberation movement.[3] Divisions among the National Liberation Front of Angola (FNLA), the Popular Movement for the Liberation of Angola (MPLA), and the National Union for the Total Independence of Angola (UNITA) flowed in part from the fact that each of these movements had its primary political and military base in a different segment of Angola's African population.[4] These ethnic divisions were exacerbated by ideological differences between the Marxist MPLA and the FNLA and UNITA, which had few established programmatic positions.[5] Another important source of conflict was personal animosity and ambition among the leaders of the three movements.[6] As the pace of Portuguese decolonialization efforts quickened, the leaders of all three movements began to shore up their traditional sources of external support in anticipation of an armed struggle for power.

Holden Roberto's FNLA could rely on its traditional base of support in neighboring Zaire.[7] In addition to the Bakongo ethnic overlap in southwestern Zaire and the FNLA's traditional stronghold in northwestern Angola, Roberto was related by marriage to Zairean president Mobutu Sese Seko. Their relationship was close, and Zaire served as both sanctuary and conduit for external aid to the FNLA throughout the Angolan crisis. There is also considerable evidence that Mobutu committed units of the Zairean regular army to fight alongside the FNLA at various times during the civil war.

The African connections of the MPLA and UNITA were not as well established as the FNLA's connection with Zaire. However, the MPLA leaders had taken refuge in Brazzaville, the capital of the People's Republic of the Congo, during certain periods of the war against the Portuguese. The MPLA's Marxist ideology and ties with European socialist countries also provided a basis for good relations with Congo President Marien Ngouabi and other leftist African leaders. UNITA had no important African alliances, having remained largely isolated within the interior of Angola.

The FNLA and the MPLA had also developed international ties beyond the African regional environment.[8] After a brief period of cooperation with the United States during the early days of the Kennedy administration, Holden Roberto had turned to North Korea and the People's Republic of China (PRC) as the principal external supporters of the FNLA. The MPLA had received support from the Organization of African Unity (OAU), the Soviet Union, Eastern Europe, Cuba, Yugoslavia, China, Sweden, and leftist Portuguese political parties. By contrast, UNITA had no important non-African sources of support, although the PRC is reported to have unsuccessfully attempted to establish an arms supply relationship with UNITA.

These external connections were to prove crucial because, at the time of the Lisbon coup, none of the Angolan liberation movements enjoyed decisive military superiority. Although the FNLA probably had more trained and armed guerrillas, the forces of all three movements lacked training, discipline, and modern arms.[9] Since all sides knew that even a relatively small increment of modern arms and well-trained combat troops could be decisive, the pressure on all groups to seek outside assistance was intense. Both the Portuguese and the African leaders realized that a political settlement was the only hope of avoiding a bloody civil war, and they undertook a series of diplomatic initiatives to head off the impending conflict.

Portuguese efforts to organize a smooth transition of power culminated in the Alvor Agreement of January 15, 1975, which set the Angolan independence date for November 11 and provided for a transfer of power to a coalition government composed of representatives of the FNLA, the MPLA, and UNITA. The Alvor Agreement also provided for a transitional government in which representatives of all three movements would share power with the Portuguese administration until independence day. The transitional regime was established in Luanda, the capital of Angola, on March 28, 1975.[10]

Portuguese efforts to organize a coalition government received broad political support from individual African governments and the OAU. President Jomo Kenyatta of Kenya chaired a meeting at Mombasa, Kenya, on January 5, 1975, at which all three Angolan movements agreed on a coordinated strategy for the talks with the Portuguese that led to the Alvor Agreement. When conflicts among the movements began to undermine the transitional government, Kenyatta summoned the Angolan leaders to Nukuru, Kenya, in June 1975 for a repeat of the Mombasa unity negotiations. Under Kenyatta's prompting, the Angolan leaders again agreed to a coalition government, but this agreement also quickly fell apart. As conflict escalated into full-scale civil war, the OAU summit that met in July 1975 again appealed to the MPLA, the FNLA, and UNITA to unite in an effective coalition regime.[11]

However, a critical distinction must be made between the position of the OAU as a whole and the actions of the African states most directly concerned with the outcome of the struggle in Angola. The policies of Zaire and the Congo were particularly important to the success of OAU policy because these states controlled the flow of external arms to the FNLA and the MPLA. The success of OAU efforts to organize a coalition regime also depended upon the willingness of Mobutu and Ngouabi to use their leverage over the Angolan movements to induce them to accept a political settlement. Zaire and the Congo did join with Zambia in mid-1974 to urge the three movements to form a unified ruling coalition.[12] However, as 1974 wore on, Zaire and later the Congo began to encourage and facilitate unilateral bids for power by the individual movements. Thus, the only OAU members who had the power to enforce the decisions of the organization actually began to undermine them.

The other regional factor that was beyond the control of the OAU was the policy of the Republic of South Africa. Pretoria viewed the emerging struggle as a potential challenge to the "détente" policy of Prime Minister John Vorster, which sought to ensure South Africa's security through links with moderate African regimes.[13] Although this policy had enjoyed a measure of success in the early 1970s, the unexpectedly rapid collapse of Portuguese colonialism seemed to pose new and more pressing security concerns. In particular, the emergence of a radical regime in Angola would provide a new base for African guerrilla assaults into the neighboring South African–ruled territory of Namibia. Thus, if the MPLA appeared on the verge of victory, Pretoria would be faced with the choice of accepting increased guerrilla pressure along the northern border of Namibia or intervening at the cost of its carefully conceived détente policy toward black Africa.

The erosion of OAU control over events and the drift toward civil war were exacerbated by the activities of non-African actors. U.S. officials were preoccupied with the collapse of South Vietnam in early 1975, and there were virtually no public expressions of U.S. support for the Alvor Agreement. The first favorable reference to the idea of a coalition government for Angola by a high U.S. official took place during congressional testimony by Assistant Secretary of State Nathaniel Davis on July 14.[14] Secretary of State Kissinger's first public endorsement of a coalition regime came at a news conference on November 25, nearly two weeks after the date of Angolan independence and well after the outbreak of full-scale civil war.[15]

The PRC responded to the Alvor Agreement more favorably, but Beijing's endorsement was hedged with serious doubts concerning the long-term prospects of a coalition government. Chinese commentaries called the agreement "an important victory in their [the liberation movements'] fight against imperialism and colonialism" but sharply criticized the USSR for "sabotaging the African People's unity and sapping their fighting will."[16] In a separate message to the leaders of the three movements, Premier Chou En-Lai warned that "the agreement is still something on paper, and it takes arduous struggle to achieve full implementation of its provisions." The message added that "neo-colonialist forces of various descriptions" were bound to "seek opportunities to make trouble and carry out sabotage."[17]

Soviet commentaries in early 1975 praised the Mombasa agreement among the three movements and plans for a tripartite transitional government but made no reference to the Alvor Agreement or the Portuguese role in the transition process.[18] Moreover, Soviet support for a coalition government was always accompanied by references to the MPLA as the movement that "bore the brunt of the armed struggle for independence."[19] Thus, while supporting the idea of a coalition regime, Soviet commentaries left no doubt of Moscow's preference should cooperation among the Angolan movements break down.

The cycle of intervention and response among the external supporters of the various Angolan movements is difficult to sort out, particularly because of the problem of identifying the important escalation "saliencies" at various stages of the conflict.[20] The MPLA had been receiving small amounts of Soviet and Cuban military assistance since the mid-1960s, although Soviet support to the Neto faction was actually suspended from 1972 to early 1974.[21] Similarly, the FNLA received small amounts of Chinese aid after the reestablishment of relations between the PRC and Zaire in 1973. With the

Portuguese coup and the approach of Angolan independence, both
the USSR and the PRC began to increase shipments of supplies to
their respective client movements. From June to August 1974, Chinese
assistance to the FNLA increased dramatically with the delivery of
a large shipment of arms and the arrival in Zaire of approximately
one hundred twenty-five military instructors.[22]

The influx of Chinese assistance was particularly important to the
FNLA because the MPLA enjoyed effective control of Luanda due
to the greater historical influence of the MPLA in urban areas. Luanda
became a prime military objective because control of the capital
would give any liberation movement prima facie claim to status as
the legitimate successor to the Portuguese administration. The problem
facing the FNLA and UNITA was to translate their control of specific
rural areas into an effective challenge to MPLA hegemony in the
capital. Arms from the PRC and Zairean support gave Holden Roberto
the resources necessary to expand FNLA influence beyond its traditional northwestern stronghold into the Luanda area.

The political aspect of this struggle for the capital stimulated the
first direct U.S. involvement in the conflict. As his forces began to
be more active in the Luanda area, Roberto moved to establish a
greater FNLA political presence in the capital. In order to provide
financial support for this effort, the U.S. National Security Council's
40 Committee allocated $300,000 of covert assistance for the FNLA.
This program, which was approved in January 1975, did not provide
military assistance and did not include any assistance for UNITA.[23]
For its part, the MPLA reacted to the FNLA challenge by requesting
increased assistance from the USSR and Cuba. Soviet arms shipments
to the MPLA increased very significantly after October 1974.[24]

The extreme volatility and sensitivity of the military situation to
relatively small increases in external assistance was reflected in the ebb
and flow of the conflict after January 1975. As the year opened, the
FNLA drive for influence in the capital provoked violent clashes
with the MPLA throughout the spring of 1975, and UNITA was
drawn into the battle in June when its offices were attacked by MPLA
supporters.[25]

The seriousness of the FNLA challenge to the MPLA's control of
Luanda was reflected in Soviet commentaries in May and June.
These articles emphasized the need for unity among the three movements and specifically called for an assertive Portuguese role in
heading off a civil war.[26] Soviet statements favorably mentioned
OAU advocacy of a coalition government and criticized assistance
by any "outside force" to any of the liberation movements.[27] During
this period, Soviet commentaries began to identify the MPLA as the

"general national movement" of Angola and to denounce the FNLA and UNITA as reactionary organizations that had played no real role in the armed struggle against the Portuguese.[28] In May and June, Soviet articles began to accuse the PRC and the United States of planning "direct intervention" in the conflict.[29]

By early July, the MPLA's military position had begun to improve due to the increasing flow of Soviet arms and the improvement in performance of MPLA troops brought about by the presence of Cuban military advisers. MPLA leader Augustinio Neto reportedly requested Cuban advisers in May 1975 to instruct his troops in the use of Soviet weapons then being received in large quantities via staging areas in the People's Republic of the Congo. During June, approximately two hundred fifty Cuban advisers arrived in Angola and established four training camps for MPLA troops.[30] The overall improvement of Neto's forces permitted the MPLA to go on the offensive in early July, and, by the end of the month, the MPLA had driven its rivals completely out of the Luanda area.

The MPLA's battlefield success was reflected in greater optimism in the Soviet media concerning the outcome of the conflict. During this period, Soviet commentaries dropped advocacy of a coalition government and questioned the wisdom of having included the FNLA and UNITA in the transitional government. According to Soviet sources, this mistake had been made because of a tendency in "certain circles" to "artificially exaggerate" the role of the FNLA and UNITA in the liberation struggle.[31] Soviet statements claimed that the MPLA represented "all the people" regardless of ethnic affiliations[32] and labeled the FNLA a "truly reactionary" movement, calling Roberto's forces an "occupation army" supported by the PRC and Zaire.[33]

The military situation of the FNLA continued to deteriorate throughout July and August, and the PRC began to waver in its support of Roberto. The process of Chinese disengagement began after the OAU summit in July, and, by late October, all Chinese advisers had been withdrawn from FNLA camps.[34] The July crisis was the stimulus for the U.S. 40 Committee's decision of the same month to authorize a program of covert military assistance to the FNLA and UNITA to be channeled through Zaire. The large size of this program compared with the January program, the shift from political to military assistance, and the inclusion of UNITA represented qualitative changes that transformed the U.S. role from that of a bit player to that of a major actor in the crisis.[35]

The July crisis also prompted Roberto to contact the South African Bureau of State Security in Namibia concerning the possibility of South African assistance for the newly formed FNLA-UNITA coalition.[36] On August 11 and 12, a small contingent of South African troops crossed into Angola from Namibia to provide security for the Cunene River hydroelectric power complex. In late September, as the MPLA thrust on the battlefield began to run out of steam and more small South African patrols appeared in Angola, the first Cuban combat troops arrived in the country. These troops are reported to have functioned as advisers for MPLA units that clashed in early October with UNITA troops assisted by South African advisers.[37] The uncertainty of the situation in early October may have prompted a temporary revival of Soviet interest in a coalition government. Despite Moscow's bitter denunciations of the "reactionary" FNLA and UNITA during July and August, a Soviet article of September 27 maintained that the MPLA was still ready to hold "businesslike talks" with the other movements on "normalizing the situation in the country."[38]

The crucial action of this phase of the war occurred on October 23 when a South African column of fifteen hundred to two thousand troops crossed into southern Angola from Namibia. Although it was relatively small, the South African force, which was equipped with armored cars and helicopter gunships, played a decisive role in turning the tide of battle against the MPLA. The South African column linked up with UNITA forces in a drive on Luanda from the south, while a coordinated FNLA offensive pressed in on the capital from the northwest. At this point the tables had turned completely, and it was the MPLA that faced a military crisis.

Within a week of the South African intervention, four ships carrying Cuban combat troops had departed for Angola.[39] Cuban aircraft began an airlift of combat troops in early November, and, by December, Cuban troops were arriving at the rate of four hundred per week. By January 1976 the arrival rate had increased to a thousand per week for a total of fourteen thousand in early 1976. The Soviet role in providing arms and strategic airlift for Cuban troops was crucial to the reversal of the MPLA's military fortunes. After several small but sharp battles in which Cuban forces reportedly sustained tactical defeats, MPLA-Cuban troops managed to halt the UNITA-South African advance south of Luanda. The FNLA offensive in the north also began to run out of steam as Cuban gunners using Soviet 122mm rocket launchers took a heavy toll on Roberto's forces.

By mid-December it was apparent that the South African intervention and the U.S. covert aid program would have to be quickly and dramatically increased if they were to achieve the desired objectives. However, the adverse political impact of the South African intervention and the revelations in the United States of the covert

U.S. aid to the FNLA and UNITA were beginning to erode the will to persevere in both Pretoria and Washington. The Portuguese simply withdrew as scheduled on November 11 without formally handing over power to any of the warring factions. The South African intervention had shattered the OAU consensus on the desirability of a coalition government, and a number of "progressive" African governments recognized the government established by the MPLA.[40] In the United States, opposition to finding the United States on the same side as South Africa and a generalized fear of "another Vietnam" combined to provoke a December 19 vote in the Senate to cut off all U.S. aid for the FNLA-UNITA coalition.

These events touched off a U.S.-Soviet confrontation over the meaning of détente and its operational relevance for the management of conflicts in the Third World. Kissinger told Congress that the USSR had rejected U.S. offers to negotiate mutual restraint and labeled Soviet actions a clear violation of the 1972 Basic Principles Agreement. He warned that Soviet behavior in Third World areas would become more aggressive unless the United States demonstrated the will to turn back the Soviet challenge in Angola. Kissinger pointed to the Soviet use of Cuban troops in a conflict far from the traditional spheres of Soviet influence as a particularly ominous development.[41] Despite Kissinger's arguments, Congress remained adamant in its refusal to fund further U.S. involvement in the Angolan conflict.

The impact of the Angolan crisis on the overall course of U.S.-Soviet relations is difficult to assess. Certainly the crisis significantly undermined public and congressional support for détente and made it more difficult for the Ford administration to maintain domestic support for its SALT negotiating position. Kissinger visited Moscow in January 1976 for negotiations on both SALT and Angola but made little progress in either area. With the onset of the 1976 presidential primary campaign, this visit was probably the last opportunity to complete negotiations on a SALT agreement before early 1977. Moreover, Angola served as a grim reminder that the Basic Principles Agreement had not changed the fundamentally conflictual character of U.S.-Soviet relations in the Third World.

With the United States' withdrawal from the conflict, South Africa decided not to attempt to match the influx of Soviet arms and Cuban troops. The last South African troops left Angola on March 27, but the military position of the FNLA-UNITA coalition had already collapsed. The MPLA steadily consolidated its hold on urban areas and began to make inroads in many areas previously controlled by the FNLA and UNITA. As part of the price for improved relations with the MPLA regime, Mobutu ultimately halted FNLA operations in Zaire, but UNITA resistance in southern Angola has been more tenacious. More than six years after independence, the MPLA government is still unable to exercise effective control over the entire country and remains dependent on Soviet and Cuban security assistance.[42]

Rhodesia: Avoidance of Superpower Crisis

With the independence of Angola and Mozambique, the focus of African liberation efforts shifted to southern Rhodesia, where black nationalists had engaged in a protracted guerrilla war against the white government headed by Prime Minister Ian Smith. Prior to the Portuguese coup, little progress had been achieved by either the United Kingdom or black Rhodesians in their efforts to replace the Smith regime with a majority rule government. British efforts to negotiate an end to the Rhodesian Unilateral Declaration of Independence had failed because of the refusal of the Salisbury authorities to move toward majority rule and the refusal of Africans to accept anything less than majority rule as a resolution of the crisis. Despite this record of diplomatic frustration, successive British governments continued to search for a Rhodesian settlement.

African armed struggle against the Smith regime had also made little progress before 1974, primarily because of the overwhelming military superiority of the Rhodesian army.[43] In addition to their own impressive military resources, the Rhodesians could rely on supplies of arms, ammunition, and petroleum from South Africa, which ignored UN economic and military sanctions against the Salisbury regime. These formidable Rhodesian forces were opposed by an African nationalist movement weakened by internal divisions. The oldest Zimbabwean liberation movement was the Zimbabwe African People's Union (ZAPU), founded in 1961 by Joshua Nkomo. The Zimbabwe African National Union (ZANU) emerged in 1963 from an internal dispute within ZAPU, and ZANU itself later split into two factions headed by the Reverend Ndabaningi Sithole and Robert Mugabe. ZANU began a guerrilla campaign against the Smith regime in 1972, and, by 1974, both ZANU and ZAPU had established guerrilla training camps in Tanzania.[44]

The demonstration effect of successful armed struggle against colonial rule in Angola and Mozambique provided an important psychological reinforcement for Rhodesian blacks who advocated armed struggle. The FRELIMO victory in Mozambique provided new sanctuary and infiltration routes for black guerrillas along the Rhodesian-Mozambican border. Moreover, the South African government began to pressure the Rhodesian regime to reach some accommodation with the black nationalists that might avoid a pro-tracted war on South Africa's northern border. Constitutional talks organized by South African Prime Minister Vorster and Zambian President Kenneth Kaunda continued throughout 1975 but achieved no progress because of continued disagreement between Smith and the black nationalists.[45]

While these negotiations were continuing, black nationalist groups began to prepare for an escalation of the armed struggle. However, allegiance among guerrilla trainees in the Mozambican camps was divided between ZAPU and ZANU, and these disputes flared into armed clashes in late 1975 and 1976.[46] The two movements were deeply divided by differences in tribal composition, divergent ap-proaches to the roles of ideology and armed struggle in the liberation process, and most importantly by the personalities and ambitions of their leaders.[47] In March 1976, Joshua Nkomo broke off negotiations with Ian Smith and announced that ZAPU would intensify the armed struggle from bases in Zambia. Thus, the political divisions among Zimbabwean liberation movements crystallized into a physical sep-aration of the movements' military forces. ZANU, now under the leadership of Robert Mugabe, remained in Mozambique, while Nkomo and ZAPU relocated to Zambia.

In early 1976, the drift toward conflict among Zimbabwean lib-eration movements was partially offset by the increasingly assertive role of the African Frontline Presidents. The presidents of the countries most directly affected by the Rhodesian conflict—Tanzania, Zambia, Mozambique, Botswana, and Angola—assumed a key role in the conduct of the guerrilla war, particularly because Zambia and Mozam-bique provided sanctuary for ZAPU and ZANU guerrillas operating against the Salisbury regime. The Frontline Presidents repeatedly declared their dedication to the elimination of white minority rule in southern Africa, through peaceful means if possible, but through armed struggle if necessary. The five African leaders further agreed that black Rhodesians would have to accomplish their own liberation, and they explicitly announced their determination to avoid a repetition of the Angola debacle. In a postmortem on Angola, President Kaunda of Zambia said, "Our failure to find a solution here confirms that the Organization of African Unity has no power to shape the destiny of Africa. Power is in the hands of the superpowers, to whom we are handing Africa by our failure."[48] The overwhelming unifying purpose of the Frontline Presidents was to reaffirm African power to shape African events and to reclaim the initiative that had been lost to the superpowers in Angola.

The ability of the Frontline Presidents to impose unity on the Zimbabwean nationalist movements and control the activities of external powers was not absolute, and it depended heavily upon the maintenance of unity among the five African leaders.[49] In early 1976, the Frontline Presidents prevailed upon Nkomo and Mugabe to form the Patriotic Front, linking ZAPU and ZANU, although the military forces of the two movements remained under separate command. The African presidents took a concrete step to restrain external involvement in the conflict by insisting that all arms for ZAPU and ZANU be channeled through the OAU Liberation Committee in Dar es Salaam. These initiatives did not resolve the problems of disunity among Zimbabwean movements or ensure complete control over communist arms supplies, but they did give the Frontline Presidents important leverage over the course of the conflict. In particular, the Frontline Presidents retained control over the introduction of new weapons systems, such as surface-to-air missiles, and preserved the right of veto over deployment of any external combat troops on their territories.[50]

Direct U.S. involvement in the search for a diplomatic solution began with trips to southern Africa by Secretary of State Kissinger in April and September 1976. Kissinger's shuttle diplomacy led to the Geneva Conference of December-January in which the United Kingdom and the United States attempted to bridge the gap between the Smith regime and the black nationalists.[51] The Geneva Conference adjourned on January 23, 1977, having made no significant progress toward a Rhodesian settlement. The "moderate" black participants in the conference, Bishop Abel Muzorewa and the Reverend Ndabaningi Sithole, returned to Rhodesia, where they began negotiations with Smith toward an "internal settlement" of the conflict. Nkomo and Mugabe announced their determination to intensify the armed struggle and received the endorsement of the Frontline Presidents.

As the guerrilla war began to escalate, it became apparent that the military balance was slowly beginning to turn against the Smith regime. The potential manpower pool on which the black nationalists could draw was much larger than that available to the Rhodesian army. Moreover, Rhodesian whites began leaving the country in increasing numbers as the war intensified during 1976 and 1977.[52] Despite this bleak long-run prognosis, the Rhodesian army repeatedly demonstrated its ability to keep the guerrilla forces off balance by raiding their sanctuaries in Zambia and Mozambique. Although the Rhodesian forces were clearly unable to win the war, they could prolong it at great cost to the guerrilla movements and to the Zambian and Mozambican regimes that supported them. Thus, the agonizingly slow and costly progress of the liberation struggle prompted both sides to consider proposals for a negotiated settlement. As the war intensified, Sino-Soviet competition for influence with the liberation movements escalated sharply. The PRC had been the principal arms supplier of ZANU since early 1975, while Nkomo and ZAPU had established an arms supply relationship with the USSR.[53] After the March 1977 visit to southern Africa of Soviet Politburo member Nikolai Podgorny, Soviet aid to ZAPU sharply increased. Soviet assistance to Nkomo included large-scale deliveries of weapons to ZAPU camps in Zambia and training of Nkomo's recruits at Cuban camps in Angola. Despite a marked improvement of Soviet ties with Mozambique, Podgorny's visit apparently led to little progress in overcoming the traditional gap between the USSR and ZANU.[54]

Faced with the necessity of matching Nkomo's growing strength while maintaining ZANU's military pressure against the Smith regime, Mugabe visited Beijing in July 1977. While in the PRC, Mugabe was received by Chinese Communist party General Secretary Hua Guofeng and, according to Chinese sources, delivered a stinging condemnation of Soviet "social-imperialism."[55] Upon Mugabe's return to southern Africa, a ZANU party congress declared that the movement was "ever more firmly committed to Marxism-Leninism–Mao Tse-Tung thought."[56] Thus, by mid-1977 the Sino-Soviet competition threatened to assume the same divisive role in the Rhodesian conflict that it had played in Angola.

Conflict among Zimbabwean liberation movements and Sino-Soviet competition were somewhat muted during the latter half of 1977 and early 1978. The United Kingdom and the United States on September 1 announced a new joint proposal for a negotiated settlement.[57] The proposal emerged from discussions between the British Labor government, anxious to rid itself of the Rhodesian albatross, and a new team of U.S. policymakers who were eager to try their hand at negotiating a settlement. Although the Patriotic Front leaders initially condemned the proposals, the Frontline Presidents prevailed upon them to negotiate with the United Kingdom and the United States. The consensus among the Frontline Presidents that the British-U.S. proposals were a "basis for negotiation" made it possible for the proposals to receive the endorsement of the UN Security Council.[58] During the council's debate, both the USSR's and the PRC's representatives expressed extreme skepticism concerning the proposals; however, both abstained on resolutions endorsing the plan, citing the African consensus in favor of giving it a try.[59]

With the announcement of the British-U.S. proposals, a pattern began to emerge whereby the United Kingdom and the United States would agree on initiatives and then discuss them with the Frontline Presidents. When agreement was reached in these ad hoc consultations, the Western negotiators would try to obtain the agreement of the Rhodesian authorities, sometimes attempting to exercise leverage on Salisbury through South Africa. Meanwhile, the Frontline Presidents would attempt to sell the proposals to the Patriotic Front leaders, usually with more success than the British and U.S. negotiators achieved with the Rhodesians. At times, the Western negotiators would meet directly with the Patriotic Front leaders, with the Frontline States and Nigeria enjoying observer status. Such direct negotiating sessions took place on Malta (January 1978); at Maputo Mozambique (April 1978); and on several occasions at the United Nations. Although some progress was achieved in these negotiations, Western diplomats resisted Patriotic Front demands that the Rhodesian army and police be disbanded and replaced by Patriotic Front forces during the proposed transition to majority rule. Nkomo and Mugabe also insisted that their movements should play the leading role in any political structures set up to oversee the transition. Predictably, the Smith regime rejected these demands and placed increasing reliance on negotiations with "moderate" black leaders toward an "internal settlement."[60]

Smith and three internal black leaders announced on March 3, 1978, that they had reached agreement on an "internal settlement." The Patriotic Front leaders immediately denounced the "internal settlement" and vowed to topple the new Salisbury regime. During the latter half of 1978 and early 1979, British and U.S. diplomats shifted from promotion of their own settlement plan to an effort to convene an all-parties conference to which both the Salisbury leaders and their Patriotic Front adversaries would be invited. The British and U.S. negotiators were unable to obtain agreement from the "internal settlement" leaders to such a conference, and momentum toward a negotiated settlement seemed to grind to a halt.[61]

Encouraged by this diplomatic stalemate, the Salisbury authorities moved to consolidate their "internal settlement" by holding the first national elections under the new constitution. Despite Patriotic Front efforts to disrupt the elections, Rhodesians went to the polls in April 1979 to elect the country's first biracial government. Bishop Abel Muzorewa's UANC party won a majority in the new Parliament, and Muzorewa became the prime minister of the new government. Muzorewa's government was not recognized by any African state, and the new Conservative government in the United Kingdom announced its intention to maintain economic sanctions and withhold diplomatic recognition. Despite mounting public and congressional pressure from conservative supporters of the Muzorewa government, President Carter declared in June that the changes in Rhodesia had not met the criteria set earlier by Congress for lifting sanctions and recognizing the new regime.[62] These widely criticized decisions by the Thatcher government and the Carter administration kept open the possibility of one last attempt to settle the Rhodesian crisis through negotiation.

The British Commonwealth Conference of forty-two heads of state held in Lusaka, Zambia, in the first week of August 1979 ended in agreement to convene another round of talks on September 10 in London. The Frontline Presidents pressured the Patriotic Front leaders to attend the London conference and make the concessions necessary to reach agreement. Under the skillful leadership of British Foreign Secretary Lord Carrington and the unrelenting pressure of the Frontline Presidents, the two sides reached agreement in early December on a plan for transition to majority rule after British-supervised elections.[63]

The elections provided for by the Lancaster House agreement were held in February 1980. Robert Mugabe and ZANU achieved an overwhelming electoral victory by winning fifty-seven of the one hundred seats in the new legislature. Joshua Nkomo's ZAPU party won twenty seats, while Bishop Muzorewa's UANC party won only three seats. The Rhodesia Front party of former Prime Minister Smith won all twenty parliamentary seats reserved for whites.

It is still uncertain whether Mugabe will be able to translate his electoral victory into effective rule of Zimbabwe while avoiding both a destructive black civil war and an economically disastrous mass exodus of whites. However, the Rhodesian election was a crucial step in the resolution by negotiation of a civil war that cost twenty thousand Rhodesian lives. The settlement also provided a hopeful precedent for peaceful political change in Namibia and possibly even in South Africa itself. Moreover, the settlement was achieved without a U.S.-Soviet confrontation, and both superpowers were far from center stage when the settlement was reached and implemented.

The African Terrain: Some Comparisons

These case studies demonstrate the critical importance of conditions and variables of the African political terrain as determinants of the character and intensity of superpower conflict (see Table 8.1). U.S.-Soviet differences in Angola escalated into a bilateral confrontation

TABLE 8.1

African Terrain Variables: A Comparison of Angola and Rhodesia

	Angola	Rhodesia
Effectiveness of African regional organizations	Zaire and Congo undermine OAU policy of imposing unity on liberation movements and controlling external intervention.	Frontline States much more successful in imposing a degree of unity on ZANU and ZAPU and more effective controls on external intervention.
Nature of decolonialization process	Portuguese withdraw at height of civil war without organizing transition of power.	Despite long history of failure, British remain involved in Rhodesia negotiations and play major role in settlement.
Local military situation	Distribution of power among liberation movements very sensitive to small increments of external assistance. High tendency toward escalation; little counterpressure toward accommodation.	Liberation struggle makes slow progress at great cost. In short run, battlefield situation relatively insensitive to increments of external assistance. Strong pressures for accommodation balance pressures toward escalation. United States undertakes no arms supply effort.
Role of Republic of South Africa	Highly visible South African military intervention that temporarily reversed situation on the battlefield.	Lower-profile RSA involvement that was not meant to reverse ultimate outcome of conflict. RSA willingness to support political settlement.
Sino-Soviet competition	PRC competes with USSR at early stages of conflict but withdraws at crucial phase, leaving United States and USSR in direct confrontation.	PRC more tenacious in supporting ZANU. Pro-ZANU ties prevent USSR from establishing arms supply relationship with both wings of Zimbabwe Patriotic Front.

that exacerbated the regional conflict and damaged the entire fabric of U.S.-Soviet relations. Although the policies of the United States and the USSR also differed in Rhodesia, no bilateral crisis took place, and the impact of superpower conflict on the African scene was less destructive.

The difference in outcome was significantly affected by the strength and activities of African regional organizations. In Angola, OAU efforts to control conflict among the liberation movements and restrain external intervention were undermined by the policies of Zaire and the Congo. In Rhodesia, however, the Frontline Presidents were much more successful in imposing a modicum of unity on the Zimbabwean liberation movements and in maintaining control over the flow of external arms to ZAPU and ZANU. The Frontline Presidents also forged a diplomatic consensus at the United Nations that discouraged Soviet interference and pressured the United Kingdom and the United States to continue their diplomatic initiative, particularly during the period of Western wavering after the "internal settlement" election. If the Rhodesian settlement was a "victory" for Western diplomacy, it was an even greater triumph for the Frontline Presidents, who achieved their goal of majority rule in Rhodesia while asserting greater African control over the activities of the superpowers.

A second major feature of the African terrain was the character and pace of the decolonialization process in Angola and Rhodesia. Portuguese colonial rule in Angola collapsed so quickly and completely that there was little opportunity for transfer of power to a united majority-rule government. By contrast, the United Kingdom never abandoned its responsibility for the decolonialization process in Rhodesia. The negotiations that led to the Lancaster House agreement and the February 1980 election were the ninth major round of negotiations on Rhodesia since 1965. The fact that a Conservative party government was able to organize and administer an election won by the self-avowed Marxist Robert Mugabe demonstrated that the British retained a unique ability to mediate the long and bitter civil war. The leading role played by the United Kingdom also served to restrain the involvement of the superpowers and reduce the probability of a U.S.-Soviet crisis.

Another important feature of the African terrain was the different military situations that existed in Angola and Rhodesia. The military balance among contending liberation movements in Angola was so volatile and sensitive that each shipment of arms or deployment of advisers by one external power generated an immediate response by the other side. The possibility of organizing a stable coalition government under such conditions was extremely remote, and the probability of escalation to a superpower crisis was high. In Rhodesia, however, the tenacity of the Rhodesian army meant that a total military victory by the Patriotic Front could have been achieved only after a protracted war that would have destroyed the economy and decimated the population of Rhodesia. The agonizingly slow progress of the war contributed to a willingness on both sides to consider a negotiated settlement. From the U.S. perspective, there was never a real possibility that U.S. military assistance would be given to the Rhodesian regime. Moreover, the low probability of a military victory by Soviet-backed guerrillas gave the Carter administration time and the internal political breathing space to permit a joint settlement initiative with the British.

The role played by the Republic of South Africa also differed significantly in the Angolan and Rhodesian conflicts. In Angola, South African forces intervened during a military crisis in a direct and highly visible manner, thus shattering any possibility of organizing an effective coalition government. The South African intervention undermined the legitimacy of U.S. aid for the FNLA-UNITA coalition, justified Soviet-Cuban involvement in the eyes of many Africans, and helped set the stage for a U.S.-Soviet confrontation. South Africa also played a key role in the Rhodesian conflict by providing extensive economic and military assistance to the Smith regime. However, the generally lower profile of South African activity in Rhodesia did not preclude Western negotiating efforts and made it possible for Africans to cooperate with these initiatives without contradicting their fundamental antiapartheid positions.[64]

Finally, the different roles played by the PRC in Angola and Rhodesia help account for the different levels of U.S.-Soviet conflict in the two crises. After playing a key role in stimulating the escalatory spiral in the Angolan conflict, the Chinese withdrew, leaving the United States and the USSR in a direct confrontation. In the Rhodesian case, Sino-Soviet competition again exacerbated conflict between African liberation movements, but the Chinese proved much more tenacious in sustaining their relationship with ZANU. This PRC-ZANU relationship prevented the USSR from establishing an arms supply relationship with the movement that ultimately came to power in Zimbabwe. Thus, greater Chinese determination to persevere in Rhodesia represented an important impediment to the achievement of Soviet objectives and probably helped to deflect pressures toward a direct U.S.-Soviet crisis.

The Nexus of African Terrain and Superpower Policy

African terrain variables do not entirely explain why the Angolan conflict became a U.S.-Soviet confrontation with global implications but the Rhodesian conflict did not provoke a bilateral superpower crisis. Information about events in Angola and Rhodesia had to be processed by decisionmakers in Washington and Moscow who operated within sets of perceptions, expectations, and assessments about the meaning of these conflicts for their national interests in Africa and the overall state of U.S.-Soviet relations. The intersection of African political-military realities and the policy choices of superpower decisionmakers determined the nature and intensity of U.S.-Soviet conflict in the two situations.

The tendency of the Ford administration to interpret African events in terms of East-West conflict played an important role in the Angolan crisis. Kissinger's interest in the conflict seems to have been stimulated almost entirely by his conviction of the necessity to curb aggressive Soviet behavior in the Third World. Thus, the possibility of inflicting a defeat on the USSR by assisting the FNLA (and later UNITA) to win a clear victory over the Soviet-supported MPLA may have stimulated the January 1975 authorization of covert support for the FNLA. The plausibility of this explanation would appear to be supported by the absence of high-level U.S. support for the Alvor Agreement and the failure of U.S. officials to approach the USSR with a timely proposal to head off the spiraling cycle of internal violence and external assistance.

Another plausible explanation for the January decision is that U.S. officials planned to undertake a limited commitment designed to assist the FNLA in building the political and propaganda base in urban areas (particularly Luanda) that was considered essential for effective participation in a coalition government. In the wake of the MPLA victory, Assistant Secretary of State William Schaufele indicated that a limited-involvement strategy of this type may have influenced the 40 Committee's decision to recommend the January program to President Ford.[65] The small amount of aid authorized and the limitations reportedly placed on its use suggest that U.S. objectives may not have initially involved all-out support for an FNLA bid for total power in Angola.

Whatever the calculations surrounding the January decision, U.S. policymakers seem to have concluded by mid-July that more U.S. aid would have to be authorized to help the FNLA and UNITA weather the immediate crisis facing them in Angola. The increase of Soviet arms deliveries to the MPLA, the appearance of Cuban advisors in Angola, and the impending disengagement of the PRC were also important factors in the approval of a covert military assistance program for the FNLA and UNITA, a step that had been under consideration in Washington throughout May and June. This decision was taken despite the advice of the State Department's Africa Bureau and "most agencies participating" in an interagency National Security Council task force that a "diplomatic-political" alternative was preferable to an arms assistance program for the two movements.[66]

The same variables of the Angolan political-military terrain that frustrated U.S. decisionmakers conferred certain advantages on their Soviet counterparts. From the earliest stages of the conflict, the pro-Soviet MPLA enjoyed important advantages over its rivals, including its historical primacy in urban areas, its overall organizational effectiveness, and its status as the preferred movement of the more radical elements within the post-coup Portuguese regime. Thus, Soviet policymakers probably anticipated that, in the absence of a significant change in the local political-military balance, the MPLA would be in a good position to dominate other parties in a coalition government.

This relatively favorable situation probably accounted for the Soviet support for the Alvor Agreement and the tendency of Soviet commentaries to emphasize the value of a coalition during periods when MPLA control of Luanda seemed threatened by FNLA-UNITA offensives. By contrast, during periods when the battlefield situation favored the MPLA, Soviet statements downplayed the idea of a coalition regime. The appearance of South African advisers in Angola during August and September 1975 and the subsequent deterioration of the MPLA's military position probably convinced Moscow that the strategic utility of the coalition idea was exhausted in an increasingly militarized and internationalized conflict. At this point, the Soviet leaders probably decided to give their full support to a Cuban expeditionary force, which had already begun initial deployments to Angola.[67] Thus, the intersection of superpower policies and Angolan political-military realities meant that, by the time the United States became more receptive to the idea of a coalition regime (mid-October), Soviet policymakers had already abandoned the coalition idea in favor of a military solution.

The result was a U.S.-Soviet confrontation played out in an arena where Soviet advantages were maximized and U.S. weaknesses were critical. Soviet strategists were under no effective domestic constraints on their ability to deliver large quantities of military assistance on a timely basis. By contrast, U.S. policymakers quickly reached and exceeded the level of military involvement that could be kept secret or that, having been made public, could acquire sufficient congressional and public support. The result was the worst of all possible outcomes for the United States—a highly visible superpower confrontation in which the United States backed down.

The new team that assumed control of U.S.-Africa policy in January 1977 was determined to follow through on Kissinger's belated activism on Rhodesia. President Carter was, at least initially, less likely than his predecessors to view Third World problems entirely in the context of East-West relations. This greater willingness to be responsive to Third World concerns was reflected in Carter's choice of Andrew Young as UN ambassador and the rising stock of "Africanists" within the State Department. Moreover, the Carter team faced a more favorable set of African circumstances in Rhodesia than had confronted the Ford administration in Angola. Despite the bewildering complexity of Rhodesian politics and the rising tide of civil war, pressures toward accommodation as well as conflict were inherent in the Rhodesian political-military situation. Thus, the intersection of U.S. policy and African terrain led to active U.S. involvement in the search for a negotiated settlement through close coordination of policy with the United Kingdom and an effective working relationship with the Frontline Presidents.

The decision to place greater emphasis on African terrain variables helped determine the U.S. view of the Soviet role in the conflict. It was decided early that the USSR could be safely excluded from the search for a political settlement, primarily because the Soviets themselves had geared their policy to the likelihood of an all-out liberation war. Moscow's estrangement from the white minority regimes in Pretoria and Salisbury and its insistence that any political settlement be based on terms laid down by the Patriotic Front effectively precluded Soviet participation in the search for a negotiated resolution of the conflict. The option of military intervention, which had been so effective in Angola, was foreclosed by the unwillingness of the Frontline Presidents to permit a Soviet-Cuban expeditionary force to operate from their territories. Even if the Frontline Presidents had been willing to permit deployment of such a force, the USSR and Cuba might have been hard pressed to respond in view of their commitments in Angola and Ethiopia. Finally, the risk of military intervention against the tough Rhodesian army and a probable counterintervention by South Africa would have been far higher than the risks run in Angola.

Thus, the combination of African political-military realities and Western diplomacy left the USSR with only one viable option, the continued arming of Zimbabwean liberation movements. Even this option proved to be of limited utility because the PRC's relationship with ZANU left Moscow in the position of having to support the weaker ZAPU wing of the Patriotic Front. The successful implementation of a negotiated settlement in which the USSR played no role and Mugabe's (ZANU's) decisive electoral victory over Nkomo (ZAPU) represented a setback for Soviet policy that could have long-term adverse implications for the Soviet strategic stake in Southern Africa.

Some Implications for Future Crisis-Prevention Efforts

The Angola crisis demonstrates that, under certain circumstances, it can be extremely difficult to design a policy that achieves U.S. objectives while avoiding a confrontation with the USSR. The Ford administration has been criticized for not adopting an alternative strategy including the following elements: (1) strong U.S. support for OAU efforts to organize a coalition regime, (2) an approach to the USSR in early 1975 to determine whether mutual restraints on arms shipments to Angolan liberation movements could be negotiated, and (3) avoidance of U.S. military involvement with any of the Angolan liberation movements. It is important to realize, however, that adoption of this alternative strategy probably would not have significantly raised the probability of achieving a stable governing coalition involving equitable powersharing among all three movements. Given the distribution of political and military capabilities among the three movements, it is likely that the MPLA would have dominated a coalition organized under OAU auspices or that the new government would have quickly disintegrated in renewed civil strife. The result in either case would probably have been MPLA control of the Luanda government and the elimination of its rivals as contestants for power in Angola. Thus, it is difficult to argue that adoption of a different policy would have resulted in greater probability of a U.S. policy success.

However, it is also important to realize that the costs of failure associated with the administration's attempt to employ coercive diplomacy were much greater than the likely costs of a failure of the alternative strategy advocated at the time by Africanists within the State Department.[68] The conditions necessary for the effective use of covert military assistance as the primary element of U.S. policy simply did not exist either on the Angolan terrain or within the U.S. domestic environment after Vietnam, Watergate, and the CIA revelations. Therefore, the strategy of relying on military involvement raised the stakes of the conflict without greatly increasing the likelihood that the struggle could be resolved on terms favorable to the United States. The administration's apparent failure to calculate accurately the "downside" risks and costs meant that U.S. policy initiatives during the Angola crisis made a bad situation worse.

The Carter administration confronted a more favorable set of African circumstances in the Rhodesian conflict. It concluded that an effective strategy to achieve the U.S. objective of majority rule in Rhodesia, while avoiding a U.S.-Soviet crisis, required active participation of the United States as one of the architects of a negotiated settlement. The initial success of the Rhodesian settlement suggests that this judgment was correct, although other actors figured in the final negotiations much more prominently than did the United States. In fact, the Rhodesian settlement suggests that regional international organizations, such as the Frontline Presidents group, and extraregional middle-rank powers, such as the United Kingdom, can sometimes make crucial contributions to resolution of pressing Third World problems and avoidance of superpower crises.

A comparison of the Angola and Rhodesia conflicts suggests that crisis-prevention policies can take many forms and impose many different requirements on policymakers. These cases indicate that the following sets of questions are likely to confront U.S. leaders in future Third World conflicts:

1. What is the correct role of force in U.S. policy? Do the preconditions for effective use of "coercive diplomacy" exist on the Third World terrain and in the U.S. domestic environment?[69] What is the likelihood of success if a military option is selected, and what are the risks and costs of failure?

2. How should U.S. policy deal with the problem of Soviet interests in the conflict? Do circumstances permit the exclusion of a potentially troublesome Soviet presence from the search for a resolution of the crisis? Are Soviet interests and prestige so deeply engaged that participation by the USSR is essential to a lasting settlement of the conflict? If so, would negotiation of an explicit U.S.-Soviet crisis-prevention arrangement be possible and desirable? What are Soviet options, and what is the Soviet view of the utility of force as a potential policy option?

3. How will the political-military terrain of the Third World affect U.S.-Soviet interaction? Do terrain variables make a direct superpower confrontation more or less likely? What role could Third World regional organizations or extra-regional middle-rank powers play in resolution of the conflict and avoidance of U.S.-Soviet confrontation? Are there important pressures for accommodation as well as conflict

inherent in the Third World political terrain? Can U.S. diplomacy build on these forces for accommodation to help promote a settlement of the conflict without provoking a U.S.-Soviet crisis? The history of superpower conflicts in Angola and Rhodesia suggests both the difficulty and the critical importance of the search for good answers to these questions. These cases also suggest that learning from past successes and failures, good timing, and a keen sensitivity for the political terrain of the Third World are essential ingredients of a strategy designed to achieve U.S. objectives while minimizing the risk of superpower crisis.

Notes

1. For the text of the Basic Principles Agreement see *Department of State Bulletin* 67, no. 1722 (June 26, 1972):898–899.

2. These terms are borrowed from an address by Secretary of State Cyrus Vance's adviser on Soviet affairs, Marshall D. Shulman, in *Department of State Bulletin* 80, no. 2034 (January 1980):17–20.

3. The initial decolonialization proposals of the Portuguese Armed Forces Movement are in "Program of the Movement of the Armed Forces" and "General Spinola's Statement on Transfer of Powers in Africa" in Colin Legum, ed., *Africa Contemporary Record: Annual Survey and Documents 1974–75* (London: Rex Collings, 1975), pp. C34-C38.

4. The FNLA had its ethnic base in the 1.2 million people of the Bakongo tribe of northwestern Angola and southwestern Zaire. The MPLA drew much of its support from the 700,000- to 800,000-member Mbundu ethnic group of western Angola, and UNITA had its ethnic base in the 2-million-member Ovimbundu tribe of the Central Benguela Highlands. The total population of Angola in 1975 was approximately 5.5 million people. Despite the obvious importance of these ethnic divisions, it would be a gross oversimplification to see the Angolan conflict as a "tribal war." Each of the movements contained members of all three major population groups, and members of the white community provided support for all three movements. Probably the most important implication of these ethnic divisions was the tendency of the FNLA and UNITA to have their roots in specific geographical areas of rural Angola. By contrast, the MPLA tended to be strongest in urban areas, particularly among the important mestico (mixed African-Portuguese) inhabitants of Luanda. For a discussion of the ethnic factor in the Angolan conflict see John A. Marcum, "Lessons of Angola," *Foreign Affairs* 54, no. 3 (April 1976):409–412.

5. Although most of the MPLA's leaders espoused "scientific socialism," it would be a mistake to assume that their ideology blinded them to pragmatic political and economic concerns. For instance, the MPLA and Gulf Oil Company reached an understanding concerning the continuation of Gulf's role in the oil-rich Cabinda enclave at the same time that U.S. foreign policy

was supporting rival liberation movements. See Legum, "Foreign Intervention in Angola," in Colin Legum, ed., *Africa Contemporary Record: Annual Survey and Documents 1975-76* (London: Rex Collings, 1976, pp. A5–A6).

6. Each of the liberation movements was beset by internal disputes, such as the split within the MPLA between a faction headed by Dr. Augustinio Neto and a dissident group headed by Daniel Chipenda. In early 1975, Chipenda deserted the MPLA to join the rival FNLA, headed by Holden Roberto. FNLA had its own history of factional conflict, including the breakaway of Dr. Jonas Savimbi, which led to the establishment of UNITA in 1964. For a discussion of factionalism within the Angolan liberation movement see Legum, "Foreign Intervention in Angola," pp. A5–A6.

7. Marcum, "Lessons of Angola," pp. 410–411.

8. Legum, "Foreign Intervention in Angola," pp. A4–A7; and Marcum, "Lessons of Angola," pp. 410–412.

9. The U.S. State Department provided the following estimates of the military strength of the various movements in January 1975: FNLA—five to six thousand trained and armed troops, MPLA—five to seven thousand trained and armed troops, UNITA—two thousand guerrilla trainees. See U.S., Congress, Senate, Committee on Foreign Relations, Subcommittee on African Affairs, *US Involvement in Civil War in Angola, January 29–February 3–5, 1976* (Washington, D.C.: Government Printing Office, 1976), p. 191. Marcum estimates FNLA strength at fifteen thousand by mid-1974, while MPLA had only three thousand trained guerrillas at the time of the Portuguese coup. He estimates that UNITA strength in the combat areas of Angola was approximately eight hundred trained guerrillas (see Marcum, "Lessons of Angola," pp. 411–413). Legum emphasizes that an important potential source of trained manpower for the MPLA was the thirty-five hundred–to six-thousand–member Katanga gendarmerie, which had gone into exile in Angola after the defeat of the Katanga secession. Roberto and Mobutu feared the Katanga gendarmerie as a potential threat to both the FNLA and the Mobutu regime in Zaire. See Legum, "Foreign Intervention in Angola," p. A8.

10. For the text of the Alvor Agreement see Legum, *Africa Contemporary Record 1974-75*, pp. C221–C226.

11. For the text of the July 1975 OAU resolution on Angola see Legum, *Africa Contemporary Record 1975-76*, pp. C16–C17.

12. Legum, *Africa Contemporary Record 1974-75*, pp. B573–B574.

13. For a discussion of South Africa's détente policy see Colin Legum, "Southern Africa: The Secret Diplomacy of Detente," in Legum, *Africa Contemporary Record 1974-75*, pp. A3–A15.

14. The text of the testimony by Assistant Secretary Davis is in *Department of State Bulletin* 73 (August 11, 1975), pp. 212–213.

15. *Department of State Bulletin* 73 (December 15, 1975), p. 856.

16. *Renmin Rabao* editorial of January 22, 1975 (*Peking Review,* no. 5, January 31, 1975, p. 15).

17. Chou En-Lai message of January 27, 1975 (*Peking Review,* no. 6, February 7, 1975, p. 4).

18. TASS International Service, Moscow, January 13, 1975 (*Foreign*

Broadcast Information Service Daily Report, Soviet Union, February 4, 1975, p. H-1).

19. *Pravda,* February 26, 1975, p. 5 (*Foreign Broadcast Information Service Daily Report, Soviet Union,* March 3, 1975, pp. H1–H3).

20. The term "saliency" was first developed by Thomas Schelling in *The Strategy of Conflict* (Cambridge, Mass.: Harvard University Press, 1960) and *Arms and Influence* (New Haven, Conn., Yale University Press, 1966) to denote any limit in war mutually agreed upon, explicitly or tacitly, by the belligerents. Thus, the crossing of such a saliency by either side represents an escalation of the conflict. For a useful summary of Schelling's discussion of saliencies see Richard Smoke, *War: Controlling Escalation* (Cambridge, Mass.: Harvard University Press, 1977), pp. 32–34. Smoke suggests that saliencies are "objective" and in some way "discrete and discontinuous." Thus, the crossing of a saliency by either party is noticeable to all parties, although the party crossing a saliency may not be able to anticipate the full consequences of its action. In the Angolan conflict, however, saliencies were difficult to identify with any degree of certainty. For example, when does an increase in a long-standing flow of military assistance from an external patron to its liberation group client represent the crossing of a saliency that "justifies" a response by the other side? Does the introduction of foreign military advisers represent the crossing of a saliency, or should some level of such assistance be regarded as an integral part of training guerrillas to use advanced military equipment? At what point does participation by advisers cross a critical saliency to become intervention by combat troops? The fact that saliencies in the Angolan conflict were not "discrete" and "discontinuous" contributed significantly to the escalatory pressures on all participants. Smoke anticipated some of the problems associated with this "blurring" of saliencies (see *War: Controlling Escalation,* pp. 32–34), but more work needs to be done on applying the theory of escalation to low-level conflict in the Third World. (For further discussion of the problem of escalation control see Chapter 15.)

21. Colin Legum, "The Soviet Union, China, and the West in Southern Africa," *Foreign Affairs* 54 (July 1976):749–750.

22. William J. Durch, "The Cuban Military in Africa and the Middle East: From Algeria to Angola," *Studies in Comparative Communism* 11, nos. 1 and 2 (Spring/Summer 1978):63. Legum believes that some Chinese advisors arrived at FNLA camps in Zaire in late 1973; see Legum, *Africa Contemporary Record 1975–76,* p. A16.

23. Statement of William E. Schaufele, Jr., Assistant Secretary of State for African Affairs, in U.S., Congress, Senate, Committee on Foreign Relations, Subcommittee on African Affairs, *Hearings on Angola* (Washington, D.C.: Government Printing Office, 1976), p. 175.

24. Durch, "The Cuban Military in Africa," pp. 63–64.

25. For a discussion of this phase of the war see Legum, *Africa Contemporary Record 1975–76,* pp. B423–B425.

26. TASS International Service, Moscow, May 14, 1975 (*Foreign Broadcast Information Service Daily Report, Soviet Union,* May 16, 1975, p. H-2).

27. *Izvestia,* May 21, 1975 (*Foreign Broadcast Information Service Daily Report, Soviet Union,* May 22, 1975, p. H-3).

28. Sergei Kulik, Untitled commentary, *TASS,* June 11, 1975 (*Foreign Broadcast Information Service Daily Report, Soviet Union,* June 12, 1975, p. H-1).

29. *TASS,* June 21, 1975 (*Foreign Broadcast Information Service Daily Report, Soviet Union,* June 24, 1975, pp. H-1–H-2).

30. Durch, "The Cuban Military in Africa," p. 64.

31. B. Pilyatskin, "A Time of Alarms and Expectations," *Izvestia,* July 19, 1975, p. 4 (*Foreign Broadcast Information Service Daily Report, Soviet Union,* July 24, 1975, pp. H-1–H-3).

32. Valery Churin, untitled commentary, *TASS,* July 16, 1975 (*Foreign Broadcast Information Service Daily Report, Soviet Union,* July 22, 1975, p. H-1).

33. Sergei Kulik, "Peking's Subversive Actions in Angola," *TASS,* July 17, 1975 (*Foreign Broadcast Information Service Daily Report, Soviet Union,* July 18, 1975, p. H-1).

34. Legum, "The Soviet Union, China, and the West," p. 751.

35. For a discussion of the bureaucratic struggle surrounding U.S. approval of this program see Nathaniel Davis, "The Angola Decision of 1975: A Personal Memoir," *Foreign Affairs* 57, no. 1 (Fall 1978):109–124.

36. Roberto's emissary to South Africa was Daniel Chipenda, the former MPLA leader who had defected to the FNLA. Legum, "Foreign Intervention in Angola," p. A8.

37. The best treatment of this crucial period appears in Durch, "The Cuban Military in Africa," pp. 64–67. Durch presents convincing evidence for his contention that Cuban troops served as advisers for MPLA units until the large-scale South African intervention of October 23. Cuban troops organized in their own combat units then began to assume a direct combat role.

38. Ye. Kubichev, "The Situation Is Becoming Complex," *Sotsialisti-cheskaya Industriya,* September 27, 1975 (*Foreign Broadcast Information Service Daily Report, Soviet Union,* October 8, 1975, p. H-3). It is interesting that this temporary revival of Soviet interest in a coalition government should appear in a journal not usually associated with authoritative comment on foreign policy. The idea of a coalition with the FNLA and UNITA did not reappear in *Pravda, Izvestia,* or other more authoritative Soviet publications. The *Sotsialisticheskaya Industriya* article may have reflected some Soviet ambivalence about the outcome of the murky struggle then in progress in Angola. If so, this ambivalence seems to have been resolved by October 20, when the Soviet media favorably reported Neto's statement that the Mombassa and Alvor agreements "cannot now be implemented because of the treacherous policy of the FNLA and UNITA." *TASS,* October 20, 1975, (*Foreign Broadcast Information Service Daily Report, Soviet Union,* October 21, 1975, p. H-1).

39. Durch, "The Cuban Military in Africa," pp. 67–68. The Cubans themselves provided the aircraft for the initial deployments of their combat

troops to Angola. Durch suggests that Soviet strategic airlift of Cuban troops did not begin until early January. A good summary of Soviet activities in support of MPLA/Cuban activities is given in Jiri Valenta, "The Soviet-Cuban Intervention in Angola, 1975," *Studies in Comparative Communism* 11, nos. 1 and 2 (Spring/Summer 1978):27.

40. The MPLA-dominated People's Republic of Angola (PRA) was recognized by a number of African "progressive" regimes, the USSR, and the USSR's East European allies as well as Brazil and Yugoslavia. Nigeria and Tanzania later recognized the PRA, citing the South African intervention of October 23 as justification. At a special OAU summit held in January 1976, twenty-two members favored recognition of the PRA while twenty-two favored further efforts to organize a coalition. The summit deadlock symbolized the OAU's total inability to maintain control over events in Angola. *African Research Bulletin* 12, no. 11 (December 15, 1975):3820.

41. Statement of Secretary of State Henry A. Kissinger, in U.S., Congress, *Hearings on Angola,* pp. 14–23, and replies to supplemental questions submitted by Senator Clark, pp. 50–55. Kissinger's accusation of a Soviet violation of the Basic Principles Agreement ignored the fact that, according to the secretary's own account, the United States first attempted to invoke the agreement in October 1975. The initial approach to the USSR took place after two covert assistance plans had been approved by the United States and well after the situation in Angola had deteriorated into civil war.

42. As of April 15, 1980, there were still some 20,000 Soviet and Cuban military technicians in Angola. See National Foreign Assessment Center, U.S. Central Intelligence Agency, *Communist Aid Activities in Non-Communist Less-Developed Countries, 1979 and 1954–79,* October 1980, page 15.

43. In 1974, the Rhodesian armed forces of 4,700 well-trained and well-equipped regular troops were backed up by 10,000 Territorial Force reserves. The army was equipped with armored cars, light artillery, and other modern weapons. The air force of 1,200 men was equipped with forty-two combat aircraft, including light bombers, Hawker Hunter, and Vampire fighter aircraft, and Alouette helicopters. Whites made up only about one-third of all active duty personnel, with the rest coming from Rhodesia's African population. *The Military Balance 1974–75* (London: International Institute for Strategic Studies, 1974), p. 43.

44. "Zimbabwe" is the name chosen to replace "Rhodesia" after the recent majority rule elections. The terms "Zimbabwe" and "Rhodesia" will be used interchangeably in this paper. For a brief discussion of the history of the Zimbabwean liberation movement see Colin Legum, *Southern Africa: The Year of the Whirlwind* (London: Rex Collings, 1977), pp. 17–26.

45. Ibid., p. 10.

46. Richard W. Hull, "Rhodesia and Her Neighbors," *Current History* 73, no. 432 (December 1977):218–222.

47. John Day, "The Divisions of the Rhodesian Nationalist Movement," *The World Today* 33, no. 10 (October 1977):392–394.

48. Quoted in Legum, "Foreign Intervention in Angola," p. A-1.

49. During the course of the conflict there were important instances of

Frontline disunity. Probably the most serious occurred in August 1978 when President Kaunda of Zambia sponsored a secret meeting between ZAPU leader Joshua Nkomo and Prime Minister Ian Smith of Rhodesia. Nkomo did not inform his Patriotic Front coleader of the plan for a meeting with Smith, nor did Kaunda inform his colleagues within the Frontline Presidents group. When the meeting became public, the result was further disunity between the two wings of the Patriotic Front and the first serious break in Frontline unity. A thorough account of this affair is provided in Garrick Uttley, *Globalism or Regionalism: United States Policy Towards Southern Africa,* Adelphi Paper no. 154 (London: International Institute for Strategic Studies, 1979), pp. 13–15. These tensions were further exacerbated when President Kaunda reopened Zambia's border with Rhodesia in October 1978, citing his country's severe economic crisis as justification. Despite these serious disputes among themselves, the Frontline Presidents were able to restore their unity in support of the critical phase of the 1979 Lancaster House talks on Rhodesia.

50. Legum, *Southern Africa: Year of the Whirlwind,* pp. 14–17. Frontline efforts to exercise control of Communist arms supplies are illustrated by reports from Lusaka that, even during Rhodesian air raids, ZAPU guerrillas often had difficulty in obtaining access to weapons stored under guard of the Zambian army. In addition to their desire to retain leverage over Rhodesian events, the Frontline Presidents needed to maintain control over Communist arms deliveries in order to assure control over their own territories. In the absence of such controls, the armies of Zambia and Mozambique might have been overwhelmed by the guerrilla armies of ZAPU and ZANU.

51. Concerning Secretary Kissinger's shuttle diplomacy and the Geneva Conference see Elaine Windrich, "Rhodesia: The Road from Luanda to Geneva," *The World Today* 33, no. 3 (March 1977):101–111.

52. The total white population of Rhodesia in 1974 was about 270,000. The net loss of economically active white men and women through emigration in 1976 was 1,801. *Strategic Survey 1977* (International Institute for Strategic Studies: London, 1978), p. 32. The figure for 1978 was 13,709. *Strategic Survey 1978* (London: International Institute for Strategic Studies, 1979), p. 93.

53. Legum, "The Soviet Union, China, and the West," pp. 753–757.

54. Hull, "Rhodesia and Her Neighbors," p. 222.

55. "Zimbabwe Friendship Delegation," *Peking Review* 20, no. 27 (July 1, 1977):4–5, 25.

56. *Zimbabwe News,* Maputo, 9, no. 56 (July-Dec. 1977), quoted in Legum, *Africa Contemporary Record 1977–78,* p. B1037.

57. Great Britain, Parliament, *Proposals for Settlement,* presented by the Secretary of State for Foreign and Commonwealth Affairs (London: H.M. Stationery Office, 1977).

58. On the origins and early reception of the "Anglo-American Plan" for a settlement, see Uttley, *Globalism or Regionalism,* pp. 8–9.

59. *New York Times,* September 29, 1977, p. 10, and *New York Times,*

184   *Larry C. Napper*

September 30, 1977, p. 5. The Chinese actually chose not to participate at all in the Security Council vote.

60. Useful accounts of these negotiations are in Uttley, *Globalism or Regionalism*, pp. 9–11, and *Strategic Survey 1978*, pp. 89–93.

61. Uttley, *Globalism or Regionalism*, pp. 14–15. For the text of the "Internal Settlement" agreement see Legum, *Africa Contemporary Record 1977–78*, pp. C73–C76.

62. *New York Times*, June 9, 1979, p. 4.

63. David Ottaway, "Africa: US Policy Eclipse," *Foreign Affairs: America and the World 1979* 58, no. 3: 641–644.

64. Richard Smoke's notion of "expectation levers" is particularly helpful in understanding the difference between South Africa's participation in the Angolan and Rhodesian conflicts. Smoke defines an "expectation lever" as an action that "involves both the crossing of a saliency and the alteration of policy makers' expectations about the course and outcome of the war." Smoke suggests that such actions play the crucial role in escalation of a conflict (*War: On Escalation*, p. 275). The South African intervention in Angola crossed a saliency by initiating intervention by foreign combat troops operating as discrete units is an unambiguously combat (non-advisory) role. Moreover, the advance of the relatively small South African column changed policymakers' expectations concerning the outcome of the conflict. By contrast, South African ties with Rhodesia simply continued despite the imposition of UN sanctions against the Salisbury regime; thus no *new* actions were taken to cross established saliencies. Moreover, South African assistance did not change the expectations of policymakers that the white regime in Salisbury could not "win" its counterinsurgency war. South African assistance to Rhodesia was never an "expectation lever," even though the amount of aid extended to Rhodesia over the course of the war dwarfed the resources devoted to the brief, ill-fated Angolan campaign.

65. U.S., Congress, *Hearings on Angola*, p. 175.

66. Davis, "The Angola Decision of 1975," p. 116.

67. The best analysis of Soviet decisionmaking in the Angola crisis is Valenta, "The Soviet-Cuban Intervention in Angola," pp. 19–26.

68. In addition to the obvious damage to U.S. prestige flowing from an unsuccessful confrontation with the USSR, the costs of failure were the following: (1) U.S. relations with OAU members were strained by American failure to heed OAU calls for non-intervention; (2) U.S. and South African activities served to legitimize the deployment of a Soviet-Cuban expeditionary force, making it possible for the USSR to avoid paying the full political cost of its own intervention; (3) U.S. relations with the MPLA became so strained that effective diplomatic contact could not be readily established with the PRA after the conflict, an estrangement that had the effect of deepening Angolan dependence on the USSR; and (4) by avoiding its own obligations under the Basic Principles Agreement, the United States lost whatever leverage invocation of the agreement might have yielded over Soviet behavior. It is possible to argue that an attempt early in the conflict to hold the USSR to its obligations would have failed because of Soviet

eagerness to seize an inviting opportunity in Angola. However, the validity of this assertion cannot be tested because the effort was not made.

69. Alexander L. George has defined coercive diplomacy as "a strategy that calls for employing military threats in an effort to persuade an opponent to halt or undo an encroachment in which he is already engaged." According to George, the successful use of coercive diplomacy requires creating in the opponent's mind (1) a sense of urgency for compliance with the demand, (2) a belief that there is an asymmetry of motivation that favors the coercing power, and (3) fear of unacceptable escalation if the demand is not accepted. See Alexander L. George, *Presidential Decisionmaking in Foreign Policy: The Effective Use of Information and Advice* (Boulder, Colo.: Westview Press, 1980), pp. 246–247. U.S. policymakers are likely to find it increasingly difficult to create these preconditions for the effective use of coercive diplomacy against the USSR in Third World conflicts because of (1) the rapid narrowing of the gap between U.S. and Soviet military capabilities suitable for intervention in the Third World, (2) the fact that U.S. policymakers must deal with significantly greater domestic constraints in the use of coercive diplomacy than their Soviet counterparts, and (3) the existence of Third World terrain factors that often make the use of coercive diplomacy more difficult and costly.

9
Missed Opportunities for Crisis Prevention: The War of Attrition and Angola

Alexander L. George

Competition between the two superpowers in a third area can escalate unexpectedly into confrontation. A mere desire to limit their competition to "safe" levels will not suffice; in addition, the two sides must be able to control the dynamics of escalation inherent in many of their contests for influence in a third area. Factors not clearly recognized or easily controlled may operate to draw the United States and the Soviet Union further and further into a local conflict. Difficulties in achieving escalation control have been experienced in many cases. In this chapter we will examine the escalation dynamics in two strikingly different cases: the events that led to Soviet military intervention in the Egyptian-Israeli War of Attrition in 1970, and the low-level competition for escalation dominance in the Angolan civil war of 1975 that was climaxed by the decisive Soviet-assisted Cuban military intervention. Each of these two cases has already been discussed from an analytical perspective that differs from the one taken in the present chapter. In Chapter 4 George Breslauer included the War of Attrition in his assessment of Soviet policy in the Middle East. In Chapter 8 Larry C. Napper showed how neglect of the local political terrain contributed to the failure of U.S. policy in Angola. The present chapter, on the other hand, focuses attention on the "missed opportunities" in both cases for avoiding escalation of superpower involvement to the level of a confrontation.

U.S.-Soviet competition in situations of this kind often takes the form of an effort first by one side, then by the other, to introduce and maintain a set of "ground rules" that is likely to result in a favorable outcome. This process may involve signaling and some degree of bargaining that may be subtle and tacit rather than explicit. As with other forms of bargaining and strategic interaction, there are dangers of misperception and miscalculation. Signaling may lack clarity and be beset with "noise," or it may be poorly timed. Offers and threats may be lacking in credibility or may be insufficiently potent. The result, as in the two cases examined here, is that the superpowers may be drawn further into a local conflict than they wanted or expected to be. And this possibility is much increased, of course, if local actors seek to manipulate the behavior of the superpowers for their own advantage.

Soviet Military Intervention in the War of Attrition, 1970

Shortly after President Nixon came into office in January 1969, he decided to invite the Soviet Union to participate in informal two-power talks to explore the possibility of developing a joint U.S.-Soviet approach for settling the Arab-Israeli conflict. This was, as Lawrence Whetten notes, "an important step in granting the Soviet Union the recognition she desired that she was co-responsible for regional stability and security."[1] Intensive discussions took place between the Soviet ambassador to Washington, Anatolyi Dobrynin, and Assistant Secretary of State Joseph Sisco to ascertain whether the two countries could develop a joint proposal setting down general principles to guide the search for an overall settlement. In the midst of these discussions in early April President Nasser of Egypt abrogated the existing cease-fire and launched a campaign of limited military action across the Suez Canal, comprising mainly heavy artillery shelling and commando raids, in what came to be called the War of Attrition.[2] At first, the two superpowers appeared to be encouraged that Nasser's initial success seemed to provide an opportunity for orchestrating a joint diplomatic effort. However, repeated efforts to move along this track in the next year proved unsuccessful for a variety of reasons.

Each superpower was reluctant to pressure its Middle East ally into making concessions beyond a certain point. Similarly, the two superpowers could not coordinate their views as regards the balance between Arab and Israeli military forces that would be most propitious for furthering their diplomatic efforts, a task rendered all the more difficult as the War of Attrition passed through different phases. It was difficult for either the United States or the Soviet Union to deny its ally additional military equipment when the ally suffered a serious setback in the ongoing war or when the regional military balance seemed to be tipping in an adverse direction. The Egyptians were receptive to U.S.-Soviet proposals in the early phase of the War of Attrition when Egyptian forces achieved a semblance of military parity, but the Israelis saw this development as reducing their bargaining leverage and decided to escalate the war by calling upon their air force in order to reassert military superiority. Coupled with this difficulty was the inability or unwillingness of either of the superpowers to go beyond a certain point in trying to control its ally's behavior or in pressing efforts to impose a settlement.

The pursuit of a joint U.S.-Soviet approach was not helped by the lack of coherence and consistent direction of U.S. policy towards the Middle East in the first years of the Nixon administration. The priority concerns of the White House were the Vietnam War and the development of a strategy for restructuring relations with the Soviet Union. The situation in the Middle East was regarded by Nixon as enormously complicated and somewhat less urgent; he was content therefore to allow the State Department to take the lead in developing and implementing policy for dealing with the Arab-Israeli dispute. As William Quandt relates, the State Department had for some time advocated an "evenhanded" approach to the Arab-Israeli conflict, whereas the White House was less committed to this view. Under the circumstances it is not surprising that Israeli diplomats soon began to bypass Secretary of State William Rogers in order to deal directly with Nixon and Kissinger.[3] Rogers tried to develop a joint U.S.-Soviet approach for settling the Middle East conflict with energy and persistence, even though his efforts did not enjoy enthusiastic or consistent support from the White House.

As for Kissinger, Nixon's special assistant for national security affairs, he was even more skeptical of the State Department's approach and zeal than was the president, who generally went along with its initiatives. Kissinger was dubious as to the feasibility of an overall settlement and the possibility of effecting an acceptable joint approach with the Soviet Union. As Kissinger makes clear in his memoirs, he favored a fundamentally different long-range strategy in the Middle East, one that would prolong the stalemate in the Arab-Israeli conflict in ways that would eventually lead Egypt to turn to the United States, reversing its alliance with the Soviet Union when it realized that the Soviets lacked the leverage to enable the Arab states to recover territories taken by Israel during the Six-Day War of 1967.[4] A consistent, coherent U.S. policy in the Middle East was hampered also by fundamental disagreements within the administration regarding the role of the Soviet Union in the Middle East. As Quandt reports: "Some felt that the Soviet Union, for global-strategy reasons, would be prepared to cooperate with the United States in the Middle East, even if this might cause Moscow some strain in its relations with Nasser. . . . Others doubted that the Soviet leaders would be prepared to sacrifice regional interests for the sake of improved U.S.-Soviet relations."[5]

The Soviet Union provided substantial military supplies and diplomatic support to Egypt and Syria after the Six-Day War, but its aid was rather carefully limited to enabling the Arab countries to acquire a defensive capability. However, Soviet leaders were either not able or not willing to prevent Nasser from utilizing his refurbished military forces to launch the campaign of limited military action across the Suez Canal in March and April of 1969 that became known as the War of Attrition. Nasser's aim was to gain footholds on the eastern shore of the canal and to wear down Israel's strength by means of heavy artillery bombardments and commando raids, thereby, he hoped, setting into motion political-diplomatic pressures that would lead to Israeli withdrawal from the Sinai. However, events were to proceed in a quite different direction. Confronted with rising losses to its forces and the possibility that Egyptian units would manage to seize footholds east of the canal, Israel responded in late July 1969 with air attacks against Egyptian artillery and other targets on the western side of the canal.[6] The limited war across the canal continued throughout the rest of the year.

Diplomatic efforts to secure a cease-fire and a political settlement of the Arab-Israeli conflict were undertaken through the United Nations and in bilateral U.S.-Soviet talks. With the failure of the so-called Rogers Plan in December, the Israeli government decided to escalate the war in a major way, both in the objectives it pursued and in the military strategy employed to achieve its goals. In early January 1970 the Israeli air force began deep penetration attacks against military targets near urban centers in Egypt in an ambitious effort to bring the war home to the population, hoping thereby to demonstrate Nasser's impotence and to bring about either his downfall or an end to the war.[7]

Israeli escalation of the war at this time, it should be noted, was not opposed and may have been tacitly supported by Washington. The arrival of Phantom aircraft from the United States in the preceding months indeed made the extension of Israeli air attacks possible. In his memoirs Kissinger gives no indication that the administration either disapproved of the Israeli decision to undertake and persist in deep penetration attacks or sought to persuade the Israeli government to call the attacks off. Evidently Washington did not believe that this Israeli action would provoke Soviet military intervention, a dangerous miscalculation, as events were to make clear.

Nasser was faced with the prospect of another serious military defeat only three years after the disastrous 1967 war, with the survival of his regime now at stake. In desperation Nasser flew secretly to Moscow on January 22. In a meeting with the top Soviet leaders, he was offered and accepted direct intervention by Soviet military forces sufficient to provide effective air defenses against Israeli air raids. A month elapsed, however, between Nasser's visit to Moscow and the movement of Soviet air defense systems and personnel into Egypt. In the meantime, Soviet leaders made some efforts to persuade the United States to curb the Israeli deep penetration air operations; at the same time, the Soviets were assessing the risk that the United States might react strongly to Soviet military intervention on Egypt's behalf, if that step became necessary.

On January 31 Ambassador Dobrynin delivered a letter from Premier Kosygin to President Nixon. Similar communications were sent to British Prime Minister Harold Wilson and French President Georges Pompidou. Kosygin warned that if Israeli air attacks on Egypt continued, "The Soviet Union will be forced to see to it that the Arab states have the means at their disposal, with the help of which a due rebuff to the arrogant aggressor could be made."⁸ As Kissinger reports in his memoirs, Kosygin also called on the four powers (the United States, the Soviet Union, England, and France) "to 'compel' Israel to cease its attacks and to establish a lasting peace beginning with the 'speediest' withdrawal of Israeli forces from all the occupied Arab territories."⁹

It may be noted that Kosygin did not specify what action the Soviet Union would take by way of ensuring that Egypt would have "the means" at its disposal to cope with Israeli air attacks. This vagueness weakened, of course, the thrust of Kosygin's effort to induce the United States to curb Israeli air attacks on Egypt and contributed to Washington's miscalculation of Soviet willingness to enforce its demand. Kosygin's threat, deliberately ambiguous in this respect, nonetheless committed the Soviet Union to take some kind of effective action, be it only stepped-up delivery of military supplies. One can only speculate as to the various reasons why Kosygin did not refer to, or imply more clearly, the possibility of direct Soviet military intervention. Soviet leaders may have believed that an explicit threat would be considered provocative by U.S. leaders and, if it were so interpreted, that it would make them unwilling to put pressure on Israel to halt the raids lest they appear to have been coerced into doing so by the threat of Soviet intervention. Another possibility is that the threat was left ambiguous so that the Soviet Union would not be committed to an intervention that it might decide later to forego for any reason (for example, if Washington issued counterthreats to deter Soviet intervention). Still another possibility is that the threat was left ambiguous for security reasons, to enable Soviet air defense personnel and equipment to be introduced into Egypt covertly so as not to be discovered prematurely by the United States or Israel.

In any event, it is clear from Kissinger's account that he did not initially regard Kosygin's letter as a threat of military intervention but rather that he saw it as still another effort to induce the United States to exert pressure on the Israelis to withdraw to pre-1967 borders. In fact, Kissinger admits that he interpreted the Soviet note as evidence that the U.S. policy of holding firm was creating just the kind of dilemma for the Soviets that would work to the advantage of the United States eventually, as Kissinger's preferred strategy predicted. In a memorandum to Nixon on February 6, 1970, Kissinger expressed scarcely concealed pleasure at what he regarded as evidence of Soviet impotence to help Nasser: "Now that he [Nasser] has turned to Moscow to lean on us to press Israel to stop the bombing, he is about to demonstrate Soviet inability to get him out of his box."[10]

The administration quickly agreed on "a firm reply" that, however, reflected a fundamental misreading of the Soviet note as threatening no more than expanded arms shipments to the Arab states. Ignoring the major escalation of the war by Israel, Nixon's reply of February 4 rejected the Soviet effort to put the blame for the fighting on Israel alone and warned that the Soviet threat to expand arms shipment could further stimulate the arms race in the Middle East and draw the United States and the Soviet Union more deeply into the conflict: "The United States is watching carefully the relative balance in the Middle East and we will not hesitate to provide arms to friendly states as the need arises."[11]

The administration's position at this time was that it would not, and indeed need not, take any steps to persuade the Israelis to halt their deep penetration raids. Evidently U.S. leaders were not aware that Nasser had traveled secretly to Moscow with an urgent plea for immediate assistance. And available sources do not reveal whether U.S. intelligence had alerted top policymakers that the Israeli raids had placed Nasser—and therefore the Soviets who were backing him—in a desperate position. Be that as it may, Nixon's response to Kosygin may well have encouraged Moscow to believe that it had no choice but to proceed with its direct intervention on Egypt's behalf and that such a move was acceptable as a calculated risk that could be monitored and controlled by observing the U.S. reaction.

Upon further reflection, Kissinger tells us, he began to wonder whether the Soviets might be contemplating sending their own military personnel into Egypt and called this possibility to Nixon's attention. The president responded, "I think it is time to talk directly with the Soviets on this."[12] But it is not clear from this reaction that Nixon took the possibility of Soviet intervention seriously, seeing in the developing situation, rather, a possible opportunity to work out an advantageous deal with the Soviets. To probe this possibility Kissinger instructed Ambassador Jacob Beam in Moscow to convey to Gromyko that the United States was prepared to work for restoration of a cease-fire and mutual limitation of arms supplies by the two superpowers to their Middle East allies. When Gromyko replied, on February 11, it was to assert, as Kissinger recalls, that the USSR "could not consider a cease-fire unless Israel first stopped its deep penetration raids."[13]

In the meanwhile, on February 10, Kissinger met with Dobrynin and, as he recalls in his memoirs, told him "on behalf of the President . . . that 'we want Soviet leaders to know that the introduction of Soviet combat personnel in the Middle East would be viewed with the gravest concern.' "[14] In his memoirs Kissinger does not suggest that either he or the president was seriously concerned over the possibility of Soviet intervention; but, it would appear, they regarded it as prudent to undertake this kind of low-cost deterrence effort through diplomatic channels. "Nothing more," Kissinger indicates, "was heard from Soviet leaders for nearly a month"; one infers, though Kissinger does not say so, that he and Nixon drew the conclusion that they had succeeded in discouraging any temptation to intervene that the Soviet leaders may have experienced.

It may be assumed that in the interim Soviet leaders closely observed U.S. behavior for any indication that the administration would force the Israelis to halt their raids or was preparing to take action to back up Kissinger's deterrence statement to Dobrynin. It may be further assumed that Soviet leaders were carefully assessing the risks of their plan for sending Soviet military personnel and equipment to shore up Egypt's air defenses. What, then, was the administration prepared to do to back up and lend credibility to Kissinger's threat? Available sources do not indicate any alert or movement of U.S. forces, nor even any heightened intelligence effort to monitor Soviet actions. In his memoirs Kissinger credits himself with having attempted, however unsuccessfully, to persuade other administration officials that the United States must resist in some

way in case the Soviets threatened Israel with retaliation and that
it should take "measures to prevent the attrition of the Israeli air
force should the Soviets introduce sophisticated equipment manned
by their own personnel."[15] However, "most in the government blamed
the impasse on Israeli intransigence" and opposed any large-scale
aid to Israel at that juncture; some went so far as to favor pressing
the Israelis to pull back. As for Nixon, Kissinger reports that he too
was skeptical as to the merits of Kissinger's advice, leaning to the
view that Israel's policies were the basic cause of the difficulty.[16]
During February, too, the administration was faced with the annual
Israeli request for additional military assistance, and it soon became
evident that there was general reluctance among policymakers to
undertake new arms deliveries. At the end of the month, annoyed
by demonstrations in several U.S. cities against visiting French
president Pompidou by protestors who objected to his recent arms
deal with Libya, Nixon directed that consideration of the Israeli
arms package be deferred indefinitely.[17]

Ample indications, it may be surmised, were available to Soviet
intelligence that the administration was not preparing forceful action
in the event of the introduction of Soviet air defense forces into
Egypt. Nonetheless, Moscow moved cautiously, trying once again to
persuade Nixon to force a cessation of Israel's air attacks and to
further reduce any risk of a U.S. overreaction to Soviet intervention.
On March 11 Ambassador Dobrynin told Rogers that the Soviet
Union had been able to obtain political concessions from Nasser in
return for new arms shipments then arriving in Egypt.[18] And on
March 10 Dobrynin had finally responded to Kissinger's warning of
February 10 that the United States would not ignore the introduction
of Soviet combat forces in Egypt. Dobrynin took what appeared to
be a conciliatory position, no doubt to head off any move toward
a harder U.S. position. A de facto cease-fire could be arranged, the
Soviet ambassador indicated, if the Israelis could be persuaded to
halt their air encroachments against Egypt. Coupled with this proposal
was an offer to resume bilateral talks with the United States aiming
toward an overall Middle East settlement, at which, Dobrynin stated,
the Soviet Union was prepared to make important concessions.
Kissinger does not indicate what response he made to Dobrynin's
conditional cease-fire offer and seems to have failed to note that the
Soviets required cessation of Israel's air attacks as a precondition
also to the offer of bilateral talks. So impressed was Kissinger with
the new Soviet interest in a possible overall settlement, he confesses,
that he failed to notice that Dobrynin had not really responded to
the earlier U.S. warning against introduction of Soviet combat per-

sonnel. Kissinger's account indicates not only that he had failed to grasp the significance of Dobrynin's emphasis that a de facto cease-fire was dependent on a cessation of the Israeli air attacks but that he had also been taken in by Dobrynin's conciliatory reference to a resumption of U.S.-Soviet bilateral talks. Elated by this seeming turn of events, Kissinger rushed to report to Nixon that the Russians had made a "significant concession" and that "our policy of relative firmness has paid off on all contested issues."[19]

Two days later Kissinger met with Israeli ambassador Yitzhak Rabin to inform him of Dobrynin's cease-fire proposal and to convey Nixon's decision to replace Israeli aircraft losses, coupling this information with a request that Israel stop its deep penetration raids against Egypt. This, evidently, was the first such U.S. request to the Israelis. It followed Dobrynin's demarche of March 10, but Kissinger's account leaves uncertain whether his request to Rabin was in fulfillment of an understanding arrived at with Dobrynin. In any event, within a week, on March 17, Rabin returned from a quick trip to Jerusalem with his government's reply that it would agree to the Soviet de facto cease-fire proposal provided that the United States double the figure for replacement of Israeli aircraft and publicly commit itself to maintaining Israeli air strength and the military balance in the Middle East. Before this issue with Israel could be resolved, Kissinger's account continues, the United States learned from the Israelis that substantial Soviet arms, including the SAM-3 surface-to-air defense missile, and 1,500 Soviet military personnel had arrived in Egypt.[20]

Alarmed by this development and fearing it to be the first installment of a larger Soviet military move, Kissinger states that on March 20 he called in Dobrynin for "a tough dressing down. I said that we had taken the Soviet communication of March 10 extremely seriously. We had, in fact, recommended a cease-fire to Israel; Israel had accepted in principle. But at the precise moment I was getting ready to approach him [Dobrynin] to settle on an agreed time for the cease-fire we had learned about the introduction of SAM-3 missiles and Soviet combat personnel. The troops had been sent despite my explicit warning of the dangers of such a step." Kissinger does not indicate what Dobrynin's reply was. No doubt the Soviet ambassador was relieved, if not altogether surprised, to learn how limited the U.S. response to the Soviet intervention in Egypt would be: "We had no choice," Kissinger reports he told Dobrynin, "except to terminate all our efforts for the cease-fire and to inform Israel accordingly."[21]

Kissinger deplores the fact that the administration did not follow up on his "tough" talk to Dobrynin. What did he have in mind? Was the administration in a position to mount stronger deterrence threats against introduction of additional Soviet forces and weapons into Egypt or to undertake coercive threats to induce withdrawal of the SAM-3s and the 1,500 Soviet military personnel? It must be recalled that these developments in the Middle East were taking place at a time when the administration was, as Kissinger himself notes, deeply preoccupied with the Vietnam War and developments there that were to lead shortly to the incursion into Cambodia. Moreover, many U.S. officials tended to the view that Israeli belligerence had provoked Soviet intervention. Besides, it dawned on American policymakers that they could not really object to direct Soviet assistance limited to preventing the collapse of its Egyptian ally.

Even Kissinger himself did not argue for any direct U.S. military response. Missing in his account is any indication that he advocated an alert or a deployment of U.S. forces. Rather, he says, "the proper response to the introduction of advanced Soviet missiles and combat personnel would have been to increase military aid to Israel—not just to promise a few replacement aircraft." Such a step, Kissinger professes to believe, "would have shown that we would match any Soviet escalation and that Soviet military pressures were not the road to solving the political problems of the Middle East...."[22] Although Kissinger refrains from acknowledging the fact, a threat of U.S. military intervention at some point would have been necessary to impress the Soviets. A mere step-up of military supplies to Israel could hardly be expected to suffice as a signal of U.S. determination to "match any Soviet escalation."

Whether the introduction of Soviet military forces into Egypt could have been avoided had the administration been more alert to this possibility and had it either pressed Israel to call off its air attacks so as to remove the necessity for Soviet intervention or taken steps to effectively deter the USSR's move cannot, of course, be known. It is certain, however, that the presence of Soviet air defense forces in Egypt, soon to be augmented by Soviet fighter aircraft and advanced equipment, altered the political as well as the military equation. Subsequent developments need not concern us; eventually, in September, after considerable difficulty and additional tensions, a stable cease-fire was established.

In retrospect, it is clear that a series of misperceptions, miscalculations, and misjudgments on the part of the administration combined to produce unfortunate developments in the War of Attrition that might have been avoided. In the first place, U.S. leaders grossly underestimated the risks of the Israeli resort to deep penetration raids. The administration condoned, if it did not tacitly support, this major escalation of Israeli war objectives and strategy. Kissinger and other officials appear to have discounted the possibility of any effective Soviet response to the Israeli move. Washington also appears to have underestimated the severe impact of Israel's deep penetration raids and the pressure Nasser's desperate situation in turn would generate for Soviet intervention. On the contrary, Kissinger took pleasure in anticipating that the Israeli air raids would demonstrate to the Egyptian leader that his superpower ally could not render effective assistance and that this lesson would lead Nasser eventually to contemplate a rapprochement with the United States once he realized that the United States was the only power possessing adequate diplomatic leverage vis-à-vis Israel. Kissinger, Nixon, and other U.S. officials did not take seriously or attempt to clarify Kosygin's veiled warning that the Soviets would intervene if the United States did not force the Israelis to stop their deep penetration air attacks. Afterward, most U.S. officials understood that Israel's escalation of the air war had provoked Soviet intervention; but at the time they failed to perceive that Israel's action might constitute just such a provocation, and they failed to act quickly and decisively to persuade the Israelis to call off the deep penetration air attacks.

Even though the opportunity to prevent Soviet intervention by removing the provocation was missed or shunted aside, U.S. officials might still have deterred the Soviets by generating credible threats of a strong U.S. response. Certainly the Soviet Union, though it was highly motivated to support its endangered Egyptian ally, proceeded cautiously, as it usually does, to monitor and control the risks of its intervention. If U.S. leaders had squarely faced the fact that the United States would not want to take measures strong enough to deter Soviet intervention, U.S. policymakers would have had to conclude that the only alternative was to exert sufficient pressure on the Israelis to make them call off their air attacks. By the time U.S. policymakers realized that the latter option was their only choice, it was too late for them to implement their decision. In part the reason for their failure was that the threat of Soviet intervention was not taken seriously enough until it was rather late to draw the proper implications for U.S. policy towards Israel's war strategy. And in part, one may assume, Washington shied away from recognizing the need to undertake coercive pressure against Israel, a step that almost surely would have generated controversy within the administration and among the public.

For all these reasons, Washington failed to take seriously the threat of Soviet intervention, and the opportunity to avoid that step was missed. This case is a sobering example, therefore, of the inability of the two superpowers to prevent their involvement in a third-area conflict from escalating into a confrontation. At the same time the case illustrates the difficulties of establishing ad hoc ground rules for limiting U.S.-Soviet competition. Moscow's military intervention in the War of Attrition was an important new departure in Soviet foreign policy. It set a precedent that enhanced the credibility of Brezhnev's threat two years later to intervene in the Arab-Israeli war of October 1973. And the successful intervention of 1970 no doubt encouraged Soviet leaders to believe that the growing global reach of their military forces would provide new opportunities for their foreign policy in the future.

The Struggle for Angola, 1975

Developments in Angola during 1975, it is generally agreed,[23] constituted a particularly important instance of the failure of the United States and the Soviet Union to manage their rivalry so as to avoid a confrontation. Even though the ensuing crisis did not entail the danger of war between the superpowers, it was nonetheless highly damaging to their overall relationship. Why, one may ask, did the United States and the Soviet Union fail to restrain their competition in Angola, a locale in which each had only limited interests? As John Marcum notes, Angola "was an improbable locus for a superpower collision."[24] Marcum's own explanation for the occurrence of this collision emphasizes Kissinger's insistence upon defining the Angolan issue in global terms, an attitude that resulted in an "obsessive, self-defeating preoccupation with superpower global antics. . . ."[25] Other observers have also stressed this factor, and it was of undoubted importance. However, Kissinger's global preoccupations do not suffice as an explanation, particularly for the earlier phase of U.S. covert involvement in Angola. In addition, there was poor policy planning and inept policy implementation that, coupled with a certain arrogance that led Kissinger to downgrade the advice and judgment of area specialists, eventually created a desperate situation in Angola that caused him openly to define the stakes in terms of a compelling need for containment of the Soviet Union. The indictment of Kissinger's policy in Angola for its insensitivity to local and regional realities is well justified; the case has been impressively argued by other observers as well, most notably by Gerald Bender.[26] And it forms a central theme in Larry C. Napper's effective contrast in Chapter 8 of U.S. policy in Angola and Rhodesia.

As Napper implies and as earlier critics noted, Kissinger quickly drew from his experience in Angola the lesson that his policies in Africa would have to be more sensitive to local and regional factors, and he attempted to adapt his approach to African problems accordingly.

One emerges from a study of the origins and development of this crisis with the conclusion that a U.S.-Soviet confrontation over Angola was not preordained and could have been avoided. Neither side foresaw or planned the scenario that unfolded during 1975. U.S. policy in Angola developed incrementally through a series of improvisations and adjustments to unexpected developments. That policy was fundamentally flawed in both conceptualization and implementation. It is more hazardous to characterize and explain Soviet policy; at some point, though it is not clear just when, Soviet leaders decided to seize the opportunity that had emerged—that Kissinger's policy had provided—to "win" the superpower contest in Angola. The temptation to score at the expense of the United States, to pay that country back for squeezing the USSR out of the peace process in the Middle East after the October 1973 war, to obtain compensation for having backed the losing side in Portugal, to outdo and outcompete the People's Republic of China in backing liberation movements— all these motivations came into play when the opportunity arose during the course of 1975 to inflict a humiliating setback on the United States.

From the standpoint of overall Soviet interests, however, the success reached for and attained in Angola was surely an example of shortsighted opportunism. For a marginal gain in influence in Africa the Soviets paid a heavy price; their behavior in Angola inflicted heavy damage on what remained of the détente relationship with the United States. If one assumes that maintaining the détente process engaged interests to which Soviet leaders assigned higher priority than to marginal gains in Africa, Soviet policy in Angola emerges as a blunder of the first magnitude.

It is quite possible that the two superpowers could have agreed at the outset on a mutually acceptable formula for arranging a transition from Portuguese rule to an independent Angola. The formula—a coalition government composed of the three contending Angolan resistance movements—was already available; it did not need to be invented by the superpowers. The formula, embodied in the Alvor Agreement of January 1975, was accepted, moreover, by the three Angolan liberation movements and had the support of both the Organization of African Unity and the Portuguese government. The Alvor Agreement was endorsed and supported at first by the

Soviet Union; Washington's response was perfunctory and its support
lukewarm because it did not regard the accord as a promising way
of ensuring an acceptable outcome.

U.S. policymaking in the Angola case will be particularly difficult
for the historian to describe and explain. There are several reasons
for this difficulty. U.S. policy developed in stages and was characterized
by a series of improvisations and adjustments to unexpected developments. The objectives pursued changed during the course of
the highly unstable internal contest for power in Angola. At the
outset and for some months thereafter U.S. policymakers pursued,
and expected to secure, a favorable outcome for the noncommunist
side in Angola. Kissinger chose to rely on a covert policy of assisting
the FNLA in its internal competition with the Marxist-oriented
MPLA. He seems to have acted on the basis of an unquestioned
and unchallenged assumption that elements of the situation in Angola
favored the United States and that the Soviets would not have the
incentive and leverage to achieve a communist-dominated Angolan
state. When the Soviets responded with additional military assistance
to the MPLA, Kissinger continued his policy improvisation. In July
he escalated U.S. assistance to the FNLA and UNITA. Later, by
condoning if not actually encouraging intervention by South African
military forces, Kissinger made it possible for the Soviets to legitimize
Cuban military intervention and alienated the support of African
states that he would desperately need in the future when he sought
a political solution to the conflict. Kissinger also miscalculated Soviet
motivation; he did not anticipate that substantial Cuban forces,
assisted logistically by the Soviet Union, would intervene in the nick
of time to reverse the expected outcome of the civil war when the
FNLA and UNITA were on the verge of ousting the MPLA from
Luanda, the capital of Angola. Rather, expecting and working toward
a victory for the FNLA and UNITA, Kissinger waited too long in
approaching the Soviet leaders to work out a compromise solution.

Faced in November with a dramatic reversal of the expected
outcome of the war, the Ford administration finally modified its
objective and its strategy. Its major concern now was to prevent a
clearcut MPLA victory. Kissinger now attempted to apply diplomatic
pressure on the Soviets to induce them to cooperate in bringing
about a compromise settlement that would take the form of a coalition
government for Angola. To obtain leverage for this purpose, the
administration attempted to obtain congressional approval of $28
million for additional military assistance for the anti-MPLA forces
in Angola. The request boomeranged and resulted in a congressional

cutoff of any additional covert aid to the Angolan movements the administration had been supporting.

Although a joint U.S.-Soviet diplomatic formula for dealing with the internal Angolan struggle may have been possible earlier in 1975, Kissinger's belated effort toward the end of that year to convert the competitive game, which he had by then clearly lost, into a cooperative U.S.-Soviet solution came too late. As a result, the Ford administration needlessly suffered a humiliating setback in Angola that posed severe damage to the international position of the United States, to the administration's détente policy more generally, and to détente's domestic political support.

Important aspects of the development of U.S. policy in Angola are difficult to reconstruct with confidence. Practically all of the statements Kissinger has made by way of describing and explaining the developments of the administration's policy were made *after* the unexpected Cuban intervention in November confronted the United States with a losing situation. Much of what Kissinger then said about the origins and development of his policy was influenced by the requirements of the "damage-limiting" strategy he hastily improvised in November and December, which will be described later in this chapter. There was a tendency in his statements, for example, to obscure the fact that the administration moderated its objectives and modified its strategy in Angola after the large-scale Cuban intervention took place. The administration's statements thereafter were shaped by a need to justify policies that had unexpectedly led to defeat and to deflect blame away from itself. Besides, the trauma of policy failure itself no doubt resulted in an unconscious tendency to repress the recollection of erroneous assumptions, calculations, and expectations that had accompanied the development of policy up to that point. We turn now to a more detailed analysis of the development of U.S. policy in Angola.

The U.S. Decision to Give Covert Support
to the FNLA in January 1975

The coup in Portugal by the Armed Forces Movement in April 1974 brought into power a regime that committed itself to liquidating its colonial possessions in Africa. Guinea-Bissau was granted independence in September, and in Mozambique the independence movement, FRELIMO, took control at about the same time. The policy of the United States with respect to these two developments was one of noninterference; indeed, little by way of an alternative was realistically available since the socialist-oriented liberation movements in these two colonies had no important internal rivals. The situation was otherwise, however, in Angola, where the Marxist-oriented MPLA not only was quite weak but was contested by two nonsocialist independence movements, the FNLA and UNITA. The Portuguese government's efforts to bring about an orderly transition to independence took the form of a plan for a transitional coalition government to be composed of these three rival movements. Portuguese authorities themselves would also participate in the transition, and, according to the Alvor Agreement signed by all the parties on January 15, Angola would become independent on November 11, 1975. This plan had the backing of the Organization of African States, but some of that group's member states actively favored one or the other of the Angolan movements. In fact, each of these numerically weak, poorly armed and trained liberation movements had been drawing support for its struggle against the Portuguese for a number of years from outside sources, both from other African states and from the Soviet Union, the People's Republic of China, the United States, and, in due course, from South Africa. We need not concern ourselves here with the details of the complex involvement of outside actors as events unfolded before and after the Alvor Agreement.[27]

The strong ideological and other differences that divided the three Angolan movements provided ample basis for concern as to the viability of the coalition government and its future once Angola achieved independence in November. Not surprisingly, the external backers of the MPLA, the FNLA, and UNITA moved to strengthen them so that they could compete effectively in the jockeying for power that was very likely to take place.

As for the United States, in late January, within two weeks of the signing of the Alvor Agreements, the high-level 40 Committee for covert operations approved a CIA request to channel $300,000 to the FNLA to enable it to strengthen its political organization.[28] This decision was made almost casually, as a routine matter, in part because of past ties with the FNLA, and certainly without any apprehension whatsoever that it might prove to be the first step on a slippery slope. Roger Morris, at the time Kissinger's specialist on Africa, has provided the most detailed account of the 40 Committee's decision. Morris states that the CIA request was routinely approved.[29] As several top U.S. officials interviewed for this study recalled, at that time no one in the administration expected or wanted a big brouhaha over Angola. Indeed, Angola attracted a very low level of attention among high-level foreign policy officials in Washington, who were mainly preoccupied by Vietnam, the danger of communism in Portugal, the Helsinki conference, and other issues.

Compared to the importance of the stakes in Portugal, Angola was a sideshow, and it would remain so for much of 1975 until the quite unexpected cycle of escalating involvement resulted in a crisis. The United States had no vital interests at stake in Angola, and neither did the Soviet Union. U.S. policymaking for Angola was marked by a notable lack of careful planning, only sporadic high-level attention, and remarkably loose policy implementation.

Another ranking official interviewed for this study, agreeing that the January decision was a "routine" one, recalled that in regard to Angola top officials in Washington were more concerned about how Portuguese authorities would handle the transition to independence than about the role that the Soviet Union was playing or would come to play. They were worried particularly over the possibility that, given the closeness of Portuguese authorities to the MPLA, Portuguese weapons might find their way into the hands of the MPLA.[30] But, on the whole, a vaguely optimistic expectation prevailed. Although Kissinger probably had little confidence that this or any other coalition government containing a Marxist party was either desirable or viable, such concern did not dominate U.S. policy calculations in January because policymakers expected that the FNLA, based in and supported by the pro-United States Mobutu government in neighboring Zaire, should be able to more than hold its own against the weak MPLA.

Hence, it seemed prudent and desirable for the United States to provide covert assistance to the FNLA that would enable it to do well, or even to win eventually, in the competition with the MPLA.[31] This attitude of relative unconcern, if not optimism, was evidently reinforced by the belief that the Soviet Union, despite its having resumed modest assistance to the MPLA in the preceding autumn, had quite limited interests and ambitions in Angola. Soviet involvement on behalf of the MPLA was seen as minimal, lukewarm, and hesitant. Gerald Bender, summarizing numerous interviews with Washington officials, reports that "the general perception in the State Department" as to the relative balance between the MPLA and its rivals "was [that] the U.S. had little cause for concern. . . . An MPLA recovery was thought to depend upon Soviet assistance, which was considered to be unlikely."[32] Confidence in this view of Soviet intentions was perhaps strengthened by the Soviet Union's public endorsements of the Alvor Agreement. In any case, as Assistant Secretary of State William Schaufele told Senator Dick Clark, U.S. policymakers operated on the assumption until March and April of 1975 that the Soviet Union intended to observe the Alvor Agreement.[33]

In retrospect it is clear that U.S. policymakers initially underestimated Soviet motivation and willingness to give enough assistance to the MPLA to enable it to compete quite effectively with its rivals and, if possible, to attain a dominant position in the coalition government. The MPLA, although narrowly based in Angolan society, beset with internal frictions, and relatively weak militarily and numerically, did have certain assets and advantages. Its nucleus consisted of intellectuals and civil servants who had close ties with the Portuguese Communist party and other African movements and enjoyed considerable support within the Organization of African Unity. The MPLA was also more strongly entrenched in Luanda, the Angolan capital, than were its competitors, and this factor was to give it significant advantages in the struggle that ensued.

Soviet motivation to aid the MPLA was importantly strengthened by concern over the role that the People's Republic of China (PRC) had been playing in the Angolan struggle for independence against Portugal. As Colin Legum emphasizes, the collapse of the Portuguese dictatorship in April 1974 initiated "a new phase in the Sino-Soviet struggle." The PRC initially made greater gains in the decolonialization process in the Portuguese colonies, particularly in Mozambique. As for Angola, given the strong position the Chinese had established with the FNLA and UNITA as well as with Mobutu's regime in Zaire, "the cards were heavily stacked in the Chinese favor at the end of 1974. . . ."[34]

The PRC had been channeling assistance to the FNLA in Zaire, which bordered on Angola, and would continue to do so for some months after the Alvor Agreement was signed. At one time, in mid-1974, PRC aid to the FNLA had given it the prospect of achieving military primacy over the MPLA, and this possibility may have played a role in the resumption of Soviet aid to the MPLA later that autumn. It should be noted, however, that in June 1975 the PRC made the decision to withdraw support from the FNLA and terminated its involvement by October. Evidently the Chinese were disappointed with the military performance of the FNLA and its prospects, given the increasing scale of Soviet support for the MPLA. Rather than continue to back the losing side, they decided to cut their losses.[35] As Bender suggests, Kissinger "stumbled into a Sino-Soviet dispute apparently without realizing it. . . . The result was that many Soviet actions in response to China were incorrectly perceived as being directed against the United States."[36]

In addition to underestimating the impact that rivalry with the PRC would have in strengthening Moscow's commitment to the MPLA, Washington also seems to have failed to take into account that growing Soviet disappointment with détente probably reduced its incentive to operate with restraint in third areas such as Angola.

By January 1975, many of the expectations and hopes generated in Moscow by the détente package embodied in the Basic Principles Agreement of 1972 had turned sour (see Chapters 2, 5, and 6). Important benefits that Soviet leaders expected had not been delivered by Washington. Kissinger's success in excluding the Soviets from equal or meaningful participation in the Middle East diplomacy after the October War in 1973 was a source of deep frustration. U.S. policy in the Middle East was not consistent, in the Soviet view, with the principles of "equality" and "reciprocity" that, according to the BPA, were to govern the relations of the two superpowers in the era of détente. Moreover, the promise that détente would yield the Soviets substantial trade and credits had foundered on the administration's inability to moderate Senator Henry Jackson's determination to link détente with Soviet policy on emigration of Jews from the Soviet Union, even after substantial concessions by Moscow on the issue. By early 1975, moreover, prospects for a SALT II agreement also had dimmed as a result of increasing controversy over this issue within the United States, extending to the highest levels of the Ford administration itself. Observing these developments in Washington affecting strategic arms limitations as well as trade and credits, Soviet leaders would have had ample reason for believing that Ford and Kissinger were not able, even when they wanted to, to deliver on the commitments and promises woven into the détente package that Nixon and Brezhnev had agreed to.

In any event, U.S. leaders initiated covert assistance to the FNLA in late January without much concern that this action would trigger increased Soviet aid to the MPLA. In retrospect, and perhaps at the time as well, U.S. officials seemed to believe that because the $300,000 they covertly allocated to the FNLA was not intended for military supplies but for political activities, their action did not justify and would not lead to an increase in Soviet military assistance to the MPLA. But such a fine distinction, even if it were perceived by the Soviets, could hardly be expected to induce the USSR to act with restraint in supplying arms to the MPLA in view of the fact that the FNLA, receiving arms from Zaire (which, in turn, was receiving military assistance from the United States), had adopted a principally *military* strategy to counter the MPLA.

There is nothing in the available historical record to indicate that U.S. policymakers considered that it might be prudent to assure the Soviets that U.S. objectives in Angola were consistent with the Alvor Agreement, that U.S. aid to the FNLA was limited to assuring it a viable role in the coalition government, and that U.S. policy was not designed to deny the MPLA a similar role in the coalition government.[37] Assurances of this kind would have been virtually obligatory had the administration decided upon a policy of lending strong support to the Alvor Agreement and had it wished to avoid a competitive contest with the Soviet Union in Angola. Such private diplomatic assurances could have been accompanied with and tied to a request for similar assurances from the Soviet Union.

Overlooked by U.S. officials was the possibility that Moscow might well suspect that the United States was maneuvering, in cooperation with Zaire and the PRC, to assist the FNLA to come out on top in the internal struggle for power. Such a suspicion could only have been reinforced when on March 23 the FNLA, supported by Zairean troops, captured a town only thirty-five miles north of the capital city of Luanda, killing and mutilating over sixty MPLA partisans in the act.[38] As viewed in Moscow, even the modest covert financial assistance that the United States was providing the FNLA for strengthening its political and organizational structure could put the FNLA on top because that party was already in the process of acquiring enough of a military advantage through assistance from Zaire and the PRC.

Finally, to round out this reconstruction of Washington's policy calculations, U.S. officials did not view the $300,000 allocated to the FNLA as merely the first installment of what would be required. To the extent that U.S. leaders thought at all about how events would unfold in Angola, they did not anticipate that they would soon be confronted by increased Soviet military assistance to the MPLA and an escalating arms race in a highly volatile internal situation. As Kissinger was to put it in his testimony before the Senate Foreign Relations Committee's Subcommittee on African Affairs the following January, the magnitude of the Soviet effort and the lengths to which Moscow was prepared to go were not clear to him until later in October.[39]

So it was that in late January and in the months to come, Kissinger let the United States drift into low-level but gradually escalating competition with the Soviets in Angola. At various times en route to the debacle in November he appears to have believed that various asymmetries in the situation either already favored the United States or could easily be made to do so and that he would in the end secure a highly favorable, certainly a quite acceptable, outcome to the Angolan struggle. Indeed, Kissinger seems not to have seriously entertained the alternative of seeking a timely understanding with the Soviets to head off further escalation and to work for a compromise solution until catastrophe loomed in late October–early November.

The July Decision for Military Assistance
To FNLA and UNITA

In the spring of 1975 it became evident to Washington that the Soviets had stepped up military supplies to the MPLA and that this support had enabled the MPLA to turn back the challenge from the FNLA and to mount effective counteroffensives in May and June. The FNLA was evicted from Luanda, and the transitional government collapsed. Under pressure from the Organization of African Unity (OAU) the three Angolan liberation movements renewed in June their earlier agreement to form a coalition government, but this accord proved short-lived, and Angola was plunged once again into civil conflict.

Under strong pressure from Zaire and Zambia to give more support to the FNLA and also to initiate assistance to UNITA, Washington undertook a review of the Angolan situation and considered its options. As early as May 1 the new assistant secretary of state for African affairs, Nathaniel Davis, in a memo to Kissinger, cautioned against initiating aid to UNITA leader Savimbi, warning that U.S. assistance could not long be kept secret and expressing concern over a possible link between Savimbi and South Africa. Davis also expressed concern that the United States could soon find itself drawn deeper into the internal conflict. An interagency National Security Council task force on Angola submitted a report on June 13 that strongly opposed military intervention and came out in favor of an attempt to achieve a peaceful solution through diplomatic and political measures. The task force also recommended that the Soviet Union be approached through diplomatic channels and urged support for a U.N. or OAU mediation effort. Such a diplomatic option, the task force report argued, would reduce the likelihood that Soviet arms would determine the outcome and avoid the danger of a superpower confrontation. The report argued against sending covert military supplies into Angola because such an action, it warned, would commit U.S. prestige in a situation whose outcome was in doubt and risk public exposure of U.S. involvement with highly adverse domestic political consequences. In a later memorandum of July 12 Davis continued to argue against covert intervention on the grounds that it would be ineffectual and would lead to further escalation; he called attention to the fact that the CIA itself had noted that the Soviets could escalate the level of military aid more readily than could the United States and, hence, that unless Washington was prepared to go as far as necessary, it stood to lose out in Angola.[40] This was a clear and explicit warning that in the competition with the Soviets in Angola the United States lacked escalation dominance and would find it difficult to establish favorable ground rules.

Despite the task force's strong recommendations, President Ford and Secretary of State Kissinger in the end decided to provide $30 million in military assistance to the FNLA and UNITA. It is important to take note of the domestic political context in which this decision was made, for it may well have strongly reinforced the existing disposition to contest the Soviets in Angola and constrained consideration of alternatives. During the spring the administration had been preoccupied with what turned out to be the denouement of the Vietnam conflict. Having failed to persuade Congress to authorize assistance to the Saigon regime in its hour of desperate need, Kissinger and Ford were deeply troubled by the damage that would accrue to the image of U.S. resolve and to the ability of the administration to conduct a vigorous foreign policy. However, shortly after the collapse of the South Vietnamese government, the administration was heartened and fortified by the strong congressional and public support that greeted its use of force to secure the release of the *Mayaguez*, a U.S. ship that had been seized by the Cambodians. It is quite possible, as Roger Morris has reported,[41] that Kissinger and Ford were encouraged thereby to believe that domestic support for a more assertive foreign policy was once again on the upswing, and this belief may have figured in their decision in July to furnish substantial military assistance to the FNLA and UNITA.

If Kissinger's motivation to accept the challenge in Angola needed reinforcement, a subterranean controversy over policy toward the Soviet Union at the highest levels of the administration provided additional incentive. Suspicions that the Soviets were acquiring a foothold in Somalia received a powerful endorsement in early June when Secretary of Defense James Schlesinger, appearing before the Senate Armed Services Committee in a closed hearing, disclosed aerial photographs that seemed to reveal the emplacement of Soviet missile sites in Berbera. The story quickly leaked to the press amidst indications that Schlesinger, dissatisfied with Kissinger's reluctance to contest Soviet encroachment, was mustering support both within and outside the administration for a stronger policy towards the Soviets. There was plainly an incentive in this situation, Roger Morris suggests, "for Kissinger to prove that he could stand up to the Russians."[42]

In any case, the available record does not provide data adequate for an authoritative reconstruction of the estimates and policy calculations behind the July decision to provide $30 million in covert military assistance to the FNLA and UNITA. It would appear that the Soviet step-up in military supplies to the MPLA in March, though it was not expected by Kissinger, was not regarded by him as indicating a strong Soviet commitment on behalf of the MPLA, one that implied a willingness to engage in further escalation, if needed, to assure the MPLA's victory. Rather, it appears that Kissinger remained sanguine about the prospects in Angola. During the Senate subcommittee hearings in January 1976 the secretary of state recalled that ". . . the magnitude of the Soviet effort and the lengths to which the Soviet Union was prepared to go were not clear to us until later in October. . . ."[43] Again, "it appeared to us that the early shipments of Soviet arms to the MPLA were merely part of an effort to strengthen that group so it could compete militarily with the then much stronger FNLA. It wasn't until later that the Soviet arms deliveries to the MPLA seemed to do more than achieve parity with the FNLA."[44]

Kissinger evidently believed that the contest with the Soviets in Angola would remain a low-level covert game, one that he accepted with a certain optimism and one that he viewed as carrying no real danger of erupting into a serious confrontation. He and his close associates deemed it quite likely that the Soviet leaders had not yet understood that the United States had seriously committed itself on behalf of the FNLA. It was necessary to make that commitment clear now. The Soviets must be sent a signal of the United States' resolve to oppose an MPLA victory in the internal Angolan struggle. Assistant Secretary of State for African Affairs William Schaufele testified with respect to the July decision to provide covert military support to strengthen the FNLA and UNITA that "we hoped at the same time to signal the seriousness of our concern by the decision to the Soviets to allow them to scale down their intervention without open confrontation."[45]

The decision in July, therefore, was intended not only to create a position of strength in Angola for the anti-MPLA forces but also to deter further Soviet involvement. And it is quite possible that Kissinger and Ford believed that their new signal of U.S. commitment in Angola would gain additional credibility in Soviet eyes as a result of the willingness to use force the administration had displayed in the recent *Mayaguez* crisis.

Kissinger's Belated Diplomatic
Conversations with the Soviets

Months later, when his policy on Angola collapsed, Kissinger was criticized for not having taken up the Angolan problem with the Soviets earlier instead of waiting until the end of October to do so.

This criticism, although it is justified, benefits of course from hindsight. Given Kissinger's sanguine view of the situation in June and July and his gross miscalculation of how the Soviets would behave in Angola in the months that lay ahead, it is easier to understand Kissinger's grave error in putting off private diplomatic conversations with the Soviets. Pressed in the Senate subcommittee hearings of January 1976 to explain why he had not approached the Soviets diplomatically when he first discovered in March 1975 that they were providing substantial military assistance to the MPLA, Kissinger gave a revealing if also ambiguous answer:

> Once the Soviets had committed resources on that scale, there would have been no point in our raising the issue with them until we had shown by our actions the seriousness with which we viewed the situation. Having shown our willingness to counter Soviet actions, and having demonstrated to them the consequences of these actions, we could then discuss the situation with some hope of a satisfactory resolution. This point was reached late last year.[46]

This statement was consistent, it is true, with Kissinger's long-standing belief that one could not expect to negotiate effectively with the Soviets from a position of inferiority but must first act to remove the situation of military inferiority and/or to impress the Soviets with one's resolution. What Kissinger skirted in his answer to the Senate subcommittee was the precise objective he had in mind in escalating military intervention in mid-1975. Did he intend that the flow of U.S. supplies to the FNLA and UNITA should merely restore a rough parity between the contending Angolan movements, at which point Kissinger would initiate private discussions with Moscow aiming at a compromise settlement that would accommodate both sides in the Angolan civil war? Or was the July decision part of a strategy aiming at placing the MPLA in a distinctly inferior military position, a development that would enable Kissinger to persuade the Soviets to accept an unfavorable outcome in Angola?

The latter interpretation is favored here, but available data on the point is sparse, and one must reconstruct Kissinger's thinking at the time from circumstantial evidence, such as the timing of his initiation of private diplomatic conversations with the Soviets. It is possible that Kissinger's preoccupation with other matters and, in particular, his trip to the PRC in mid-October were partly responsible for the delay. Be that as it may, by October 29, when Kissinger finally did approach Dobrynin, U.S. military supplies to the FNLA and UNITA had already turned the military situation around to a remarkable extent. Within another week or ten days the MPLA would be on the verge of defeat. Thus, be it noted that on October 14 South African troops (which had entered the conflict covertly) and UNITA and FNLA troops had launched a major attack from the south that soon closed in on Luanda. At the same time FNLA and Zairean troops pressed toward the capital city from the north in a pincers movement. The MPLA was placed in a desperate situation.[47]

But before proceeding we should pause to inquire what Kissinger told Dobrynin on October 29. By then, quite plainly, he had achieved not merely a military balance but what appeared to be an emerging superiority on the battlefield. In the Senate subcommittee hearings of late January 1976 Kissinger revealed remarkably little regarding the substance of the private diplomatic conversations he held with Soviet Ambassador Dobrynin beginning on October 29 and gave the impression that he followed a consistent line in this and subsequent diplomatic conversations with the ambassador. However, it is possible that on October 29, confident that U.S. assistance and the South African intervention had decisively tipped the scales against the MPLA, Kissinger approached Dobrynin with the objective of deterring further Soviet escalation in Angola and working out a diplomatic formula that would seal the success and provide the Soviets with an exit from a losing situation. Kissinger may indeed have proposed, as he claimed to have done in the Senate subcommittee hearings, that both powers cease supplying arms to the Angolan combatants. Given the military advantage that the anti-MPLA forces had now gained on the battlefield, the ground rules for deescalating superpower involvement that Kissinger proposed were clearly advantageous to the United States. "Since October," Kissinger stated at one point in the hearings, "we have consistently offered to stop all military supplies on our side, provided all other countries would do the same thing, and have made repeated proposals for an end of all foreign military intervention."[48]

It is also possible that Kissinger finally went to Dobrynin on October 29 out of concern lest the military advantage and the prospect of a favorable outcome be jeopardized by an incipient Soviet escalation of the ground rules. Thus, Kissinger may have received intelligence indications[49] that a substantial augmentation of Cuban military forces was underway and that it was urgent to try to head off this significant escalation by dealing with the Soviets. If so, then quite obviously Kissinger failed to deter the Soviets or to persuade them not to engage in this important counterescalation.

It is also possible that the line Kissinger took and the proposals he made in diplomatic conversations with the Soviets changed substantially after his initial conversation with Dobrynin on October 29. It was only some days later, in early and mid-November, that the MPLA, with the assistance of a new influx of Cuban troops and Soviet heavy weapons, dramatically and decisively reversed the battlefield situation, setting into motion developments that were to lead to an eventual victory for the MPLA.

Kissinger's Complex "Damage-Limitation" Strategy:
November-December 1975

In November Kissinger was suddenly faced with the prospect of a humiliating and highly damaging collapse of his Angolan policy. The effort to compete in Angola by furnishing limited covert support to anti-MPLA forces had blown up in his face, and he was in danger of being seen as having presided over a badly misguided, adventuristic policy. The fact that the emerging MPLA victory was dramatically assisted by the flagrant Soviet airlift of weapons and Cuban troops could not be hidden from either the U.S. public or international audiences. The adverse consequences of such a humiliating setback for the Ford administration in the arena of domestic politics and for its foreign policy would be formidable. Kissinger's own personal and professional reputation was also on the line.

Faced with the certain prospect of paying a heavy price for the emerging failure in Angola, Kissinger displayed remarkable agility in hastily improvising a complex "damage-limiting" strategy.[50] What he needed was a policy and a strategy that would enable him to deflect blame for the policy catastrophe, minimize the domestic political damage to the Ford administration from both "hawks" and "doves," pressure the Soviets if possible into arranging some kind of compromise settlement in Angola, warn the Soviets against undertaking additional Angola-type interventions, and also retain as much domestic support as possible in order to continue uninterrupted the détente process with the Soviets.

The first requirement for so ambitious and complicated a damage-limiting strategy was to convince himself, the president, and the many audiences he wished to influence that there was indeed some way to recoup the losing situation in Angola. From the ashes of the fire in Angola Kissinger emerged with a new policy and proceeded to try to convince the interested audiences, domestic and foreign, that it was feasible. Faced with the threat that his policy of attempting to outcompete the Soviets in Angola would end in a fiasco, Kissinger quickly shifted gears, attempting to convert the competitive game into a cooperative one. He now sought to persuade the Soviets to cooperate with the United States in order to work out a compromise settlement in Angola, even one that might provide no more than diplomatic face-saving for the United States. In late November and December Kissinger and President Ford attempted to persuade the Soviets to endorse an agreement for withdrawal of all external forces—Cuban and South African—from Angola. They belatedly discovered the virtues of the Alvor Agreement and the potential utility of the Organization of African States for bailing the United States out from a losing situation in Angola.

"In the hope of halting a dangerously escalating situation," Kissinger told the Senate subcommittee that he "undertook a wide range of diplomatic activity pointing toward a summit of Organization of African Unity scheduled for January 1976. Starting in October we made several overtures to the Soviet Union, expressing our concern over the scale and purpose of their intervention. We offered to use our influence to bring about the cessation of foreign military assistance and to encourage an African solution if they would do the same."[51] In other words, Kissinger offered to persuade the South Africans (and perhaps the Zairean forces as well) to withdraw if the Soviets would secure the withdrawal of Cuban forces. Later in his statement to the subcommittee Kissinger added that "indeed we have formally proposed that the removal of outside forces begin with those of South Africa and have asked—in vain—for an indication of how soon thereafter Soviet and Cuban forces would be withdrawn."[52]

It will be recalled that in late October Kissinger had finally approached Dobrynin to discuss the Angolan situation. At that time Kissinger could still speak to the Soviets from a "position of strength" on the Angolan battlefield; as we have already speculated, his purpose at this first meeting with the Soviet ambassador may have been to persuade Moscow to accept its imminent "loss" in Angola and, certainly, to dissuade it from any further escalation of assistance to the MPLA. After the massive and unexpected Cuban intervention of November dramatically reversed the battlefield situation, Kissinger's conversations with Dobrynin were conducted from a position of weakness. Kissinger was now reduced to invoking the Basic Principles Agreement of May 1972, claiming that Soviet behavior in Angola (but not U.S. behavior there) was in violation of the principles, and to issuing private and public warnings that détente would be severely damaged if the Soviets did not agree to a compromise settlement in Angola. His warnings to the Soviets and those of President Ford were carefully hedged; they did not commit the United States to do anything, a fact that would have been duly noted in Moscow.

But Kissinger's ability to reinforce his demand for a cooperative solution was severely handicapped by his inability to generate credible threats of additional U.S. escalation in Angola. It was perhaps largely for this reason that in late November the administration requested Congress to reprogram $28 million in defense funds for additional covert assistance to the FNLA and UNITA. The administration initially regarded this as a routine, noncontroversial request; it was shocked and dismayed when senatorial critics of its Angolan policy vehemently opposed the request fearing that it would lead to direct U.S. involvement in Angola. Such concerns were not based on mere suppositions. Senators Dick Clark and John Tunney may well have learned of a CIA recommendation that U.S. military advisers be dispatched to the Angolan battlefield.[53] The Clark amendment to the Foreign Assistance Act opposing the transfer of $28 million from Department of Defense funds to the CIA was vetoed by President Ford, but a subsequent amendment cutting off all assistance in Angola offered by Senator Tunney was passed by the Senate on December 19.

The additional $28 million for "covert" assistance was hardly an essential—and in the eyes of some administration officials not even a very important—part of the diplomatic strategy that was in process aiming at a compromise solution in Angola. In the Senate subcommittee hearings of late January 1976 Kissinger had considerable difficulty explaining how the $28 million could possibly have been used in time to enable the FNLA and UNITA to cope with the superior weaponry and manpower of the Cuban troops in Angola. Evidently Kissinger saw it as of largely symbolic importance, as another signal to the Soviets of U.S. resolution that would presumably provide some leverage at least for applying diplomatic pressure to get Moscow to go along with the administration's proposal for withdrawal of all foreign troops and use of the Organization of African Unity to facilitate an internal Angolan settlement. Interestingly, in an effort to head off the Tunney amendment Kissinger persuaded Ford to propose a compromise whereby $9 million would be made available for additional aid to the FNLA and UNITA in return for Ford's agreeing to submit any additional proposals for assistance to the Senate for approval. The compromise proposal failed to prevent Senate passage of the Tunney amendment.

In his testimony Kissinger claimed that at first, in response to his diplomatic pressure, the Soviets had given some indication of being receptive to his proposed compromise solution. He drew attention in this connection to what he claimed to have been a temporary cessation of the Soviet airlift to Angola from December

9 to 24.⁵⁴ Kissinger argued that his last-minute diplomatic effort might have succeeded had not the U.S. Senate voted to cut off all aid to the FNLA and UNITA in Angola. Thus, as one arm of his damage-limitation strategy, Kissinger attempted to place the blame for the failure of his policy in Angola upon the Senate: "Our diplomacy was effective," Kissinger told the Senate subcommittee, "so long as we maintained the leverage of a possible military balance." After the Senate vote cutting off further aid, "The Cubans more than doubled their forces and Soviet military aid was resumed on an even larger scale. The scope of Soviet-Cuban intervention increased dramatically; the cooperativeness of Soviet diplomacy declined."⁵⁵

Right-wing domestic critics of the administration's détente policy were presumably to be assuaged by the spectacle of Kissinger's heroic effort to adopt a hard stance towards Soviet-Cuban intervention in Angola. At the same time, Kissinger attempted to moderate the damage to the administration stemming from "dovish" critics of his Angolan policy. Obscuring the fact that he had earlier hoped and expected that covert aid to the noncommunist side in Angola would ensure its success in the internal struggle, Kissinger attempted to portray the administration as having all along sought an African solution—the coalition government of the Alvor Agreement—through the auspices of the Organization of African Unity and as having consistently pursued the objective of ending all foreign military intervention in that country. U.S. military assistance to the FNLA and UNITA, he explained, had been necessary to achieve a "military balance" so that compromise settlement could be worked out. And the administration had chosen covert means to this end simply "because we wanted to avoid creating a pattern of overt intervention by outsiders and because we wanted to avoid a public confrontation with the Soviet Union."⁵⁶

In other words, the United States may have lost in Angola, but it had followed the only possible policy from the beginning, and, so far as blame for the setback in Angola was concerned, it rested with the U.S. Senate and the Soviets, not the administration.

The administration's failure in Angola carried with it, of course, the likelihood of additional damage because Soviet leaders might be encouraged to assert their new global military reach with similar boldness in the future. As were so many others, Kissinger was genuinely shocked and dismayed by the unexpected magnitude and boldness of the Soviet-assisted Cuban military intervention in Angola, and he was seemingly unable to appreciate its linkage with the earlier South African intervention. He perceived that the setback in Angola would severely erode domestic support for his détente policy and was dismayed by the prospect of additional Angolas elsewhere should Soviet leaders draw the conclusion that Washington's ability to conduct a firm foreign policy would continue to be constrained by the Vietnam aftermath. Rather than seeking to limit the damage by minimizing the importance of the setback in Angola, an option probably no longer available to him in November and December, Kissinger decided to give dramatic emphasis to the potentially grave consequences for détente of allowing the Soviets to win in Angola. This interpretation enabled him to denounce Soviet behavior in Angola and to warn Moscow against attempting to create future Angolas—an important objective of his damage-limiting strategy. At the same time, his denunciation of and warning to the Soviets, Kissinger hoped, would enable him to get some credit from hawks in the United States for being tough with the Soviet Union, certainly another objective of his damage-limiting strategy. "The United States must make it clear," Kissinger proclaimed "that Angola sets no precedent; this type of action will not be tolerated elsewhere. . . ."[57]

At the same time that Kissinger attempted to assuage and reassure domestic hawks as to his toughness towards the Soviets he had to be careful not to exacerbate their reservations over his détente policy. He had somehow to convey that whatever the significance of Soviet behavior in Angola, that behavior did not mean that détente was no longer a desirable and viable policy. Reprisals for Soviet boldness in Angola, such as Kissinger's doctrine of linkage might seem to call for, were not advisable. Instead, contenting himself with verbal protests and warnings, Kissinger on his trip to Moscow in late January turned quickly in his discussion with Soviet leaders to the subject of making progress toward a new SALT agreement. And President Ford, speaking to a convention of the American Farm Bureau in St. Louis on January 5, 1976, gave an explicit assurance that he would not withhold the sale of grain to the Soviet Union in retaliation for its behavior in Angola.

With his foreign policy under increasing attack—but for different reasons—from both hawks and doves at home, Kissinger was caught in an increasingly powerful whiplash. Détente strategy called for a sophisticated use of a combination of carrots and sticks to obtain leverage on Soviet behavior. The exposure of the administration's covert intervention in Angola had agitated and effectively mobilized the doves, who feared that it portended a step-by-step involvement as in Vietnam. When Kissinger attempted to brandish a "stick"— his request for $28 million for Angola from Congress—to reinforce his last-minute diplomatic efforts to pressure the Soviets into a compromise settlement in Angola, the doves in the Senate succeeded in defeating it.

If, as Kissinger complained to the doves, his carrot-and-stick strategy was weakened by their depriving him of a much-needed stick at a critical moment in the Angolan crisis, hawk critics were also gently reprimanded—and tacitly partly blamed for the failure in Angola—for having earlier deprived him, through the Jackson-Vanik and Stevenson amendments, of the "carrot" the administration needed in order to moderate Soviet behavior by holding out the prospect of increased trade, credits, and most-favored trading status.

Thus did Kissinger attempt to put the best face possible on the policy of covert intervention in Angola in ways that would deflect blame from the administration itself to other targets: the Soviets, the U.S. Senate, and both the dove and hawk critics of his policies.

Most of Kissinger's public statements about Angola—including his detailed testimony to the Senate Foreign Relations Committee on January 29, 1976—were made in the late autumn and winter of 1975–1976, so they were inevitably influenced by his desperate efforts at that time to limit the damage of the Angolan fiasco. Accordingly, the historian must exercise caution in relying upon Kissinger's statements and testimony to reconstruct and explain the origins and development of the administration's policy in Angola during the course of 1975. Kissinger and other U.S. policymakers did provide considerable factual data on events in Angola. But because they were defending themselves against the charge that they had led the United States into a humiliating and possibly avoidable setback in Angola, their characterization and explanation of how this situation had developed during 1975 was distorted by a desire to portray their policy as having been both desirable and feasible. There was no element of self-criticism in Kissinger's remarks, no admission that his Angolan policy was in any way mistaken either in its objective or in the means employed, no willingness to admit that it would have been wiser to have followed a different policy or strategy in Angola. The blame for defeat, Kissinger charged, lay elsewhere.

A Missed Opportunity?

It is interesting to speculate on whether the ground rules for the Angolan conflict that Ford and Kissinger proposed to the Soviets in November might have been better received in January–February or even in June and might have led then to a less damaging outcome in Angola. It should be noted that their belated proposal for withdrawal of all external forces from Angola constituted an effort to deescalate the conflict and to establish ground rules that had, as it were, been already violated. Generally speaking, and certainly in this case, deescalation to a lower level of involvement is more difficult to achieve than limiting involvement before it occurs. It was all the more difficult to rewrite the ground rules in December because acceptance of the proposal by the Soviets at that time would have required the USSR both to forego the advantages it had gained and to undertake to persuade the Cuban forces to withdraw from Angola. Not only did the United States lack sufficient leverage—either in threats or in promises—to persuade the Soviets to accept the U.S. proposal, the costs to Moscow of appearing to back away from victory in Angola and of pressuring the Cubans to do the same would have been substantial.

Similarly, had Kissinger given the kind of strong, active support for an "African solution" to the Angolan conflict that characterized his efforts in December much earlier—in January-February, or even in mid-summer *before* the South African intervention—it might have been possible to avoid the damaging defeat that eventuated.

A strong case can be made, then, that an opportunity to avoid a confrontation had existed and that, if utilized, the chance might well have enabled the administration to avoid a highly damaging setback. The case of Angola, as has been noted, has important lessons to offer with regard to the extremely important but also very difficult task of establishing effective ground rules to limit U.S.-Soviet competition in a third-area conflict. Other lessons can also be drawn from this case.

With Angola a remote sideshow in the scale or priority of foreign policy concerns in early 1975, the administration failed to take the crisis seriously enough to do the necessary policy planning—the systematic preparation and analysis of alternative options that Kissinger prided himself on—until June-July. Instead, in January the administration almost casually entered into a commitment, the importance and costs of which were to become known only months later, to secure a favorable outcome of the enormously complex and opaque situation. Within a few months, fueled by a step-up in Soviet involvement that was somehow unforeseen by U.S. policymakers in January, developments in Angola drew Washington further into the quagmire of additional incremental involvement. This time, at least, a well-considered alternative option was produced by the National Security Council (NSC) policymaking system for Kissinger's and Ford's consideration. Despite clear warnings of the risks of continuing the competitive game with the Soviets in Angola provided by the NSC task force, Kissinger and Ford decided on a major but still covert escalation of their involvement. The option they chose to pursue, however, was poorly conceptualized and ineptly implemented. If indeed they had in mind, as Kissinger later claimed, the intention of moving the contest with the Soviets into the diplomatic track in order to work out a cooperative solution once they had signaled the U.S. commitment and corrected the local military imbalance, they waited much too long.

If the option chosen in July was ineptly implemented in this critical respect, it was also poorly conceived. A competitive low-level contest of this kind should be entered into only under one or the other of two conditions. The first of these conditions is that there be a reasonable basis for assuming that one can impose satisfactory ground rules on the conflict, either because there are strong grounds for believing that the opponent attaches little importance to the situation and will not be motivated to escalate, or because one has the ability and willingness to employ coercive threats and/or persuasion, if necessary, to deter the opponent from seeking to change the ground rules to its advantage. Instead of facing up to the need for soberly assessing whether either basis existed for enabling the United States to impose its preferred ground rules on the Angolan situation, Kissinger and his close associates engaged in wishful thinking. They blithely assumed—ignoring reasons for thinking otherwise and dismissing arguments to the contrary made by middle-level officials—that the Soviets had little interest in the outcome in Angola, that the asymmetries in the situation would somehow operate to favor the United States in the competitive game, and that the Soviets would be forced to restrain themselves for fear of damaging their relationship with the United States. Particularly questionable was Kissinger's assumption that Washington, even though itself obliged by domestic pressures to restrict its involvement to covert assistance, could somehow coerce the Soviets to refrain from escalating their own involvement.

In brief, it should have been evident from an early stage that the United States lacked the capacity for escalation dominance over the Soviet Union in Angola and that U.S. officials were taking a great risk in assuming that Washington could establish and maintain favorable ground rules. Without substantial diplomatic support, which the South African intervention destroyed, the United States simply lacked the leverage to force or persuade the Soviets to accept ground rules that would favor the anti-MPLA coalition of internal forces.

Uncertainty as to whether this first condition (assurance of the ability to impose ground rules) could be met need not have prevented Kissinger from entering into the low-level competitive game had he been willing to meet a second condition—namely, that the administration be prepared to accept defeat in the competition should the Soviet Union refuse to be bound by ground rules that favored the United States. Indeed, it appears that this second condition could have been met. The fact that the United States had nothing resembling vital interests at stake in the Angolan sideshow and intended to keep U.S. involvement covert and quite limited appeared to give Washington the option of dropping out of the contest if it could not impose its preferred ground rules and things went badly. Thus, in June-July the United States could have cut its losses instead of escalating its involvement. Perhaps Kissinger and Ford thought that they could fall back on this option should the July decisions fail to secure a favorable outcome. But, if so, they failed to reckon with the fact that their July decisions increased what was at stake for them politically both within their own administration and their own party and in the larger arena of domestic politics.

They also failed to foresee that the involvement in Angola decided upon in July was on too large a scale to be kept from becoming public if things went badly and that the impossibility of secrecy, coupled with the entanglement of U.S.-Angolan policy in the complex web of domestic, intraadministration, and intra-Republican party politics, would deny them the hypothetical option of quietly accepting a loss in Angola.

Kissinger and Ford also failed to foresee that if, contrary to their expectations, the Soviets decided to outcompete the United States in Angola, the administration would find it extremely difficult to minimize the importance of a Soviet- and Cuban-assisted victory by the MPLA. Instead of considering the grave consequences, both domestic and international, should this seemingly unlikely scenario take place, Kissinger in effect recklessly gambled that it would not occur. When the roof fell in and he was confronted in November by the catastrophe to which his policy had led, Kissinger was forced to improvise a desperate damage-limiting strategy to minimize the adverse domestic and international effects.

Conclusion

The two cases examined in this chapter illustrate the built-in tendency of superpower competition in third-area conflicts to escalate unexpectedly, ending in confrontations not desired by either side at the outset. If the superpowers are to avoid such outcomes they must somehow cooperate to control the dynamics of escalation inherent in their involvement in regional conflicts, such as the Egyptian-Israeli War of Attrition, or in civil wars, such as the Angolan case.

In the absence of advance agreement on "rules of engagement" to limit their involvement to a safer level, the two powers are forced to improvise ad hoc ground rules in each case in which they enter into competition. Stable ground rules, however, are difficult to achieve because each side, first one and then the other, is tempted to escalate its involvement in order to avoid a setback and to increase the likelihood of achieving its objective. In other words, each side is motivated to achieve "escalation dominance"—i.e., a set of ground rules that favor its side in the competitive struggle. We shall return to the problem of escalation control in our concluding chapter.

Notes

1. Lawrence L. Whetten, *The Arab-Israeli Dispute: Great Power Behavior,* Adelphi Papers no. 128 (London: International Institute for Strategic Studies, 1977), p. 15.

2. The most detailed factual and analytical study of the War of Attrition is Yaacov Bar-Siman-Tov's *The Israeli-Egyptian War of Attrition, 1969–1970: A Case Study of Limited Local War* (New York: Columbia University Press, 1980). It should be noted, however, that this book was written before Kissinger's memoirs became available. For additional discussion of the War of Attrition see the sources cited in Chapter 7, n. 2. However, all of these studies, too, were prepared before the publication of Kissinger's memoirs, which contain much relevant information not to be found in other sources.

3. William B. Quandt, *Decade of Decisions* (Berkeley: University of California Press, 1977); especially pp. 79–81.

4. Henry Kissinger, *White House Years* (Boston: Little, Brown & Co., 1979); see, for example, pp. 351, 354, 361, 368–369, 372, 376, 378–379.

5. Quandt, *Decade of Decisions,* pp. 86–87. In his memoirs Kissinger makes amply clear that Nixon was not convinced of the correctness of his views of Middle East strategy and limited the special assistant's role in Middle East policy until 1971. (*White House Years,* pp. 379, 558–559).

6. Bar-Siman-Tov, *The War of Attrition,* pp. 81–115.

7. Ibid., pp. 117–144.

8. Quandt, *Decade of Decisions,* pp. 95–96; Kissinger, *White House Years,* p. 560. As noted by Quandt, a full text of Kosygin's letter appears in *Arab Report and Record,* March 1–15, 1970, p. 167.

9. Kissinger, *White House Years,* p. 560.

10. Ibid., p. 561.

11. Ibid.

12. Ibid., p. 562.

13. Ibid.

14. Ibid.

15. Ibid., p. 563.

16. Ibid., pp. 563–564.

17. Quandt, *Decade of Decisions,* p. 97; Kissinger, *White House Years,* p. 565.
18. Quandt, *Decade of Decisions,* p. 97.
19. Kissinger, *White House Years,* pp. 567–568.
20. Ibid., pp. 568–569.
21. Ibid., p. 570.
22. Ibid.
23. This account of the Angolan crisis draws upon a number of published analyses, the hearings conducted in early 1976 by the Subcommittee on African Affairs of the Senate Committee on Foreign Relations, and interviews with several of Kissinger's close associates. The Angolan crisis is not dealt with in the first two volumes of Kissinger's memoirs; it will presumably be taken up in a third volume. On Soviet policy in the Angola crisis see Jiri Valenta, "Soviet Decision-making on the Intervention in Angola," in *Communism in Africa,* ed. David E. Albright (Bloomington: Indiana University Press, 1980).
24. John Marcum, "Lessons of Angola," *Foreign Affairs* 54 (April 1976); 407.
25. Ibid., p. 418.
26. Gerald Bender, "Kissinger in Angola: Anatomy of Failure," in *American Policy in Southern Africa* ed. Rene Lemarchand, 2d ed. (Washington, D.C.: University Press of America, 1981), pp. 65–143.
27. External actors, their interests, and their involvement in Angola are discussed in detail in several sources; see, for example, Colin Legum, "Angola and the Horn of Africa," in *Diplomacy of Power,* ed. Stephen S. Kaplan, (Washington, D.C.: Brookings Institution, 1981), pp. 574–580; Arthur Jay Klinghoffer, *The Angolan War: A Study in Soviet Policy in the Third World* (Boulder, Colo.: Westview Press, 1980), pp. 9–29.
28. John Marcum has called attention to the testimony of John Stockwell, former head of the CIA's Angola task force, in which Stockwell indicated that in July 1974, without approval from the National Security Council's 40 Committee on covert operations, the CIA reportedly began making covert payments in $10,000 to $25,000 increments to the FNLA and that these payments became widely known (John Marcum, "Communist States and Africa: The Case of Angola," ms., June 30, 1980, p. 7). Stockwell's testimony, cited by Marcum, appears in U.S., Congress, Committee on International Relations, Subcommittee on Africa, *Hearings Before the Subcommittee on Africa of the Committee on International Relations: United States–Angola Relations* (Washington, D.C.: Government Printing Office, 1978), p. 12.
29. Roger Morris, "The Proxy War in Angola: Pathology of a Blunder," *New Republic* 174, no. 5 (January 31, 1976):21.
30. William G. Hyland, a close associate of Kissinger at the time, recalls that the administration's concern that the Portuguese Communist party might gain a dominant position in Portugal was linked increasingly with developments in Angola where "Portuguese authorities were conspiring with indigenous communists . . . to mount a severe challenge to the agreed settlement, the Alvor Accord of January 1975" (Hyland, "Soviet-American

Relations: A New Cold War?" [Santa Monica, Calif.: Rand Corp., R-2763-FF/RC, May 1981], p. 32; see also p. 43).

31. Marcum interprets available information on the administration's behavior in January as indicating that it "chose to press for a victory by its clients and a shut-out for the Soviets" ("Communist States and Africa," p. 15).

32. Bender, "Kissinger in Angola," pp. 72–73.

33. U.S., Congress, Senate, Committee on Foreign Relations, Subcommittee on African Affairs, *Hearings on Angola* (Washington, D.C.: Government Printing Office, 1976), p. 193.

34. Colin Legum, "The Soviet Union, China, and the West in Southern Africa," *Foreign Affairs* 54 (July 1976):749-750; see also Marcum, "Lessons of Angola," pp. 413–415.

35. Bender, "Kissinger in Angola," pp. 109–115.

36. Ibid., p. 114.

37. These points were emphasized by John Marcum in his testimony before the Senate Subcommittee on Africa on February 4, 1976 (U.S., Congress, Senate, *Hearings on Angola*, pp. 126–130).

38. According to John Stockwell, in February Zairean President Mobuto and the United States had encouraged FNLA leader Holden Roberto to move "his well armed forces into Angola from Zaire and to begin attacking the MPLA in Luanda and Northern Angola" (Stockwell, *In Search of Enemies* [New York: Norton, 1978], p. 67). The importance of the escalation of the internal Angola conflict and its ominous implications regarding the viability of the Alvor Accord is noted in most accounts. Kissinger himself, in his statement to the Senate subcommittee, referred to the FNLA attack of March 23 as "the first of repeated military clashes" (U.S., Congress, Senate, *Hearings on Angola*, p. 17).

39. Ibid., p. 38.

40. Nathaniel Davis, "The Angola Decision of 1975: A Personal Memoir," *Foreign Affairs* 57, no. 1 (Fall 1978):109-124. Additional details on the July decision are provided in Stockwell, *In Search of Enemies*, pp. 52-55, 68.

41. Morris, "The Proxy War in Angola," pp. 21–22.

42. Ibid., p. 22; Bender, "Kissinger in Angola," pp. 81–82.

43. U.S., Congress, Senate, *Hearings on Angola*, p. 38.

44. Ibid., p. 52.

45. Ibid., p. 175.

46. Ibid., p. 52.

47. There is evidence to suggest that Kissinger may have encouraged the South African intervention. See, for example, John Marcum, *The Angolan Revolution*, 2 vols. (Cambridge, Mass.: MIT Press, 1978), 2:268-273. Whether he did or not, it is quite likely that the two prongs of the military attack on Luanda were coordinated and timed to take the capital city before November 11, the date that the Portuguese authorities had designated for the turnover of power to an Angolan government. For a detailed account see Stockwell, *In Search of Enemies*, pp. 163-168.

48. U.S., Congress, Senate, *Hearings on Angola,* p. 8.

49. According to Stockwell (*In Search of Enemies,* pp. 169–170), in early October the CIA learned that 700 Cuban soldiers had arrived in Angola via sea transport and became worried over the possibility of a major Cuban intervention.

50. According to Stockwell (*In Search of Enemies,* pp. 21, 216), Kissinger's first reaction to the bad news from the Angolan battlefront was to ask the CIA in mid-November to come up with plans for winning the war. However, the agency's secret funds for aiding the anti-MPLA force in Angola were now exhausted. Late in November the CIA presented the 40 Committee with options that would cost an additional $30, $60, or $100 million, whereupon the 40 Committee requested the CIA to outline a cheaper "bare bones proposal for keeping the conflict alive." In response the CIA, according to Stockwell's account, "recommended not only the introduction of American advisors into the Angolan battlefields, but also more sophisticated and powerful weapons." When this CIA paper was read by Kissinger he "just grunted" without giving any answer and shortly thereafter embarked on a trip to China. What the account by Stockwell (not verified by other sources) suggests is that Kissinger realized that the administration could provide only very limited additional assistance to the FNLA and UNITA and that, therefore, he must improvise as best he could the damage-limiting strategy described in the remainder of this chapter.

51. U.S., Congress, Senate, *Hearings on Angola,* p. 10.

52. Ibid., p. 20.

53. See note 50.

54. Whether there was indeed a deliberate cessation of the Soviet airlift in early December and, if so, what explains this cessation remains an unsettled question. It is possible that the Soviet government was reevaluating its position in the light of U.S. diplomatic pressure, as Kissinger and other administration officials have contended. But John Marcum reports that "some U.S. government officials have quietly conjectured that the pause in the airlift was attributable to technical difficulties." Marcum reports that when he questioned William Colby about the incident in March 1979, the former CIA director had no memory of it and could not recall its having played any role in political-strategic calculations (Marcum, "Communist States and Africa," p. 3 and n. 3).

In any event, an immobilization of Soviet aircraft on that occasion would have reflected Moscow's typically cautious manner in situations of the kind, where risks must be monitored and weighed. A similar cautious approach, it may be recalled, characterized the introduction of the Soviet air defense capability into Egypt in February–March 1970. Tht , Moscow may have halted the airlift temporarily not because it was interested in Kissinger's proposal for Angola but, rather, because it was waiting to see how the Senate would respond to the administration's request for additional funds for Angola and did not want to risk provoking the Senate into giving its approval.

55. U.S., Congress, Senate, *Hearings on Angola,* p. 18.

56. Ibid., p. 40.

57. Ibid., p. 21.

10
The Ogaden War: Some Implications for Crisis Prevention

Larry C. Napper

The Ogaden War of 1977–1978 led to a second large-scale Soviet-Cuban intervention in an African conflict and a marked increase in U.S.-Soviet tensions. Although there was never a real danger of a physical U.S.-Soviet confrontation, the protracted Ogaden crisis provided another graphic example of the inability of the détente framework to prevent or to effectively regulate U.S.-Soviet conflict in the Third World. Moreover, after the Soviet-Cuban intervention on the side of Ethiopia, it became increasingly apparent that the entire structure of the U.S.-Soviet bilateral relationship, even in the arms control area, could not be insulated from the shocks of superpower conflicts in the developing world.

The following case study of the Ogaden War is in three sections: (1) a historical overview of the crisis; (2) a discussion of how the political-military terrain of the Horn of Africa influenced superpower decisionmaking; and (3) a discussion of factors that inhibited serious U.S.-Soviet crisis-prevention efforts. The case study concludes that the attitudes, patterns of behavior, and analytical and intelligence shortcomings that were major factors in the failure of the superpowers to reach a crisis-prevention understanding in the Ogaden conflict remain major impediments to future crisis-prevention efforts.

Conflict on the Horn: The Origins of the Ogaden War

The outbreak of the Ogaden War in July 1977 should have surprised no one who was acquainted with the international politics of the Horn of Africa. Despite their common status as two of the poorest

Opinions expressed in the article are the author's and do not necessarily reflect those of the U.S. government.

nations on earth, Ethiopia and Somalia had long been engaged in conflict over control of the thinly populated and barren Ogaden region of eastern Ethiopia. The two antagonists fought a series of sharp border struggles over the area in the early 1960s and had subsequently engaged in a competitive arms race fueled by the unresolved dispute. The uneasy truce that had lasted for more than a decade began to erode after 1974, largely due to the onset of revolution within Ethiopia.[1]

On the eve of war in 1977, Ethiopia was wracked by internal violence, threatened with disintegration along ethnic lines, and virtually without reliable regional allies. Between February and August 1974 a shadowy group of young Ethiopian army officers and NCOs called the Dergue had carried out a "creeping revolution" against the increasingly ineffective and corrupt regime of Emperor Haile Selassie. In the early stages of the revolution, the Dergue enjoyed the support of many Ethiopians for whom the old regime's failure to cope with the effects of the great drought of 1973 provided the immediate justification for some form of revolutionary change. However, the young officers of the Dergue had no shared ideological conception beyond their preference for direct military rule and a desire to improve the lives of the poorest strata of the Ethiopian population. Differences over power and policy often escalated into purges and even shootouts among members of the Dergue throughout 1976 and 1977. When the smoke cleared from one of these gun battles in February 1977, Lieutenant Colonel Mengistu Haile Mariam emerged as chairman of the Provisional Military Administrative Council with Lieutenant Colonel Atnafu Abate as his second in command.[2]

Mengistu moved to consolidate his position within the Dergue and as military ruler of Ethiopia while explicitly embracing "Marxism-Leninism." Mengistu's regime was challenged from the right by the Ethiopian Democratic Union, an amalgam of former landowners, clerical leaders of the Coptic Christian Church, and other groups that had enjoyed power under Haile Selassie.[3] A more serious threat was posed by a coalition of radical students, workers, and civil servants, called the Ethiopian People's Revolutionary party, which was skeptical of the Dergue's commitment to socialism and demanded a return to civilian rule. Conflict between the Dergue and its internal opposition escalated into a bloody cycle of assassination and reprisal that reached crisis proportions during 1977. Thus, throughout the crisis with Somalia over the Ogaden, Mengistu's hold on power in Addis Ababa was threatened by conflict within the Dergue itself and a virtual civil war in urban areas between the military regime and its internal opposition.[4]

The regime in Addis Ababa also confronted secessionist movements in border areas that threatened the disintegration of the Ethiopian empire. In Eritrea, a secessionist movement of impressive size, strength, and organizational ability appeared to be on the verge of establishing the region's independence. The loss of the Red Sea littoral province of Eritrea would have deprived Ethiopia of its only access to the sea and established a compelling precedent for other ethnic groups seeking to break away from Ethiopia's multinational empire.[5] Among the areas most likely to join Eritrea in secession was the Ogaden, which was inhabited almost entirely by nomads of Somali ethnic origin. Despite its virtually homogeneous Somali population, the Ogaden had been incorporated into Ethiopia as a result of colonial settlements among the Ethiopians, British, French, and Italians at the end of the nineteenth century. Throughout the early 1970s, the indigenous Western Somali Liberation Front conducted a low-level insurgency against Ethiopian rule, but, more importantly, the Ogaden question had been at the root of a longstanding confrontation between Ethiopia and the Somali Democratic Republic.[6]

By contrast with Ethiopia's long history of political independence, the Somali Democratic Republic achieved its independence only in 1960 with the merger of Italian and British Somaliland. However, the Somali people remained divided, with important segments in the Ogaden region of Ethiopia, the French colonial territory of the Afars and the Issas (Djibouti), and the northeastern province of Kenya. The most important national objective of Somalia, enshrined in its constitution and symbolized by the five-pointed star on its national flag, was the unification of all ethnic Somalis within a "Greater Somalia." Thus, Somali nationalism came to represent a threat to the territorial integrity of Ethiopia and Kenya and to the prospects for independence of tiny Djibouti.[7]

Since a bloodless military coup in September 1969, President Mohamed Siad Barre had held power in Somalia.[8] Siad Barre's rhetorical commitment to "scientific socialism" was shaped by his preference for one-man rule and Somalia's Islamic heritage, but by 1977 the military regime had made some progress in dealing with Somalia's overwhelming economic problems. Despite his dictatorial style, Siad Barre's hold on power was tenuous, and it depended upon his ability to maintain the support of the Somali army. The degree of support for Siad Barre among his generals depended importantly on their judgment of his success in advancing the cause of Somali national unification and in ensuring an adequate supply of weapons for the army. With Ethiopia descending into chaos, Siad Barre saw what appeared to be a historic opportunity to achieve Somalia's highest national objective while solidifying his own hold on power. His determination not to allow the opportunity to pass plunged the Horn of Africa into a regional crisis that ultimately led to superpower intervention.

The Ogaden crisis took place within a complex and often unpredictable regional environment. As an Islamic nation and the first non-Arab state to join the Arab League, Somalia enjoyed the support of Saudi Arabia, Iran, the Sudan, Egypt, and other conservative Arab or Islamic states. Radical Arab states, such as Iraq and Algeria, indirectly aided the Somali cause by providing assistance to Islamic liberation movements in Eritrea. However, Arab support for Somalia was not unanimous, since the self-proclaimed Marxist government of the People's Democratic Republic of Yemen (South Yemen) supported Ethiopia throughout the conflict. Ethiopia also received small quantities of arms from Israel, which saw the maintenance of Ethiopian rule in the Ogaden, and particularly in Eritrea, as preferable to Arab control of the entire Red Sea littoral. Finally, pro-Western Kenya supported Ethiopia against Somalia because of its fear that Somali irredentism would shift to the northeastern province of Kenya as its next target if the Ogaden were successfully absorbed into the Somali Democratic Republic.[9]

The relations of the superpowers with Ethiopia and Somalia were in a state of flux on the eve of the Ogaden War. The United States had been closely allied with Ethiopia since the signature of a mutual defense agreement in 1953, and Ethiopia had received more than half of all U.S. military assistance to sub-Saharan Africa during that period.[10] Moreover, the United States had consistently supported the territorial integrity of the Ethiopian Empire, even to the extent of acquiescing in Haile Selassie's 1962 annexation of Eritrea. In return for this U.S. largesse, Ethiopia provided the United States with an important communications facility at Kagnew (in Eritrea) and supported the United States on a wide variety of international political questions.[11]

Despite Haile Selassie's fall from power, the United States sought to maintain its close ties with Ethiopia, and military assistance allocations actually increased during the first two years of military rule in Addis Ababa.[12] However, the Dergue's increasingly radical ideology and repressive internal policies began to cool the enthusiasm of U.S. officials for their relationship with Ethiopia. Meanwhile, the more radical members of the Dergue apparently concluded that more could be gained through an association with the USSR than through a continuation of exclusive ties with the United States. In December 1976, the USSR and Ethiopia reached an agreement that provided for delivery of Soviet military equipment to the Dergue.[13]

The bloody events of February 1977 that raised the pro-Soviet Mengistu to leadership within the military government apparently were the last straw for the newly elected Carter administration. On February 24 Secretary of State Cyrus Vance announced that Ethiopia would be among the first countries singled out for reduction of U.S. military aid because of human rights violations.[14] The Ethiopian government retaliated by expelling the U.S. Military Assistance Group and ordering the immediate closure of the Kagnew communications facility.[15] Relations between the United States and Ethiopia further deteriorated after April 28 when the State Department announced that all weapons shipments to Ethiopia had been suspended.[16]

The decline in Ethiopia's relations with the United States was offset by improving ties between Addis Ababa and Moscow. Mengistu visited the USSR in early May for the signature of new agreements that formalized the improvement in political relations between the USSR and Ethiopia and provided for "all-round" cooperation between the Soviet Union and the Mengistu regime. In Moscow, Mengistu was received by Soviet President Brezhnev and Defense Minister Ustinov; the Ethiopian leader reiterated Ethiopia's determination to crush all secessionist movements.[17] Throughout the spring of 1977, Ethiopia's relations with Cuba also began to improve, particularly after an unpublicized visit to Ethiopia by Fidel Castro in March.[18] During April, two hundred Cuban "commandos" arrived in Ethiopia to assist in the training of Ethiopian troops.[19]

The improvement of political relations between the USSR and Ethiopia and the beginning of a Soviet-Cuban military assistance program for the Dergue placed a growing strain on Moscow's long-standing alliance with Somalia. The USSR had supplied weapons to Somalia since 1963, and by the mid-1970s, the Somali army had overcome its historic inferiority to the U.S.-supplied Ethiopian army. The close political ties and security link between the Soviet Union and Somalia had been codified in July 1974 with the signature of a Treaty of Friendship and Cooperation, the first such treaty between the USSR and a sub-Saharan African state. In return for its military assistance and political support, the USSR received access to bases on Somali territory, an arrangement that greatly facilitated the forward deployment of Soviet naval and air forces in the crucial Red Sea–Persian Gulf area. After a decade of close Soviet-Somali collaboration, it appeared by 1975 that the USSR had no more reliable and useful Third World ally than the Somali Democratic Republic.[20]

Soviet affinity for revolutionary Ethiopia probably began to cause concern in Mogadishu, the Somali capital, soon after the fall of Haile Selassie, but the Soviet-Ethiopian arms agreement of December 1976 was the immediate cause of serious intraalliance conflict. Soviet President Podgorny visited Mogadishu in March 1977, probably in an effort to mollify Siad Barre and elicit Somali cooperation with Soviet-Cuban efforts to head off a war between "progressive" Ethiopia and Somalia.[21] On the eve of Mengistu's May visit to Moscow, Siad Barre announced a unilateral extension of Somali naval facilities to the Soviet fleet.[22] If the purpose of this gesture was to remind the Soviet leaders that Somalia was the USSR's true friend in the Horn, the gesture failed to prevent the signature of new political and military agreements between the Soviet Union and Ethiopia. A visit to Moscow in June by Somali Vice President Mohamed Ali Samantar apparently failed to slow the gathering momentum of Soviet-Ethiopian cooperation, and it did not affect the decision of the Somali leadership to intervene in the Ogaden.[23]

These obvious signs of strain in Soviet-Somali relations were welcomed and encouraged by policymakers in Washington. On June 12 President Carter told a group of magazine editors that he intended to "aggressively challenge" the USSR for influence in areas "crucial or potentially crucial" to the United States. Somalia was among the countries singled out for particular attention in this projected competition with the USSR.[24] By early July, U.S. determination to compete with the USSR for influence in Somalia was extended to the military sphere by Secretary Vance's announcement that the United States would consider "sympathetically" appeals for assistance from countries threatened by "a build-up of foreign military equipment on their borders, in the Horn and elsewhere in Africa."[25] During early July, the Carter administration "agreed in principle" to supply arms to Mogadishu for "defense of Somalia's internationally recognized borders."[26]

Despite their demonstrated willingness to arm Ethiopia and Somalia, both superpowers supported efforts to create ad hoc regional security arrangements that might have headed off the Ogaden War. Moscow gave its support to Cuban President Castro's effort to induce Ethiopia and Somalia to subordinate their bilateral feud and join with Marxist South Yemen in a Red Sea "progressive front."[27] Castro reportedly made the proposal during a meeting with Mengistu, Siad Barre, and Yemeni President Salem Robaye Ali in Aden during the Cuban leader's March 1977 trip to Africa. According to Siad Barre, Somalia rejected the idea of a confederation because of Ethiopia's "intransigence," presumably on the Ogaden issue.[28] Despite Castro's failure to reconcile Ethiopia and Somalia, the USSR continued to urge that the "progressive" states of the Horn bury the hatchet and cooperate to frustrate the plans of the United States and its conservative Arab allies.

Soviet concerns over Somali involvement in a potential grouping of conservative Red Sea littoral states were stimulated by a meeting at Ta'iz in the Yemen Arab Republic (North Yemen) among Saudi Arabia, the Sudan, Somalia, and both South Yemen and North Yemen in May 1977.[29] Soviet commentaries also expressed concern over Sudanese President Jaafar Numeiri's trip to Beijing in May as evidence of the People's Republic of China's support for the idea of turning the Red Sea into an "Arab lake" at the expense of Ethiopia and the USSR.[30] While these ineffectual efforts to organize regional political arrangements went forward, the Western Somali Liberation Front, with encouragement and assistance from Mogadishu, intensified its activities in the Ogaden. By early July, Siad Barre had decided on an all-out effort for a military solution of the conflict before the arrival of Soviet and Cuban assistance to Ethiopia made a successful war in the Ogaden impossible.

War and Superpower Intervention in the Ogaden

Somalia's intervention in the Ogaden was not acknowledged by Mogadishu, which steadfastly maintained that the war was being prosecuted by the indigenous Western Somali Liberation Front. However, the active participation of "volunteers" from the Somali army and the commitment of Somali tanks and other heavy equipment to the war made it clear that Mogadishu was actively directing the conflict. Somali forces were committed to the war in strength in mid-July, and these forces proceeded to drive Ethiopian troops out of much of the disputed territory. The Somali advance finally bogged down in mid-November after a successful but bloody battle for the Ethiopian tank base at Jigjiga. The Somali army had planned to move through the mountain passes beyond Jigjiga to take the ancient walled city of Harar, thereby effectively blocking any counterattack from the Ethiopian highlands into the Ogaden. However, a combination of heavy rains, Ethiopian air strikes, and Ethiopian counterattacks aided by Cuban advisers halted the Somali advance before Harar. After this period of movement, the war settled into an extended Somali siege of Harar throughout December 1977 and the first half of January 1978.[31]

Somalia's decision to fight for the Ogaden precipitated an open break with the USSR and Cuba and provoked the deployment of another Soviet-supported Cuban expeditionary force in Africa. In early August, Soviet commentaries accused Somalia of permitting itself to be used by Western imperialists and "bourgeois-feudal Arabs" in a conspiracy to destroy "revolutionary Ethiopia."[32] On August 7, a statement by the Soviet Committee for Solidarity with Afro-Asian Countries called for OAU mediation and a political solution of the conflict in a spirit of "anti-imperialist solidarity."[33] By mid-August, Soviet commentaries expressed the "serious concern" of "leading circles" in the USSR over the "invasion" of the Ogaden under the "noble pretext" of self-determination.[34]

Despite the escalation of anti-Somali rhetoric from Moscow, Somali leaders continued to emphasize their desire to maintain ties with the USSR. On August 18, it was announced that the USSR and Somalia had signed a new economic agreement,[35] and on August 31, Somali President Siad Barre arrived in Moscow for talks with Soviet leaders. Apparently the Soviet leadership made little progress in convincing Siad Barre to call off the Ogaden invasion, and the Somali leader was not able to convince his hosts of the need for restraint in their support of Ethiopia.[36] Somali dissatisfaction with the Soviet policy emerged clearly in a September 14 warning from Mogadishu that continued Soviet and Cuban support for Ethiopia could have "serious consequences."[37] For its part, the USSR on October 19 announced that it had suspended arms shipments to Somalia because of the Ogaden invasion.[38] Siad Barre signaled an impending crisis in Soviet-Somali relations on October 21 by stating that Soviet support for Ethiopia and the presence of Cuban troops in the Ogaden placed relations between Somalia and its Communist allies in "great jeopardy."[39] On November 14, Siad Barre announced the expulsion of all Soviet advisers from Somalia, the withdrawal of all base rights that had been extended to the USSR, the renunciation of the Soviet-Somali treaty, and the breaking of diplomatic relations between Somalia and Cuba.[40]

Despite his open break with the USSR, Siad Barre found that Somalia's invasion of the Ogaden had cooled the enthusiasm of U.S. policymakers for supplying arms to Mogadishu. As soon as it became apparent that Somali troops and equipment had been committed to the Ogaden fighting, the State Department announced that the United States would not provide arms for Somalia as long as the war in the Ogaden continued. These statements of U.S. policy were accompanied by appeals for Soviet and Cuban restraint in arming Ethiopia.[41] This position was maintained throughout the conflict, despite repeated pleas for assistance and expressions of frustration from Siad Barre. In an effort to keep open its channels of communication with both sides of the conflict, the United States even negotiated with Ethiopia in mid-September for a possible resumption of embargoed U.S. arms shipments.[42] Throughout the remainder of 1977, the United States advocated OAU mediation of the conflict, Somali withdrawal from the Ogaden, and Soviet-Cuban restraint in arming Ethiopia.

U.S. government reluctance to arm Somalia was reinforced by congressional opinion. Representatives Don Bonker and Paul Tsongas visited the area in December 1977 and subsequently published a report that strongly opposed arming Somalia as long as Somali troops remained in the Ogaden. The Bonker-Tsongas report and policy recommendations almost certainly reflected the prevailing congressional consensus on the issue.[43] Thus, congressional opinion seems to have played an important role in sustaining a U.S. policy limited to support for OAU mediation of the conflict, appeals for Somali withdrawal from the Ogaden, and calls for Soviet-Cuban restraint in assisting Ethiopia. By the end of 1977, U.S. officials were reportedly frustrated by their inability to achieve any of these objectives.[44]

The OAU effort to head off the building crisis on the Horn also ended in frustration. The OAU summit of May 1973 had created a committee of eight nations to mediate the dispute, and the committee met in emergency session on August 5 to discuss Ethiopian charges of a Somali invasion of the Ogaden. However, Somalia refused to participate in sessions of the committee unless its mandate was widened to include an in-depth investigation of the problems of the Ogaden under Ethiopian rule. Somalia also demanded that representatives of the Western Somali Liberation Front be invited to participate in the deliberations of the committee. Ethiopia predictably refused to agree to these conditions, and Nigerian efforts to persuade Somalia to reconsider its boycott of committee sessions failed. Unable to perform its role as mediator, the committee could only issue the ritual OAU statement calling for respect of borders existing at independence and maintenance of the territorial integrity of member states. For the remainder of the war, the OAU and its member states could only issue statements repeating these maxims and calling for restraint on the part of external powers.[45]

In January, the Ogaden War began to enter a critical phase as Somali forces launched a final assault on Ethiopian positions in front of Harar. By mid-January, a massive influx of Soviet equipment and Cuban troops had begun to turn the tide, and the Somali drive fell short of its objectives.[46] Cuban and Ethiopian troops fighting under the command of Soviet generals then went over to the offensive and began to drive back the Somali forces. In a well-conceived tactical maneuver, the Cuban-Ethiopian forces chose not to fight their way

back up the mountain passes in a direct assault on the former
Ethiopian tank base at Jigjiga. Instead, they swung south and east
to bypass and cut off Somali forces in the Gara Marda pass and at
Jigjiga. The Somali units thus trapped were virtually destroyed,
although Ethiopian officers later complained that Soviet commanders
had withheld attacks long enough to permit the escape of some
Somali units.[47]

The Superpowers Organize a Cease-Fire

The success of the Cuban-Ethiopian counterattack raised fears in
Somalia and the West that the USSR would sponsor an invasion of
Somalia itself once the Ogaden had been retaken. An invasion of
this type, which would probably have been militarily feasible given
the momentum of the Cuban-Ethiopian force and the disarray of
the Somali army, would almost certainly have led to the fall from
power of Siad Barre and might have threatened the independence
of the Somali Democratic Republic. It might also have enabled the
USSR to attain through military intervention what had proved to
be beyond the reach of Soviet diplomacy—the organization of a
subservient Red Sea "progressive front" and the total exclusion of
U.S. influence from the Horn of Africa.

Whether such far-reaching objectives actually motivated Soviet
policy is uncertain, but the military victories of the Soviet-Cuban-
Ethiopian coalition made such a strategy seem feasible and generated
pressures for an active response in Washington. The U.S. response
involved two related initiatives: (1) the creation of a diplomatic and
military deterrent to a Soviet-sponsored invasion of Somalia, and
(2) direct approaches to the USSR that sought to promote a cease-
fire. The construction of a political-military deterrent began with a
January 21 meeting in Washington of the United States, the United
Kingdom, the Federal Republic of Germany (West Germany), and
Italy to discuss the crisis. The Western powers publicly favored a
negotiated settlement under OAU auspices, and the next day West
Germany announced a grant of $11.8 million worth of credits to
Somalia.[48] Secretary of State Cyrus Vance warned in a February 10
news conference that the United States would reconsider its policy
on arms shipments to Somalia if the Soviet-Ethiopian counterattack
crossed the Somali border.[49]

While the United States tried to construct an effective deterrent
to a Soviet-sponsored invasion of Somalia, public and private diplomatic efforts to end the war intensified.[50] The Soviet airlift of
Cuban troops and combat equipment that made possible the successful

Ethiopian defense of Harar during the last week of November precipitated the first direct U.S.-Soviet diplomatic exchanges on the conflict. The impetus came from the U.S. side, which was worried that the November influx of Soviet and Cuban troops might signal Soviet consolidation of its foothold in Ethiopia. However, there appears to have been little immediate concern among U.S. officials in November and December over a possible Ethiopian invasion of Somalia, backed by the USSR and Cuba.

At the same time, U.S. officials were concerned about the implications of successful use of force by Somalia in the Ogaden for other African territorial disputes. This concern and the belief that an early end to the war would help limit opportunities for Moscow on the Horn stimulated a search for formulas that might bring about Somali withdrawal from the Ogaden in exchange for an Ethiopian grant of autonomy to that province within the Ethiopian state.

During the period between the last-ditch Ethiopian defense of Harar in the final week of November and the Ethiopian-Cuban counterattack that began in the first week of February 1978, the United States approached the Soviets on several occasions to express concern about the influx of Cuban troops and Soviet equipment. These approaches also included requests that Moscow use its influence with Addis Ababa to obtain Ethiopian agreement to the withdrawal-and-autonomy formula for a cease-fire and a political settlement.

Probably buoyed by the successful Ethiopian-Cuban defense of Harar in November and the OAU consensus against Somalia, Moscow refused to discuss a political settlement or even a cease-fire in advance of Somali withdrawal from the Ogaden. The Soviets also consistently maintained that their assistance to Ethiopia was defensive in nature. To bolster this claim, the Soviets in private repeated their public assurances that Ethiopia had no intention of pushing its counterattack across the prewar Somali boundary. As early as November 21, the Soviet media had announced that Ethiopia had "no intention whatsoever" of invading Somali territory,[51] and Mengistu himself gave similar assurances during a December 13 meeting with visiting U.S. Congress members Bonker and Tsongas.[52] Moscow also urged that the United States not provide arms for Somalia or permit arms to be transferred to Mogadishu by U.S. allies in the region.

At a news conference on January 12, President Carter predicted that Somalia would soon call for a negotiated end to the conflict, even though Somali forces were still deep in the Ogaden.[53] On January 25, Carter used the occasion of a previously scheduled meeting with visiting Soviet candidate Politburo member Boris Ponamarev to advocate a negotiated settlement and call for restraint of Soviet-

Cuban arms assistance to Ethiopia.[54] However, by late January, it had become clear that Somalia was facing a deteriorating military situation in the Ogaden and that Soviet-Cuban assistance might soon permit Ethiopia to go over to at least a limited counteroffensive.

At this point, one option considered by U.S. officials was a joint U.S.-Soviet initiative to end the war. This initiative would have involved a U.S. decision to drop the withdrawal-and-autonomy formula in favor of parallel U.S. and Soviet public statements on the crisis. The Soviet government would be asked to make public its private statements of nonsupport for any Ethiopian attempt to cross the Somali border. In return, the United States would publicly urge Somali withdrawal. This proposal was not adopted, however, in part because the Somalis remained unwilling even to acknowledge the presence of their forces in the Ogaden.

U.S. assessments that any Ethiopian counterattack in the Ogaden would achieve only limited results changed dramatically in the first week of February as the Ethiopian-Cuban counteroffensive began to roll back Somali forces at a startling rate. As the overwhelming success of the offensive again seemed to raise the prospect of an invasion of Somalia itself, Siad Barre accused President Carter of reneging on his promises to Somalia and warned that "nothing could now prevent a declaration of war" between Ethiopia and Somalia.[55] On February 12, Somalia announced full mobilization of its forces and for the first time acknowledged that its regular troops were being committed to the Ogaden fighting.[56] Meanwhile, Mengistu accused the United States of "active political and military support of Somalia" and warned that Ethiopia might break off diplomatic relations with the United States, the United Kingdom, and West Germany.[57] Soviet statements during this period warned that U.S. naval deployments in the Red Sea area and alleged U.S. plans to funnel arms to Somalia via Egypt could provoke a wider war.[58]

With the Cuban-Ethiopian advance beginning to generate new escalatory pressures, the Soviets made the first substantive change in their position since the beginning of direct U.S.-Soviet diplomatic exchanges on the war—an offer to use their influence to ensure that, if Somalia would agree to withdraw its forces from the Ogaden, those forces would not be attacked as they withdrew. The Soviets still insisted that Somali-Ethiopian negotiations would be appropriate only *after* Somali withdrawal and that the question of autonomy for the Ogaden was an internal matter for Ethiopia.

On February 10, Secretary Vance told a news conference that the United States had received Soviet assurances that the counterattack would not cross the Somali border.[59] Vance on February 15 repeated

U.S. assurances that it would not arm Somalia unless the counterattack crossed the prewar borders of Somalia.[60] In order to be sure that this message was accurately understood in Ethiopia, a U.S. team headed by the deputy assistant to the president for national security affairs, David Aaron, visited Addis Ababa February 17–19 for the first high-level U.S. talks with Ethiopian leaders since the crisis began. During his talks with the U.S. delegation, Mengistu repeated his earlier assurances that the counterattack would stop at the Somali border, and in return the United States agreed to release for shipment to Ethiopia a quantity of "non-lethal" military equipment that had previously been embargoed by the United States.[61]

Despite Soviet and Ethiopian assurances that the counterattack would not cross the Somali border, Washington was alarmed enough by mid-February to suggest to the Soviets privately that the crisis be referred to the UN Security Council. However, Moscow turned aside this suggestion, continuing to emphasize the necessity for Somali withdrawal before discussion of a cease-fire or political arrangements in the Ogaden. During this period the United States, for the first time, suggested that the Soviet intervention in the Horn might damage prospects for progress in other areas of U.S.-Soviet relations. On February 22, Siad Barre denounced U.S. pressure for a Somali withdrawal as "unfair and misinformed" but indicated that Somalia would be willing to negotiate an end to the war.[62]

By early March, the situation of retreating Somali forces in the Ogaden had become desperate. The collapse of Somali forces in the Ogaden apparently convinced the Somali leadership that withdrawal would be necessary to obtain a cease-fire and avoid a possible Ethiopian-Cuban-Soviet invasion of Somalia. Having obtained a Somali commitment to withdraw, Washington relayed this information to Moscow privately and publicly warned Moscow and Addis Ababa not to cross the Somali border. At the same time, Washington dropped its effort to link Somali withdrawal from the Ogaden to an Ethiopian grant of autonomy to the province. This change of policy was combined with the request that Ethiopian forces exact no reprisals against ethnic Somalis in the reconquered Ogaden.

On March 2, President Carter announced that he had received assurances directly from Soviet Foreign Minister Gromyko that the counterattack would not cross the Somali border. Carter again pledged U.S. restraint in arming Somalia as long as the prewar borders of the Somali Democratic Republic were respected.[63] Although Siad Barre was still reluctant to give up the hope of acquiring the Ogaden for Somalia, the deteriorating battle situation and U.S. pressure induced him to acquiesce in the positions taken by the two superpowers. At a news conference on March 9, Carter announced that Somalia had agreed to withdraw from the Ogaden, and the withdrawal was completed on March 15.[64] The Cuban-Ethiopian attack did stop at the Somali border, thus ending the most dangerous phase of the conflict without a direct military confrontation between the super-powers.

The Impact of the War: Diplomatic Realignment on the Horn and a New Blow to Détente

The short but violent Ogaden War had a profound effect on international political alignments in the Horn of Africa and a sig-nificant adverse impact on the entire fabric of U.S.-Soviet relations. Soviet ties with Ethiopia were cemented by a successful campaign against rebellious Eritrea after the conclusion of the Ogaden War, and a Treaty of Friendship and Cooperation between the USSR and Ethiopia was signed in November 1978. Mengistu's Soviet and Cuban connections have helped him to maintain his rule in Ethiopia and to suppress much of the internal opposition that threatened to unseat the Dergue in early 1977. However, the potential for renewed civil unrest and ethnic tension is never far from the surface in Ethiopia, and Mengistu's repressive policies in the Ogaden and Eritrea are certain to create lasting resentment toward the military regime. Moreover, Ethiopia continues to be plagued by enormous economic problems, which its ties with Moscow have done nothing to alleviate. Thus, Soviet strategic gains earned by timely assistance to Ethiopia during the Ogaden War could still be eroded by the political uncertainty that is endemic to the Horn of Africa.

The United States also moved somewhat belatedly and reluctantly to consolidate the diplomatic realignment that emerged from the Ogaden War. The primary impediments to U.S. action were opposition among U.S. officials to Somali irredentism and concern that a closer U.S. relationship with Mogadishu would be opposed by other African states that feared Somali territorial ambitions. Siad Barre was almost overthrown by a military coup within a month of the Somali withdrawal from the Ogaden, and some Western commentators speculated that Somalia might be forced to repair its damaged relations with Moscow on Soviet terms.[65] The Iranian crisis quickened U.S. interest in obtaining access to Somali military facilities, and this shift in U.S. perceptions was reinforced by the December 1979 Soviet invasion of Afghanistan. After extended negotiations, Somalia agreed "in principle" to U.S. use of the former Soviet military facilities in Somalia in exchange for arms aid and economic assistance.[66] The key understanding that paved the way for conclusion of the access agreement was a formula limiting Somali use of U.S. weapons to within the "recognized international boundaries of Somalia"—i.e., not in the Ogaden or by the Western Somali Liberation Front. This arrangement was formalized in a bilateral U.S.-Somali access agreement concluded in August 1980.

The Ogaden War was another important signpost on the road to collapse of U.S.-Soviet détente. The deployment of another Soviet-Cuban expeditionary force in an African war convinced many U.S. citizens that the Soviet Union had begun to implement a far-reaching master plan for expansion in key areas of the Third World. The fact that Soviet advisers and Cuban troops did not withdraw from Ethiopia after the conclusion of the Ogaden War was often cited as evidence of a long-range Soviet campaign to dominate the strategic Horn of Africa and control the oil supplies of the Persian Gulf.[67] Despite its often-repeated intention not to link Soviet behavior in the Third World with other aspects of U.S.-Soviet relations, the Carter administration began to make such linkages after the Ogaden War. Negotiations with the USSR for a limitation of military deployments in the Indian Ocean area were suspended because of Soviet behavior in the Ogaden War, and National Security Adviser Zbigniew Brzezinski warned that Soviet aggressiveness in the Third World could adversely affect the negotiation of the SALT II agreement. While Secretary Vance continued to deny that Third World conflict would be linked to SALT, it became clear in the wake of the Ogaden War that superpower conflict in the Third World could undermine the entire edifice of détente.[68]

The Political-Military Terrain of the Ogaden War

The superpowers confronted a military and political terrain on the Horn of Africa that was, in some respects, similar to the situation that had prevailed in Angola. The failure of the OAU to serve as an effective mediator of the dispute made external intervention in some form virtually inevitable. Superpower efforts to organize regional peacekeeping structures for the Horn also failed, primarily because the proposed structures could not reconcile or transcend the clash of Ethiopian and Somali nationalisms. Despite Castro's plea for reconciliation on the basis of a shared commitment to "scientific socialism," neither Ethiopia nor Somalia was willing to make the concessions on the Ogaden question needed to make a "progressive" confederation plan work. The U.S.-supported effort by conservative Arab states to draw Somalia into their plan for a regional group of

Red Sea littoral states had even less chance of success because it totally excluded Ethiopia.

As had been the case in Angola, the military balance on the Horn was volatile and sensitive to timely increments of external military assistance. Despite their long history of competitive arming, both Ethiopia and Somalia found that the war quickly began to exhaust their reserves of trained manpower and equipment. During the November 1977 battle for Jigjiga, the Ethiopian army suffered crippling losses of personnel and U.S.-made tanks. With the U.S. source of supply cut off, the Dergue had little choice but to rely on Soviet equipment and Cuban troops to halt the Somali advance on Harar. The contribution of the Cubans was particularly important because of the relative unfamiliarity of U.S.-trained and -equipped Ethiopian troops with the Soviet equipment arriving daily on Soviet transport aircraft. By all accounts, Soviet leadership and Cuban troops were vital to the successful defense of Harar and the counterattack that drove the Somali army out of the Ogaden. Lacking similar timely assistance from any outside power, the Somali army had no choice but to retreat to the prewar borders of the Somali Democratic Republic.

The internal weakness of the Ethiopian regime also proved to be a crucial element of the local political-military terrain. At the height of the mid-November Somali advance on Harar, tensions within the Dergue erupted in another bloody purge of the military government. Although few details of the conflict are known, it appears that Mengistu was almost overthrown by a group of dissident officers headed by his deputy, Lieutenant Colonel Atnafu Abate. The dissident group was accused of seeking to weaken the regime's commitment to socialism and of opposing the creation of a mass socialist political party. It is also probable that Atnafu and his supporters opposed Mengistu's growing reliance on Soviet and Cuban security assistance. After an intense struggle, Mengistu emerged on top and successfully ordered the execution of Atnafu and his closest supporters. Although Mengistu was victorious, the crisis within the Dergue must have been a grim reminder to Moscow that Soviet access and influence in the Horn now depended entirely on the unpredictable balance of forces within the Dergue.[69]

Despite the volatility of the military balance and the political crisis in Addis Ababa, the potential for escalation of the conflict was limited in important ways. Somalia's territorial objectives appear to have been limited to the detachment of the Ogaden from Ethiopia; therefore, no advance into the central Ethiopian highlands was contemplated in Mogadishu. Similarly, Ethiopian aims during the counterattack phase of the war were limited by the desire of the

Dergue to achieve a favorable settlement as quickly as possible on the Somali front so that the Ethiopian army could turn its attention to suppression of the highly successful national liberation movement in Eritrea. Despite a constant flow of bellicose rhetoric from Addis Ababa and Mogadishu throughout the crisis, these limited war aims provided important raw material for a negotiated cease-fire.

The roles of extraregional middle-rank powers and the PRC were relatively minor in the Ogaden War, particularly when compared with the important roles of these actors in the Angolan and Rhodesian conflicts. The United Kingdom, West Germany, and Italy did join with the United States in urging a negotiated end to the war, but only West Germany actually made any tangible contribution to the creation of a deterrent to a possible invasion of Somalia. The PRC's support for Somalia was almost entirely rhetorical and probably of minor significance as a determinant of Soviet policy. Conservative Arab states and Iran did deliver limited assistance to Somalia during the crisis, but they were deterred from providing more aid by U.S. unwillingness to arm Somalia while its troops occupied the Ogaden.

An important difference between the Ogaden War and the conflicts in Angola and Rhodesia was that the Ethiopian-Somali war involved two sovereign states that were members of the United Nations and the OAU. Thus the OAU's established norms for upholding the territorial integrity of member states and the inviolability of borders established during the colonial period played a crucial role in the conflict. Although the OAU could do nothing to enforce its will on either the combatants or the superpowers, the existence of these norms undermined the legitimacy of the Somali invasion of the Ogaden and served to justify Soviet-Cuban intervention in the eyes of many Africans. Moreover, both the United States and the Soviet Union were extremely reluctant to be seen in violation of these norms and the expressed preferences of the OAU throughout the conflict.

The Nexus of African Terrain
And Superpower Policy

Some analysts of Soviet policymaking have tended to view the USSR's activity in support of Ethiopia as a continuation and extension of a Soviet "master plan" begun earlier in Angola. In this formulation, Soviet decisionmakers are believed to have undertaken an enhanced arms supply program and the deployment of a Cuban expeditionary force as a way of binding Ethiopia to the service of Soviet strategic objectives in the Red Sea–Persian Gulf area. By virtue of its timely assistance, the USSR is said to have acquired greater strategic advantages than it had previously enjoyed on the Horn, primarily because of the presence of Cuban troops and Soviet advisers in Ethiopia. Soviet strategists are said to have calculated that the U.S. response to Soviet-Cuban military initiatives would be ineffective and that the risk of escalation to a dangerous superpower crisis would be low. The emphasis in such analyses is on Soviet initiation of aggressive policies, and the impact of distinctive features of the political-military terrain of the Horn is minimized. The conclusion usually reached in analyses of this type is that the USSR is likely to repeat this scenario in other Third World trouble spots, particularly as Third World elites come to believe that an association with the USSR pays more dividends than an association with the United States.[70]

Although such analyses correctly identify Soviet aggressiveness as a major factor in the conflict, they obscure the influence of the specific political and military features of the Ethiopian-Somali conflict on Soviet policy and downplay many of the important and interesting differences between Soviet policy in Angola and in the Ogaden War. The USSR's support for the MPLA in Angola was the outgrowth of a decade of assistance to that movement and a long Soviet association with Augustinio Neto. If Moscow had followed this pattern on the Horn, Soviet support would have gone to Somalia and the radical Arab liberation movements in Eritrea. The Somali Democratic Republic was among the USSR's most consistent and useful Third World allies in the mid-1970s. Certainly the USSR had derived more tangible benefits from its alliance with Somalia than from that with any other Third World ally, with the possible exception of Egypt during the height of USSR-Egyptian military cooperation. Moreover, both the USSR and Cuba had for many years supported the Eritrean liberation movements, even to the extent of providing weapons and guerrilla training in Cuba. In view of this history of Soviet support for Somalia and the Eritrean liberation movements, why did Moscow come to support the unpredictable and embattled Dergue in the Ogaden War?

Soviet policymakers may have made a rational calculation that, despite its current difficulties, Ethiopia would be a more valuable ally than Somalia in the long term. The basis for this possible Soviet calculation is that Ethiopia has a much greater land area than Somalia and nine times the population of the Somali Democratic Republic as well as a strategic location on the Red Sea and in East Africa. However, this view of Soviet policy ignores the alternative option that Soviet strategists had in 1976—that of supporting Somali designs on the Ogaden and the independence of Eritrea. If the USSR had adopted this policy, in all probability Somalia would have been successful in its Ogaden campaign and Eritrea would have achieved its independence from Ethiopia. Soviet relations with both states would probably have been excellent, the Soviet navy would still be operating from Berbera, and an independent Eritrea might well have been willing to accord base rights to its Soviet benefactor. Ethiopia would have been truncated and landlocked, and its large population would have become more a burden than an asset. In all probability, internal violence would have continued to sap its strength, and the United States would have been saddled with the economic and political support of a basket case. If this scenario had been followed, the Soviet strategic position in the Red Sea–Persian Gulf area would have been at least as good as it is today without the damage to détente that was caused by the actual events of the Ogaden War.

The fact that this option was not selected suggests that Soviet policy was not governed by an iron logic of strategic rationality and that it was the product of a variety of disparate, sometimes conflicting, elements. There was an obvious affinity among Soviet leaders for the expressed commitment of Mengistu and the other radical members of the Dergue to socialism. By contrast, Siad Barre's commitment to Soviet-style socialism had always been questionable, and the close Soviet relationship with Somalia had always risked damage to the USSR's relations with other African states that opposed Somali irredentism. The opportunity to challenge U.S. influence in a country that had long been the most important U.S. ally in Africa probably also played a role in Soviet calculations.

The most important factor in Soviet policymaking may well have been the hope that the USSR (with Cuban assistance) could somehow bridge the gap between "progressive" Ethiopia and Somalia through appeals to shared ideological commitments and promises of Soviet military assistance for all members of the proposed Red Sea "progressive group." By the time Moscow realized that its scheme for a "progressive block" on the Horn was a failure, arms supply agreements with Ethiopia had already been reached, and the depth of Somali resentment was manifest. When Siad Barre forced the issue by invading the Ogaden, Moscow's effort to straddle the conflict by arming both Ethiopia and Somalia quickly became untenable. Faced with the necessity of choosing, the Soviet leaders, probably thoroughly exasperated with Siad Barre and influenced by the African consensus favoring Ethiopia, decided to throw their support to the Dergue. With Somali troops already deep in the Ogaden and on the verge of victory, the only military strategy capable of pulling victory from the jaws of defeat was the deployment of a Cuban force supported by massive deliveries of Soviet equipment. Having bailed out the Dergue in the Ogaden, the USSR and Cuba, apparently somewhat reluctantly, acquiesced in a subsequent Ethiopian campaign to crush the Eritrean liberation movements.

Thus, Soviet policy in the Horn appears to have been plagued by overconfidence and an important analytical failure to comprehend the depth of Somali determination to unite the Ogaden with the Somali Democratic Republic. Having alienated the Somalis by its attempt to straddle the Ogaden issue, the Soviet Union ultimately had little choice but to support the Dergue to the hilt in order to maintain the degree of access to and influence in the region that it had enjoyed prior to 1977. This interpretation of Soviet policymaking accords with the evidence that the USSR tried throughout early 1977 to head off a war between its two clients on the Horn. It also may explain why the USSR effectively failed to follow through on its promises of arms aid to Ethiopia until the October–November 1977 crisis precipitated by the Somali advance on Harar and the power struggle within the Dergue.[71] Indeed, Moscow seems to have given up on Somalia only after Siad Barre made clear his demand that the USSR break off its military supply relationship with Ethiopia in order to keep its alliance with Somalia. This the USSR was unwilling to do under pressure from Mogadishu, even if its actions meant the disintegration of the Soviet-Somali alliance and the rise of a threat to the Soviet strategic position on the Horn.

U.S. policymakers also faced a number of dilemmas in shaping their policy on the Horn, including the fact that U.S. military power did not seem to be an effective policy instrument during the crisis. Critics of U.S. policy have suggested that U.S. officials missed numerous opportunities to use United States military assistance as a lever to achieve U.S. policy objectives vis-à-vis Ethiopia and Somalia and to counter aggressive Soviet-Cuban behavior. It has been suggested that the United States did not supply Ethiopia with sufficient arms during Haile Selassie's rule to ensure that Somalia would be deterred from war in the Ogaden. It has also been suggested that the U.S. decision to cut military assistance to Ethiopia on human rights grounds in early 1977 was poorly conceived and counterproductive. Finally, some Western analysts have criticized the Carter administration for first offering to provide Somalia with "defensive" weapons and then withdrawing the offer when the Cuban-Ethiopian forces drove the Somali army out of the Ogaden.

It is true that U.S. arms deliveries to Ethiopia during Haile Selassie's last years did not keep pace with Soviet arms aid to Somalia.

However, the traditional balance of power on the Horn was not decisively upset until revolution and secessionist pressures eroded the internal stability of Ethiopia. It is doubtful that greater U.S. arms aid to the increasingly isolated and unpopular Haile Selassie regime would have arrested those processes of internal decay that eventually gave Somalia the opportunity it had been waiting for. The decision of the Carter administration to cut arms aid to Ethiopia on human rights grounds was obviously an important irritant in U.S.-Ethiopian relations, but it was not decisive. The first arms agreement between the USSR and the Dergue was concluded almost three months before the U.S. arms aid cut was announced. Moreover, relations between Ethiopia and the United States had already become strained during the Ford administration, in part because of congressional concern over Ethiopian human rights violations. This initial deterioration in U.S.-Ethiopian relations took place despite record arms allocations to Ethiopia during the last years of the Ford administration. Thus, there is much evidence to suggest that disagreements over human rights and arms supplies were symptoms rather than the root of conflict between Ethiopia and the United States.

The question of possible U.S. arms assistance for Somalia is one of the most important and controversial aspects of the Ogaden War. Siad Barre may have believed that these offers were a signal that the United States would come to Somalia's aid if the USSR and Cuba intervened on the side of Ethiopia. Thus, the amount of actual arms aid that might have been received from the United States was not nearly as important as the assurances Siad Barre thought he had received of U.S. political support in the event of an East-West confrontation over the Somali invasion of the Ogaden. From this perspective, U.S. offers of weapons to Somalia in mid-1977 probably contributed to the Somali decision to escalate the conflict by committing regular troops and equipment to support the Western Somali Liberation Front.

After Somali forces joined the fight in the Ogaden, transfer of U.S. weapons would probably have had very little military impact because Somali forces had been totally organized and equipped by the USSR. Moreover, there existed no quickly deployable force comparable to the Cuban troops that could have trained the Somalis to use U.S. equipment while leading them in combat. Probably the only viable military option open to the United States would have been to encourage conservative Islamic states, such as the Sudan, Egypt, and Iran, to transfer weapons from their stocks of Soviet-made equipment to the Somalis. Several such transfers did take place, but they did not match the quantity and quality of Soviet weapons flowing to Ethiopia, nor did they provide any combat counterweight to the Cubans.

Even if an effective military response to the Soviet-Cuban intervention had been available, the use of force on behalf of Somalia would have entailed very high political costs. Somalia was clearly engaged in an act of aggression against a neighboring state, and a U.S.-sponsored program of assistance would have been condemned by virtually all OAU members and many other UN members. Moreover, U.S. arms aid to Somalia might have led to a crisis in U.S. relations with Kenya, the only openly pro-Western state on the east coast of Africa. Finally, it is extremely doubtful that a military aid program large enough to be really helpful to Somalia could have gained sufficient congressional and public support in the U.S. as long as Somalia occupied the Ogaden. These considerations appear to have been major factors in U.S. decisionmaking throughout the conflict.

U.S. policymakers were probably correct in concluding that no useful role could be played by an *actual* U.S. military aid program during the Ogaden War. However, once the Cuban-Ethiopian counterattack had begun, the *threat* of a U.S. military program for Somalia if the counterattack did not stop at Somalia's prewar boundaries proved to be a useful deterrent measure. It confronted the USSR with the likelihood of a superpower confrontation if the counterattack were not restrained, thus reinforcing the escalation saliency represented by the prewar boundary. Moreover, Soviet strategists probably realized that any postwar attempt to repair their relations with Somalia would be greatly complicated if wartime pressures led to the establishment of a U.S.-Somali arms supply relationship. Finally, Moscow's Ethiopian allies were themselves prepared to halt at the Somali border because of the Dergue's eagerness to shift its attention to Eritrea. Thus the same measure (threat of a U.S. arms supply program for Somalia) that had served to escalate the conflict in July 1977 served to strengthen existing tendencies toward a cease-fire in January–February 1978.

The Ogaden War: Implications for Future U.S.-Soviet Crisis-Prevention Efforts

At least three factors appear to have had a critical impact on U.S. and Soviet consideration of possible crisis prevention arrangements during the early stages of the Ogaden crisis:

U.S. Fears of Legitimizing a Soviet Role on the Horn. The Ogaden crisis took place against the backdrop of the disastrous October 1,

1977, joint U.S.-Soviet statement on the Middle East. The Carter administration's explicit recognition of a major Soviet role in the Middle East peace process had generated a storm of opposition from Israel and on the U.S. domestic political scene. President Sadat's November 1977 trip to Israel and the beginning of the Egyptian-Israel peace process had then forced the administration to jettison its joint initiative with Moscow in favor of a new negotiating process that appeared to freeze the USSR out of a role in the area. This maneuver in turn left the administration vulnerable to a flood of public and private Soviet accusations of bad faith that frayed the entire fabric of détente.

Thus, there was little support within the U.S. foreign policy bureaucracy for joint U.S.-Soviet efforts to head off a war on the Horn of Africa. In particular, there appears to have been considerable concern among U.S. policymakers that a U.S. approach urging Moscow to use its influence with Ethiopia to help bring about a cease-fire and a negotiated political resolution of the Ogaden dispute would legitimize a Soviet political-military role in the Horn and help the Soviets to entrench themselves in Addis Ababa. In fact, throughout the early stages of the war Somalia seemed likely to win, undermining the entire Soviet position in the strategic Horn of Africa. U.S. reluctance to engage the Soviets in direct contacts on the war changed only after the initial Soviet-supported deployments of Cuban combat troops to the Ogaden in mid-November. This reluctance appears to have been a major reason why the first direct U.S.-Soviet exchanges on the crisis took place only in December 1977—six months *after* the deployment of Somali troops in the Ogaden and *after* the beginning of a massive Soviet-Cuban military intervention on behalf of Ethiopia.

Soviet Readiness to Use Force. The Soviet Union was clearly riding the crest of its successful intervention in Angola as the Ogaden crisis began. Whether it was acting according to a "master plan" or opportunistically responding to events, Moscow was prepared to support to the hilt its new Ethiopian allies and a Cuban expeditionary force that turned the tide of battle in the Ogaden. There is little doubt that Soviet calculations were importantly influenced by the low probability of an effective U.S. military response. Throughout the Ogaden crisis, the United States appeared saddled with an unattractive Somali client and hamstrung by internal weakness in the wake of Vietnam, Watergate, and the CIA revelations. Soviet support for Ethiopia could also be portrayed as based on the principles of refusal to reward aggression and of the legitimacy of defensive assistance to the victim of an unprovoked attack. Thus, the Soviets were able to justify their intervention in terms that were persuasive to many African and other Third World governments. Moscow therefore had few incentives to work for a crisis-prevention arrangement or to press its Ethiopian ally to consider an autonomy scheme for the Ogaden when Soviet objectives seemed attainable through a low-risk military intervention.

Analytical and Intelligence Failures. Soviet faith in the USSR's ability to convince Ethiopia and Somalia to subordinate the Ogaden dispute to the requirements of a joint "anti-imperialist" crusade in the Horn may have contributed to Moscow's indifference toward a possible crisis-prevention understanding with the United States. Similarly, U.S. policymakers had little incentive to seek a crisis-prevention arrangement with the USSR as long as Somalia appeared capable of forcing the regime in Addis Ababa seriously to consider its demands for a change in the political status of the Ogaden. As late as the first week in February, U.S. analysts believed that Somali forces in the Ogaden could contain the expected Ethiopian-Cuban counteroffensive. Only when the counterattack unexpectedly crushed the Somali army and began to push it out of the Ogaden did the United States drop its demands for an autonomy scheme for the Ogaden in favor of a cease-fire on the basis of Somali withdrawal and Soviet-Ethiopian commitments to respect Somalia's prewar boundaries.

Due to the influence of these and other factors, the United States and the USSR never seriously discussed a *crisis-prevention* arrangement that might have headed off the Ogaden War or brought it to a close before the superpowers became militarily involved. Thus, the U.S.-Soviet discussions that did finally take place were directed toward *crisis management* and avoidance of a direct military confrontation between the superpowers. The attitudes, patterns of behavior, and flaws in analysis and intelligence that impeded U.S.-Soviet discussion of a crisis-prevention understanding in the period leading up to the Ogaden War remain deeply ingrained in the respective approaches of the superpowers to conflict in the developing world. Thus, a comprehensive crisis-prevention regime for regulation of superpower conduct in such situations is probably not feasible for the foreseeable future. There may, however, be scope for understandings of limited geographic scope and duration, which could contribute to the avoidance of future superpower confrontations in third areas. The attainment of even this limited objective will require that both Moscow and Washington learn from the experience of the 1970s, including the Ogaden War of 1977–1978.

Notes

1. For a good account of the situation in the Horn on the eve of the Ogaden War see Tom J. Farer, *War Clouds on the Horn of Africa: A Crisis*

for Detente (New York: Carnegie Endowment for International Peace, 1976). See pp. 1–4 for a brief but vivid physical description of the Horn of Africa.

2. A detailed discussion of the Ethiopian Revolution is Marina Ottaway and David Ottaway, *Ethiopia: Empire in Revolution* (New York: Africana, 1978). See also Farer, *War Clouds on the Horn*, chap. 3.

3. Ottaway and Ottaway, *Ethiopia: Empire in Revolution*, pp. 82–90. The conservative reaction against the Ethiopian Revolution was weakened by class and ethnic divisions and by the fact that the EDU at first did not receive significant foreign assistance. However, Sudanese President Jaafar Numeiri decided in mid-1976 to extend his support to the EDU, and by early 1977 the movement launched a major offensive against Ethiopian garrisons along the Sudanese border.

4. The clash between the Dergue and its "leftist" opposition is detailed in Ottaway and Ottaway, *Ethiopia: Empire and Revolution*, pp. 99–148.

5. For a sympathetic view of the Eritrean liberation struggle see Gerard Chaliand, "The Horn of Africa's Dilemma," *Foreign Policy* no. 30 (Spring 1978):124–131. See also Farer, *War Clouds on the Horn*, pp. 20–35, and Ottaway and Ottaway, *Ethiopia: Empire in Revolution*, pp. 151–162.

6. On the background of the Ogaden dispute see Farer, *War Clouds on the Horn*, pp. 49–103, and Ottaway and Ottaway, *Ethiopia: Empire in Revolution*, pp. 162–164.

7. For a sympathetic view of Somali nationalism as an expression of the desire for "Wilsonian" self-determination see Raymond L. Thurston, "The United States, Somalia, and the Crisis in the Horn," *Horn of Africa* 1, no. 2 (April/June 1978):11–20.

8. On Somalia under military rule see Farer, *War Clouds on the Horn*, pp. 93–103, and Chaliand, "The Horn of Africa's Dilemma," pp. 121–122.

9. The tangled regional alignments on the Horn were full of paradoxes, including: (1) Israel and the USSR both supported the Dergue; (2) Libya supported Ethiopia despite the Dergue's suppression of the Islamic insurgency in Eritrea; and (3) Soviet ally Iraq actively supported Somalia and the Eritrean liberation movements. See *Strategic Survey 1977* (London: International Institute for Strategic Studies, 1978), p. 18.

10. U.S. military aid to Ethiopia amounted to more than $400 million in credits and grants, while economic aid reached more than $200 million. The Military Assistance Advisory Group in Ethiopia numbered three hundred men at its height, and approximately twenty-five thousand Ethiopians had received military training in the United States (*Strategic Survey 1977*, p. 18).

11. On Ethiopian rejection of the UN autonomy scheme for Eritrea see Ottaway and Ottaway, *Ethiopia: Empire in Revolution*, p. 153. Ethiopian troops fought with the UN command in Korea, and, at one point, Haile Selassie offered to send an Ethiopian contingent to Vietnam.

12. *Strategic Survey 1977*, p. 19. The level of U.S. assistance actually doubled in 1975 because of Ethiopian requests for new equipment, such as M-60 tanks and F-5E aircraft. The United States authorized the sale of $53 million worth of military equipment to Ethiopia over a two-year period and permitted Iran to transfer a squadron of F-5A aircraft to Ethiopia.

13. *Strategic Survey 1977*, p. 19. The USSR is reported to have promised Ethiopia $385 million worth of military equipment, but actual deliveries were held in abeyance while Soviet-Cuban plans to promote a regional organization of Red Sea "progressive" states went forward.

14. *New York Times*, February 25, 1977, p. 1.

15. *New York Times*, April 24, 1977, p. 1. The United States had already scaled down both the scope of its operations at Kagnew and the size of the Military Assistance Group to reflect the reduction of U.S. arms aid programs to Ethiopia. Nevertheless, the expulsion of U.S. personnel and the closure of activities on very short notice reflected growing strains in U.S.-Ethiopian relations. See Ottaway and Ottaway, *Ethiopia: Empire in Revolution*, p. 166.

16. *New York Times*, April 28, 1977, p. 43. On the same day the Ethiopian government ordered the closure of the consulates of all Western countries and the Sudan in Asmara (Eritrea) and the expulsion of all Western journalists from Ethiopia.

17. *Pravda*, May 7, 1977, p. 1 (*Current Digest of the Soviet Press* 29, no. 8 [June 1, 1977]:10). For the text of the Soviet-Ethiopian "Declaration of Friendship" signed in Moscow see *Pravda*, May 9, 1977, pp. 1, 4 (*Current Digest of the Soviet Press* 29, no. 8 [June 1, 1977]:11).

18. *New York Times*, May 20, 1977, p. A5.

19. *Strategic Survey 1977*, p. 136.

20. On the history of Soviet-Somali military cooperation see Farer, *War Clouds on the Horn*, p. 98, and *Strategic Survey 1977*, p. 19. Throughout the period 1974–1977, Somalia's extension of base facilities to the USSR was a source of considerable concern to Western military planners. These facilities included a deep-water port at Berbera, a thirteen thousand-foot runway, communications facilities, and quarters for fifteen hundred troops.

21. *Pravda*, April 4, 1977, p. 1 (*Current Digest of the Soviet Press* 29, no. 13 [April 27, 1977]:27–28). Soviet coverage of Podgorny's brief stopover in Somalia emphasized the intention of both states to expand cooperation in accordance with the 1974 alliance. However, the brief communiqué contained nothing of the enthusiasm that accompanied reports of previous Soviet-Ethiopian high-level contacts during 1976–1977.

22. *Strategic Survey 1977*, p. 136.

23. The Samantar visit to Moscow received sparse coverage in the Soviet press, although the Somali vice president was received by Brezhnev; see *Pravda*, June 2, 1977, p. 1 (*Current Digest of the Soviet Press* 29, no. 22 [June 29, 1977], p. 25).

24. *New York Times*, June 12, 1977, p. 1.

25. *Department of State Bulletin* 77, no. 1989 (August 8, 1977):170.

26. See speech by the director of the State Department's policy planning staff, Anthony Lake, on October 27, 1977, in *Department of State Bulletin* 77, no. 2007 (December 12, 1977):844–845.

27. See, for example, K. Kudryavatsev, "Shadows Over the Red Sea," *Izvestia*, April 16, 1977, p. 4 (*Current Digest of the Soviet Press* 29, no. 15 [May 11, 1977]:5).

28. *New York Times*, May 20, 1977, p. A5.

29. *Strategic Survey 1977*, p. 18.

30. S. Kulik, "Numeiry in Peking," *Izvestia*, June 14, 1977, p. 3 (*Current Digest of the Soviet Press* 29, no. 24 [July 13, 1977]:21).

31. The summary of this phase of the war is based on the account given in *Strategic Survey 1977*, pp. 21–22.

32. V. Kudryavatsev, "The Colonialists' Strategy," *Izvestia*, August 2, 1977, p. 4 (*Current Digest of the Soviet Press* 29, no. 31 [August 31, 1977]:18).

33. *Pravda*, August 7, 1977, p. 4 (*Current Digest of the Soviet Press* 29, no. 32 [September 7, 1977]:15).

34. *Pravda*, August 14, 1977, p. 4 (*Current Digest of the Soviet Press* 29, no. 33 [September 14, 1977]:6).

35. *New York Times*, August 18, 1977, p. A2.

36. There were several indications that Siad Barre's visit to Moscow did not go well. The Somali president was not received by Brezhnev (he did see Kosygin, Gromyko, and Suslov), even though Somali Vice President Samantar had been received by Brezhnev for a "friendly conversation" in June. The Soviet report of the visit said only that "the sides exchanged opinions on questions of mutual interest," a formulation that indicates that there were probably disagreements between Siad Barre and his hosts. Finally, there was no mention of the 1974 Soviet-Somali treaty. See *Pravda*, September 1, 1977, p. 1 (*Current Digest of the Soviet Press* 29, no. 35 [September 28, 1977]:19–20).

37. *New York Times*, September 15, 1977, p. A3.

38. *Strategic Survey 1977*, p. 138.

39. *New York Times*, October 22, 1977, p. A5.

40. *New York Times*, November 14, 1977, p. 1.

41. *New York Times*, September 2, 1977, p. A2.

42. *New York Times*, September 16, 1977, p. A2.

43. See *War in the Horn of Africa: A Firsthand Report on the Challenges for United States Policy, Report of a Factfinding Mission to Egypt, Sudan, Ethiopia, Somalia, and Kenya, December 12–22, 1977 to the Committee on Foreign Relations, US House of Representatives* (Washington, D.C.: Government Printing Office, 1978).

44. *New York Times*, December 29, 1977, p. A3.

45. On OAU efforts to mediate the conflict see *Africa Research Bulletin* 14, no. 8 (September 15, 1977):4525–4526.

46. Soviet transport aircraft made some fifty flights during the first sixty days of the airlift, which began in mid-November. The number of flights later dropped as more supplies began to come by sea. Soviet and Cuban civilian passenger aircraft were used to move Soviet advisers and Cuban troops to Ethiopia, and Soviet aircraft violated the airspace of several countries by conducting unauthorized overflights. Four Soviet generals are reported to have helped command the Cuban-Ethiopian forces in the Ogaden War. *Strategic Survey 1978*, pp. 13, 14.

47. Ibid., pp. 94–96.

48. *New York Times*, January 23, 1977, p. 9. The Ethiopian government

expelled the West German ambassador in retaliation for Bonn's extension
of credits to Somalia.

49. *Department of State Bulletin* 78, no. 2012 (March 1978):13–14.

50. The discussion of U.S.-Soviet contacts contained in this section of
the chapter is based on the author's interviews with a number of U.S. officials
who are familiar with these exchanges. These interviews took place during
the period 1980–1981 when the author was an officer of the State Department's
Office of Soviet Union Affairs.

51. V. Korovikov, "The People's Resolve," *Pravda,* November 21, 1977,
p. 3 (*Current Digest of the Soviet Press* 29, no. 46 [December 14, 1977]:5).

52. *War in the Horn of Africa,* p. 11.

53. *Department of State Bulletin* 78, no. 2011 (February 1978):21.

54. *New York Times,* January 26, 1978, p. A3.

55. *New York Times,* February 11, 1978, p. A3.

56. *New York Times,* February 12, 1978, p. A15.

57. John Darnton, "Ethiopia Chief Says US Backs Somalia," *New York
Times,* February 15, 1978, p. A9.

58. "Whipping Up Tension," *Izvestia,* February 7, 1977, p. 4 (*Current
Digest of the Soviet Press* 30, no. 6 [March 8, 1978]:19).

59. *Department of State Bulletin* 78, no. 2012 (March 1978):18.

60. *New York Times,* February 15, 1978, p. A9.

61. Graham Hovey, "Ethiopia Sends US Promise on Somalia," *New York
Times,* February 22, 1978, p. 1. See also *New York Times,* February 23,
1978, p. A14.

62. *New York Times,* February 23, 1978, p. A14.

63. *Department of State Bulletin* 78, no. 2013 (April 1978):20.

64. Ibid., p. 21.

65. See, for example, Steven David, "Realignment in the Horn: The
Soviet Advantage," *International Security* 4, no. 2 (Fall 1979):69–90.

66. *Africa Research Bulletin* 17, no. 3 (April 15, 1980):5631. See also
New York Times, January 10, 1980, p. A15, and *New York Times,* January
11, 1980, p. A8. On the access agreement between the United States and
Somalia see Department of State announcement of August 22, 1980, and
statement by Assistant Secretary of State for African Affairs Richard Moose
of August 26, 1980, in *Department of State Bulletin* 80, no. 2043 (October
1980):19.

67. See, for example, Peter Vanneman and Martin James, "Soviet Thrust
Into the Horn of Africa: The Next Targets," *Strategic Review* 6, no. 2 (Spring
1978):33–40.

68. The Vance-Brzezinski division was *not* over whether the concept of
linkage should be applied after the Ogaden War. The disagreement involved
whether Soviet behavior should be linked to other regional issues (the Indian
Ocean talks), as Vance advocated, or whether the linkage should be made
to SALT, as Brzezinski seemed to favor. See Bernard Gwertzman, "Top
Carter Aides Seen in Discord on How to React to Soviet Actions," *New
York Times,* March 3, 1978, p. 3.

69. For a discussion of the abortive coup against Mengistu and the

executions of Atnafu and his supporters see *Africa Research Bulletin* 14, no. 11 (December 15, 1977):4633–4634.

70. For a good argument of this case see David, "Realignment in the Horn." See also W. Scott Thompson, "The American-African Nexus in Soviet Strategy," *Horn of Africa* 1, no. 1 (January/March 1978):42–46.

71. *Strategic Survey 1977*, p. 20.

11
Negotiated Limitations on Arms Transfers: First Steps Toward Crisis Prevention?

Barry M. Blechman
Janne E. Nolan
Alan Platt

A decision to transfer deadly weapons of war from one nation to another is often a significant political act. As Moshe Dayan once said, "F-15s ain't washing machines." Because of their deadly character, weapon transfers suggest, and are understood to reflect, the taking of sides. A willingness to sell or grant arms to a certain government implies support of the policies of that government and the individuals that lead it, at times estranging the seller both from nations in conflict with the buyer and from the buying government's domestic opponents. Similarly, decisions not to sell or grant arms, when arms have been requested, also have significant consequences; they are perceived as indicating disapproval of either the policies of the potential recipient or of the people in charge or of both.[1]

Both the United States and the Soviet Union have long understood the political significance of arms sales, employing them as central instruments of their foreign policies throughout the post–World War II period. Until the mid-1950s, arms transfers to the superpowers' respective allies in Europe were most important, but for the last twenty-five years emphasis in U.S. and Soviet arms transfers has been increasingly on the Third World.

Indeed, arms transfers have become an increasingly important aspect of the struggle between the great powers for influence in the Third World. Arms transfers often serve as the leading edge of great-power involvement in local conflicts in developing regions, aggravating U.S.-Soviet relations and complicating the superpowers' attempts to reach accommodation in the strategic competition and in Europe. Occasionally, great-power involvement in local conflicts stemming from arms sales to rival Third World nations has escalated, resulting in confrontation and a serious risk of military conflict between the United States and the Soviet Union.

Recognizing these complications and dangers, the Carter administration in 1977 initiated talks with the Soviet Union aimed at finding a basis for cooperation in limiting arms transfers to the Third World. But there was more to the CAT (conventional arms transfer) talks, as these discussions became known, than that. Some in the administration saw the negotiations as a way to begin to engage the Soviets in a dialogue about limits on the roles of U.S. and Soviet military power in the Third World, as a way to reach mutual understanding of the boundaries between proper and improper behavior in developing regions. Although the negotiations fared poorly, eventually becoming both the victim of and a contributor to the deterioration of U.S.-Soviet relations that took place during the Carter administration, enough progress was made in the four rounds of talks that were held to provide practical lessons in both the promises and the problems of negotiations to restrain arms transfers as a means of reducing the risk of U.S.-Soviet confrontation.

In this chapter, we seek to describe the U.S.-Soviet conventional arms transfer negotiations, both the progress that was made and the problems that eventually led to the collapse of the talks in 1978; we will do this in the second section of the chapter. The chapter begins with a brief discussion of why U.S. and Soviet arms transfers to the Third World have become a political problem. It concludes with an analysis of the lessons of CAT and an outline of the strategies that might be more effective if such efforts were resumed at some future time. There is also a brief appendix describing trends in U.S. and Soviet arms transfers to the Third World.

Arms Transfers as Political Instruments

Both the United States and the Soviet Union utilize arms transfers as levers to gain influence in the developing world, influence that at times can be used to secure such tangible benefits as military facilities. Sometimes this tradeoff is made explicitly, as in recent years when continued U.S. access to bases in the Philippines, Spain, Somalia, and Oman has been linked directly to sales of military equipment. More often, however, the exchange is more subtle, and often the gain achieved by the United States or the USSR has little to do with military capabilities. Basically, both superpowers seem to value greater influence, or steps that they see as potentially convertible into greater influence, for their own sake.

Often, arms sales agreements signal the beginning of a new relationship between a great power and a recipient. In the summer of 1955, for example, the first serious Soviet foray into the Middle East was indicated by an arms deal between Egypt and Czechoslovakia, the latter acting on behalf of the Soviet Union. This unexpected Soviet initiative was widely regarded in the West as a bold effort to "leap-frog" over NATO and other then-budding U.S. alliances. Twenty years later, the shifting fortunes of the great powers in the Middle East were signaled by the termination of military assistance agreements between Egypt and the Soviet Union and the beginning of the resupply of the Egyptian armed forces with U.S. military equipment. Although the ultimate extent of U.S. arms sales to Egypt remains to be seen, the United States clearly intends, as did the Soviet Union before it, to make arms sales a key element in the construction of cooperative relations with Egypt.

Both great powers see continuing arms sales relationships as an important long-term source of influence with recipient nations. In addition to explicit or tacit quid pro quos between supplier and recipient, dependency of the recipient nation on the donor for maintenance, spare parts, and replacements for its major items of military equipment is seen as a potential source of influence in difficult situations. The arms donor need not actually threaten to curtail needed supplies; knowledge of this dependency is believed to subtly condition decisions taken by the recipient long before such threats would be contemplated.

It is during crises that the security commitment that is implied by a decision to sell arms is brought to the test, and thus such a decision carries with it the danger that a local conflict could escalate into a superpower confrontation. Having agreed to provide weapons of war to a Third World nation, the donor nation must decide, once a military conflict involving that recipient begins, whether to sustain its commitment by replacing weapons lost during the war and whether to make available additional weapons so that its client can continue to prosecute the client's war aims. A decision not to continue to supply weapons, such as that made by the French with regard to Israel after the Six-Day War, is as significant, or perhaps more so, than a decision to continue, no matter what legalistic interpretation of neutrality is cited as justification. A decision to go ahead, however, pointedly involves the supplying nation in a real or potential military conflict. In effect, that decision concentrates in one dramatic moment all that was implied in the arms sales relationship throughout more peaceful times. It is the most decisive taking of sides; the expectation must be that the weapons transferred will be used to kill citizens of the opposing nation or to destroy their property. It is, in fact, the penultimate association of the donor with the war aims of the recipient, and it is perceived as such by all those involved.

When the superpowers are involved, respectively, in arms sales relationships with rival nations, each conflict that erupts between their clients carries the potential of involving them militarily on the opposing sides and thus contains the seeds of confrontation between them. During such conflicts, deliveries of weapons are often hurried and necessarily facilitated by use of the donor's armed forces to deliver them into the war zone. Although this sort of involvement does not inalterably commit the donor nation actually to fight on the recipient's side of the military conflict, it is just a short step from the involvement of the donor's own armed forces in the conflict itself. The potential for involvement in the actual fighting should be apparent; the potential for conflict between the armed forces of the great powers is equally evident.

Sometimes, the great powers can reach arrangements, often tacitly, that can ease the potential dangers of their arms transfer relationships. Throughout the Vietnam War, for example, by exercising considerable mutual restraint the United States and the Soviet Union were able to avoid the evolution of that conflict into one between themselves. On the U.S. side, the United States chose not to interdict the flow of military supplies to North Vietnam, by sea or land, until near the very end of the U.S. involvement. On the Soviet side, the USSR did not supply certain types of weapons to Vietnam that might have threatened the sanctuary accorded to U.S. naval vessels operating in the Gulf of Tonkin. Neither land-based surface-to-surface missiles nor fast patrol boats equipped with antiship missiles were transferred to North Vietnam until well after the United States had disengaged from that war.

The United States and the Soviet Union have demonstrated mutual restraint in other situations as well. In the Korean Peninsula, for example, neither superpower until recently made available to its Korean ally certain types of military equipment that it had already transferred to recipients in other regions. Both powers seem to have perceived the dangers of the situation on the Korean Peninsula and the likelihood that certain types of arms transfers could have had a destabilizing effect on the military balance there, with the potential of implicating them in any conflict that might have been the result. Thus, for example, the Soviet Union did not supply mobile air-defense systems to North Korea, such as those it had supplied to several states in the Middle East, which would have greatly strength-ened North Korea's ability to mount an invasion in the face of U.S. and South Korean air superiority. This restraint made it possible for the United States, at least through 1980, to resist domestic pressures and South Korean requests for the transfer of the most advanced models of U.S. fighter aircraft. In turn, this U.S. restraint permitted the Soviets to resist North Korean demands for both mobile air defenses and advanced fighter aircraft of their own. Also, neither the United States nor the Soviet Union has been willing to supply surface-to-surface missiles to their respective clients on the Korean Peninsula, except for the shortest-range weapons of strictly tactical utility. These tacit arrangements existed throughout the 1970s, although they now seem likely to erode because of the Reagan administration's decision early in 1981 to sell F-16s to Korea.

At other times and in other situations, circumstances, ambition, and perceptions of national interest have combined to make arms sales relationships evolve into dangerous confrontations between the superpowers. More often than not, these situations seem to take place in the Middle East. From 1967 through 1973 there was a clear pattern of escalating involvement of the superpowers in four crises in the Middle East, each of which contained the potential for conflict between them.[2] In 1973 both superpowers took actions that brought them closer to actual involvement in the fighting than had ever been the case previously.

Although the Soviets had denied certain types of weapons[3] to both Egypt and Syria prior to the 1973 war, when hostilities broke out massive arms deliveries were quickly initiated. These deliveries continued throughout the war and were raised to such high proportions that they clearly implied continued Soviet support to and encour-agement of the belligerents. When Israeli air strikes on Syrian ports damaged Soviet merchant ships delivering munitions, the Soviet navy was deployed along the air and sea routes between Eastern Europe and the Middle East in such a fashion as to suggest Soviet willingness actively to defend these lines of communication. Further, when Israel threatened major strategic defeats for the Soviet clients—the possibility of an attack on Damascus on October 17 and the possibility of totally destroying the encircled Egyptian Third Army on October 24—the Soviet Union threatened by word and by active military preparations to intervene in the situation with its own forces.

On the U.S. side, arms deliveries were delayed for a while, in part because of opposition from certain Defense Department officials, but also because Secretary of State Kissinger saw advantages for the United States over the long term in maintaining distance between the United States and Israeli war aims. Eventually, however, U.S. arms were shipped by sea and airlifted to Israel, the latter method of transport necessitating the deployment of some U.S. military personnel at Lod airfield near Tel Aviv and, perhaps, at Sinai airbases as well. The airlift was supported and protected by the U.S. Sixth Fleet in the Mediterranean. And, at the most dramatic point of the confrontation, on October 24, the United States responded to a threatened Soviet intervention by advancing the readiness of all its armed forces and by taking certain actions indicating a willingness, if necessary, to counter the Soviet moves with an escalatory process that could result in nuclear war. Simultaneously, the United States persuaded Israel to conform to the terms of the cease-fire, relieving pressure on the besieged Egyptian army; thus, a way was found out of the 1973 confrontation shortly after the U.S. alert. How far the confrontation might have evolved and what specific steps each superpower might have taken had tensions not been relaxed at that point is difficult to estimate.

In short, seemingly routine decisons to sell arms in peacetime led gradually, yet inexorably, to a situation in which the risk of actual military conflict between the superpowers was not insignificant. Indeed, both the advantages and the disadvantages of arms sales as instruments of great power policies in the Third World come to the fore during crises. It is at times of confrontation that the potential leverage resulting from arms sales is most sorely tested; it is also at times of confrontation that the potential of arms sales to involve the great powers in military conflict with each other becomes important.

Given the instability of politics in the Third World, the possibility that arms transfer relationships will lead to dangerous situations can be ruled out only rarely. Moreover, the problems of arms transfers during crises cannot be abstracted from the problems of arms transfers on a routine basis; the former follows inevitably from the latter. As time passes and the superpowers accustom themselves to greater and greater military involvement in Third World crises, the escalation that has been witnessed already in the Middle East is likely to continue there and to be replicated elsewhere. This eventuality will be particularly worrisome in the event of continued deterioration in overall U.S.-Soviet relations.

Consequently, steps to regulate U.S. and Soviet arms transfers can be seen as one means of blunting the leading edge of the superpower military competition in the Third World and therefore as a potential means of preventing confrontation between the United States and the USSR. Such steps would follow directly from the obligations incurred by the United States and the Soviet Union in the 1972 Basic Principles Agreement and reinforced by the more specific 1973 Agreement on Prevention of Nuclear War. Both documents sought to spell out general codes of behavior necessary to sustain and promote cooperative relations between the superpowers and to avoid the development of situations that eventually might lead to nuclear war.

It was with these considerations in mind that the conventional arms transfer negotiations were convened by the two great powers in 1977 and 1978. To the point, the U.S. approach to these talks was founded specifically on an appreciation of the implications of arms transfers for the risk of U.S.-Soviet conflict in the Third World.

U.S.-Soviet Conventional Arms Transfer Talks

The Carter administration entered office in 1977 determined to reduce the quantity and technological sophistication of arms being transferred to the Third World. There were many reasons for the high priority accorded to this objective, not least of which were the personal beliefs and commitments of President Carter, Vice President Walter Mondale, Secretary of State Cyrus Vance, and many members of Congress, as well as the prominence that Carter had accorded to the desirability of limiting arms sales during his campaign for the presidency. Most importantly, however, many of the new administration's senior decisionmakers were well aware of the implications of certain arms transfers for the risk of U.S.-Soviet conflict, as was discussed previously. These same officials also perceived that the degree of international political attention being devoted to problems associated with arms sales suggested that multilateral discussions on ways to limit arms transfers were feasible. In addition, for Secretary Vance and others, there was hope that such talks could spark a process through which the two superpowers could begin to regulate their competition in the Third World and, thus, ease an increasingly troublesome source of U.S.-Soviet friction. As we shall see, there was certainly no unanimity on these prospects within the administration, but in 1977 the weight of opinion within the government— in both the executive and legislative branches—did support some kind of effort.

The Carter administration adopted a three-part strategy to bring about a reduction in the world's arms trade.[4] A new unilateral U.S. policy on arms transfers was declared that, the administration maintained, would reverse the previous policy by shifting the burden of proof from those who opposed a particular arms transfer to those who advocated it. The policy consisted of technical criteria against which all prospective weapon sales had to be tested and an annual ceiling on the total dollar value of all U.S. transfers to the Third World.[5] Second, the administration pledged to seek the involvement of the Soviet Union and major Western suppliers in multilateral negotiations to limit arms sales. And, third, the administration sought to encourage potential purchasers of weapons to curb their appetites for new arms.

Demarches to suppliers were initiated at the very beginning of the administration's term. The idea was broached at the highest levels of government by Vice President Mondale on his trip to Western Europe in late January 1977. It was later explored in unpublicized, lower-level meetings among U.S., British, French, and German officials. While stating their general support for multilateral arms transfer restraint as a desirable foreign policy objective, the Europeans argued that serious discussions on this subject should not be pursued by the West until the Soviets had demonstrated concretely their interest in restraining arms transfers. In part, this position reflected the Europeans' skepticism about the seriousness of Soviet interest in the subject. The Europeans particularly asked why the Soviet Union would agree to limit an important foreign policy instrument in which it frequently had a comparative advantage over the West. The Europeans' position was also somewhat self-serving, however, in that it permitted them to avoid beginning a process that might lead to restrictions on their own weapon sales without appearing to be uncooperative with the new administration. The French, particularly, were reluctant to become involved, a fact that seems to have had most to do with the importance of foreign sales to their own armaments industries and their desire to pursue an independent foreign policy in the Third World.

Accordingly, the United States turned its attention to the Soviet Union. In March 1977, during Secretary Vance's trip to Moscow, conventional arms transfers was one of eight subjects on which the United States and the USSR agreed to establish working groups.[6] At the initiative of the United States, preliminary consultations were held in Washington in mid-December 1977. This first round of talks was exploratory. The U.S. delegation, headed by Leslie Gelb, director of the State Department's Bureau of Politico-Military Affairs, explained to the Soviets in some detail the new U.S. arms transfer policy.[7] The point was made that this unilateral restraint policy, if it were to be sustained over time, would require multilateral cooperation. The relationship of these talks to the 1972 Basic Principles

Agreement was also emphasized, a point that seemed to impress the Soviets.

Essentially, the Soviet delegation listened carefully during this first round but did not make a significant contribution to the dialogue. After considering what the U.S. representatives had said, however, they requested further talks.

The second round of negotiations was held in Helsinki in May 1978. In preparing for this session, U.S. officials had decided that it was important for both domestic and international reasons to produce some tangible, public sign of progress. It was agreed that at the minimum a joint communiqué that contained certain specific points indicating Soviet, as well as U.S., seriousness was required. Such a document, it was argued, could be used to galvanize interest and cooperation on the part of the major European suppliers as well as recipients in the Third World. This emphasis on obtaining concrete results also reflected growing skepticism within segments of the administration about Soviet motives for entering the talks.

In the second round of talks, the U.S. delegation tied the conventional arms transfer negotiations to the 1972 Basic Principles Agreement even more explicitly; the final joint communiqué, issued on May 11, 1978, unmistakably reflected this strategy. Along with the United States, the Soviet Union acknowledged that "the problem of limiting international transfers of conventional arms is urgent" and that "these meetings, being a component of the Soviet-American negotiations on cessation of the arms race, are held in accordance with the Basic Principles Agreement." Both sides also pledged support for efforts to restrain arms transfers at the then-forthcoming United Nations Special Session on Disarmament and agreed that it would be useful "to hold regularly scheduled meetings in order to explore concrete measures that could be taken to limit international transfers of conventional arms."[8] Soviet behavior during this round of talks and the wording of the final communiqué convinced most of the U.S. participants and many foreign observers who were briefed on the talks that the Soviets—for whatever reasons—were indeed willing to pursue these negotiations seriously. Such great optimism surrounded the talks at this point that a third round was scheduled for July, only ten weeks after the previous one.

In preparing for the third round of talks, however, a crucial difference of opinion developed within the executive branch over the approach to be pursued in the negotiations. This issue bears directly on the question of whether the regulation of arms sales can be used—in some future context—to help dampen U.S.-Soviet competition in the Third World.

The Arms Control and Disarmament Agency (ACDA) took the lead in arguing that strategy for the CAT talks, as for other ongoing arms control efforts such as SALT and the comprehensive test ban negotiations, would best be approached by minimizing the issue's political content, particularly in the initial stages. This plan meant focusing the talks on such technical issues as detailed lists of weapon systems whose transfer might be limited or banned on a global basis and whose exclusion from the international traffic in arms would not be very controversial. Emphasis would be placed on precluding sales of weapons not typically considered for widespread transfer in any event, such as long-range surface-to-surface missiles, napalm, or small, lightweight air defense systems that could be used by terrorists. Indeed, a whole family of such weapons—known to the cognoscenti as weapons of ill repute—was outlined that, for one reason or another, could probably be banned without raising too much dissent. Admittedly, for the same reasons, such agreements would not have made much of an impact on world arms sales. But that was not the major point. The underlying objective of this strategy was to acclimate the bureaucracies in both the United States and the Soviet Union to the idea of restricting arms transfers and, in so doing, to develop and institutionalize the mechanisms and procedures necessary to make more substantial progress toward the regulation of arms transfers. This approach also seemed to offer the best hope for early concrete progress, which was seen to be a prerequisite for European participation and greater interest on the part of recipients in multilateral negotiations.

The ACDA strategy envisioned moving eventually to the more common and significant currency of the world's arms trade, such as high-performance aircraft or ground combat vehicles, and accepted that those later discussions necessarily would have to be on a regional, rather than a global, basis (e.g., aircraft considered technologically advanced, and thus prohibited, in Latin America would not necessarily be considered very advanced in the Middle East). But even then, under the terms of this approach, the focus of the talks would be on specific weapons, with necessary asides about specific regions, rather than on the totality of weapon transfers to a region with asides about specific weapons. This approach had the advantage, according to ACDA officials, of deemphasizing the sensitive political relations between suppliers and recipients that would complicate any regional talks.

Secretary of State Vance and the chief U.S. negotiator, Leslie Gelb, favored a different approach. They viewed CAT as more a political than a technical (or arms control) negotiation. Through these talks, these officials hoped, the United States and the Soviet Union might begin to discuss and reach mutual understandings about their rivalry in the Third World; eventually, their competition might then begin to be controlled. At a minimum, it was hoped, the two sides might reach implicit agreement about appropriate norms of behavior in the parts of the Third World. Furthermore, State Department officials argued, if the talks were to be meaningful, if they were to make real progress, it was necessary that they focus on specific regions or subregions, in order to permit consideration of the full political and military scope of U.S.-Soviet competition. Weapon systems would be discussed, but only as conduits. The ACDA approach, it was feared, would make the talks drag on for years and would distract attention from the real motive for arms transfers: the political struggle between the superpowers for influence in the Third World.

Gelb shed some further light on this approach to the talks when he remarked:

> We have justified our arms sales to most of our friends and allies in the Third World over the years, in terms of what the Soviets were doing in this area. Presumably, the Soviets were doing this too, which in turn affects our behavior. We have an interest in trying to influence Soviet policy, if that is possible, and we certainly had an interest in seeing that they don't miscalculate our intentions and responses. I think we understood from the beginning that CAT was a foreign policy negotiation. . . .[9]

The State Department's approach to the talks ultimately was endorsed by the president, who was increasingly concerned with Soviet inroads in the Third World, or at least was concerned with the effects of these inroads on his political standing and thus on his ability to accomplish other policy objectives. CAT was to be viewed largely as a political negotiation, designed mainly to explore the possibility of parallel U.S.-Soviet interests in lessening tensions and reducing the risk of military confrontations in certain regions of the Third World through the medium of restraint in arms transfers.

In line with this concept, the U.S. side brought to the third round of talks, held in Helsinki in July 1978, an approach that emphasized the need for discussions of arms transfers to specific regions. The U.S. delegates suggested the establishment of a working group on regions and put forward Latin America and Africa south of the Sahara as the best regions with which to begin discussions, given the relatively low level of arms transfers by either side to these regions. Although the U.S. approach also envisioned negotiations on specific criteria to guide weapon transfers on a global basis, its principal focus was shifted to the regional working groups and achieving restraint agreements specific to particular regions.

In its presentations during the third round, the Soviet delegation began to emphasize the primacy of the need to agree on legal principles to govern arms transfers globally, particularly those needed to establish eligibility criteria for potential recipients. For example, the Soviets argued that criteria should be established stating that arms might be transferred for self-defense against aggression and other unlawful uses of force but might not be transferred for violation of the territorial integrity of another country. In their proposals, the Soviets drew heavily on a variety of international legal documents, most importantly the UN charter. The U.S. delegation accepted the need for such legal guidelines but emphasized the concurrent requirement for more technical criteria, criteria that would define the permissible levels and types of weapons that could be transferred to "legitimate" recipients. Not surprisingly, the types of norms favored by the U.S. delegation were in keeping with guidelines already incorporated in the new unilateral U.S. arms transfer policy.

It quickly became apparent that the Soviet Union was intent upon according precedence to agreement on broad legal principles, whether or not progress was achieved on more detailed, technical criteria. Although they accepted the need for legal guidelines, the U.S. delegates wanted to pace the discussions of legal questions with those of military or technical questions, so that progress in each area would be seen as interdependent. It was during the third round that the U.S. side gained explicit Soviet acceptance of the necessary equality of both sets of guidelines, at least for the operational purpose of the negotiations. The U.S. recognized the CAT effort would be at best meaningless—and at worst dangerous—if it were allowed to become an exercise in delineating broad guidelines devoid of enforceable restraint criteria. Some U.S. officials thought that Soviet concentration on general legal principles revealed the essentially propagandistic Soviet motives in CAT. At the same time, the Soviets' eventual agreement to hold the two sets of discussions and their active participation in both working groups represented a strong indication of Soviet seriousness. In the end, both sides tabled proposed language for both technical and legal criteria, and they began detailed negotiations on common language for both types of guidelines.

Most importantly, though, and to the surprise of the U.S. delegation, the Soviets agreed in the third round of the talks to the U.S. proposal to discuss restraint in specific regional contexts. The Soviets even accepted the possibility suggested by the United States that interim regional restraint agreements could be negotiated in advance of any final decisions on overall criteria. They indicated also that these interim agreements could consist of lists of specific weapons that would be restrained—the position hoped for by the U.S. side to ensure rapid progress. Accordingly, a working group on regions was convened, and, at the initiative of the United States, Latin America and sub-Saharan Africa were discussed at some length. The Soviet delegation, for its part, did not propose any regions for discussion.

By the end of the July round, both sides were in agreement on a three-part arms transfer restraint framework, including: commonly agreed-upon political and legal criteria to determine recipients' eligibility, commonly agreed-upon military and technical criteria to govern types and quantities of arms permitted to be transferred, and arrangements to implement these principles and guidelines in specific regional situations. The purpose of this framework was to establish "a common set of criteria and a common approach to their implementation, which can serve as models for both suppliers and recipients in framing arms transfer policies and designing regional restraint agreements."[10] In short, U.S.-Soviet agreement on general guidelines was to be only one step toward more comprehensive agreements.

In preparing for the fourth round of the talks, to be held in Mexico City in December 1978, U.S. officials again concentrated on regions. Preliminary diplomatic contacts indicated that the Soviets would raise "East Asia" (by which they meant the People's Republic of China) and "West Asia" (by which they meant the Persian Gulf) as regions to be considered in the next round of talks. From the point of view of some U.S. officials, discussing these regions with the Soviets, particularly at the end of 1978, would be a risky undertaking. In East Asia, normalization of relations with the People's Republic of China was in its delicate final stages. In West Asia, the stability of the shah's government in Iran was deteriorating daily. A number of senior U.S. officials, including National Security Adviser Zbigniew Brzezinski and Secretary of Defense Harold Brown, felt that even pro forma discussions with the Soviets about these areas could lead to problems in U.S. relations with key nations and damage U.S. security interests. Brzezinski argued strongly that the U.S. delegation should be instructed to break off the negotiations if the Soviets brought up these regions, and that the USSR should be so informed before the talks began. Others, like Leslie Gelb, felt that the United States, although it was clearly uninterested in the short term in restraining arms transfers to either East Asia or West Asia, was obliged at least to listen to Soviet proposals about these regions, even if its only response was to reject the proposals. Never before, it was noted, had one side refused even to listen to the other's presentation at a U.S.-Soviet arms control negotiation. Moreover, in gaining Soviet agreement to discuss Latin America and sub-Saharan Africa, the U.S. side had pledged to discuss any legitimate geographic region suggested by the USSR. In the end, President Carter was persuaded by the arguments of Brzezinski and others. Instructions to the delegation were to discuss Latin America and sub-Saharan Africa only and, if other regions were brought up by the Soviets, to walk out of the talks.

In Mexico City, Gelb presented the U.S. position to his astonished Soviet counterpart before the formal opening of the talks. After nearly one week of strained procedural meetings regarding an agenda for the negotiations, the delegates reached a compromise. The regional working group was not convened, and no regions were discussed at any of the sessions. Both sides subsequently tabled candidate lists of political or legal and military or technical criteria, worked on common texts, and agreed on the need to establish a consultative mechanism to oversee the implementation of these guidelines. But the talks had foundered on the regional issue, and neither the Mexico City round nor subsequent diplomatic exchanges were able to resolve the issue. For all practical purposes, the CAT talks ended in Mexico City in December 1978.

Why did CAT fail? Fundamentally because the talks were conducted against a backdrop of deteriorating U.S.-Soviet relations, a volatile scene in the Middle East, and an increasingly difficult political situation for the Carter administration in the United States. To be sure, these problems were complicated by bureaucratic snafus, personal rivalries, and tactical errors. Most importantly, in 1978 President Carter made two contradictory decisions: first, that CAT should be a political rather than a technical negotiation; but second, that the international political relations upon which it would impinge were too sensitive from the standpoint of the U.S. to discuss with the Soviet Union. It was this contradiction that, more than anything, ensured the failure of CAT. The contradiction, however, resulted from more basic problems with CAT—problems that would have to be avoided in the future should limitations on conventional arms transfers ever be the subject of negotiations again.

An a priori requirement for success in such an effort would be a tolerable level of cooperation between the United States and the Soviet Union. The holding of CAT talks did follow from the 1972 Basic Principles Agreement, but by 1977 the spirit behind both the agreement and the U.S.-Soviet détente that spawned it had seriously waned. Arms transfers are likely to continue to be an integral element in the great powers' struggle for influence in the Third World, but they will be restrained only when—for whatever reasons—the U.S. and Soviet Union mutually decide that in at least certain contexts the dangers and costs of that competition exceed its potential benefits. From 1975 onward, Soviet actions in Africa, Asia, and Latin America increasingly demonstrated that the USSR had not reached such a judgment and that, even though the Carter administration had reached such a decision, the dangers of the competition were not clearly recognized by a durable political consensus in the United States.

Moreover, the CAT experience makes it clear that any U.S. administration that wishes to pursue such negotiations must be unambiguous about the purposes of the talks and must take the time and effort necessary to build appropriate domestic political support behind them. If the purpose is to limit arms transfers per se, then a relatively noncontroversial, technical approach, such as that proposed by ACDA in the spring of 1978, seems most appropriate even though the results achieved may be limited. Such an approach can accomplish what is doable and delay or otherwise deemphasize the more difficult tasks—those that would impinge on sensitive political relations.

If the purpose of such talks, however, is to begin to manage U.S.-Soviet competition in the Third World, primarily to reduce the risks of confrontation and conflict between the superpowers, the essentially political nature of the problem must be faced and the effort must not be initiated until necessary constituencies have been developed and nurtured at home and abroad. In short, it must be made clear that the talks involve the identification of respective interests in specific regions and the discussion of respective perceptions of acceptable and unacceptable behavior. Such a forthright approach in U.S.-Soviet discussions would necessarily have diplomatic implications for each power's relations with other countries since it would worry foreign leaders dependent on U.S. (or Soviet) support. However, only by managing these potential adverse international consequences directly could bureaucratic and political opponents be preempted and domestic support be sustained.

Furthermore, by facing up to the real character of the problem, the United States could avoid the subterfuges through which it previously sought to make conventional arms transfer negotiations politically acceptable. This approach means managing bureaucratic and political problems in anticipation of prolonged, complicated, and difficult negotiations, rather than setting short deadlines to produce concrete results (such as the approximately one-year deadline set on the CAT effort). But meaningful progress in this sensitive area cannot be expected without a firm commitment at the highest levels of government on both sides to the overriding importance of the objective and to the general desirability for U.S. and Soviet leaders to develop patterns of restraint in their competition in the Third World.

Prospects and Problems for Future Negotiations

Against today's backdrop of deteriorating U.S.-Soviet relations and continuing pressures to restructure U.S. and NATO military strategy to counter Soviet military involvement in the Third World more effectively, any proposal to initiate bilateral or multilateral negotiations aimed at developing restraints on arms transfers has all the credibility of a reported sighting of flying pigs. The limitations of the CAT experiment, moreover—in particular its inattention to the requisite development of a political and bureaucratic infrastructure to sustain the effort—clearly have contributed quite extensively to skepticism and misconceptions about the utility and feasibility of negotiated restraint in arms transfers. Overlooked, of course, are the tangible steps toward the elucidation of a framework for restraint that were in fact achieved during CAT; these measures could suggest contours, albeit in a limited way, for future efforts. Still, restoring credibility to such an effort would take time even under the best of circumstances. Since CAT, initiatives for conventional arms transfer restraint will have to transcend the image of failure and naiveté associated with previous ventures.

The competitive aspects of arms transfers have clearly overshadowed any sense of mutuality or durable coincidence of interest between the two countries. This viewpoint has tended to relegate the whole subject of arms transfer negotiations to the category of idealistic ventures or at best of unenforceable initiatives motivated largely by transitory political concerns.

Nevertheless, the continuing escalation of the quantity and quality of arms being transferred to countries in the Third World, countries increasingly autonomous from superpower influence, threatens both global stability and U.S. national interests in a real and pragmatic sense. Both the United States and USSR have experienced arduous object lessons indicating that no matter how central to foreign policy the motivation for arms transfers may be, the results will be at best unpredictable. This common experience would suggest that existing notions of the leverage and influence afforded by arms transfers should be substantially revised. Yet, paradoxically, actual arms transfer behavior has maintained an escalatory momentum seemingly unresponsive to fundamental changes in international conditions and repeated demonstrations of the dangers and inefficiencies that seem to be associated with arms transfers.

To the extent that escalatory trends in arms transfers are fueled by competitive expectations of other suppliers' likely behavior—expectations frequently manipulated successfully by recipients—neither the United States nor the Soviet Union can be expected to take unilateral steps of any duration aimed at curtailing the quality or quantity of the arms they transfer abroad. As long as the environment in which national arms transfer decisions are taken has as its primary facet the struggle of the great powers for political supremacy in the Third World, each power will continue to transfer arms of types or in quantities or to particular recipients that may threaten its own national interests over the longer term. As in strategic force planning, the absence or distortion of information concerning rivals' intentions leads inexorably to exaggerated, compensatory behavior by the competitors. The absence or distortion of information about the other side's prospective arms transfers to local rivals of the great power's clients frequently results in "preemptive" transfers and makes both of the great powers susceptible to manipulation by recipients.

Ironically, it is in part through this very effort to secure competitive political advantage through the transfer of increasingly sophisticated weapons that the great powers themselves are undermining their ability to dominate conflicts in certain regions of the Third World. The growing diffusion of advanced military capabilities clearly presages a growing circumscription of superpower influence and diplomatic maneuverability.

Moreover, regardless of these considerations of stability and political competition, there are sound military reasons to take steps to reduce pressures to export certain types of military equipment, particularly those types that incorporate advanced technologies and whose export thus could compromise existing U.S. military advantages. Important elements of the U.S. policy community, more often in the military than the diplomatic sector, have often recognized the extent to which efforts to gain short-term political advantages by releasing advanced weapons to certain recipients can pose potentially serious long-term threats to U.S. security. In the absence of a coordinated multinational approach to arms transfers, however, the military inadvisability of certain types of exports is frequently overshadowed by ad hoc political decisions, particularly, but not only, during times of political crisis.

In principle, at least, negotiations between the great powers that created consultative channels for discussing arms transfers could have a stabilizing effect on this aspect of their rivalry; actual agreements to restrict certain types or quantities of weapons transferred, at least to certain regions, could have even more dramatic effects. At the very least, any approach that began to elucidate norms for arms transfers would enhance national decisionmaking by adding to the body of empirical information needed to assess recipients' security requirements realistically, lending some measure of predictability to what is, at present, an environment of virtually complete uncertainty.

In the case discussed previously, for example, the fact that the great powers for many years seemed tacitly to recognize a mutual desire to restrain arms transfers to the Korean Peninsula demonstrates the possibility of a mutual interest in restraint in specific circumstances. The several instances in which the superpowers have come close to confrontation in the midst of conflicts over which they had no direct control of course underscore the inherent dangers of a continued unchanneled rivalry. And finally, as was noted, the two sides have a mutual interest in protecting certain types of advanced military technologies, thereby prolonging their ability to dominate militarily a variety of potential situations in the Third World.

Are these reasons for revitalizing a dialogue on arms transfer restraint sufficient to overcome the short-term political advantages of total flexibility in transfers and CAT's legacy of failure? Probably not, at least not in the present political atmosphere. Whether or not this assessment might change and, if so, how soon, is problematic; a new demonstration of the problems that sometimes result from unrestrained arms transfers, however, ironically might have salutary effects.

The legacy of CAT, moreover, suggests a number of points about possible strategies for future efforts at arms transfer restraint. Clearly, there is a complex agenda underlying the question of superpower competition, of which weapon transfers form only a part. What the CAT experiment showed was that it is not possible to discuss U.S.-Soviet competition in the Third World under the guise of negotiating limits on arms transfers, or, for that matter, any other subterfuge. This fact suggests that a multiple-track approach to the problem is necessary, an approach that segregates the ostensible agenda (limiting arms transfers) from the hidden agenda (curbing the risks of U.S.-Soviet competition in the Third World) of the CAT experiment. Differentiated strategies, perhaps undertaken concurrently, are clearly required both to address the general aspects of great power rivalry effectively and to devise a pragmatic approach to arms transfer restraint.

For now, arms transfer limitations are probably best pursued in a multilateral context in which the superpower rivalry could be ameliorated by the influence and problems of other nations. Negotiations of this type, moreover, would be best served by an initial focus on technical issues of arms restraint—discussions of characteristics of candidate weapon systems for inclusion in a restraint regime, for instance—that kept in abeyance more politically volatile issues until a durable infrastructure for negotiation was developed. These talks would aim at the outset at the establishment of global restraint guidelines, without reference to the highly contentious issues involved in applications to specific regions or countries. This approach is discussed in the next section.

At the same time, however, other approaches aimed more explicitly at regulating superpower competition could reinforce these efforts, political conditions permitting. Initially, these other approaches could take the form of concurrent bilateral discussions on weapon restraint guidelines, again largely technical in nature. Given that generalized codes of conduct for arms restraint might only be effective, or in fact desirable, for the most technologically advanced or militarily insignificant types of weapon transfers, more thorough or far-reaching restraint efforts ultimately would require guidelines of a more detailed and differentiated kind, and other arms suppliers would have to be brought into such arrangements. Region- or even country-specific measures, tailored to particular security requirements and concerns of particular recipients and to variations in level of interest and commitment of suppliers, could, over time, supplement initial broad guidelines applied on a global basis.

To this end, a bilateral U.S.-Soviet dialogue aimed at elucidating norms of great power conduct in particular areas, if the dialogue identified mutually acceptable patterns of behavior and types of restraint, might be initiated, either as a concurrent effort or after initial agreement on broad guidelines had been reached. Such an approach could be undertaken through a series of ad hoc country- or region-specific measures, leading ultimately perhaps to diplomatic understandings between the powers tailored to specific areas. Although arms transfers as a specific issue would only be a part of the agenda of these exchanges, the exchanges could reinforce and even facilitate the comprehensive restraint agreements being negotiated multilaterally.

Another possibility for great power restraint, alluded to earlier, would be the sort of tacit agreement that has already been exhibited in certain sensitive areas. Whether it was pursued as an alternative or as a supporting measure to formal or explicit restraint measures, such a tacit agreement could be an important instrument for ameliorating superpower competition, regardless of the success or failure of future CAT efforts or even without the resumption of formal arms transfer efforts.

None of these strategies is mutually exclusive. Their relative feasibility, however, clearly varies. The CAT experiment has shown that a differentiated approach to the regulation of superpower competition is indeed required. Yet the experiment has also shown that an incremental (technical) approach to arms transfer restraint—one that minimizes difficult political issues at the outset—is preferable to an effort that attempts to grapple with fundamental political differences before delineating a framework for sustained negotiations. For several reasons, discussed in the next section, there are clear advantages to the multilateral, largely technical, approach if arms restraint is the priority objective. Coincidentally, if the political atmosphere improved, broader measures to reduce the dangers of U.S.-Soviet competition would clearly augment this effort.

Multilateral Negotiations

The United Nations Committee on Disarmament in Geneva would provide a convenient forum to establish a working group to discuss arms transfer negotiations. The talks would include not only all major suppliers but, from the outset, major Third World arms purchasers. There may be difficulty interesting some nations in such discussions, but the international community is on record at the first UN Special Session on Disarmament as recognizing the severity of the problems caused by arms transfers and the need to take steps to alleviate those difficulties. If these words mean anything, all nations—not only the United States and the USSR—should be willing to address the problem directly; if they chose not to, responsibility for failure would not rest solely with the great powers.

Although the complexity of discussions would grow with an increase in the number of participating countries, the costs of this extra complication are far outweighed by the benefit of avoiding some of the political frictions that emerged from a strictly supplier-oriented framework. A forum that engaged recipients as well as suppliers would avoid exacerbating recipients and eliminate purchasers' fears of superpower paternalism originating in the necessary secretiveness and cartel-like structure of a suppliers' conference. The direct participation of recipients is likely to be a precondition to developing any kind of international consensus on arms transfer problems.

It can be assumed, a priori, that any discussion between the United States and other suppliers on conventional arms transfers to Third World countries would invoke intense suspicions among recipients.

Some recipients would fear a loss of flexibility in their relations with supplier countries if the talks seemed to be leading to a supplier condominium. Negative reactions of this type would mitigate the success of efforts to defuse political tensions within the talks themselves. (The Soviets, particularly, are extremely sensitive to the appearance of condoning any agreements that would provoke such reactions.) Even global restraints on weapons that no Third World country had in its arsenal could cause recipients to fear that the restraint process ultimately would become mechanistic and therefore that their supplier would become insensitive to their security requirements. Underlying these suspicions, of course, would be a realization that it might become less likely that suppliers would meet demands for weapons on the basis of exaggerated perceptions of the recipient's security needs—perceptions now frequently created by manipulating one superpower against the other.

If these concerns became severe enough, some recipients might be provoked sufficiently to seek more arms from alternative suppliers. Countries such as Israel, Argentina, and Brazil in the short run, and several other countries in subsequent years, may be able to provide major combat equipment to recipients that would sorely test the effectiveness of any restraint regime. The extent to which these alternative suppliers could be brought under the aegis of a restraint regime or would be sensitive to the international opprobrium that could ensue if any multilateral agreement were deliberately circumvented is problematic. Particularly if during the negotiations the superpowers were viewed as paternalistic, this could invoke more pronounced schisms in the current North-South debate. Of course, third-party suppliers would still be critically dependent on the larger powers not only for security guarantees but also for the technological inputs needed to maintain their defense industries. These dependencies might mitigate this problem to a degree.

Another political problem concerns reactions of European arms suppliers. Without the support of the countries in Western Europe, no negotiated limits on arms transfers between the great powers could be of anything but limited scope and duration. Although the United States and the Soviet Union might still have an interest in monitoring each other's high-technology exports and developing norms that could lend some predictability to their own relationship, continued opposition from other suppliers could quickly undermine the value of any agreement. At the same time, the United States would have to decide if the potential benefits of an arms restraint initiative were worth engendering frictions in the NATO alliance.

Conversely, it is equally important to question some of the reasons given in Europe for resisting multilateral arms restraint efforts. Largely motivated by a fear that a multilateral arms restraint agreement would unduly penalize their industries and economies, given their disproportionate dependence on arms exports, major Western suppliers have tended to overdramatize the negative impact that such agreements could have. For the types of restraints outlined here, however (those aimed most directly at selective types of weapons), there is no evidence that European suppliers would encounter major economic dislocations. Especially in the earlier stages of an agreement, when technological sophistication would serve as the major basis for restraint, the economic impact would probably be marginal. To illustrate this point: Of French weapons, candidates for restraint would probably include only the most advanced surface-to-surface missile, the Matra, which is just now being deployed with French forces, and the Mirage 2000 aircraft. Although the French may, in fact, plan for these systems eventually to be transferred to Third World arsenals, in most recipient countries being able to absorb, far less pay for, such equipment is a fairly distant prospect.

Additionally, multinational efforts for advanced technology sharing in NATO may provide an avenue for greater coordination of arms export guidelines among the NATO countries. The United States, regardless of the political climate, will continue to place restrictions on European exports of advanced coproduced equipment. In essence, these restrictions are a form of diplomatic tradeoff that elicits European compliance with U.S. export restrictions in return for access to advanced technologies, a high priority for most NATO countries. Europeans' sharing in such state-of-the-art technology will always be contingent on their adoption of rules to protect this technology from possible compromise. Although this issue already has led to considerable political friction in the alliance, it has not been unmanageable. There is a pragmatic coincidence of interest among NATO countries in this area that could lead to more explicit cooperative measures for arms export restraint.

Returning to our concept for multilateral negotiations, the initial focus should remain on weapons that could be restrained on a global basis, without requiring direct reference to specific regional contexts, so as to provide the least complicated avenue for agreement on an initial restraint framework. Once momentum was achieved, the multilateral working group could consider organizing supplier-recipient conferences for specific regions, in which broader issues of security and arms transfers could be addressed. This stage might also be a propitious time to initiate bilateral U.S.-Soviet discussions on these matters, as was previously discussed.

Multilateral discussions would focus on selecting candidate weapons for global restraint and developing guidelines to govern their transfer. Although these talks might be linked eventually to the effort to develop consultative channels between the great powers for crisis prevention, it is critical that the multilateral arms transfer negotiations not be tasked from the outset with moderation of U.S.-Soviet rivalry in the Third World. It is in keeping with the traditional logic of arms control that these initial efforts be assigned only modest objectives. They should seek agreement on what is feasible, conservatively speaking, and avoid the more complex and potentially explosive political issues. Given the novelty of conventional arms transfer diplomacy, the development, as a first step, of a negotiating framework and, subsequently, of procedures and consultative mechanisms based on technical, rather than political, factors is a necessary precondition for success.

Specifically, the most advantageous strategy for developing some momentum in these negotiations would likely be one that focused on weapon systems whose transfer was not central to either side's foreign policy and that had been recognized mutually as of particularly high risk: long-range surface-to-surface missiles, for instance, as was discussed above, or weapons particularly susceptible to diversion to terrorists, such as air defense systems that can be easily transported. As auxiliary measures, weapons that have been the subject of international attention for their indiscriminate effects and that have marginal military utility, such as incendiary or fragmentary weapons, could be included for discussion. As the technical issues of definition and capabilities of systems were resolved, these arms could make up the beginning of a "trigger list" of weapons whose potential transfer would be subject to an a priori ban on a global basis or would require consultation among the suppliers before transfers took place.

Diplomatic precedents for such a structure are not abundant. The London Suppliers' Group, designed to monitor exports of items related to nuclear technologies, is perhaps the closest approximation extant. The COCOM structure, used by the West for monitoring technology transfers of potential military significance to Communist countries, provides a more vague example. Both precedents suggest a variety of limitations in enforcing and interpreting guidelines, too lengthy to be discussed here.

The definitional and verificational problems attending global arms restrictions would be significant. Even if these problems were successfully resolved, the results of such multilateral efforts would be modest. If all weapons that conceivably could be regulated on a global basis were prohibited from transfer, their disappearance would hardly make a dent in the volume of weapon transfers to the Third World. Still, restriction could ease some specific problems, such as access by terrorist organizations to advanced military technologies, and could make infeasible the introduction of certain new technologies into the arsenals of the Third World, a development that otherwise might eventually occur. Moreover, any successful effort would demonstrate the practicality of negotiated restraint and would create the procedures and institutions necessary to implement it. From such a base, it would then be feasible to contemplate more ambitious efforts, such as regional conferences to consider limiting the more common currency of the Third World arms trade—aircraft, ground combat vehicles, and so forth—combined with broader initiatives between the great powers for regional discussions.

Conclusion

Most discussions of the problems posed by the escalation of arms transfers are profoundly pessimistic about prospects for solving these problems through negotiation. Having paid homage to the litany of obstacles that would be brought to bear on such an endeavor, however, these analyses beg the question of alternatives. A major conceptual flaw in these critiques is that they take as a point of departure the objective of a comprehensive restructuring of supplier and recipient arms transfer behavior to achieve significant reductions in the global arms trade. When the focus of analysis is on an achievement of such awesome ambition, clearly the obstacles must predominate in the ensuing discussion. It is odd that, in the absence of any concrete diplomatic precedents for conventional arms control, so little attention is paid to the obvious need to focus on incremental and relatively modest objectives until an infrastructure for more ambitious efforts has been established.

As was stated earlier, bilateral efforts to negotiate arms restraint require a clear differentiation between efforts to achieve specific guidelines on arms transfers for global application and more diffuse, politically complex efforts to reach agreement on acceptable norms for great power actions in specific regions or countries. In the initial stages, successful bilateral discussions for the latter objective would probably be easiest to achieve if talks were tailored at first to the pursuit of similar objectives delineated in the multilateral forum, modest and mostly technical. Successes at this level would serve to enhance—although they would not substitute for—agreements reached multilaterally. At the same time, momentum in these talks could provide the impetus for reaching more ambitious goals related more directly to crisis prevention: the series of possible, ad hoc agreements or understandings applied to specific areas or situations, as discussed previously. The exchange of views on security concerns, commitments, and likely future behavior could, in time, provide the parameters for regionally differentiated arms transfer restraint proposals that could be submitted for multilateral consideration. Whether or not multilateral agreement on such measures was reached, however, the bilateral exchanges in themselves could have a beneficial effect on U.S.-Soviet relations and global stability generally.

If any such discussions are to have a chance for success, the domestic and international constituencies necessary to sustain them must be developed carefully. Such constituencies will not arise unless the importance of the subject and the potential benefits of the negotiations, bilateral and multilateral, to national security are carefully explained. Otherwise, the risks will seem much greater than the benefits; the short-term costs to U.S. relations with traditional clients in the Third World will seem to dominate whatever longer-term political and security benefits may be inferred from the discussions. Because of this apparent balance, those who oppose U.S.-Soviet talks or arms restraint initiatives generally, for whatever reason, are able to mobilize resistance to the discussions both within the U.S. bureaucracy and abroad—resistance sufficient, first, to place undue and hasty demands on the talks and, eventually, to cripple them.

Perhaps the major lesson of the CAT experiment that should guide future endeavors is that any such initiative must be the product of a carefully elucidated framework, not just for the strategy of the negotiations, but for U.S. foreign policy as a whole. Negotiations cannot be an afterthought to foreign policy with which they are not consonant. Aside from sending contradictory signals to both adversaries and allies, such ill-conceived ventures undermine the credibility of U.S. diplomacy and set difficult precedents to transcend. The achievement of a constituency for arms restraint and for crisis prevention generally is not a precondition for undertaking initiatives. Such a constituency is rather the outgrowth of a coherently conceived and carefully articulated foreign policy of which such measures form a part. Clearly, the sensitivity and controversial nature of such initiatives invite opposition and, sometimes, sabotage, a fact that underscores even further the need for consistent and firm leadership from the highest levels of the U.S. foreign policy apparatus. Without such endorsement, CAT and all related efforts to mediate U.S.-Soviet

rivalry risk becoming the domain of advocates—perhaps correct in
vision, but fatefully flawed in any operational sense.

Notes

1. Throughout this paper, the terms "arms (or weapon) transfers," "arms
(or weapon) sales," and, to a lesser extent, "military grants (or assistance)"
are used interchangeably. The authors of course recognize the distinctions
among transfers, grants, and sales, as well as those among weapons, arms,
and military equipment.
2. The Six-Day War (1967), the War of Attrition (1969–1970), the
Jordanian crisis (1970), and the October War (1973).
3. For example, long-range surface-to-surface missiles.
4. For details on this three-part strategy see Lucy Wilson Benson,
"Controlling Arms Transfers: An Instrument of U.S. Foreign Policy," *Department of State Bulletin,* August 1, 1977, pp. 157–158. See also testimony
of Leslie Gelb in U.S., Congress, House of Representatives, Committee on
Foreign Affairs, Subcommittee on International Security and Scientific Affairs,
Review of the President's Conventional Arms Transfer Policy (Washington,
D.C.: Government Printing Office, February 1, 1978).
5. The Carter administration policy, enunciated in Presidential Directive
13 of May 1977, set forth controls for arms transfers to be applied to all
countries outside of Japan and the members of NATO and ANZUS. In
addition to an annual ceiling on the dollar volume of government-to-
government arms transfers, these categories included: (a) prohibition of
transfers of advanced equipment that would introduce a qualitatively higher
combat capability into a region; (b) a ban on the development of weapons
solely for export; and (c) restrictions on coproduction agreements and
retransfers of U.S. equipment and on the promotion of weapon sales by
agents of the U.S. government or private manufacturers. All of these provisions
were to be subject to exceptions only in "instances where it can clearly be
demonstrated that the transfer contributes to national security interests."
6. The other working groups were on chemical weapons, antisatellite
weapons, limitations on military forces in the Indian Ocean, civil defense,
radiological weapons, prior notification of missile test firings, and comprehensive nuclear test ban negotiations. See "News Conference of Secretary
of State Cyrus Vance, Moscow, March 30, 1977," *Department of State
Bulletin,* April 25, 1977, p. 401.
7. In addition to Gelb, the U.S. delegation was composed of representatives of the Arms Control and Disarmament Agency, the National Security
Council staff, the Department of Defense, and the staff of the Joint Chiefs
of Staff. Regional specialists and weapons experts supplemented the delegation
as necessary.
The Soviet delegation was led by two career diplomats successively,
Ambassadors Khlestov and Mendelevich. Its deputy was a Red Army general,

Galkin. Various specialists, some with practical field experience in negotiating arms sales, rounded out the Soviet delegation.

    8. "Joint U.S.-U.S.S.R. Communique, May 11, 1978," *Department of State Bulletin,* July 1978, p. 36.

    9. "Interview with Leslie Gelb," *Arms Control Today* 10 (September 1980):4.

    10. Barry Blechman, "Controlling the International Trade in Arms," address to the Woodrow Wilson International Center for Scholars, May 21, 1979, p. 10.

APPENDIX

Patterns in U.S. and Soviet Arms Transfers to the Third World

The first direct deliveries of Soviet weapons to the Third World took place in 1956, when both Syria and Egypt received Soviet aircraft, armor, warships, and other military equipment. Soviet weapon deliveries have grown relatively steadily since then, amounting to some $35 billion worth of equipment by 1979. Growth has been particularly apparent since 1974, and existing agreements suggest that annual deliveries will continue to increase into the 1980s.

Most of this equipment has gone to the Middle East and North Africa. The former region accounts for more than one-half of all Soviet weapon deliveries, the latter for an additional 20 percent; but North Africa is growing increasingly important. The distribution of Soviet weapon deliveries over time and by region is shown in Table 11.1.

Although fifty-four nations in the Third World have received Soviet weapons, deliveries have been highly concentrated. Nine nations account for 85 percent of the value of all sales. India, Syria, and Iraq have been important customers throughout the period. Indonesia was an important customer until 1965, as was Egypt until 1974. Libya, Algeria, South Yemen, and Ethiopia all became important customers in the 1970s.

U.S. arms transfers to the Third World also have grown considerably since the mid-1950s, particularly in the 1970s. The average value of U.S. military equipment delivered to Third World nations, which was around $1.2 billion between 1955 and 1969, rose to around $3.6 billion during the next five years and then soared to $5.7 billion during the last five years reported (1975–1979). U.S. deliveries totaled nearly $65 billion over the entire twenty-five-year period; 45 percent took place during the past five years. Inflation in the price of weapons

TABLE 11.1

Value of Soviet Weapon Deliveries to the Non-Communist Third World,
by Region, 1955-1979 (In Billions of U.S. $)

Region	1955-1974 Value	%	1975 Value	%	1976 Value	%	1977 Value	%	1978 Value	%	1979 Value	%	1955-1979 Value
Middle East	9.4	70	1.1	55	1.2	39	1.7	36	1.9	35	3.4	52	18.7
North Africa	0.7	5	0.5	25	1.0	32	1.3	28	1.7	31	2.1	32	7.2
South Asia	2.1	16	0.2	10	0.5	16	0.8	17	0.3	6	0.5	8	4.4
Sub-Saharan Africa	0.4	3	0.3	15	0.3	10	0.6	13	1.4	26	0.6	9	3.5
East Asia[b]	0.9	7	0		0	0	0	0	0		0	0	0.9
Latin America[c]	neg.	neg.	0.1	5	0.1	3	0.4	9	0.1	2	neg.	neg.	0.7
Worldwide[a]	13.5		2.0		3.1		4.7		5.4		6.6		35.3

[a]Components may not add to totals because of rounding.

[b]Excludes China, North Korea, and North Vietnam throughout; also excludes Laos and Cambodia after 1975.

[c]Excludes Cuba.

Source: Communist Aid Activities in Non-Communist Less Developed Countries, 1979 and 1954-1979 (Central Intelligence Agency, ER80-10318U, October 1980).

TABLE 11.2

Value of U.S. Weapon Deliveries to the Non-Communist Third World, by Region, 1955-1979 (In Billions of U.S. $)[a]

Region	1955-1974 Value	%	1975 Value	%	1976 Value	%	1977 Value	%	1978 Value	%	1979 Value	%	1955-1979[e] Value	%
Middle East	6.2	17	2.3	62	4.2	82	5.6	88	6.0	81	4.7	77	28.9	45
North Africa	0.2	1	neg.	neg.	neg.	neg.	0.1	2	0.1	1	0.2	3	0.6	1
South Asia	0.9	3	neg.	neg.	neg.	neg.	0.1	2	0.1	1	0.1	2	1.2	2
Sub-Saharan Africa[b]	0.2	1	neg.	neg.	0.1	2	0.1	2	0.1	1	neg.	neg.	0.6	1
East Asia[c]	27.1	75	1.2	32	0.6	12	0.3	5	1.0	14	1.0	16	31.4	48
Latin America[d]	1.3	4	0.2	5	0.2	4	0.2	3	0.1	1	0.1	2	2.1	3
Worldwide[e]	35.9		3.7		5.1		6.4		7.4		6.1		64.8	

[a] Includes foreign military sales, grant aid, and commercial sales (after 1970).

[b] Excludes Republic of South Africa.

[c] Excludes Japan, Hong Kong, New Zealand, and Australia.

[d] Excludes Cuba.

[e] Components may not add to totals because of rounding.

Source: U.S., Department of Defense, Foreign Military Sales and Military Assistance Facts (Washington, D.C.: Department of Defense, Defense Security Assistance Agency, Data Management Division, Comptroller, December 1980).

accounts for only a small portion of this increase. Existing contracts indicate continuing, if not so dramatic, increases in the future.

Like those of the Soviet Union, the most important U.S. customers have been in the Middle East. The region accounts for 45 percent of all U.S. arms transfers to the Third World and nearly 80 percent of such weapon deliveries since 1974. The three largest purchasers of U.S. arms in this region are Iran (17 percent of the worldwide total), Saudi Arabia (14 percent), and Israel (10 percent). East Asia accounts for another 48 percent of the U.S. total, but most of this amount took place before 1974, when Vietnam accounted for 28 percent of all U.S. transfers. Korea continues to be an important customer for U.S. arms, accounting for about 10 percent of total American grants and sales to the Third World.

Table 11.2 contains data describing U.S. weapon deliveries to the Third World by time and region.

12
Crisis Prevention in Cuba

Gloria Duffy

By exacting a U.S. promise during the missile crisis not to invade
Cuba or interfere in its internal affairs, Nikita Khrushchev boasted
in his memoirs, the Soviet Union had forced the "American imperial
beast" to "swallow a hedgehog, quills and all." Although the Soviet
premier's memory of the outcome of the 1962 crisis was self-serving,
Cuba's quills have periodically pricked the United States as new
Soviet military equipment has appeared on the island and the Cuban-
Soviet military relationship has grown so close as to support joint
operations in Africa and the Middle East. Yet although Cuba was
the scene of the most dangerous crisis between the United States
and the Soviet Union, it has also been the locus of a largely successful
effort to prevent recurring confrontations over the sensitive subject
of Soviet forces deployed on the territory of an ally next door to
the United States. The legacy of the 1962 missile crisis was an
understanding governing the military uses of Cuba by the USSR and
the terms of U.S. tolerance for this Soviet protégé state ninety miles
offshore. Although it is ambiguous, that agreement has provided a
reference point for coping with a succession of later controversies
over Soviet military use of the island and has evolved into a broader
set of rules recognized by both sides.

But if the definition of crisis prevention is achieving diplomatic
solutions to disagreements in a region or over a particular issue, the
observance of the set of principles that had helped moderate tensions
over Cuba for seventeen years lapsed seriously in 1979. The circumstances that converted potential confrontations into accommodation in the cases of an apparent Soviet effort to build a base for
nuclear submarines in Cuba in 1970 and of MiG-23 fighter aircraft
deployed on the island in 1978 changed to promote a standoff over

the much more mundane issue of a Soviet troop brigade, discovered in 1979 to have been stationed near Havana.

Ambiguity is the nature of tacit agreements. Neither the imprecision of the 1962 Kennedy-Khrushchev exchanges about Cuba nor the fact that their understanding was officially recognized by the United States only in 1970 are matters of common knowledge. The 1962 understanding is remembered as a U.S. pledge not to invade Cuba if Moscow forebore from introducing offensive nuclear weapons onto the island. But President Kennedy's promise in return for Soviet retraction of medium- and intermediate-range ballistic missiles and forty-two Ilyushin-28 fighter-bombers was actually couched in somewhat different terms.

In his October 26 letter to President Kennedy, Chairman Khrushchev had written, "I propose: we, for our part, will declare that our ships bound for Cuba are not carrying any armaments. You will declare that the United States will not invade Cuba with its troops and will not support any other forces which might intend to invade Cuba."[1] The letter continued, implying that such declarations by the two sides could then lead to removal of the missiles, a proposal made more explicitly at about the same time by a member of the Soviet embassy staff in Washington in a conversation with John Scali, a U.S. journalist, with the understanding that Scali would communicate it to high levels in the Kennedy administration.

President Kennedy responded the next day:

> ... the key elements of your proposal—which seem generally acceptable as I understand them—are as follows: 1) You would agree to remove these weapons systems from Cuba under appropriate United Nations observation and supervision; and undertake, with suitable safeguards, to halt the further introduction of such weapons systems into Cuba. 2) We, on our part, would agree—upon establishment of adequate arrangements through the United Nations—to ensure the carrying out and continuation of these commitments—a) to remove promptly the quarantine measures now in effect, and b) to give assurances against an invasion of Cuba.[2]

A month later, Kennedy made the U.S. position public. "If all offensive weapons systems are removed from Cuba and kept out of the hemisphere in the future," he said in his November 1962 press conference, "... we shall neither initiate nor permit aggression in this hemisphere."[3]

In addition, in the months following the missile crisis, the Kennedy administration expressed its objection to the continued presence of

Soviet ground troops in Cuba, the residuum of forces that accompanied the missile deployment. In his November 20, 1962, press conference, the president specified that "the importance of our continued vigilance is underlined by our identification of a number of Soviet ground combat units in Cuba, although we are informed that these and other Soviet units were associated with the protection of offensive weapons systems and will be withdrawn in due course."[4]

Secretary of State Dean Rusk noted on January 27, 1963, that "we have seen some outtraffic of Soviet military personnel in recent weeks, but we are very much interested in the continuation of that outtraffic."[5] As a matter of policy, Rusk added, "we must anticipate that these forces would be removed. . . ."[6]

Neither the Soviets nor the Cubans acquiesced to Kennedy's demand for UN verification on Cuban territory that the missiles and aircraft had been removed, and neither offered safeguards to preclude deployment of offensive forces in the future.[7] Raymond Garthoff, State Department special assistant for Soviet bloc politico-military affairs in 1962, argues that the agreement did not officially go into force in the early 1960s because the Soviets did not fulfill all the U.S. conditions. The final, authoritative statements on the status of the understanding, Garthoff reports, came at a November 29, 1962, meeting between Kennedy and Soviet First Deputy Prime Minister Anastas Mikoyan. At the meeting, Garthoff recalls, "Mikoyan repeatedly pressed for clarification and confirmation that the United States accepted a commitment not to invade Cuba. President Kennedy reassured him that the United States had no intention to invade Cuba, but stressed that the conditions called for in the exchange of letters in late October (international verification in Cuba and safe-guards) had not been met. Without making the unequivocal future commitment the Soviets wanted, Kennedy would only state that if the Soviet Union abided by the exchange of correspondence, so would the United States."[8]

The ambiguity over whether the understanding was actually in force between the two sides proved relatively insignificant in succeeding years. After the Bay of Pigs exercise, the United States was not disposed to attempt another invasion of Cuba, with or without an agreement. A combination of a perception of strong U.S. commitment and local military superiority, as well as Soviet domestic factors, caused the USSR to refrain from again testing U.S. sensitivities about deployments of offensive weapons in Cuba until 1969. And, of course, the independent U.S. ability to check on the type of Soviet forces on the island was a further deterrent to Soviet activity.

But three key imprecisions in the official U.S. position in 1962 left unclear the definition of an "offensive" weapon system, whether the prohibition extended to Soviet forces deployed near but not actually on Cuban soil, and how strongly the United States objected to Soviet troops stationed in Cuba. Two potential crises and a third actual confrontation over the Soviet military presence in Cuba during the 1970s arose from Soviet probing of these ambiguities and U.S. response, each episode defining more concretely the level of U.S. concern on these various points.

Submarines, 1970

On July 11, 1969, a Soviet naval group, composed of three surface combatants, three support ships including a submarine tender, and two *Foxtrot*-class conventionally armed, long-range diesel attack submarines steamed into Havana harbor.[9] A *November*-class, nuclear-powered attack submarine, carrying nonnuclear torpedoes, was simultaneously cruising the Caribbean but did not enter a Cuban port.[10] This activity represented the first venture by Soviet submarines into a port in the Caribbean, and the flotilla cruised for over a month before leaving the area. A second deployment from May to June of 1970 stopped in both Cienfuegos and Havana harbors. It included an *Echo II*–class nuclear-powered cruise missile submarine and two *Foxtrots*. The *Echo II* is capable of carrying eight SS-N-3 nuclear cruise missiles or the same number of nonnuclear cruise missiles.[11]

A tender also accompanied a third visit not involving submarines in September 1970, and it remained in Cuban waters until early January 1971. This third visit deposited two barges, identified by U.S. intelligence as associated exclusively with disposal of effluents from the reactors of nuclear-powered submarines, in Cienfuegos harbor.[12] These Soviet naval vessels engaged in exercises in the Gulf of Mexico and the Caribbean and showed the Soviet flag in several Caribbean ports. Thus far, the Soviets did not seem to have violated the 1962 agreement. Although it watched the submarine visits carefully, the Nixon administration did not protest to the Soviets.

On August 4, 1970, Soviet chargé d'affaires Yuli Vorontsov called on Henry Kissinger, then White House national security advisor. Vorontsov asked for a reaffirmation of the 1962 Kennedy-Khrushchev understanding. A bit puzzled by the Soviet request, seemingly unconnected with any new developments in Cuba, Kissinger nevertheless complied on August 7. His reply "noted with satisfaction the assurance of the Soviet government that the understandings of 1962 were still in full force. We defined these as prohibiting the emplacement of any offensive weapon or any offensive delivery system on Cuban territory. We reaffirmed that in return we would not use military force to bring about a change in the governmental structure of Cuba."[13] This was the first official U.S. statement that this country considered the agreement in force, superseding Kennedy's qualified position of 1962.[14]

But U-2 reconnaissance flights executed over Cienfuegos at the start of the third visit on September 15 revealed that construction of a variety of structures in Cienfuegos harbor had begun and had progressed since a previous overflight.[15] Kissinger describes what the intelligence revealed, in his memoirs:

> What the photography showed was that in less than three weeks the Soviet Union had rushed to complete a fairly significant shore installation. Two new barracks and administrative buildings suddenly stood on Cayo Alcatraz, which had been barren only a month earlier. Recreation facilities had quickly risen on the island, including a basketball court and a soccer field. In my eyes this stamped it indelibly as a Russian base, since as an old soccer fan, I knew Cubans played no soccer. More important, the submarine tender had moored in permanent fashion to four buoys in the bay. Alongside the tender were the two support barges, which had been unloaded from the amphibious ship. The tender was thus in a position to service submarines. Antisubmarine nets guarded the entrance to the harbor. On the mainland, a few miles from the town of Cienfuegos, there had arisen a new dock, a fuel storage depot, and the early stages of a major communications facility, undoubtedly the radio link to Moscow, guarded by anti-aircraft missiles and surveillance radar. What we saw, in short, had all the earmarks of a permanent Soviet naval base."[16]

In mid-September, the submarine tender moored one mile north of Alcatraz Island, where it periodically returned after cruises to other Cuban ports until late December. The two support barges were moored alongside the tender.[17] The Defense Intelligence Agency concluded that "the combination of the submarine tender and the construction on Alcatraz Island appears to be intended to provide the Soviets with an increased capability to support the naval operations in the Caribbean area, including those of submarines."[18]

Beyond the possible contravention of the 1962 agreement and incremental introduction of new Soviet military capabilities into an area of high U.S. interest, establishment of a submarine support facility at Cienfuegos threatened to disadvantage the United States militarily in two ways. First, refueling, repair, and crew relief facilities at Cienfuegos would have allowed the Soviets to increase the time that strategic submarines could patrol on station off Bermuda, saving the time they normally expended to return to their home bases on the Kola peninsula in the USSR.

Second, a base in Cuba would allow the Soviets to reduce the frequency with which their submarines had to pass between Greenland, Iceland, and the United Kingdom, where NATO forces could fairly easily detect their passage.[19] In sum, as Brookings Institution analyst Barry Blechman testified in a 1974 congressional hearing, "The fact that there are Soviet submarines off the coast which are capable of striking targets virtually anywhere in the U.S. is part of the reality we have to accept; just as they have missiles within the Soviet Union that can strike us. Having the base in Cuba doesn't change that situation. It just makes it a little cheaper to pose the same threat."[20]

Pentagon spokesmen leaked word of the intelligence about Cienfuegos to the press on September 24, 1970.[21] At an afternoon briefing on September 25, Kissinger issued a stern public warning to the Soviets. The United States was watching the situation "very closely," he said, and the establishment of a Soviet base to service missile-firing submarines in Cienfuegos would be regarded with "utmost seriousness" as a violation of the 1962 agreement.[22]

Kissinger summoned Soviet Ambassador Anatolyi Dobrynin to the White House. Contrary to the restraint that he recalls was advocated by the State Department and President Nixon, Kissinger then embarked upon what he calls his "preferred course" for dealing with the Soviets. On September 25, Kissinger told Dobrynin that the United States considered the construction at Cienfuegos "unmistakably a submarine base."[23] "Moscow should be under no illusion," he said; "we would view continued construction with the utmost gravity; the base could not remain. We would not shrink from other measures including public steps if forced into it; if the ships—especially the tender—left Cienfuegos, we would consider it a training exercise."[24]

On October 5, Dobrynin urgently requested an appointment with Kissinger. On October 6, he conveyed Moscow's written reply, promising to uphold the Soviet part of the 1962 bargain.[25] Kissinger remembers that Dobrynin gave him a verbal commitment that ballistic missile–equipped submarines would never call in Cuban ports in an operational capacity.[26] A "President's Note" Kissinger later sent Dobrynin defined five types of Soviet activities in Cuba that the United States would find objectionable.[27] The Soviet news agency TASS affirmed on October 13 that the USSR was "not building a base or doing anything to contradict the 1962 understanding."[28] With the exception of the submarine tender and a tugboat, the Soviet ships left Cuban waters on September 16, within a few days of the warning. The vessels departed the Caribbean on September 21.[29]

But the September public White House statements had been vague, leaving to Soviet interpretation what constituted a "base," whether the warning applied to Cuban ports other than Cienfuegos, and which "missile-firing submarines" were of concern to the United States. Most servicing for submarines, with the exception of crew relief, may be accomplished by a submarine tender moored offshore. The question of whether a tender constitutes a "base" is thus ambiguous. Not only did the Soviet submarine tender remain in Cuba, the naval visits soon resumed. A fourth Soviet navy cruise to Cuba, beginning in December 1970, involved visits by a *Foxtrot*-class conventionally powered and armed attack submarine to Antilla, Havana, and Cienfuegos.

To specify that servicing submarines from a tender was functionally equal to doing so from shore facilities, and that the United States objected to such activity from anywhere in Cuba, not just from Cienfuegos, the White House issued another statement in December. The U.S. position, the announcement said, was to oppose servicing "in or from bases in Cuba."[30]

Unfortunately, a month later President Nixon muddied the waters that were in the process of being clarified. On January 4, 1971, Nixon stated that " . . . in the event that nuclear subs were serviced either in Cuba or from Cuba, that would be a violation of the understanding. That has not happened yet. We are watching the situation closely."[31] Whether the Nixon administration meant nuclear-powered submarines or nuclear missile submarines was left ambiguous, although it was clearly the latter that were of concern.[32] The White House had acknowledged this distinction in its earlier September statement.[33]

In the face of U.S. statements open to a variety of interpretations, the Soviets chose to continue probing. In February 1971, a *November*-class nuclear-powered cruise missile submarine with a tender visited Cienfuegos.[34] In April 1972, a *Golf II*–class diesel-powered ballistic missile submarine called at Antilla. In August 1973, an *Echo II*–class cruise missile–equipped nuclear-powered submarine visited Havana and Cienfuegos. In April and May 1974, a *Golf II*–class diesel-powered ballistic missile submarine put into Havana harbor. These visits sometimes included tenders and surface combat ships and were interspersed with visits of the much older, conventionally powered and armed *Foxtrot*-class submarines.[35]

The pattern of the visits indicated a clear qualitative escalation on the part of the Soviets, from *Foxtrot* in 1969 to *Echo II* in 1970 to *November* in 1971 to *Golf*-class ships in 1972 (see Table 12.1.) Even after calling off the September 1970 deployment and ceasing work on the facilities at Cienfuegos, the Soviets were clearly testing the limits of the 1970 understanding.

In November 1974, the Inter-American Affairs subcommittee of the House Foreign Affairs Committee held its annual hearing on the Soviet naval presence in Cuba, drawing attention to the continued Soviet visits and steady escalation of the class of submarines involved. In particular, Barry Blechman, in his statement before the subcommittee and in a subsequent *New York Times* article, called for a formal U.S. protest about the visits and consideration of linking Soviet behavior to progress in the SALT negotiations, if necessary.[36]

No formal objection was issued by the United States in 1974, but when the twelfth deployment left Cuban waters on November 11, Soviet submarine visits to Cuba ended as abruptly as they had begun five years earlier. Naval deployments continued regularly, but apparently no Soviet submarine entered a Cuban port again until late in 1977. Connecting the change in Soviet behavior to the rise in 1974 of U.S. public concern over the visits is conjectural and perhaps misguided. In fact, no Soviet naval vessels at all visited Cuba for fourteen months, between June 1975 and August 1976, a notable gap in the pattern of regular visits every few months from 1969 to 1974.[37]

A variety of factors could account for Soviet behavior. From 1975 until 1978, the Soviet navy performed operations along the West African coast and in the Indian Ocean, supporting the Cuban-Soviet military actions in the Angolan and Eritrean civil wars. Surface ships in particular may simply have been more urgently needed elsewhere.

The U.S. objection to servicing of submarines in Cuba rendered the military rationale for Soviet visits less important. If one intent of Soviet naval visits to the Caribbean was to establish precedents for acceptable behavior, that objective had already been accomplished from 1969 to 1974. If part of the reason for the Soviet visits was to demonstrate both Soviet solidarity with and watchfulness over the Castro regime, the joint Cuban-Soviet activities in Africa underscored the same points. Soviet interest in continuing progress in the SALT negotiations, which had received a boost from the Ford-Brezhnev meetings at Vladivostok in November 1974, may have increased Soviet sensitivity to U.S. concern about Cuba, independent of any U.S. statements.

In late 1977, the submarine visits to Cuba resumed. In late December–early January a *Foxtrot* visited for over a month. Between September and December 1978, a deployment including a *Foxtrot* submarine visited Cuban ports for a total of eighty-two days, the longest stay on record.[38] The deployments have continued at regular intervals since then, according to U.S. intelligence sources.

Despite the ambiguity of U.S. statements about the types of Soviet submarines it could not abide in Cuba, the central point of Nixon and Kissinger's protest was clear. The United States objected to the servicing of Soviet submarines in or from Cuba. The U.S. stance was limited to this specific military concern, not extended to broader discomfort with the sign of Soviet support for Cuba represented by the port visits themselves. This circumscription and Kissinger's strong but measured private approach to the Soviets, assuring Dobrynin that no U.S. press campaign was planned and leaving steps open for a Soviet retreat, may have convinced the USSR of the seriousness yet specificity of the U.S. objection.

U.S. restraint was most likely motivated by the priority given by the Nixon administration to the overall détente relationship with the USSR. Greater importance was attached to maintaining the cordial tones of the broader association than to confronting the Soviets over these relatively trivial violations of an ambiguous agreement.

The Soviet Union, for its part, has refrained from provoking the United States into initiating a crisis by never deploying the USSR's most advanced *Yankee-* or *Delta-*class nuclear-powered, ballistic missile–carrying submarines in Cuba. These submarines can each carry missiles with a total of between sixteen and forty-eight nuclear warheads, and they are capable of ranges of up to five thousand nautical miles.[39] Both nuclear-powered and nuclear-armed, they would be in violation of any possible interpretation of the 1962 agreement and its 1970 codicil.

More to the point, deployments after the 1970 U.S. protest never took the pattern of regularized servicing of any class of Soviet submarines, such as is conducted from Soviet bases in Murmansk and Petropavlovsk or for U.S. submarines from bases in Holy Loch, Scotland, or Rota, Spain. This activity would have caused a more concrete concern for U.S. security. After 1974, with rare exceptions, the Soviet visits were by 1950s-vintage *Foxtrot* submarines. And following the Nixon protest, the Soviets immediately ceased expanding their facilities on land in Cienfuegos. So, while the Soviets clearly stretched and even violated the spirit of the U.S. position, they stopped short of what was probably their initial intention to turn Cienfuegos into a full-fledged facility to service Soviet submarines.

TABLE 12.1

Soviet Naval Visits to Cuba, 1969-1978

Visit	Dates	Submarines	Type	Armament
1	11 July-12 August 1969	2 Foxtrot 1 November[a]	long-range, diesel attack nuclear-powered	conventional nonnuclear torpedoes
2	8 May-3 June 1970	2 Foxtrot 1 Echo II	long-range, diesel attack nuclear-powered	conventional nuclear or conventional cruise missiles
3	3 September 1970- 8 January 1971	surface ships only	(time of Cienfuegos construction)	
4	30 November 1970- 8 January 1971	1 Foxtrot	long-range, diesel attack	conventional
5	10 February-11 June 1971	1 November	nuclear-powered	nonnuclear torpedoes
6	25 May-4 June 1971	1 Echo II	nuclear-powered	nuclear or conventional cruise missiles
7	31 October 1971- 24 January 1972	2 Foxtrot	long-range, diesel attack	conventional
8	7 March-17 May 1972	1 Foxtrot 1 Golf II	long-range, diesel attack diesel-powered	conventional ballistic missiles: 3 SS=N=5s/700 nm range
9	28 November 1972- 20 February 1973	1 Foxtrot 1 Echo II	long-range, diesel attack nuclear-powered	conventional nuclear or conventional cruise missiles
10	31 July-16 October 1973	1 Echo II 1 Foxtrot	nuclear-powered long-range, diesel attack	nuclear or conventional cruise missiles conventional

Visit	Dates	Submarines	Type	Armament
11	29 April-30 May 1974	1 Golf II	diesel-powered	ballistic missiles
12	24 September-11 November 1974	1 Foxtrot	long-range, diesel attack	conventional
13	25 February-5 April 1975	surface ships only		
14	23 May-6 June 1975	surface ships only		
15	16 August-21 September 1976	surface ships only		
16	27 June-22 July 1977	surface ships only		
17	13 December 1977-18 January 1978	1 Foxtrot	long-range, diesel attack	conventional
18	20 March-6 May 1978	surface ships only		
19	16 September-7 December 1978	1 Foxtrot	long-range, diesel attack	conventional

[a]Cruised in the Caribbean but did not enter a Cuban port.

Source: U.S., Congress, House of Representatives, Committee on Foreign Affairs, Subcommittee on Inter-American Affairs (annual hearings), 1971-1979.

MIG-23s, 1978

A second potential Cuban crisis was more quickly and clearly deflected by the two countries in 1978. Although Cuba has sometimes been the last of the Soviet protégé states to receive a particular weapon, the USSR has generally been evenhanded toward the countries for which it serves as military supplier, soon providing hardware to all clients comparable to that it has supplied to one. Thus Soviet shipment of MiG-23 fighter-interceptors to Syria, Iraq, Libya, and Algeria during the 1970s alerted U.S. intelligence to watch for a similar transfer to Cuba.

The MiG-23 has been produced by the Soviets in several models. The MiG-23-D, deployed only in the USSR, is a ground-attack plane with a range of twelve hundred miles. It would be capable of striking military targets in the U.S. if it were deployed in Cuba, and it can have the capacity to carry nuclear weapons. The MiG-23-F, the model exported to Egypt and other clients, is an interceptor aircraft, not configured to carry nuclear weapons.[40]

U.S. intelligence identified eighteen or twenty crated MiG-23 aircraft on board Soviet ships arriving in Cuba in late April 1978.[41] An October 23 memorandum on this development from Secretary of Defense Harold Brown to the White House was apparently leaked to newspaper columnists Rowland Evans and Robert Novak, who aired the matter on November 15, 1978.[42] In the following weeks, the U.S. press devoted considerable attention to this subject. *Pravda* responded that U.S. allegations that the MiG-23 deployment violated the 1962 agreement were "groundless and provocative" and stated that the aircraft were for defensive purposes only.[43]

Certain design characteristics distinguish the MiG-23-D from the MiG-23-F. But only the internal wiring for the bomb bays, invisible to the eye of electronic surveillance, prevents a MiG-23 from being loaded with nuclear weapons. The United States did not possess the human intelligence sources in Cuba that might have been used to confirm the mission of the new aircraft. The United States thus had no means of its own to determine conclusively whether the MiG-23s sent to Cuba in 1978 could carry nuclear weapons.

Secretary of State Cyrus Vance raised the question of the MiG-23s at a meeting with Soviet Ambassador Dobrynin on November 19, 1978.[44] U.S.-Soviet talks on the subject continued for the next three weeks.

The Carter administration had to decide what face to put on a controversy with the Soviet Union based on essentially ambiguous evidence. The administration believed that foes of the nearly completed SALT II treaty had instigated leakage of the Brown memorandum to Evans and Novak and that public support for SALT could be jeopardized by a critical view of Soviet behavior in Cuba.

In examining the negotiating history of the 1962 agreement, the State Department found that although the United States had required withdrawal of forty-two Ilyushin-28 light fighter-bombers taken into Cuba by the Soviets, the MiG-21 aircraft then under Cuban control were construed at the time as within the normal boundaries of military supply from the USSR to a client state and not threatening to U.S. security. If the MiG-23s exported to Cuba in 1978 were the F model, they were clearly replacements for the MiG-21s, were not capable of carrying nuclear weapons, and did not constitute a violation of the 1962 agreement. The State Department concluded that even if U.S. intelligence could not positively identify the aircraft as MiG-23-Fs, the limited numbers introduced did not present a significant threat to the United States and did not warrant a formal U.S. protest to the Soviets.[45]

Senior military and intelligence officials argued, however, that the 1962 agreement should not be taken as the final word on the acceptability of Soviet behavior. The threat to the United States of each Soviet action must be weighed independently from any agreements in force, they said. Almost everyone could agree, however, that eighteen or twenty MiG-23s, whatever their mission, would not markedly increase the military threat to the United States. In talks with the Soviets, the Carter administration stressed that the United States could accept Soviet assurances that the planes were not capable of carrying nuclear weapons, providing their numbers did not increase.[46]

President Carter pronounced this formula at a televised news conference on November 30:

> We would consider it to be a very serious development if the Soviet Union violated the 1962 agreement. When we have interrogated the Soviet Union through diplomatic channels, they have assured us that no shipments of weapons to the Cubans have or will violate the terms of the 1962 agreement. We will monitor their compliance with this agreement very carefully, which we have been doing in the past, both as to the quality of weapons sent there and the quantity of weapons sent there, to be sure that there is no offensive threat to the United States possible from Cuba.[47]

Indeed, the Soviets sent the Cubans no more than two squadrons, each of ten MiG-23s, first sighted in the spring of 1978. Of course, the Soviets may never have intended to provide the Cubans with more than twenty of the aircraft. But it is interesting to note that Iraq has received eighty of the planes; Syria, sixty-four; Egypt, thirty; and Libya, twenty-four. Although these countries, unlike Cuba, do pay cash for Soviet weapons, they all are more distant military clients of the Soviets than the Cubans.

The 1970 exchanges between the United States and the USSR over Soviet naval visits to Cuba had confirmed that an understanding dating from 1962 was in force between the two countries. Although it was still ambiguous in other respects, the 1970 interchange refined the nature of the U.S. objection to apply to "nuclear" forces, within the overall classes of offensive forces. The ambiguous MiG-23s transferred to Cuba in 1978 could be defined as nonnuclear by the Carter administration and thus construed as outside the terms of the understanding.

The Combat Brigade, 1979

Barely half a year passed after the MiG-23 affair before events were set in motion to provoke a major U.S.-Soviet confrontation over Cuba.[48] Called by former CIA Deputy Director Ray Cline an exercise in crisis "mangling" rather than crisis management, and contemptuously demoted to a "storm in a teacup" by the International Institute for Strategic Studies, this crisis concerned a supposed Soviet combat brigade stationed near Havana.[49]

Between fifteen thousand and seventeen thousand Soviet troops remained in Cuba after the missile crisis.[50] These included four heavily armed combat groups, according to a 1963 report by Defense Secretary Robert McNamara, totaling roughly five thousand men.[51] Each group was stationed in a different camp, and each had been encharged with site security for one of the four missile bases established during the Soviet missile deployment the year before. A group of Republican leaders, including Barry Goldwater, Richard Nixon, Nelson Rockefeller, and Kenneth Keating, made a brief fuss over the troops remaining in Cuba in the first half of 1963. These men attempted unsuccessfully to tie Senate ratification of the Test-Ban Treaty to a reduction of the Soviet troops.[52]

Early in 1963, Secretary McNamara noted in public that some of the military equipment associated with these units had been moved out of Cuba.[53] Then the Soviets removed most of the troops. Or, as one former official put it, "our surveillance recorded lots of young men in identical sport shirts on ships going out of Havana."

During the year before the missile crisis, the USSR set up a mission of several thousand military advisers in Cuba to train Cuban forces in the use of equipment exported from the USSR and to affirm the Soviet military relationship with the Castro regime. Throughout the 1960s and 1970s, the United States presumed these advisers to be the only Soviet troops on the island.

Then, U.S. intelligence obtained photographs in early 1978 showing modern Soviet military equipment located near Lourdes, sixty miles southwest of Havana.[54] The Defense Intelligence Agency and the Central Intelligence Agency concluded that the equipment was destined for Cuban forces as part of the regular process of modernization of the Cuban military that had been underway since the mid-1970s and that troop bivouac areas nearby were Cuban camps.

National Security Advisor Zbigniew Brzezinski had been alarmed about Cuban-Soviet military activities since the two countries' intervention on the Horn of Africa in 1978. His concern grew as Cuban involvement was reported in revolutions in Grenada, Nicaragua, and El Salvador. In March 1979 he ordered CIA Director Stansfield Turner to assess the size, location, capabilities, and purposes of Soviet forces in Cuba, together with Soviet and Cuban military missions elsewhere in the world.

Monitoring the "housekeeping," or administrative, communications channels of Soviet and Cuban military units from April through June 1979, the National Security Agency (NSA) unearthed Russian-language references to a Soviet unit stationed at the two sites southwest of Havana as a "brigada." Intelligence and military experts regarded a brigade as a highly irregular way to structure a training unit.

A study completed in mid-June 1979, based upon a retrospective search of NSA files, concluded that a Soviet brigade headquarters existed in Cuba as a unit separate from the acknowledged Soviet advisory group.[55] Uncertain about the mission of this unit, Army Intelligence and the NSA argued that all possible functions should be considered, including guarding nuclear weapons and conventional combat. CIA chief Turner, Defense Intelligence Agency (DIA) Director Lieutenant General Eugene Tighe, and the heads of the State Department Bureau of Intelligence and Research, Air Force Intelligence, and Navy Intelligence disagreed.[56]

CIA Director Stansfield Turner preferred a more moderate view of the new information about Soviet forces in Cuba. On July 12, the intelligence community issued a coordinated interim report that stated that a Soviet force was present as an entity separate from the advisory group but did not confirm the size, organization, or mission of the force. Reports persist that Turner ordered Army Intelligence and the NSA to abandon their more alarmist speculation about the brigade. In response, President Carter ordered stepped-up surveillance of Cuba to determine the nature and purpose of the unit.[57]

Democratic Senator Richard Stone, mindful of a large Cuban émigré population among his Florida constituency, took a particular interest in Soviet activities in the Caribbean. A swing vote in the Panama Canal Treaty debate, Stone elicited a public commitment from President Carter in January 1978 against Soviet military bases in the Western Hemisphere.[58] A member of the Foreign Relations Committee, Stone also opposed the SALT II Treaty. He was certain that the Carter administration was underrating the Soviet military threat to the United States in order to promote the treaty.

On his way to an open Foreign Relations Committee hearing on SALT II on July 17, 1979, Stone was pulled aside by a member of his staff. The aide told Stone that he had overheard a conversation between members of the executive agency staffs that were present. Apparently discussing the June NSA report, they made remarks that indicated that the intelligence community knew of the existence of a Soviet combat force in Cuba.

Stone lost no time in using the information. As soon as the hearing began, Stone asked witnesses admirals Thomas Moorer and Elmo Zumwalt whether "a direct or indirect effort to establish a military base would be established by the introduction of a large number of combat troops of the Soviet Union into Cuba." That afternoon, the committee went into a closed session to discuss verification of SALT II. Stone asked administration officials present to confirm or deny his rumor, under threat of walking out the door and announcing to the waiting press all he had been told by his aide. CIA Director Turner denied that the intelligence community had found anything new in Cuba. But Vice Admiral Bobby Ray Inman, chief of the National Security Agency, did not deny Stone's charge.

Committee Chairman Frank Church listened to the assurances of Defense Secretary Brown, DIA chief Tighe, and White House counsel Lloyd Cutler. Secretary Brown offered to put his position in writing. Fearing that Stone would release his allegations and seeking to avoid rumors damaging to SALT, Church promptly issued a committee statement, from which only Senator Stone dissented:

> In response to a question about the presence of Soviet military personnel in Cuba, Secretary Brown advised the Senate Foreign Relations Committee that there is no evidence of any substantial increase in the size of the Soviet military presence in Cuba over the past several years. Apart from a military group that has been advising the Cuban

Armed Forces for 15 years or more, our intelligence does not warrant the conclusion that there are any other significant Soviet military forces in Cuba.[59]

Stone then contacted the White House and Secretary of State Vance, asking for increased surveillance of Cuba and a formal response on the troop issue. Vance wrote Stone a letter on July 27, paraphrasing Secretary Brown's position: "There is no evidence of any substantial increase of the Soviet military presence in Cuba over the past several years or of a Soviet military base. Apart from a military group that has been advising the Cuban armed forces for 15 years or more, our intelligence does not warrant the conclusion that there are other significant Soviet forces in Cuba."[60]

Few newspapers reported Stone's charge on July 18, and the matter quickly disappeared from public view.[61] Contrary to his public expression, however, Secretary Vance decided to take the matter up with the Soviets. On July 27, the same day Vance's denial was released, State Department Special Advisor on Soviet Affairs Marshall D. Shulman called on Soviet Deputy Ambassador Bessmertnykh in Washington. Shulman noted to Bessmertnykh that the Soviets would have heard press reports that the United States had evidence that organized Soviet combat troops were in Cuba. The United States was watching developments in Cuba very closely, Shulman told the Soviet diplomat. The United States, he said, would be very concerned if there were a Soviet base in Cuba, and U.S. concern was "not theoretical."

Shortly thereafter, the monitoring of voice communications between personnel in the Soviet force and at Cuban command centers in Havana who were arranging Soviet use of Cuban military maneuvering areas yielded details of a planned field exercise by the brigade.[62] On August 17, U.S. reconnaissance satellites took photographs of a Soviet force equipped with tanks, artillery, and armored personnel carriers, in maneuvers bearing no apparent relation to training Cuban forces.

On August 23, President Carter was informed of the new intelligence when he stopped in Hannibal, Missouri, during a vacation on a Mississippi riverboat. On August 27, this observation, identifying a combat brigade, was reported in the *National Intelligence Daily,* a classified internal report with a circulation of over two hundred individuals within the U.S. government.[63] The strength, between two-thousand and three-thousand men, and structure of the unit were deduced from existing intelligence about other Soviet brigades in East Germany and the Soviet Far East.

An interagency meeting, attended by Secretaries Vance and Brown,

Brzezinski, and senior intelligence officials, was held at the White House on August 28. The decision at the meeting was to downplay the significance of the brigade by avoiding public disclosure as long as possible and to pursue the matter privately with the Soviets through diplomatic channels. Accordingly, David Newsom, the under secretary of state for political affairs, called chargé d'affaires Vladilen Vasev at the Soviet embassy in Washington. He informed Vasev that the United States now had conclusive evidence of the brigade and that the brigade was a matter of great concern to the United States.

On August 29, the contents of the *National Intelligence Daily* were leaked to the magazine *Aviation Week and Space Technology*, whose staff telephoned Newsom's office for confirmation, threatening immediate publication.

An interagency meeting of under secretaries and assistant secretaries was called at the State Department of August 30 to decide how to cope with the leak. Both to allay a sense of crisis and to protect SALT, the officials decided that State Department spokesman Hodding Carter III would make a short announcement the next day and Under Secretary Newsom would alert congressional leaders.

When he called the Senate Foreign Relations Committee to speak with Chairman Frank Church, Newsom reached a clerk, the only staff member on call while the senators and senior staff were in various parts of the world on fact-finding trips and vacations. The clerk directed Newsom to phone Church at his home in Idaho. Newsom told Church that U.S. intelligence had uncovered evidence in Cuba of a Soviet combat brigade. Church asked how large the brigade was and how long it had been there. The brigade was between two and three thousand men, Newsom replied. Not all the data were in, he cautioned, and the unit could have been in Cuba for some time. The administration believed it to be a new development that these troops seemed to have no advisory role and appeared to be a self-contained Soviet unit. Newsom explained that he was advising Church because the senator could expect to read about the new developments in the newspaper within twenty-four to forty-eight hours.

Staff members arriving at Church's home for dinner that evening found the Senator sitting on a chair by the door, hands folded, with a sorrowful look on his face. "You won't believe this," he said, "but there's a Soviet combat brigade in Cuba, exactly the opposite of what the administration told us thirty days ago." For the next two hours, Church and his staff debated how to handle the matter. Despite Church's careful management as Senate Foreign Relations Committee chairman, strong opposition to the SALT II treaty had been manifested through hearings held in July and early August. Church worried that Senator Stone, minority leader Howard Baker, and other senators would launch into frank opposition to the treaty if the brigade became public through a press leak, because the presence of the force could cast doubt on the reliability of the Soviets, the credibility of the Carter administration, and the detection capabilities of the U.S. intelligence community.

One of Church's formative experiences as a junior senator had been the 1962 Cuban missile crisis. Senator Kenneth Keating had been the target of Cuban émigré pressures and intelligence community leaks alleging the presence of missiles in Cuba in 1962, just as had Senator Stone about the brigade in 1979. Under assurances from the Kennedy administration, Church had voiced the administration's denials in the Senate in the late summer of 1962 that any offensive Soviet missiles had been placed in Cuba.

When the U-2 reconnaissance flights finally exposed the missile sites, Church was left out on a limb. Kennedy personally rescued the young senator by appointing him to accompany United Nations Ambassador Adlai Stevenson to the UN as a Senate Foreign Relations Committee delegate, to present the case there against the Soviet missile deployment. So reminiscent was the sequence of events in 1979 of the 1962 crisis that they reawakened what one former Church associate calls "tribal memories" in the senator.

Church and his staff felt that in order to prevent a crisis on the order of 1962 and to encourage a successful diplomatic solution with the USSR on the model of the dealings over Soviet submarine facilities at Cienfuegos in 1970, the affair had to be handled very carefully. Church felt that it would be politically inept to let the information be leaked rather than announced by someone in a position of authority in the government.

Finally, Frank Church had put his name on the Senate Foreign Relations Committee statement a month earlier, affirming that no change had occurred in Soviet forces in Cuba. Fighting a National Conservative Political Action Coalition campaign in Idaho, which had branded him "soft" on defense and the Soviet Union, Church was worried that the news leak would make his earlier denial of Soviet forces look either gullible or irresponsible. An anti-Church commercial on Idaho television just the night before had shown Church and Fidel Castro smoking cigars together, on Church's recent trip to Havana. Soviet Americanologist Georgi Arbatov's reported comment a day or two later, "There is nothing as dangerous as a scared dove," may be unjust, but to the extent that Church was politically sensitive, the issues of Cuba, defense policy, and Soviet behavior were particularly salient at this moment. Church's natural reaction was to take matters into his own hands.

After two hours of discussion with his staff, Church's conclusion was that if the administration didn't intend to take a stronger profile in announcing the news, he would. Church placed a call to Secretary of State Cyrus Vance. Church asked Vance whether either he or the president intended to make the announcement. No, Vance said. Church responded that "if you're not going to make the announcement, then at least the news should come by way of a responsible announcement." He told Vance that he intended to make the announcement himself. Vance replied, "We'll trust you to use your judgment on that, Senator," and cautioned Church not to blow the affair out of proportion. He reported that the State Department was "working on" the prospect of negotiations with the Soviets. Church took this response to mean that Vance had no objection if he wanted to divulge the information.

Church then placed a call, through the White House operator, to President Carter in Plains, Georgia. When he reached White House Congressional liaison Frank Moore, he was told that the president was "out of pocket," or unavailable through the weekend, and would not be returning the senator's call that evening. Church and his staff then wrote a statement that was delivered to a hastily convened press conference in the living room of Church's home an hour later. Church told the local media of the new developments and said that the brigade must be removed. When pressed by local reporters that evening and on a Boise television show the next day, Church refused to speculate on the link between the brigade and SALT II.

On September 4, Senator Church canceled the Foreign Relations Committee hearing on SALT II to hold closed interrogations of administration witnesses about the brigade. At the end of this first day of hearings, in response to a reporter's question, Church firmly tied the Cuban issue to SALT II. "There is no likelihood whatever that the Senate would ratify the SALT II Treaty as long as Russian combat troops remain stationed in Cuba," he said, stating what he thought was a political fact.[64] The press took his statement as a firm commitment.

A State Department staff meeting was called on September 4 to hammer out the department's position on the brigade. The department had conducted a review of the U.S.-Soviet interaction over Soviet forces in Cuba since 1962, and particularly of U.S. statements on record about Soviet ground forces. Although the review yielded ten statements about Soviet ground forces by top U.S. policymakers in the months after the missile crisis, there was no evidence that ground forces had been covered by the 1962 understanding or its 1970 addendum. But from these statements, as well as from President Carter's commitment in 1978 against Soviet bases in the western hemisphere, the State Department staff members drew the conclusion that a combat force could be regarded as in conflict with unilateral but publicly expressed U.S. policy.

Secretary Vance announced at a September 5 press conference that he would "not be satisfied with the *status quo* in Cuba."[65] He added that the administration might not object if SALT II were held up until the USSR met U.S. concern about the troops.

The Soviet reaction to the U.S. charge was rapid and indignant. Vasev responded to Newsom's initial questioning by demanding to know the "legal basis" for the U.S. charge. A lengthy *Pravda* editorial on September 11, entitled "Who Needed This and Why?," debunked the U.S. concern. "For almost 17 years there has been a training center in Cuba, where Soviet military personnel help Cuban military men learn about Soviet military technology which is used by the Cuban Army," *Pravda* argued.[66]

Called back to Washington from the deathbed of his father in Moscow, Soviet Ambassador Anatolyi Dobrynin met with Secretary of State Vance on September 10, and again four times in the next two weeks. On September 24 and 27, Vance met in New York with Soviet Foreign Minister Gromyko.

According to many reports, the U.S. position toward the Soviets initially was to ask for a withdrawal of the Soviet brigade. Zbigniew Brzezinski had convinced the president that the United States must take a firm position on this issue, to strike at the broader problem of Soviet-Cuban military collusion. Vance seemingly hoped for Soviet accommodation, a hope based partly on early indications from a Soviet source he trusted that the USSR might be flexible on this point. Although Secretary Vance admitted on September 19 that the United States had no right to demand that the troops be removed under the 1962 and 1970 understandings, he reiterated that their presence ran "counter to long-held American policies."[67]

The Soviets stressed repeatedly in private and in their press that the Soviet forces in Cuba had training functions. A continuing review of intelligence established the distinct possibility that this Soviet unit, although its hardware had recently been upgraded, had been in place for a number of years, if not indeed since 1962. In the words of a U.S. intelligence official, "In 1963, the Soviet units were withdrawn, and the Soviets consolidated what they had left. We observed the disappearance of these four [combat] units, and equated this with their movement out, rather than their redistribution. . . . When we searched back through all the information, we found that one camp was always a little different from the others." And while no specific training functions could be identified for the force, no airlift or sealift capabilities could be found to lend it the capability of engaging in combat outside of Cuba. Finally, a variety of other possible missions— from guarding the largest Soviet electronic intelligence-gathering facility in the world, located nearby at Los Palacios, to serving as a guarantee of Soviet commitment to the Castro regime while twenty thousand Cuban troops were fighting in Angola and Ethiopia—were identified.

The Soviets refused to consider the U.S. demand for the brigade's withdrawal or to formulate a way to alter the equipment of the brigade so that its actual status agreed with its stated training functions, as the Carter administration eventually requested. The Soviets were incapable of understanding the complex way in which U.S. domestic politics had produced the U.S. request that the brigade be removed or altered. The Soviets perceived the U.S. position as a deliberate attempt to exact concessions from the USSR in return for the ratification of the SALT II treaty. Making these concessions, they felt, could open a "Pandora's box" of other demands upon the Soviet Union. As one Soviet analyst of the United States in Moscow told *Washington Post* correspondent Murray Marder at the time, "They will end up demanding that Castro leave Cuba and that Cuba should abandon Marxism."[68]

The nature of the U.S. position, after U.S. tolerance of Soviet ground forces in Cuba for twelve years, underlined Soviet suspicions. Given the magnitude of U.S. intelligence coverage of Cuba, and the rapidity with which the submarine base construction and the arrival of the MiG-23s had been detected by the United States in 1970 and 1978, the Soviets had difficulty believing that the United States had only discovered the troop presence in mid-1979. Even if the Soviets knew that they had successfully hidden the brigade from U.S. intelligence, U.S. linkage to SALT II convinced the Soviets of U.S. designs beyond the direct issue of the military threat to the United States represented by the unit. The most the USSR agreed to accept was a series of statements reaffirming the training mission of the brigade, promising not to change its function or status, ensuring that it would not be a threat to the United States or any other nation, and reaffirming the 1962 and 1970 agreements.[69] The statements held only the force of a verbal understanding, committed to paper in the form of a diplomatic "non-letter" for purposes of clarity in communication.

In the third week of September, President Carter apparently decided that an aggressive stance towards the brigade, prolonging the crisis and deepening the public sense of confrontation with the USSR, might doom the SALT treaty in the United States. Faced with Soviet infexibility, Carter went on nationwide television on October 1 to announce a series of unilateral U.S. actions to deal with this threat. Increased surveillance of Cuba and of Soviet military activities elsewhere in the world, establishment of the Joint Caribbean Military Task Force, and expanded regular U.S. military maneuvers in the Caribbean were among the measures Carter outlined.[70] He also cited Brezhnev's assurances about the troops, received via the U.S.-Soviet hotline on September 27.

This sequence of events was indeed a "storm in a teacup," but a crisis need not threaten to provoke a direct military showdown in order to pose dangers to international peace stability. The brigade "minicrisis" of 1979 had two important consequences. First, it contributed greatly to the political demise of the SALT II treaty signed by presidents Carter and Brezhnev at Vienna in July, 1979, and under debate in the United States in the fall of 1979. Second, the U.S. position in the affair may have actually been counter-productive to the goal of frustrating Soviet military activity in the Third World, the fundamental issue that the brigade crisis brought into focus.

When the Senate Foreign Relations Committee completed several weeks of intensive hearings on SALT II on August 2, the chance of the treaty's passing looked at least even. When the brigade crisis occurred, Frank Church, the committee chairman, linked the treaty to the fate of the brigade and postponed reporting it from the committee for more than a month to hold hearings on the Cuban imbroglio and await its resolution. Not until November 9 did the committee complete its consideration and report the agreement out for floor debate. Then, in December, as Senate Majority Leader Robert Byrd sought to find the space on the Senate calendar for the treaty debate, the Soviet invasion of Afghanistan occurred, bringing in its wake President Carter's formal tabling of the treaty.

Even had the treaty come up for debate in October or November, the brigade crisis would have made its passage doubtful. Focus by the public and Congress on the brigade had shifted the terms of the national debate away from the substance of the treaty and onto the issues of Soviet foreign behavior and Soviet-Cuban military relations, of which the brigade was symbolic, where deeper emotions about the USSR could come into play. The moderate coalition in the Senate supporting the SALT agreement suffered substantial attrition as the brigade crisis allowed senators wavering on SALT to find a reason to oppose the treaty. Russell Long, a senior and influential member of the Senate, changed his vote to oppose SALT II on September 12, giving as his reason Soviet "bad faith" as evidenced by the troop brigade.[71] And linkage of SALT to the much more objectionable Soviet behavior in Afghanistan in December was nearly inevitable, given the previous linkage to the Cuban brigade.

The Brezhnev regime began in 1964 on a note of succession to a predecessor who had unsuccessfully attempted to extend Soviet military influence using Cuba as a base. In one sense, the entire import of the Brezhnev leadership in the military realm has been to build Soviet strength to the point that in a general way, if not relating specifically to establishing the sort of outpost Khrushchev attempted in Cuba, the USSR would not be obliged to curtail the promotion of its foreign influence at the behest of the United States, as it had so sharply in 1962. From the Soviet standpoint it was simply preposterous that the USSR should be asked in 1979 to agree to compromise on an issue where no hard evidence could be presented to show a change in Soviet behavior from what had been tolerated for seventeen years by the United States. For Soviet leaders to make such a concession could have had serious ramifications for the image of the reliability of Soviet commitment to military allies and would have reawakened historically painful and humiliating memories.

Three perceptions contributed more specifically to Soviet unwillingness to compromise on the issue of the brigade. Unable or unwilling to understand how the U.S. political system could irrationally or unpremeditatedly produce a demand that they alter the brigade, the Soviets suspected ulterior motives. They failed to see how the United States could regard the brigade as a genuine military threat. The linkage of the brigade's removal to SALT II, which seemed necessary for political reasons in the United States, was the kiss of death for persuading the Soviets actually to change the force.

Without access to Soviet decisionmakers, speculation about the effect that one experience in international politics has upon subsequent actions by Soviet leaders rests to a certain extent upon guesswork. But Soviet leaders most likely base their expectations for the behavior of the United States on past experiences, among which instances of great importance or recent vintage may particularly stand out.

The author's discussions with Soviet officials at the time and interviews afterward revealed a growing Soviet attitude after the brigade crisis that further positive benefits from the relationship with the United States were unlikely, given the accusatory, confrontational, and to the Soviet mind somewhat irrational face the Carter administration presented over the brigade issue. The Soviets may have made a political calculation that the Carter administration was not capable of delivering a ratified SALT treaty at a price that would be acceptable to the USSR. At the same time, the disorganized and contradictory U.S. handling of the matter, and the eventual U.S. retreat from its stated aim to ensure removal of the brigade, revealed to the Soviets an administration unwilling or unable to exert leverage upon the USSR. U.S. policy in the brigade case failed to act as either an inducement or a deterrent toward the USSR.

The Soviet invasion of Afghanistan three months after the brigade affair occurred mainly for reasons indigenous to Soviet-Afghan relations, percolating long before the fall of 1979. But U.S. behavior in the brigade case acted to remove any positive constraints that expectations for productive relations with the United States might have exerted on Soviet calculations in dealing with Afghanistan. This same U.S. behavior demonstrated the hollowness of U.S. statements of commitment against Soviet policies.

Conclusions

The historical record shows that Cuba is a source of periodic crises in U.S.-Soviet relations. How this danger is managed depends, of course, on the actions of both superpowers. But two successfully resolved quarrels and one confrontation over Cuba during the 1970s show that there is much the United States can do unilaterally to cope better with the problem, beyond the obvious need to understand Soviet interests and perceptions more accurately.

During the past decade, incidents involving Cuba have been successfully resolved when the United States has been able to present clear evidence of objectionable Soviet behavior, to limit its protest to activities representing a concrete threat to U.S. security, and to exert effective leverage upon the USSR.

In 1970 and 1978, U.S. intelligence on Soviet behavior and military hardware in Cuba was precise and timely. Therefore, the United States was able in the first instance to confidently present its objection to the Soviet construction of submarine support facilities. In the second case, although U.S. intelligence was unable finally to ascertain the payload of the aircraft, sufficient information about the arrival dates, numbers, and deployment of the MiG-23s was quickly obtained, and these data aided in determining the U.S. position on the question. Whatever the wisdom of the policies finally adopted by the U.S., these policies were taken with high confidence that the information on which they were based was accurate.

In contrast, intelligence on the combat brigade dribbled into the hands of decisionmakers in 1978 and 1979 in a fashion that fostered a political conflagration in the existing domestic climate. The problem was partly one of available intelligence, partly one of analysis, and partly one of intelligence management. Cutbacks in both overflights and peripheral intelligence gathering around Cuba during the Nixon and Carter administrations had reduced coverage of Cuba that might have more completely recorded changes in the equipment and maneuvering practices of the brigade beginning in the mid-1960s. By 1974, a variety of trends had combined to reduce the number of analytical personnel assigned to Cuba within the intelligence community to less than 25 percent of what it had been in the mid-1960s.

In the years following the Cuban missile crisis, despite the alarms over submarines and bombers in the 1970s, U.S. intelligence coverage of Cuba was steadily eroded. Sometimes the purpose of cutbacks was geared to political ends. Intrusive intelligence gathering against Cuba was a source of friction that some officials in the Carter administration thought necessary to eliminate to smooth the path to normalizing relations. U.S. dealings with Cuba, they believed, could conceivably become less troubled if relations took a more regular course.

But more importantly, the available analysts were not viewing the available data with an eye to noting changes in ground forces. Analytical filters, perhaps changing over time to align with the boundaries of tolerance drawn by a particular president or director of Central Intelligence, or established incrementally over years, seem to determine the developments an intelligence analyst regards as militarily significant. Soviet ground forces in Cuba were not deemed important between 1962 and 1979, within the mainstream of the intelligence community. When such forces were noted, their presence was not highlighted in intelligence reports.

The discovery of a Soviet unit distinct from the training mission in 1979 does not seem to be simply a case of policymakers' not paying heed to available information. In this instance, data that might have revealed a separate nontraining unit were filed away without closer examination, because the question of the troops' function and status was considered as irrelevant as their very existence. As the political climate in the United States and the context of Soviet-Cuban military operations worldwide changed to make the question pertinent, a review of the available intelligence in this new light yielded an impression of surprise and newness.

The apparent newness of the brigade, which in reality was just newly discovered by U.S. intelligence, reinforced the sense of crisis about events in the summer of 1979 and left Secretary Vance, Frank Church, and President Carter with the impression that it was something urgent that must be dealt with. On the basis of the partial and somewhat misleading information available in late August, Senator Church and the administration quickly committed themselves to the position that the status quo was unacceptable without having a clear conception of what exactly was the status quo.

The context of overall Soviet behavior within which any discrete Soviet activity must be weighed shifts constantly. Successive political leaderships may also redefine the types of Soviet actions they judge to be threatening to U.S. security. This being the case, how can any meaningful criteria be established to determine which activities are worthy of a constantly high level of attention? Even for a country with the resources of the United States, intelligence capabilities are finite and must be apportioned to various targets according to a set of priorities.[72]

A first principle should be that certain areas, due to the peculiar combination of U.S. and Soviet interests, are likely scenes for confrontation. Cuba is outstanding among these areas. Irrespective of the rise and fall in the importance to the United States of other areas of the globe, Cuba should remain a constant priority. Given the burden of evidence, as the difficult task of apportioning scarce intelligence collection and analysis resources is accomplished, Cuba is among the last areas where scrutiny should be cut back.

Even with adequate data, the problem of analysis remains. A time lag obviously occurred in 1979 between a change in the perception of policymakers like Brzezinski about the context of Soviet and Cuban military ventures abroad, within which discrete activities in Cuba were considered, and heightened sensitivity within the intelligence community. This problem suggests the need for constant review of intelligence issues in a particular region in the context of broader concerns, so that intelligence can anticipate rather than trail political necessity.

The issue of the Soviet military presence in Cuba holds a peculiar volatility in public opinion in the United States. This fact suggests that a category of intelligence may exist that is politically significant beyond its operational military importance. Based on the experience of the past twenty years, intelligence on any Soviet military activity in Cuba demands special attention in analysis and particular care from top intelligence officials in presenting the government and the public with enough background and contextual information to ensure a clear and balanced impression of the activity's significance.

Management of the intelligence on the combat brigade contributed to the difficulty of political handling of the affair. Imprecision was evident in the new designation of the brigade as a combat force in the *National Intelligence Daily* in August. Political maneuvering was apparent in Stansfield Turner's downplaying of evidence about the brigade in reports to the White House and congressional testimony in the summer of 1979. The conviction grew within some parts of the intelligence community that Turner was not considering sufficiently seriously the intelligence fragments uncovered in 1978 and early 1979, showing possible changes in Soviet forces in Cuba. The resulting refusal of Vice Admiral Bobby Ray Inman to deny Senator Richard Stone's charge in July and the leaks to the press in August tied the hands of political leaders by causing them to believe they must take immediate action. Intelligence community managers must obviously be more attuned to the political uses of information and must cope more effectively with divergent assessments of intelligence data within the community.

Clarity of information is important for any government that does not wish to be trapped by its own public, its own Congress, or its own internal bureaucratic processes. Precise, accurate intelligence and analysis, based on a clear conception of what U.S. interests are and what constitutes objectionable Soviet behavior in a particular region, is perhaps the most important ingredient of diplomatic flexibility in a time of crisis.

Henry Kissinger has proclaimed his success in halting the construction of submarine servicing facilities at Cienfuegos in 1970 as a triumph of quiet diplomacy with the USSR.[73] His feat was as much domestic as it was diplomatic, however, in maintaining a distinction between the military threat to the United States of Soviet activities in Cuba and other objectionable Soviet behavior. If a single phenomenon characterized the 1979 brigade crisis, it was the Carter administration's poor management of the intelligence on the brigade, and of the public impression of the brigade's meaning for U.S. security, that allowed the issue to become linked to SALT II.

A lack of political sensitivity in judging the effects of their acts, combined with a sense of political constraint to pursue those very courses of action, impelled Carter administration officials first to commit themselves to the position that no change in Soviet forces had occurred in Cuba, in Secretary Vance's July 27 letter to Senator Stone. Fear of appearing duplicitous as new information contradicting the assurance became available and the accident of the incident's occurring during Washington's summer vacation then drove Secretary Vance to alarm Senator Church in the midst of a campaign swing in Idaho. By involving Senator Church in its earlier denial of a change in Soviet forces in Cuba, the administration had made him vulnerable to the charge of duplicity if he did not act once the new intelligence was brought to his attention. And the president and secretary of state lost control of the situation completely by hesitating to handle the matter directly themselves in the days before the news was to become public.

The linkage to SALT II and commitment at the highest levels of the administration to remove the combat brigade was made before thought was given to how and whether this objective could be accomplished. President Carter, Secretary Vance, Senator Church, and others backed themselves into a corner from which they could escape only by gambling that the Soviets would be flexible and accommodating on the issue of ground troops in Cuba.

The Carter administration's failure to limit its objection to only those Soviet activities that were directly threatening to U.S. security decreased the credibility of the U.S. demand to the Soviets. The first two questions Soviet Ambassador Dobrynin reportedly asked Secretary Vance when they met in early September were whether the brigade was a new phenomenon and whether it was a threat to the United States. Vance was forced to reply "No" to both questions. From that point forward, the Soviet position on the issue did not deviate an inch from complete refusal to negotiate.

In Paul Nitze's words, "Our outrage should be commensurate with our leverage." In 1979, SALT II was obviously not sufficient leverage to induce the Soviets to remove the combat brigade, if the fate of the treaty turned upon the minor issue of the brigade.

Pro- and anti-détente factions in the United States have disputed whether that policy has really smoothed relations between the two superpowers. In controversies involving Soviet forces in Cuba, the tone of the overall relationship has seemed to influence the incentives of both sides to compromise in order not to jeopardize the basic association. When U.S.-Soviet relations have been relatively good or have held the promise of improvement, as in 1970, or at least the promise of an arms treaty, as in 1978, adjustment has been encouraged on both sides. The implied leverage of Soviet expectations in relations with the United States has proved effective in dealings about Cuba, but explicit linkage has only been counterproductive.

The brigade episode was merely the worst in a series of failures marking the Carter administration as the nadir of effectiveness in the execution of U.S. foreign policy in recent years. Lack of presidential leadership, a volatile political climate, and the penetration of Congress into the making of foreign policy all affected the way in which the brigade issue was handled. The revelation in early 1982 that the USSR had sent ground-attack helicopters to Cuba is evidence that future administrations will be forced to deal with the question of Soviet military relations with the island. Despite the cold war tone of Reagan's presidency, the Reagan administration may have more success in coping with this problem by virtue of greater coherence in leadership, providing proper attention is given to the necessities of intelligence, the prerequisites for credibility with the Soviets, and the limits of linkage.

Notes

The author has benefited from the suggestions of Barry M. Blechman, Alexander L. George, Arnold L. Horelick, William H. Kincade, John W. Lewis, Cynthia Roberts, and Marshall D. Shulman, who read and commented on drafts of this chapter. The Center for Foreign Policy Development at Brown University, the Arms Control and Disarmament Program at Stanford University, and the Social Science Department of the RAND Corporation arranged seminars that provided helpful discussion and criticism on this subject.

1. "Chairman Khrushchev's Message of October 26, 1962," *Department of State Bulletin,* November 19, 1973, p. 645. Khrushchev wrote a letter to President Kennedy the following day that discussed both the issues of verification and U.S. missiles in Turkey:

We are willing to remove from Cuba the means which you regard as offensive. We are willing to carry out and to make this pledge in the United Nations. Your representatives will make a declaration to the effect that the United States, for its part, considering the uneasiness and anxiety of the Soviet State, will remove its analogous means from Turkey. Let us reach agreement as to the period of time needed by you and by us to bring this about. And after that, persons entrusted by the United Nations Security Council could inspect on the spot the fulfillment of the pledges made. Of course, the permission of the Governments of Cuba and Turkey is necessary for the entry into those countries of the pledge made by each side. . . .

We . . . will make a statement within the framework of the Security Council to the effect that the Soviet Government gives a solemn promise to respect the inviolability of the borders and sovereignty of Turkey, not to interfere in its internal affairs, not to invade Turkey, not to make available our territory as a bridgehead for such an invasion, and that it would also restrain those who contemplate committing aggression against Turkey, either from the territory of the Soviet Union or from the territory of Turkey's other neighboring states.

("Chairman Khrushchev's Message of October 27, 1962," *Department of State Bulletin,* November 19, 1973, pp. 646–647.) When Kennedy responded on October 27, he addressed the chairman's remarks of the previous day, omitting reference to Turkey.

2. "President Kennedy's Message of October 27, 1962," *Department of State Bulletin*, November 19, 1973, p. 649.

3. "Statement by President Kennedy, November 20, 1962," *Department of State Bulletin*, December 10, 1962, pp. 874–875.

4. "President John F. Kennedy, News Conference, November 20, 1962," *Department of State Bulletin*, December 10, 1962, p. 874.

5. "Secretary of State Dean Rusk, Interview, *Meet the Press*, NBC-TV, January 27, 1963," *Department of State Bulletin*, February 18, 1963, p. 245.

6. Ibid., p. 245.

7. Raymond L. Garthoff, "American Reaction to Soviet Aircraft in Cuba, 1962 and 1968," *Political Science Quarterly* 95, no. 3 (Fall, 1980):436.

8. Ibid.

9. U.S., Congress, House of Representatives, Committee on Foreign Affairs, Subcommittee on Inter-American Affairs, *Soviet Naval Activities in Cuba*, Hearings, 92d Congress, 1st Session, September 28, 1971, pt. 2, p. 2.

10. Ibid., pp. 2–3.

11. International Institute for Strategic Studies, *The Military Balance* (London: International Institute for Strategic Studies, 1979–1980). p. 10.

12. U.S., Congress, House, *Soviet Naval Activities in Cuba*, pt. 2, p. 2. The barges were publicly identified as receptacles for nuclear-power-plant effluents only in 1974. See U.S., Congress, House of Representatives, Committee on Foreign Affairs, Subcommittee on Inter-American Affairs, *Soviet Activities in Cuba*, Hearings, 93d Congress, November 20 and 21, 1974, pts. 4 and 5, p. 65.

13. Henry Kissinger, *White House Years* (Boston: Little, Brown & Co., 1979), p. 634.

14. Garthoff, "American Reaction to Soviet Aircraft."

15. U.S., Congress, House, *Soviet Naval Activities in Cuba*, p. 4.

16. Kissinger, *White House Years*, p. 638.

17. U.S., Congress, House, *Soviet Naval Activities in Cuba*, p. 4.

18. U.S., Congress, House of Representatives, Committee on Foreign Affairs, Subcommittee on Inter-American Affairs, *Soviet Naval Activities in Cuba*, Hearings, 91st Congress, 2d Session, September 30, October 13, November 19 and 24, 1970, p. 2.

19. U.S., Congress, House, *Soviet Activities in Cuba*, p. 34.

20. Ibid., p. 36.

21. Highly informed officials in the State Department believe that Kissinger himself first leaked the information.

22. Kissinger, *White House Years*, p. 646; *New York Times*, September 26, 1970.

23. Kissinger, *White House Years*, p. 647.

24. Ibid.

25. Ibid., p. 649.

26. Ibid.

27. Ibid., p. 650. In his memoirs, Kissinger does not specify the nature of these five types of activity.

28. TASS International Service, Moscow, October 13, 1970 (*Foreign Broadcast Information Service Daily Report, Soviet Union,* October 13, 1970, p. A1).

29. Barry M. Blechman and Stephanie E. Levinson, "Soviet Submarine Visits to Cuba," U.S. Naval Institute, *Proceedings* vol. 101, no. 9/871 (September 1975):33.

30. George Quester, "Missiles in Cuba, 1970," *Foreign Affairs* 49 (April 1971):494.

31. Blechman and Levinson, "Soviet Submarine Visits," p. 33.

32. Diesel-powered submarines could actually benefit more from a base in Cuba, since their on-station time is far shorter than that of nuclear-powered craft.

33. *New York Times,* September 25, 1970.

34. Blechman and Levinson, "Soviet Submarine Visits," p. 33.

35. Some *Foxtrots,* including one exported to Cuba by the USSR in 1979, are newly manufactured to designs of the 1950s.

36. U.S., Congress, House of Representatives, Committee on Foreign Affairs, Subcommittee on International Political and Military Affairs, *Soviet Activities in Cuba,* Hearings, September 1976, p. 30. (Hereafter cited as U.S., Congress, House, *Soviet Activities* 1976.)

37. U.S., Congress, House, *Soviet Activities in Cuba,* p. 102.

38. U.S., Congress, House of Representatives, Committee on Foreign Affairs, Subcommittee on Inter-American Affairs, *Impact of Cuban-Soviet Ties in the Western Hemisphere, Spring, 1979,* Hearings, April 25 and 26, 1979, p. 8.

39. International Institute for Strategic Studies, *The Military Balance,* p. 87.

40. U.S., Congress, House, *Impact of Cuban-Soviet Ties,* p. 15.

41. Garthoff, "American Reaction to Soviet Aircraft," p. 438.

42. Rowland Evans and Robert Novak, "Cuba's MiG 23s," *Washington Post,* November 15, 1978.

43. "The Making of Soap Bubbles," A. Petrov, *Pravda,* November 18, 1978, p. 5 (*Foreign Broadcast Information Service Daily Report, Soviet Union,* November 20, 1978, p. B1).

44. *Washington Post,* November 20, 1978, p. 1.

45. Garthoff, "American Reaction to Soviet Aircraft," p. 438.

46. *Baltimore Sun,* December 2, 1978, p. 6.

47. "President's News Conference of November 30, 1978," *Weekly Compilation of Presidential Documents* 14, no. 48 (December 4, 1978):2101.

48. Much of the material in this section is based on interviews with individuals in the Carter administration who dealt with the brigade crisis.

49. See Ray S. Cline, "History Repeated As Farce," *Washington Post,* October 15, 1979, p. 23; *Strategic Survey,* 1979, pp. 30–31.

50. "Secretary of State Dean Rusk, Interview, *Meet the Press,* NBC-TV, January 27, 1963," *Department of State Bulletin,* February 18, 1963, p. 245.

51. "Department of Defense Special Cuba Briefing," Robert S. McNamara, U.S. Department of State, February 6, 1963, transcript, p. 39.

52. Mark Brent and William Kincade, "How Sanity Defused a Cuba Flap," *Washington Star,* October 14, 1979.

53. "Department of Defense Briefing," p. 39.

54. Don Oberdorfer, "Chapter 1: 'Brigada': Unwelcome Sight in Cuba," *Washington Post,* September 9, 1979, p. 1.

55. Ibid.

56. Ibid.

57. Ibid.

58. U.S., Senate, Committee on Foreign Relations, *Hearings and Markup on the Panama Canal Treaties,* 95th Congress, 2d Session, vol. 6, January 26, 27, and 30, 1978, p. 101.

59. "Statement Issued by Senator Frank Church (D-Idaho), Chairman of the Senate Foreign Relations Committee, and Senator Jacob Javits (R-New York), Ranking Minority Member," Committee on Foreign Relations media notice, July 17, 1979.

60. "Texts of Letter and Statements by Vance and Carter," *The New York Times,* September 6, 1979, p. 7.

61. *Washington Star,* July 18, 1979, p. 4.

62. Oberdorfer, "Chapter 1."

63. Martin Schram, "Response: Avoiding a Crisis Tone," *Washington Post,* September 9, 1979, p. 18.

64. *Washington Post,* September 6, 1979, p. 1.

65. "Press Conference by the Honorable Cyrus R. Vance," Department of State press release no. 216, September 5, 1979.

66. *Pravda,* September 11, 1979, p. 1 (*Foreign Broadcast Information Service Daily Report, Soviet Union,* September 11, 1979, p. A1).

67. Robert C. Toth, "Soviet Brigade in Cuba: No Easy Solution," *Los Angeles Times,* September 19, 1979, p. 8.

68. Murray Marder, "Soviet Views of Troop Issue Colored by 1962 Debacle," *Washington Post,* October 1, 1979, p. 1.

69. "Background on the Question of Soviet Troops in Cuba," U.S. Department of State release no. 93, October 1, 1979, p. 2.

70. "Soviet Troops in Cuba," Department of State release no. 92, October 1, 1979 (full text of Carter speech).

71. *Washington Post,* September 13, 1979, p. A1-16.

72. As a result of the Cuban brigade controversy, two internal intelligence community reviews have considered the problem of gathering and analyzing intelligence on Cuba, in particular, and on other targets of fluctuating priority. The Senate Intelligence Committee staff prepared a classified report for the Committee in late 1979 and early 1980, reviewing the coverage provided by all agencies on Cuba since the missile crisis of 1962. See "Report to the Senate of the Select Committee on Intelligence, United States Senate, Covering the Period January 1, 1979–December 31, 1980," 96th Congress, 2d Session, 1980, p. 12-13.

A senior review panel of the intelligence community, composed of three experts not currently involved in intelligence work and a staff director, completed a broader analysis in 1980. The purpose of their highly classified report was to establish criteria and make recommendations for prioritizing intelligence targets, to avoid being surprised by a "discovery" such as the Cuban brigade in the future.

73. "Kissinger Says His Quiet Diplomacy Prevented Cuban Crisis in 1970," *Washington Star,* September 24, 1979, p. 1.

13
Why Détente Failed: An Interpretation

George W. Breslauer

By any meaningful definition of the term, détente no longer exists today. If we agree that its reappearance would be a good thing, it behooves us to ponder what went wrong. One possible explanation for the demise of détente would be that Soviet bad faith undermined the embryonic collaborative relationship between the superpowers. Another explanation would be that U.S. bad faith had this effect. Still a third explanation would be that détente collapsed due to mutual misperceptions, missed signals, and misunderstandings. A fourth hypothesis would be that the failure of détente was inevitable, given the structure of the international system and the differences between the superpowers in ideology, interests, assets, needs, political structures, and stages of international involvement.

I find none of these explanations fully satisfying, though my proposed explanation will come closer to the fourth hypothesis than to any of the others. The first two explanations are too one-sided, failing to appreciate that no clear definition of obligations existed against which to measure bad faith or good faith. The third explanation places too much emphasis on accidental factors, downplaying the fact that misperceptions and misunderstandings are often a product of differences in perspective. Finally, the inevitability thesis, although it correctly emphasizes both superpower interaction and fundamental differences between the superpowers, is too quick to conclude that things could not have happened any other way. For one thing, there were accidental factors (Watergate, for example) that intruded on the détente relationship by undermining the strength and cohesiveness of U.S. leadership. For another thing, the reality of nuclear weapons gave the superpowers an overriding *mutual* interest in arms control and in defusing some of the most obvious sources of confrontation.

Yet détente failed despite this mutual interest. Why? I propose to argue in this chapter that détente was originally defined as a mixed collaborative-competitive relationship. It failed because each side tried to define the terms of competition, and the terms of collaboration, in ways more geared toward maximizing unilateral advantage than toward expanding the mutual interest in institutionalizing the relationship. I will leave it to other scholars to determine the domestic structural and ideological roots of these increasingly incompatible definitions—and to investigate whether events could have unfolded otherwise. My task is more limited: to propose an analytic framework for thinking about the nature of the superpower relationship being forged in the early 1970s; to discuss the fragilities inherent in such a relationship; and to indicate how the positions adopted by the Soviet and U.S. leaderships intensified those fragilities.

There are, in principle, four ways in which the superpowers could relate to each other in the world of the 1970s: confrontation, competition, collaboration, and avoidance. By the late 1960s, both Soviet and U.S. leaders had concluded that mutual avoidance was not a practical basis for peace; there were too many areas in which interests and aspirations clashed and overlapped. The leaders also came to realize that the periodic confrontations of the 1950s and 1960s were too dangerous in an era of strategic parity between competing global powers. Hence, Nixon and Brezhnev moved toward a détente relationship that would increase the scope of superpower collaboration, geared toward reducing the incidence of confrontation while acknowledging the reality of competition.[1] Neither side harbored great illusions that a mixed collaborative-competitive relationship would eliminate confrontations from the relationship, for each side had high-priority, frequently overlapping interests and ambitions to defend against encroachment (in the Middle East, for example). Nor did the two nations embrace such airtight grand strategies as to assume that mutual avoidance would no longer be part of their foreign policy repertoire. But their goal was to change an existing relationship of confrontational competition into one better described as collaborative competition.[2]

By definition, collaborative competition is a mixed relationship. It is based upon the *coexistence* of conflicting premises, not the harmonious resolution of such presuppositions. It assumes that these premises are at least compatible, for if they were not, an effort to coexist on the basis of each would be like trying to square the circle. (The world being what it is, it would be impossible to compartmentalize hermetically the two tracks of the relationship.) Thus, détente between global superpowers can only work if collaboration and competition are treated as conflicting premises rather than antithetical or incompatible ones.

To prevent collaboration and competition from becoming incompatible impulses requires vision and skill in the leadership of both countries. It requires conscious efforts to reinforce and expand the mutual interest in maintaining such a mixed relationship. Both powers must be committed to a measure of reciprocity and restraint in their dealings with each other. Specifically, superpower competition must be kept in bounds by mutual acknowledgment (tacit or formal) of the need for restraint, both in seizing opportunities for wins and in reacting to losses that do not threaten primary interests. In the absence of such restraint, the competitive relationship will quickly escalate to a confrontational one. And while occasional confrontations are inevitable—and the threat of confrontation to defend vital interests is necessary—no collaborative process can remain alive for long in the face of continuous confrontations (as we learned during 1958–1962).

The collaborative relationship, in turn, must be regulated by a mutual commitment to reciprocity. In the absence of such a norm, no process of collaboration could withstand the strain imposed by the competitive side of the relationship and remain legitimate for long in the eyes of both participants. In sum, for détente to take hold and survive the ups and downs of national and world politics, nothing is more important than a *mutual* commitment to ensuring that neither side *write off* the other's dedication to restraint in their competition and reciprocity in their collaboration.

Yet dismissing each other's efforts is precisely what the two powers had done by the end of the 1970s. The reason this happened, it seems to me, is that each partner in the relationship sought to skew the definitions of restraint and reciprocity in ways that would play to its own strengths, insulate its weaknesses, and maximize its comparative advantage. As détente deteriorated, each side paid less and less attention to expanding the mutual interests that would be required to ensure the longevity of the process itself.

On Competition

Great power competition is the process by which these states jockey for advantage in areas that are not vital interests of the competitor and by means that do not contain a high potential for escalation. Competition between the United States and the Soviet Union during the 1970s was a given. U.S. withdrawal from Vietnam did not signal withdrawal from the United States' role as a global power. The Soviet buildup of conventional forces—the navy, in particular—signaled the USSR's determination to fulfill the commitment it had made in 1955: to compete for presence, status, influence, and allies throughout the Third World.[3] The onset of détente, then, did not imply an end to this competition. Rather, it reflected a mutual recognition that the competition could not safely be regulated by threats of continuous confrontations or by mutual avoidance. The task, therefore, was to regulate the competition.

There was one formal effort to define rules of the game in the competition: the Basic Principles Agreement of 1972.[4] Although that document formalized certain principles on which détente was based (mutually advantageous commercial relations, avoidance of threats to each other's primary security interests, noninterference in internal affairs, and the need to prevent confrontations), it did little to define realistic rules of competition in the Third World. It expressed the hope that each side would "prevent the development of situations capable of causing a dangerous exacerbation of their relations." It called for "mutual restraint" and negotiation of differences "in a spirit of reciprocity, mutual accommodation, and mutual benefit." It raised the prospect of an ultimately "effective system of international security." And it averred that neither side would seek "to obtain unilateral advantage at the expense of the other, directly or indirectly." In endorsing these principles, each side hoped that the other was agreeing that it had no Third World interests that warranted the destruction of the budding collaborative relationship on issues of primary concern.

Yet the Basic Principles Agreement contained the seeds of disillusionment. For unless both sides proceeded to explore, separately and collaboratively, the operational meaning of these abstractions and their applicability to concrete situations, those principles would create either cynicism or false expectations of harmony in a world of *competitive* global powers. By structuring the choices as confrontation or collaboration, the superpowers set the stage for disillusionment, as each side jockeyed for position in the ongoing competitive game.

On the other hand, we should not be overly harsh in our criticism of the Basic Principles Agreement. It goes too far to call the agreement "fatuous"[5] simply because it seemed to ignore the fact that great powers compete for unilateral advantage in peripheral areas as a matter of course. One purpose of détente—to both Soviet and U.S. leaders—was to prevent the search for unilateral advantage from getting out of hand. The *mutual* hope was that each side would develop a stake in the collaborative relationship that would temper its seizure of opportunities and its backlash against losses. To accomplish this development of interest would require a dilution of the myth (previously ascendant on both sides) that Third World competition was a zero-sum game, in which each side's gain was the other side's loss. The Basic Principles Agreement would have been more realistic had the two nations spelled out this distinction between competition as jockeying for advantage and competition as a zero-sum game. But that agreement was realistic in tacitly acknowledging the need for a norm of restraint in the competitive relationship if détente were to flourish.

Even if the politicians involved had wanted to make operational the distinction between routine and unacceptable competitive behavior, they would have had a difficult time indeed. For these men were not scholars engaged in an academic exercise; they were politicians seeking simultaneously to bargain hard in defense of their countries' interests and to create a relationship of manageable expectations between competing global powers. Under those circumstances, formalizing rules of the game, and specifying a comprehensive distinction between competition and confrontation, is a tortuous process at best.

First, there is no way that either side can define for itself (let alone in public) a clear distinction between the two modes of operation. A competitive global power, for example, might define its vital interests geographically, in terms of commitments to defend certain regions or countries. But to defend them against what? Since both powers claim the right to compete for *influence* everywhere, the issue then becomes one of the means employed to project influence. On this score, clear distinctions are almost impossible to agree upon. By one accounting, economic, diplomatic, and political instrumentalities might be defined as competitive means and any form of military assistance or penetration might be defined as confrontational. By another accounting, military assistance programs, advisers, advanced weapons, or subversion might be defined as the normal tools of competition in areas of nonvital interest to either power, whereas combat troops and threats to intervene might be defined as confrontational.[6]

This obstacle might be surmountable if the assets of the competing global powers were roughly symmetrical, so that agreement on one definition or the other did not grossly disadvantage one side. Such is not the case with the United States and USSR. When it seeks to build lasting influence in Third World countries, the Soviet Union relies primarily on its ideological appeal (as "antiimperialist"), on the provision of heavy-industrial materials and expertise, on political-diplomatic support, and on military hardware and personnel. When the United States competes, it can provide all of these (except the ideological appeals), as well as large amounts of investment capital, credits, loans, consumer goods, high technology, and markets; it can also manipulate administrative and political levers that remain to U.S. allies as a legacy of the colonial era. Stated differently, the United States is much less reliant than the USSR on military instruments for influencing outcomes in the Third World.

This basic asymmetry complicates the task of agreeing upon equitable rules of the game for superpower competition. Other things being equal, the likelihood of Western "wins" (to the extent the decisive factor is outsider involvement) without the employment of overt military force is greater than the likelihood of Soviet wins that do not rely on the military instrument. Yet formalized rules of the game can only be legitimized to both parties if the question "Who wins?" is as important a criterion as "By what means?" in judging each country's value as regulators of the competition. For if rules grossly disadvantage one side, those rules are not likely to remain legitimate for long—if they are agreed to in the first place.

A third obstacle to formalizing rules of the game is rooted in the strategy of conflict and might be called "the Korea analogy." How does one admit the distinction between legitimate competition and illegitimate confrontation without in fact inviting challenges that might not otherwise have been forthcoming? Each side in a competitive relationship can be expected to manipulate the meaning of "competition" and "confrontation" to secure bargaining advantages, and neither side can afford to tip its hand too much without incurring costs. Hence, both sides have an interest in keeping the rival in some doubt about their intentions, their distinction between vital and secondary interests, and their willingness to resist encroachment.[7] This is what we mean when we say that the essence of competition is the search for unilateral advantage.

Yet, if that search is unrestrained, détente cannot possibly survive. Comprehensive rules of the game are not the way to keep the competition within manageable bounds. Alternatively, each competitor, I would argue, must communicate to the other, by its response to losses and by its level of assertiveness in exploiting targets of opportunity, a sense of proportion about the extent of the loss and the implications for other, more collaborative tracks of the relationship. Thus, more important than prior agreement about rules is the message subsequently tacitly communicated by the contestants' degree of restraint in playing the competitive game.

When we examine the course of superpower competition in the 1970s, we find that the competitive track of the relationship ultimately destroyed the collaborative track. This destruction occurred largely because neither side showed much restraint in the pursuit of unilateral advantage in the competitive relationship. Each of the superpowers defined the terms of "legitimate competition" in ways that allowed it to lean on its strengths—to employ those of its assets in which it enjoyed a comparative advantage. Moreover, each superpower engaged in best-case predictions about the compatibility of its competitive behavior with the continuance of the détente process.

Both governments signaled, by word and deed during 1969–1972, their insistence that détente did not imply a withdrawal from their global power roles. The United States did this by Henry Kissinger's eager pursuit of exclusionary diplomacy in the Middle East, by his linking of U.S.-Soviet normalization with the opening to the People's Republic of China (which implied a mobilization of new assets in international diplomacy and of new sources of political leverage on the USSR), and by President Nixon's doctrine of Vietnamization (which implied U.S. efforts to increase the capacity of the nation's Third World clients for self-help without ruling out U.S. reentry if self-help failed). Perhaps the most forceful demonstration of U.S. determination not to let détente deter the United States from maintenance of its competitive global role was the mining and bombing of Haiphong harbor only a week before the scheduled Nixon-Brezhnev Moscow summit in May 1972.[8]

Soviet words and deeds signaled an analogous determination. From the very first months of détente, Brezhnev and other Soviet leaders repeated over and over that détente would not lead the Soviets to endorse the international status quo or to opt out of generalized support for national liberation movements or anti-Western governments.[9] In the Middle East during 1969–1972, the Soviets escalated their military involvement in Egypt and Syria. In Vietnam, the Soviets continued their heavy-material supply for that country's military effort and refused to pressure Vietnam to cease its war of liberation. In the Third World more generally, the Soviets increased their rate of arms transfers from 1970 onward. Thus, both countries made clear that efforts to avoid confrontations and to expand collaboration did not mean a marked diminution of the commitment to global competition.

Marked diminution is one thing; selective restraint is another. Both countries' leaders *did* indicate an awareness that some restraint in the scope of competition might be necessary to prevent the collaborative process from collapsing. Kissinger and Nixon, for example, reassured the Soviets that the United States' recognition of the People's Republic of China (PRC) did not imply a budding anti-

Soviet alliance. In addition, the United States was steadily withdrawing troops from Vietnam during 1970–1972, a move that signaled a new era of more modest U.S. use of the military instrument in global competition. Finally, struggles in Washington between the executive and congressional branches signaled, willy-nilly, the development of a "Vietnam syndrome," i.e., a reduction in the collective will (and, therefore, the presidential ability) to use the military instrument.

The Soviets experienced no such syndrome. Their conventional military establishment was expanding steadily in pursuit of parity as a global power. Yet the Soviets did indicate a willingness to exercise selective restraint in seizing targets of opportunity. In the Middle East during 1970–1972, they exercised so much restraint (relative to their clients' demands and to U.S. indulgence of Israeli demands) that Sadat threw them out of his country.[10] In Vietnam, during 1972, they overlooked U.S. bombing and mining in order to hold the summit meeting as scheduled, and they encouraged North Vietnam to make crucial concessions in the Paris Peace Talks in January 1973. In Latin America, they acted like misers in the type and amount of support they gave the Allende regime, partly because they considered Allende a poor bet but partly because they did not want to provoke the United States.[11]

Although both sides exercised selective restraint, even as they insisted that they would remain global powers, the leaders of each nation also fashioned strategies of détente that would maximize their overall comparative advantage in the competitive game. For the United States, the main assets were economic. Kissinger's strategy of détente, therefore, sought to envelop the Soviets in a web of economic ties that would deepen the USSR's material stake in continued détente with the United States. The price for such continuation would be ever-greater Soviet restraint in the competitive game. Thus, Kissinger considered it vital to forge linkages between the economic-collaborative side of détente and the Third World competitive side. Whether Kissinger was motivated by a Spenglerian view of history or by high optimism is beside the point. It does not matter whether he was just trying to make the best of a bad situation (i.e., the Vietnam syndrome) or whether he believed that he could ultimately induce the Soviets to opt out of the competitive game entirely, leaving the United States to try to forge a conservative and stable international order in the Third World. In the short term, his strategy of linkage was simply an effort to lean on U.S. economic strengths so as to reduce U.S. vulnerability to Soviet encroachments in the Third World.

Predictably, the Soviets rejected such linkage. They pressed instead for maximization of reciprocal exchanges *within* policy realms. Hence, their emphasis on insulating the SALT treaties from events in other realms of Soviet-U.S. relations, their urge to strike "mutually advantageous" deals *within* the economic realm, and their failure to accuse the United States of violating the rules of détente by resisting forces of change in the Third World. They exuded a quiet confidence that those forces of change worked to their advantage and that U.S. efforts to resist those forces would ultimately fail. They rejected in principle a strategy of linkage that sought to make trade contingent on an end to Soviet assistance to those forces. Instead, they sought to maximize their perceived comparative advantage by compartmentalizing the competitive and the collaborative tracks of the U.S.-Soviet relationship.

This divergence in perspective contained the seeds for a breakdown of the détente relationship. Yet, through mid-1973, things appeared to be going rather well. The economic relationship was expanding, and the Soviet appetite for those economic benefits appeared to be increasing with the eating. The competitive relationship was not undercutting the collaborative, despite conflicts over Vietnam, the Middle East, and Cuba. In addition, the Soviets responded to quiet U.S. pressures by allowing tens of thousands of Soviet Jews to emigrate during 1970–1973. Yet, from 1974 onward, things went downhill. Events intruded that changed the balance of incentives for Soviet competitive restraint.

Two very different kinds of events took place. The first was Kissinger's escalation of exclusionary diplomacy in the Middle East from January 1974 onward. The shock of the October 1973 war had led to agreement on a multilateral forum (the Geneva Conference), under U.S.-Soviet cochairmanship, for negotiating a Middle East settlement. But within a matter of weeks, Kissinger perceived the opportunity once again to go it alone, and he initiated step-by-step shuttle diplomacy in the region.[12] This development resulted in the Israeli-Egyptian disengagement agreement of January 1974—an agreement that did not enrage the Soviets, for a Kissingerian effort to drive a wedge between them and Egypt was nothing new. But when, in May 1974, Kissinger negotiated a similar agreement between Israel and Syria, the Soviets perceived a real challenge. Syria had developed a special relationship with the USSR and was perceived by Moscow as more reliable than Egypt under Sadat. The Soviets had been working hard to consolidate their influence in Syria. Now the United States was seeking to disrupt that relationship as well. In Soviet eyes, this escalation of the competition was not a violation of the rules of détente, nor was it cause for confrontation. It did suggest to them, however, that Kissinger (1) was not interested in U.S.-Soviet Third World collaboration and (2) embraced a definition of restraint in the competition that did not preclude U.S. efforts to expel Soviet influence from countries in which the USSR had invested heavily. In short, the Soviets perceived Kissinger's efforts in the Middle East as zero-sum competition.[13]

A second set of events during 1974 also undermined Soviet incentives for restraint: the Jackson-Vanik and Stevenson amendments to the U.S.-Soviet Trade Agreement. Kissinger fought hard against these bills but lost. The first amendment formally linked most-favored nation status for the USSR to Soviet emigration policy. Specifically, it demanded formalized, public Soviet commitment to high levels of annual Jewish emigration. The second bill restricted credit allocation to the Soviets to a four-year total of $300 million—that is, $75 million a year, a mere drop in the bucket relative to Soviet expectations. Thus, Kissinger's strategy of linkage was being undercut at home, with a major reduction in economic incentives for competitive restraint.

From 1975 onward, the Soviets noticeably escalated their competitive activity in the Third World. They gave material and military assistance to the North Vietnamese in their final offensive. And they qualitatively escalated the means of competition, increasing the use of direct military and political involvement in the Third World by Soviet, East German, and Cuban military personnel, in order to have a decisive and lasting impact on the course of events. We are all familiar with the litany: Angola (1975–1976), Ethiopia (1978), South Yemen (1978). The dividing point, however, appears to be 1975. What motivated this change in Soviet tactics?

The usual interpretation is that the Soviets were seizing a target of opportunity, with the only means at their disposal, at a time when the risk of a U.S. confrontational response was low. However, this explanation says nothing about Soviet calculations of the impact of their actions on the larger détente relationship with the United States. Although a good study of this matter remains to be written, it seems quite plausible that the Soviets' escalation of competition was justified in their minds by the events of 1974. Little economic incentive for restraint remained. And if Kissinger would make every effort to mobilize his political and economic leverage to exclude the Soviets from the Middle East, why could they not use their primary assets (Cuban forces and military supply) to exclude the United States from Angola and Ethiopia? The point is not that they were looking for revenge but rather that they did not necessarily view their behavior as a violation of the spirit of détente.[14]

The response of the U.S. policy community, however, was to cry "Foul!" Having been led to believe that détente would result in a *reduction* of Soviet Third World activity and influence, key U.S. officials defined Soviet actions as confrontational. The fact that Soviet wins resulted from novel use of the military instrument further increased the objections. For the use of such an instrument is inherently more threatening than the mobilization of economic assets, and it was precisely in the use of the military instrument, given the Vietnam syndrome, that U.S. policy influentials felt at a comparative disadvantage in the competitive game. For this very reason, the United States did not directly confront the USSR over Angola. Instead, it reacted to Soviet wins in ways that leaned on U.S. strengths and exploited Soviet vulnerabilities. Prospects for SALT II ratification dropped sharply, as did U.S. interest in bilateral trade, and the United States began to move in the direction of a strategic relationship with the PRC. Zero-sum thinking about the competitive relationship gradually became ascendant in Washington, as did skepticism about the value of the collaborative relationship, overwhelming the continuous efforts of Cyrus Vance, the periodic efforts of Jimmy Carter, and the occasional efforts of Zbigniew Brzezinski to stem the tide. These changes in attitude, it should be noted, preceded the Soviet invasion of Afghanistan in December 1979.

The Soviets viewed these trends with alarm. And well they might, for a return to the arms race, loss of economic benefits, and a tacit U.S. alliance with the PRC were each threatening prospects in themselves.[15] But these trends were also alarming because they communicated so clearly the broad gap between Soviet and U.S. definitions of restraint in the competitive game. Specifically, the Soviets realized that the U.S. policy community had never come to accept the basic premises of détente, as *Moscow* had sought to define them in order to maximize *its* comparative advantage: greater importance of the U.S.-Soviet relationship than that of the U.S.-USSR-PRC triangular relationship; insulation of the commitments to SALT and trade from the vagaries of Third World competition; and acceptance of the Soviet claim to equal status as a global power.

In sum, at a crucial stage in the evolution of détente, the competitive track had no mutually agreed-upon norms of restraint. When events conspired to highlight this situation, each side leaned on its strengths and exploited its rival's vulnerabilities. Such a tendency created immense pressure in Washington to scuttle détente. For the two sides had, since 1969, been operating with incompatible conceptions of the linkage between the collaborative and competitive tracks of the relationship.

On Collaboration

In contrast to competition, collaboration requires an ongoing procedure for negotiating tradeoffs and explicitly coordinating definitions and policies. Superpower collaboration can take many forms, both among issues and within them. The early years of détente witnessed a series of bilateral agreements, geared toward controlling the arms race, controlling nuclear proliferation, defusing the Berlin issue, recognizing the division of Europe, expanding East-West trade, and collaborating in scientific, cultural, environmental, health, and related fields. The Basic Principles Agreement of 1972 was a first step toward defining norms of reciprocity in the Third World, but the second step was never taken.

In the Third World, there are numerous forms that collaboration could take. At one extreme, the concept of a superpower condominium implies a comprehensive, harmonious, and collusive definition of interests, geared toward jointly imposing on weaker states terms for conflict resolution that the superpowers have worked out on their own. At the other extreme, a minimalist form of collaboration would establish procedures—consultation, notification, and so on—that keep open lines of communication or seek to prevent accidents and misunderstandings. These extremes are either too much or too little; the first is utopian and the second is insufficient. But between these extremes, one can imagine (and find support in history for[16]) a panoply of collaborative formulas: exclusive spheres of influence; partial and adhoc superpower collusion at the expense of both nations' clients in a specific conflict; ad hoc agreement that both superpowers will avoid involvement in a given conflict; ad hoc agreement upon involvement by one power, but not the other, in a given conflict; agreements to restrict the use of certain means of competition in given areas or types of conflict; and development of multilateral forums for conflict resolution or amelioration.

Superpower collaboration, in most of these forms, is extraordinarily difficult, given Third World turbulence, the competing ideologies of the superpowers, and their differing stages of international involvement. Moreover, since collaboration is only a supplement to ongoing competition, the process must bear the political strain invariably arising from that competition. But for collaboration to succeed, it must also deal with still another constraint: both sides must legitimize the process at home by being able to demonstrate that some acceptable minimal norm of reciprocity is being met, either within individual agreements or among them.

For an ongoing process of superpower collaboration to remain legitimized, it must meet two criteria of reciprocity, at two levels of the relationship. At the more general level, it must ensure diffuse support for the relationship by affirming the *equal status* of the two powers.[17] Equal status means that neither power will actively seek to undermine the stability of the other's system, neither will challenge the political sovereignty of the other's government in the territory of the homeland, and neither will attempt to force the other to abandon its role as a global power. Mutual recognition of equal status is the minimal level of consensus required for a collaborative bargaining structure on more specific issues to remain intact through the inevitable ups and downs of the relationship. At this more specific level, the norm of reciprocity requires a mutual commitment to *equivalent exchange.* The definition of what constitutes equivalence, of course, can be tortuous in situations in which the assets, security needs, and ambitions of the powers involved are not symmetrical.[18] But precisely for this reason it is important that the notion of equal status be continuously reaffirmed in the course of hammering out more specific agreements.

Détente's early successes in defining reciprocity and reaching agreements may well be attributable to special features of the issues and regions in which those agreements were being forged. First, in contrast to Third World questions, issues of European security, Berlin, and German rearmament were located in arenas for either confrontation or collaboration. The ambiguities and uncertainties of superpower competition largely did not apply, for the area had been shown, through a history of confrontations, to be unmistakably of primary interest to both powers. Second, Europe and arms control were among the highest priorities of the superpowers at the time (in addition to Vietnam for the United States), thus providing what Thomas Comstock calls a "temporary confluence of priority interests" in reaching agreements through compromise.[19] Third, Europe and arms control were issues that, in the early 1970s at least, did not challenge the norm of equal status for the superpowers. The two countries reaffirmed spheres of influence in Europe and mutual recognition of what was then viewed as "reality," and, in the case of arms control, they sought to stabilize a relationship of strategic parity. Fourth, in contrast to the turbulent Third World, issues of trade, European security, and even arms control had a relatively stable frame of reference in which to hammer out mutually agreeable terms. To be sure, the pace of technological advance always threatened to outstrip that of arms control negotiations, but that pace was at least reasonably predictable, whereas the direction of Third World change was not. Fifth, the extent of superpower control over the units the two countries were seeking to regulate was much greater than superpower control in the Third World. For Nixon and Brezhnev to forge an agreement on arms control, trade, and European security required them to be able to "deliver" domestic political actors or relatively agreeable alliance partners. To forge an agreement on the Middle East required them also to deliver the leaders of Egypt, Israel, Syria, Saudi Arabia, and the Palestine Liberation Organization. Finally, the collaborative issues on which success was achieved could more easily be broken down than Third World conflicts. Agreement was reached in large part because the negotiators were able to come to terms on the easiest components of the issue, deferring the knottiest issues to future negotiations. Thus, the German treaties were made possible by the fact that they were not linked to success in the Mutual Force Reduction talks. SALT I was made possible by the deferral until SALT II of consideration of MIRVs and qualitative strategic modernization. The Helsinki Accords were made possible by an agreement to disagree about the practical definition of "human rights." All these features, then, made it considerably easier (though by no means easy) to achieve early successes in superpower collaboration than it would have been if détente's early agenda had been primarily the regulation of Third World competition.

Yet this deferral of the knottiest issues also demonstrates how very competitively each side approached the collaborative process. Each tried to lose as little unilateral advantage as possible in the exchanges negotiated. (Why they adopted these postures—because of political constraints at home, for example—is another matter.) Thus, in SALT I, the United States was determined to protect its MIRVs and to develop cruise missiles as ostensible bargaining chips, rather than trading them away in exchange for a Soviet commitment not to develop and deploy such weaponry. The Soviets, in turn, communicated to President Nixon their determination to build up in those areas not restrained by the treaty.[20] Brezhnev was committed to catching up in the qualitative race and to arming while talking. Similarly, on the European settlement, the Soviets showed little interest in making real progress on Mutual Balanced Force Reduction. Their primary—indeed, almost exclusive—goal was to reach agreements that would gain Western European and U.S. recognition of post–World War II boundaries, along with expanded inter-European trade. Western negotiators, in turn, pressed for a definition of human rights as political rights and sought to commit the Soviets to exchange liberalization in Eastern Europe for boundary recognition and economic benefits. As a result of this mutual search for the best possible unilateral deal, both sides would interpret the Helsinki agreement in self-serving ways: the Soviets stressed Baskets I and II; the U.S. stressed Basket III.[21]

When détente began to go downhill, this deferred agenda for collaboration came back to haunt pro-détente forces on both sides. The rise of the right wing in U.S. politics was facilitated by the conservatives' ability to point to Soviet strategic modernization and production of MIRVs, to the presence of SS-20 IRBMs in the European theater, and to Soviet human rights policy at home. Although they were not formal violations of any agreed-upon obligations, these tendencies helped to legitimize efforts to remilitarize NATO and to encourage a backlash against SALT per se. That backlash against détente in turn entered into Soviet calculations of the costs of invading Afghanistan.

Superpower collaboration on Third World issues did not get very far before distrust began spiralling in 1975. One reason for this lack of action was that the agenda of détente was already crowded with more pressing issues. But another reason was that each side embraced very different notions about the purposes of collaboration and the forms of collaboration that were most desirable and feasible.

The geopolitical situation in which the Soviets found themselves in the early 1970s helped to shape their perspectives on Third World collaboration. The USSR was in the position of a rising military power, but one lacking the economic capacity to compete in the international economic order (old and new). And the Soviets faced a continuing problem of border security—an unstable Eastern Europe and a hostile PRC, supplementing U.S.-led alliance systems. The combination of a latent "siege mentality," a sense of exclusion from much of the international economic community, and expanded global reach fostered in the Soviet leadership a combination of vulnerability, fear, and determination. That determination expressed itself competitively in efforts to gain allies, influence, and status commensurate with a global power and to emphasize the USSR's role as leader of the world communist movement. Collaboratively, however, that determination found expression in an urge to use collaborative forums both as instruments for selective conflict amelioration and as ways of consolidating or expanding relative Soviet access, status, and influence.

This perspective predisposed Soviet leaders toward certain forms of collaboration while biasing them against others. In various oceans, for example, they would signal their determination to compete militarily with the United States in those waters but would simultaneously propose demilitarization of the ocean, whereby the United States would retreat from established positions and the USSR would agree not to fill the vacuum thereby created. On the Arab-Israeli conflict during 1970–1977, the Soviets were eager for either of two approaches: a multilateral negotiating forum that would simultaneously tackle substantive issues and reaffirm Soviet status as a global power, a regional power, and the primary military and political patron of key Arab states; or some kind of superpower collusion that would tackle substantive issues behind closed doors and thereby ensure that pressure on client states to make concessions would not appear to be unilateral.[22] On the PRC issue, the Soviet urge for superpower collusion was strongest. Hoping to create an exclusive superpower club, but having very little leverage of its own over the PRC, the USSR hoped to enlist the United States in collusion against Chinese nuclear and ICBM development.[23]

Thus, the Soviet approach entailed a preference for forms of collaboration that would increase Soviet leverage where there previously had been relatively little. This is not to say that they acted in bad faith, viewed collaborative forums as arenas for obstructionism, or viewed Third World collaboration as a zero-sum game. Rather, Soviet leaders optimistically perceived the United States to be on the defensive in world affairs and in need of collaboration. The Soviets would often, therefore, offer the United States tradeoffs in which the Soviet concession would be not to exploit U.S. difficulties or in which the Soviets would offer to reduce the costs to the United States of accommodating to certain new "realities."

These offers were, in any case, usually their initial bargaining position. We may never know how much the Soviets would have conceded in the collaborative process, for Kissinger and Brzezinski wrote off Soviet initiatives as disingenuous and optimistically believed in the United States' ability to go it alone. U.S. economic power and military power in the international system were declining in relative terms but were still far greater, taken together, than those of any other state. Awareness of relative decline fostered a sense of vulnerability and fear in the face of Soviet wins, but the fact of hegemonic U.S. power fostered a sense of confidence about U.S. ability to outcompete the Soviets and avoid genuine collaboration— beyond agreements to keep in touch to avoid letting crises get out of hand. Moreover, U.S. leaders were not inclined to accord the Soviets status and access that the USSR had not been able to achieve without the help of the United States.

On some issues, this choice not to pursue collaboration was a predictable response, for it was a reaction to the one-sided character of Soviet proposals. When the Soviets proposed demilitarization of a region in which the United States was the only substantial military power, U.S. leaders saw this proposition as lacking in reciprocity. When the Soviets proposed demilitarization of certain waters (e.g., the Persian Gulf) in which both powers had a naval presence but where it was far more important to the United States to maintain its presence, and along the borders of states on the shores of which the Soviets enjoyed massive conventional superiority, U.S. leaders also rejected this offer as one-sided. And the Soviet wish for U.S.-Soviet collusion at the expense of the PRC was also viewed as an unequal exchange, since only the U.S. had something to lose in that situation.

But the U.S. approach to Third World collaboration was also self-serving, and therefore it was unacceptable to the Soviets. Typically, U.S. national security advisers defined collaborative reciprocity as Soviet forebearance from exploiting targets of opportunity when U.S. efforts to control a local situation were failing and the United States was in retreat. This was a definition of collaboration that the Soviets could not live with, for it appeared to them to lead to bailing out the United States after that country had tried to exclude them. The Soviets had little urge to reinforce U.S. exclusionary efforts by reducing the cost to the United States of pursuing such efforts. They were not interested, either, in forms of collaboration that involved ad hoc Soviet restraint in the face of U.S. political paralysis or retreat. Rather, they wanted explicitly negotiated tradeoffs that would reaffirm their status as coequal and through which they could feel more confident that the tables would not later be turned on them.

Thus, the failure of U.S.-Soviet collaboration to get off the ground on Third World issues was a product of clashing definitions of reciprocity. The Soviet leaders were apparently more eager for a collusive relationship than were the U.S. leaders, but they often shaped their initial bargaining positions in ways that sought to play upon the Vietnam syndrome and put the United States on the defensive. In the end, this tendency only strengthened the forces of backlash in U.S. politics. The United States, in turn, assumed from the start that the USSR was only interested in unilateral ascendancy in the Third World. U.S. presidents resisted the establishment of collaborative forums in which that proposition might be tested, for the very establishment of those forums might give the Soviets something for nothing—access and influence they might otherwise not attain. Yet it was precisely that access and influence toward which Soviet Third World policy was aimed.

Because both sides were exceedingly ambitious about Third World collaboration—the USSR seeking either collusion or one-sided deals, the United States seeking to go it alone at Soviet expense—little or no attention was paid to developing more modest building blocks for a collaborative regime. In particular, almost no attention was paid to reaching agreements that both superpowers would avoid involvement in a given conflict. To be sure, such agreements would not have been easy to achieve. But it is striking that so little diplomatic effort was invested in exploring the possibilities.

Conclusion

To summarize: détente was a mixed competitive-collaborative relationship between global superpowers possessed of contrasting ideologies, political structures, assets, needs, and stages of international involvement. It was made possible by Soviet attainment of strategic parity, which led to a perceived mutual interest in arms control and confrontation avoidance. For détente to maintain its momentum as a process, given the numerous differences between the superpowers, it had to be buttressed by norms of restraint in the competitive relationship and norms of reciprocity in the collaborative. As it turned out, the norms agreed to were rather minimal in scope and application. Each side instead shaped its approach in ways that leaned on its strengths and sought to maximize its comparative advantage. Kissinger's strategy of détente had possibilities for expanding the mutual interest in restraint and reciprocity, but the rise of the right wing, beginning in 1974, changed both the terms of exchange in the relationship and Soviet behavior. On both sides, the search for unilateral advantage escalated thereafter. The consequence of these tendencies was that competition escalated, leaving the ongoing collaborative process hostage to the political backlash. Since collaborative successes in the early years had been based on deferral of the knottiest issues, it was these issues that slowed down progress on the collaborative track. With few successes in these issues to be set against it, the U.S. backlash against détente was able to gather momentum before the collaborative process could consolidate its political base.

With this interpretation in mind, let us now return to the four alternative explanations of the failure of détente outlined at the beginning of this chapter. The notion that détente failed because the fundamental differences between the superpowers overwhelmed their mutual interests gains credibility. On the other hand, it remains for historians to determine whether détente could have ended any other way if certain "accidents," such as Watergate, had not undermined

Kissinger's promising early successes. The notion that the failure of détente was due to missed signals and poor communication does not gain credibility from our analysis. To be sure, good communication is a prerequisite for managing a mixed relationship of this sort. Better communication might have made a marginal difference during the 1970s, but given the fundamental conflicts of interest that emerged from 1974 onward, it is doubtful that such communication would have made a decisive difference.

The other explanations—U.S. bad faith and Soviet bad faith—are too one-sided, if only because the mutual obligations in the relationship were never clearly defined as standards against which to measure good faith. However, the question of which side bears the greater responsibility for the failure can be posed without reference to obligations. One can ask instead: given the mutual goal of a mixed competitive-collaborative relationship, what does the *analyst* consider to be reasonable or realistic behavior on the part of a superpower in the current international political order?

Those who lay greater blame on the United States for the failure of détente generally endorse all or some of the following propositions about reasonable behavior.

1. U.S. efforts to hold détente hostage to Soviet domestic policy (on dissidents or emigration) was an unrealistic infringement on Soviet political sovereignty.

2. U.S. willingness to punish Soviet competitive wins by under-cutting SALT II ratification and by moving toward a strategic alliance with the PRC was a disproportionate response, because: (a) Soviet competitive wins were no threat to U.S. national security, whereas the PRC is a powerful, contiguous enemy of the USSR; and/or (b) there is no way the United States can prevent the USSR from gaining a place in the sun as a global power; hence, assuming that the United States' most vital interests are not directly threatened, the United States should accommodate itself to the inevitability of some Soviet wins rather than overreacting to them; and/or (c) Soviet competitive wins were no greater than U.S. competitive wins (e.g., in Egypt, Sudan, Rhodesia/Zimbabwe); they only used different means.

3. The Soviet defense buildup of the 1970s[24] did not violate any treaty or formal understanding with the United States and did not upset the relationship of mutual deterrence between the superpowers; hence, it did not imply Soviet bad faith or the need for the United States to substitute an arms race for arms control.

In contrast, those who lay greater blame on the USSR generally endorse all or some of the following propositions about reasonable behavior:

1. Soviet competitive wins employed the military instrument in novel ways (Cuban expeditionary forces and Soviet support personnel) at a time of U.S. paralysis in the use of that instrument. This usage was unreasonable behavior because only the military instrument contains high potential for turning the competitive track into a confrontational one.

2. Soviet eager pursuit of competitive wins was bound to undermine embryonic norms of restraint in the relationship.

3. The Soviet military buildup of the mid-1970s, when coupled with the novel use of the military instrument in pursuit of Third World wins, indicated probable Soviet contempt for norms of restraint in the relationship.

There is no way to reconcile these divergent inventories. They are based upon conflicting assumptions about the nature of the contemporary international order. Yet these inventories do highlight a central theme of this chapter: that each side leaned on its very individual assets to gain for itself the best possible deal in détente. If détente is to be successfully resurrected, in some form, as an ongoing process of negotiated confrontation avoidance, there will have to be some prior change in the political, ideological, circumstantial, or structural factors that made the bargaining process so highly competitive.[25]

Notes

I would like to thank professors Alexander L. George, Nelson Polsby, and Wallace Thies for their comments on earlier drafts of this essay.

1. See Henry Kissinger, "Detente with the Soviet Union: The Reality of Competition and the Imperative of Cooperation," *Department of State Bulletin,* October 14, 1974, pp. 505–519; Kissinger, *White House Years* (Boston: Little, Brown & Co., 1979); Zbigniew Brzezinski, "The Competitive Relationship," in *Caging the Bear,* ed. Charles Gati (Indianapolis and New York: Bobbs-Merrill, 1974), pp. 157–199.

2. For the terms "cooperative competition" and "confrontational competition" see Stanley Hoffmann, "Reflections on the Present Danger," *The New York Review of Books* 27, no. 3 (March 6, 1980):18–24.

3. Robert Legvold, "The Nature of Soviet Power," *Foreign Affairs* 56, no. 1 (October 1977).

4. "Basic Principles of Relations between the United States of America and the Union of Soviet Socialist Republics," *Department of State Bulletin,* June 26, 1972, pp. 898–899. For analyses of how Soviet and American leaders interpreted these principles, see Chapters 5 and 6.

5. Stanley Hoffman, "The Crisis in the West," *The New York Review of Books* 27, no. 12 (July 17, 1980):41–48.

6. For a fuller accounting of some of the difficulties, with reference to developing restraints on conventional arms transfers, see Chapter 11.

7. On the importance of manipulation in signaling between rival powers see Thomas C. Schelling, *The Strategy of Conflict* (New York: Oxford University Press, 1963), and Robert Jervis, *The Logic of Images in International Relations* (Princeton, N.J.: Princeton University Press, 1970). I am grateful to my colleague, Wallace Thies, for drawing to my attention the relevance of this literature to the argument I am developing.

8. On U.S. foreign policy strategy during Nixon's first term see Kissinger, *White House Years.*

9. See Chapter 6.

10. See Chapter 4.

11. See Paul E. Sigmund, "The USSR, Cuba, and the Revolution in Chile," in *The Soviet Union in the Third World: Successes and Failures,* ed. Robert H. Donaldson (Boulder, Colo.: Westview Press, 1981).

12. For Kissinger's detailed account of this crucial year in Middle Eastern affairs, see Henry Kissinger, *Years of Upheaval* (Boston: Little, Brown & Co., 1982).

13. Kissinger's account (ibid., p. 1022 and chap. 23) reinforces my reading of the official Soviet reaction to his initiatives.

14. Robert Legvold, "Containment without Confrontation," *Foreign Policy,* no. 40 (Fall 1980):74–98, reports that an interviewee in the Soviet foreign policy establishment observed that "in Angola the rules were ambiguous."

15. See, for example, Strobe Talbott, *Endgame: The Inside Story of SALT II* (New York: Harper & Row, 1979); Kissinger, *Years of Upheaval,* pp. 985–998; Banning N. Garrett, "Soviet Perceptions of China and Sino-American Military Ties," unpublished (Washington, D.C., May 1981). Garrett's report is based on extensive reading of Soviet materials and interviews with Soviet officials and academics.

16. See Chapter 3; see also Alexander L. George, *Towards a Soviet-American Crisis Prevention Regime: History and Prospects,* ACIS Working Paper no. 28 (Los Angeles: University of California at Los Angeles, Center for International and Strategic Affairs, November 1980).

17. For the distinction between diffuse support and specific support in the legitimization of political regimes, see David Easton, *A Systems Analysis of Political Life* (New York: John Wiley & Sons, 1965), pt. 4.

18. For a theoretical statement on the essential but tortuous process of defining reciprocity and equivalence in social relations, see Alvin W. Gouldner, "The Norm of Reciprocity: A Preliminary Statement," *American Sociological Review* 25, no. 2 (April 1960):161–178. For practical insight, see Chapter 11.

19. Thomas Comstock, "Soviet and American Preference-Orderings During Detente, 1969–1972" (graduate seminar paper, University of California at Berkeley, Department of Political Science, March 1981).

20. Samuel B. Payne, Jr., *The Soviet Union and SALT* (Cambridge, Mass.: MIT Press, 1980), pp. 85–86.

21. For thorough documentation of this negotiating process see Thomas Krantz, "Moscow and the Negotiations of the Helsinki Accords, 1972–1975 " (Ph.D. thesis, Oxford University, 1981).

22. See Chapter 4.

23. See Garrett, "Soviet Perceptions of China." See also the discussion of the origins and the complex negotiation of the Agreement on Prevention of Nuclear War in Chapter 5.

24. "The combination of improved accuracy, greater throw-weight, and MIRV warheads led to a dramatic twelve-fold increase just from 1975 to 1978 in the destructive power of the Soviet strategic missile force" (Payne, *The Soviet Union and SALT*, p. 86).

25. For an argument that lasting détente requires that both sides overcome stereotyped myths about each other, and about international politics, see K. J. Holsti, "Detente and Peaceful Co-existence: Assessing the Possibilities," *Co-existence* 17, no. 1 (April 1980):1–19. For an earlier analysis, see Robert C. Tucker, "United States–Soviet Cooperation: Incentives and Obstacles," *The Annals of the American Academy of Political and Social Science* 372 (July 1967):1–15.

14
The Strategy of
Preventive Diplomacy in
Third World Conflicts

I. William Zartman

The United States has a reputation for coercive intervention in the Third World and a less widely held reputation for diplomatic assistance. Which policy is more productive? A comparative evaluation would require too long a list of cases for the space available here, and in any event the issue of coercive intervention has been already argued frequently.[1] But what are the advantages and limitations of preventive or conciliatory diplomatic assistance to Third World countries beset by conflict?

Material for an answer to this question can be found in a number of cases from the Middle East and Africa where the opportunity for preventive diplomacy existed and was handled in various ways, in some cases resulting in a full-scale diplomatic initiative that monopolized U.S. government attentions at the highest level, in some cases evoking lower levels of effort that were often equally effective, and in other cases attracting no response as the opportunities slid by. More important than the historical review, however, is the need to conceptualize these opportunities, in order to separate those that were ready for effective diplomacy from those that were best left to run their own course. For whatever value one can find in the preemptive attempts of a great power to help Third World parties overcome their antagonisms and resolve their disputes without dragging external allies into one side or another of the conflict, it is certain that not any conflict can be mediated at just any time but that effective diplomacy depends on understanding the evolution of a conflict and seizing the proper moment during the crisis' course.

341

Cases of Diplomacy

There are a number of recent cases that are helpful to the understanding of Third World conflict and the opportunities for preventive diplomacy.[2] A series comes from the Middle East: the Kissinger disengagements of 1974–1975, the Camp David sequence of 1977–1978, and the subsequent autonomy negotiation after 1979. Three more come from northern Africa: the Saharan dispute since 1975, the collapse of government in Chad especially since 1978, and the conflict in the Horn of Africa after 1976; each underwent an earlier mediation in the 1960s. Three come from southern Africa: the successive Shaba invasions of 1977 and 1978, independence negotiations for Zimbabwe after 1977, independence negotiations for Namibia beginning in 1977. Many of these have been subject to full-length studies elsewhere,[3] but their salient features can be noted here in preparation for an analysis of the conceptual questions of "when" and "how."

The disengagement mediation of Secretary of State Henry Kissinger began with the October 1973 war between Israel and its neighbors, notably Egypt and Syria. When the Egyptian and Israeli armies became locked in a mutual encirclement, a cease-fire became effective, direct negotiations for the conditions of the cease-fire at kilometer 101 of the Suez-Cairo road ended rapidly in success, and the stage was set for mediated negotiations to begin on a phased Israeli withdrawal that would start in motion the processes of exchanging territory for security in a final peace treaty. In its international aspects as well as in its military lines, the conflict had rapidly arrived at a stalemate intolerable to both sides; each was blocked in its attempt to achieve a unilateral solution, the formerly stronger and weaker parties saw their positions reversed, and a way was perceived to move the deadlocked conflict into a broader solution beneficial to both sides: the moment for productive diplomatic intervention had arrived.

The first Sinai disengagement was followed by a similar diplomatic exercise in the Golan Heights, where the elements of stalemate were less compelling and so greater skill of diplomacy was required. Israeli prisoners held by Syria were bargained against Syrian territory held by Israel, the mediator's threat to end his mission was used to establish the pressure of a deadline, and the Egyptian-Israeli precedent was helpful in establishing momentum toward an agreement. The same device was used in both cases: a boundary in depth with thinned-out armaments to improve the security-for-territory exchange. Unfortunately, the Golan disengagement was never followed by a second withdrawal on the Syrian front, which would have improved the momentum and increased the element of trust between the two parties. Unfortunately too, the disengagements on the two fronts were never followed by a similar movement on the West Bank between Jordan and Israel. Here, Jordanian ambiguity, Israeli demands, the absence of an attractive formula for agreement, and a domestic crisis in the United States undercutting the effectiveness of Kissinger all combined to dissipate a demarche that could have had a tremendous effect on history.[4]

Instead, the mediator returned to the Sinai for the third disengagement agreement, working against a much less favorable set of conditions. Kissinger was obliged to put the threat of his own withdrawal from the process to the test and break off his mission, backing it with an ostentatious review of U.S. policy in the region. The formula of territory for security was again applied in the final agreement, even though the stalemate between the two parties was no longer as evident or as painful. In the end, agreement was only possible through a massive injection of side payments by the mediator, and the step-by-step initiative lost its means and momentum in the sands of the Sinai.

The second part of the preventive diplomatic exercise in the Middle East came with the new Carter administration, whose policy premises declared step-by-step negotiation to be outmoded and global settlement the goal.[5] But the momentum had gone out of the process, and it bogged down in considerations of participation and venue. It took one of the parties, Egypt's President Anwar Sadat, to revive movement by his visit to Jerusalem in November 1977 in order to jump the procedural obstacles and create an atmosphere of expectation, and it took President Carter's personal summit at Camp David in September 1978 to provide the tremendous pressure of a deadline and agreement on details. The Camp David agreements were the result, but the bargaining continued. A further personal initiative by Carter in his own shuttle to the Middle East in January 1979 was needed to refine the last details of the terms of trade and to bring to bear the pressures of a personal deadline once again. The Washington Treaty, signed in March 1979, was the result.

The third part of the process is that portion of the Camp David agreements not implemented by the Washington Treaty, specifically the agreement to negotiate a settlement for the West Bank.[6] The very framework at Camp David was filled with intentional ambiguities, as was necessary for topics yet to be resolved, and with intentional deceptions, a much more regrettable aspect that may nonetheless have been the necessary price of agreement on other items. Negotiations began on the basis of disputed ground rules and soon collapsed in all but form on disagreement over the very meaning of autonomy and on mutual disillusion over the dissipation of trust and goodwill. The U.S. role in the autonomy talks was at most one of eager innovator, seeking new and acceptable ways of packaging incompatible positions, and at least that of a rather passive chaperon before whom too hostile behavior on the part of the others would have been embarrassing. Above all, the talks were frozen by the previous engagement that had still to run its course, and pressures could not be laid on the parties—particularly on Israel—for fear that the return of the remainder of the Sinai would be aborted before the final date of April 26, 1982. That date operated as a deadline in reverse, inhibiting effective diplomacy by preventing either party from achieving agreement on its own terms where both parties could not achieve agreement on intermediate terms. Both sides were bent on winning on this round, and in that frame of mind, neither concessions nor new formulas were possible lest the side appear as losing.

Unfortunately for the process, if the moment was not propitious for an agreement before April 1982, it was even less so thereafter, for quite different reasons. Israel—in the Begin government's eyes—has to show that its hard line has been effective in the area, and Egypt has to restore its ties with the other Arab countries. The lost time has worked in Israel's favor, as that country uses occupation and settlement to consolidate the hold over territory that it could not legitimize by negotiation. Its first track, or unilateral attempt at a solution, has been able to create a new reality, even if not yet a new solution. The most that can be said for the Reagan administration is that it has been wise not to press an unpromising mediation, if in fact its restraint was purposeful, but it has also lost the opportunity to position itself for a new initiative when a propitious moment arrives. That moment requires new evidence of stalemate, some renewed indication that a mutually acceptable solution is possible, a stronger role of the mediator in limiting unilateral attempts at an outcome, and some new thinking about a formula to cover a conflict area that is neither Sinai nor Golan.

The cases of preventive diplomacy in southern Africa have had various degrees of success, but each has had instructive strengths and weaknesses. In Zimbabwe, a decade of unsuccessful British attempts following the Unilateral Declaration of Independence (UDI) in 1965 preceded a U.S. demarche in 1976 and an Anglo-American initiative in 1977 and 1978, before the final successful British effort within the commonwealth in 1979. The United Kingdom and the United States brought to bear some of the important elements necessary to good mediation, notably their persistence and patience and their use of allies—the Frontline States—to help bring the Patriotic Front to agreement. But they had no leverage over the various governments of Ian Smith, no control over a deadline, no ability to demonstrate the likely catastrophe that loomed at the end of the chosen course, and no ability to block the unilateral attempts of the parties to impose a solution on each other.

South Africa was sometimes useful as an intermediary, but in general it was not as helpful on its side as the Frontline States were in working on their ally. The "mediator" in Zimbabwe lacked not only formal authority to decide but informal power to make the parties decide by effectively blocking their first or unilateral policy tracks and making another, joint track more attractive.

This situation changed in 1979 when new elements continued to give the mediator this power. A new Conservative British government showed a willingness to recognize the internal solution in Zimbabwe/Rhodesia and thereby reassured the Smith-Muzorewa government enough to bring it to agreement. The continual Rhodesian raids on the Patriotic Front bases took a heavy enough toll for the national liberation movement to see a fair agreement now as preferable to a military victory in the long run. British Foreign Secretary Lord Carrington was able to impose deadlines on the actual mediation process and to hold to them (with the necessary flexibility).

No trust between the parties was created through the suspicion-ridden process, but there was trust in the fairness of the procedural solution and the acceptability of the substantive constitutional framework, as well as faith in the equitable outcome of the elections. Britain could give assurances to the side that was stronger in the short run and put pressures on the side that was likely to be stronger in the costly longer run.

In the second Shaba crisis, in 1978, after an inconclusive round the previous year, the United States and its Western and African allies pressed their associate, Zaire, into a settlement of issues with its neighbor, Angola, just at the time when Angola was also beginning to perceive the moment to be ripe for resolution. Both the mediators and the conflicting parties in varying degrees saw the danger of escalating crises and the futility of pursuing their first-track policy of unilateral resolution through conflict. The mediators also had the means to convince their own associate of the need to reconcile, since the crisis brought them into discussions over financial and political remedies necessary to put Zaire back on its feet again. Confidence was built between the two African states through their common interest in controlling liberation movements left over from the Angolan war for independence and earlier, after both states had seen that the liberation movements were ineffective means of overthrowing each other's government.

The weakness was that all these results could have been accomplished a year and a crisis earlier, with only slightly more effort, had the U.S. government been able to see past what it perceived as the Cuban-Soviet control of the government in Angola. All the elements present in 1978 in reinforced form were present in 1977, except for the Angolan perception of a ripening moment. Yet even on this point, there were internal differences of interpretation in Luanda, and a Western demarche in favor of reconciliation, reinforcing existing African support, would have had excellent chances of success.

In Namibia, the Western Five Contact Group of U.S., U.K., France, Canada, and West Germany began in 1977 to work out an agreement for independence between South Africa and the Namibian nationalist movements, mainly the South West African Peoples Organization (SWAPO). Working through the African Frontline States, the Contact Group brought SWAPO into an agreement; working directly on South Africa, the mediators also got Pretoria to change its position three times and to abandon its first choice, of a unilateral solution, at least in its original form (annexation) and in the first variant of its modified form (the Turnhalle formula for apartheid-like independence). But once South Africa had made major concessions and had accepted a new formula based on the UN plan and quite close to the demands of SWAPO, the Western Five could not elicit those last concessions on detail, either because South Africa had crossed its fingers when it had made the basic agreement or, as is more likely, because South Africa felt that the last details were important in view of the serious concessions it had already made. In 1981–1982, the Western Five (principally the United States) made a new attempt to rework the details to suit their associate, but in the process they may have shaken up the original formula enough to lose SWAPO's adherence to it.

Confidence in the neutrality and fairness of the procedures as well as in the acceptability of the outcome was destroyed rather than built up by the mediation process. Even more serious, there was no pressure applied by the mediators on South Africa to match the pressure that the Frontline States were able to place on SWAPO alongside their assurances of support. South Africa alone has set the deadlines, and the mediators have had no credible sanctions to force cooperation or to block unilateral solutions. As a result, the mediation actually brought South Africa to believe that its modified first-track solution was a preferable and a possible option, and therefore reinforced SWAPO's belief in its own first track—continued and intensified war of national liberation—as the only way.

Three other conflicts continued unresolved from the 1970s into the 1980s, in contrast with successful but ephemeral efforts at conflict management that were applied to the same conflicts in the 1960s. The most striking lesson of these cases is that while conflict management can be fruitfully purchased with a promise of conflict resolution, this promise creates an even greater danger of reintensified conflict and crisis when raised hopes are dashed. In Chad, innumerable external attempts have been made to assist a settlement, without success. The first was in 1969, when the government of François Tombalbaye invited the French military to help overcome the rebellion of the Chadian National Liberation Front (FroLiNaT), a proposition to which the French agreed only if administrative reforms were accepted. In the short run, the dual effort was effective, but by 1972 it was clear that the Administrative Reforms Mission (MRA) had not removed basic grievances and the military mission had not defeated their spokesman. The conciliator in 1978 was again France, which brought together the government and one faction of the FroLiNaT, the Armed Forces of the North (FAN) of Hissene Habre. Those factions left out continued the struggle, and the two parties to the reconciliation themselves fell to scrapping. The conciliator in the second round in 1979 was a group of African members of the Organization of African Unity (OAU), notably Nigeria, which was host to the conciliation conferences at Kano and Lagos, with some initial help from France as well. The conciliator in 1982 was the same group, with the anxious assistance of the United States as well, all hoping to bring the FroLiNaT factions, which had now taken over the Transitional National Unity Government (GUNT), into working harmony. The struggle continues.

The lessons of Chad are all in the weakness of the conciliation process. At no time during the various attempts were the parties brought to believe that an attempt to press on to victory was impossible and that therefore they must abandon their unilateral efforts and join in a multilateral resolution of the conflict. Unable to block the parties' first tracks, the conciliators were unable to make a second track attractive. Confidence was totally absent, and its absence was reinforced by every round of conciliation in which all the parties showed themselves to be untrustworthy when an occasion arose. But whenever one party moved toward the top of the pile, it fell apart. Furthermore, there was some uncertainty about the legitimate parties, since the state itself as an entity has been in question, and in a reversal of roles, the one state that was a clear and coherent party to the conflict—Libya—was the party that all conciliators sought to exclude from the solution.

In the Horn of Africa, the potential great power mediators were in intense competition to destroy each other's power base, and therefore mediation either unilaterally or cooperatively was impossible. In fact, the USSR and Cuba never touched the basic conflict, and Podgorny and Castro had no formula for its resolution in their preventive diplomacy of 1977; like so many other Marxists, they could not understand the national question. The United States (or other Western or moderate Arab states) was unwilling to give Somalia enough help to hold on to its conquests in the Ogaden War and make Ethiopia negotiate, for a great deal of help was needed, and the Somali cause was illegitimate. Yet Somali expectations were raised high by the earlier promises of Haile Selassie in the conflict management of 1967 and then by the collapse of his government in 1974—just at the time when any Ethiopian government was least likely (indeed, least able) to be flexible.

In sum, the moment was manifestly inappropriate for mediation. In the future, an increase in Somali guerrilla activity may produce escalating crises, and the consolidation of the Ethiopian regime may gradually favor resolution, but the United States is in a poor position to produce resolution. Only the ally of the country making the concessions—here, Ethiopia—would be able to buy an agreement. However, by the same token the United States is in a good position to start the process by helping consolidate agreement between Somalia and Kenya.

In the Sahara, the situation is more ambiguous, for the conflict is neither structurally impossible to resolve, as in the Horn, nor patently ripe, as it was at some past moments. Throughout 1978, before and after the military coup in Mauritania, and around the 1979 and 1980 OAU summer summits, balanced stalemate occurred at various levels, favoring conciliation. In each case, the United States had means of pressure that France and the African and Arab states could have reinforced. As it was, individual Arab and African states undertook mediation with no encouragement or support from outside powers. The missing ingredient was either the impending catastrophe or the enforceable deadline, however. An open war between Morocco and Algeria was viewed as both avoidable and undesirable by the parties, and they concentrated efforts on holding or postponing the OAU deadline for recognition of the Saharan Republic (SADR) rather than using the deadline to promote conciliation. Deadlines could have been created by U.S. threats to recognize either the Madrid partition or the Polisario, but unfortunately the United States never considered the problem to be that serious. The United States could also have used restraint on arms supplies to Morocco as an inducement for Algeria to talk, or arms supplies themselves as an inducement for Morocco to talk. But as a result of the United States' failure to capitalize on the circumstances, its position in the region, the support it might have gotten for its Middle East policy, and possibly the strength of the Moroccan monarchy itself have all suffered.

These cases, then, provide histories of lost opportunities for preventive diplomacy—in the West Bank and Golan Heights, the Western Sahara, and Somalia—as well as examples of the way "political engineering" can work to create better outcomes—as in the Sinai, Zaire, and Zimbabwe—and some irresolubles to complete the picture—in Namibia and Chad. They clearly show—perhaps so unmistakably that the conclusion is banal—that both mediator and parties to the conflict are better off with an agreement than without. In Shaba, both parties recognize that they are in a more favorable situation because the political threat to the Zairean and Angolan governments is reduced (even if not eliminated, for reasons generally outside the accord). Both parties can turn more attention to domestic development and consolidation.

To the United States (and its Western allies), this situation is desirable; specifically, the United States gained increased leverage for reforms in Zaire and much improved relations with Angola as a result of the reconciliation, though both benefits were relative. The parties that paid the price of the reconciliation were the national liberation movements.

In Zimbabwe, things are better for all sides—with nuances, of course. Although some white settlers are losing confidence, their earlier lack of realism made this change of attitude inevitable. The outcome of the mediation was the best they could have gotten, even if not the best conceivable in their own terms. The Patriotic Front has collapsed, but half of it, ZANU, has triumphed, and the remarkable skill and balance of Prime Minister Robert Mugabe promises well for the most constructive evolution possible for Zimbabwean politics and development. As of 1982, Mugabe's stand on global relations has been much what the United States might want, and as far as the United States is concerned at least, the negotiated settlement and elected government are far preferable to a contested internal solution and a continued, externally supported guerrilla campaign. The parties who paid the price of this agreement were the African partners of the internal solution—the "black Smiths"—who played their role in history and were then passed by.

Despite the long stalemate in Namibia, the mediation effort there has produced beneficial results in averting South African annexation and destroying the Turnhalle solution as direct pressure and verbal condemnation alone could never have done. Even if South Africa were to pursue its modified first track to the end, it has so changed the original formula that the outcome would be far preferable to that of the original version. Yet the solution itself is still waiting to be found, and as long as it remains so, the dangers of explosion and Soviet penetration—and of the pernicious effects of continued conflict for Namibians—are still present. However, low-level conflict is preferable to possible political compromise for SWAPO and for South Africa as well, which is why the war goes on. Free and fair elections will show who bears the cost of agreement; until then, the costs of nonagreement are borne by the victims of the continuing conflict.

Chad is a poignant example of the way in which sectarian interests in favor of continued conflict outweigh a general but unrepresented interest of the body politic in conflict termination. Even more striking, in Chad each party thrives on the hope of gaining an upper hand rather than on benefits gained directly from the conflict: present hurt does not outweigh future hope, and the war grinds on. The external beneficiary is Libya again, and, distantly, the Soviet Union. But Chad itself, its African neighbors, and the Western allies would all benefit from the stability and security and the opportunity for some small development that successful reconciliation alone would bring. The key to a solution, if one can be found, is in destroying the perception of future hope, in increasing the present pain, or in providing a reconciliation that confers benefits on the conflicting parties in greater measure or probability than the hoped-for benefits of conflict and victory.

The Middle East experience shows the value of this formulation. Both Egypt and Israel feel better off because of the peace treaty, but for different reasons. Israel has gained recognition and neutralized a powerful opponent, Egypt has regained its territory and gained a more explicit commitment in favor of the Palestinians than was ever obtained before from Israel. War made this achievement possible, but further war is unlikely to provide any better outcome for both sides—a Pareto-optimal position. No Pareto-optimal solution is visible at the moment for the West Bank, since any outcome that makes one side more secure makes the other feel less so, and one side is currently unchecked in its means of pursuing its own security, while the other side lives in total insecurity since its very existence is denied (and the denial is then reciprocated). Similarly, as Israel moves toward a unilateral solution of the West Bank and Golan problems through annexation, Palestinians and Syrians cling to denial, unable to impose present pain or block the unilateral attempt at a solution. Not only is the conflict unpropitious for mediation but the formula is missing that would make both parties feel better off than with continuing conflict. Thus being better off is often determined by the notion of the specific solution.

In the Horn, the results of nonagreement are even more destructive. The plight of the million and a half refugees of drought and terror is catastrophic beyond imagination, one of the poisonous byproducts of political leaders' disputes carried on the backs of their suffering people. The calamity of the drought in Ethiopia in 1974, which triggered that country's revolution, was small in comparison. In formal terms, the border problem remains as it was in 1963, but history never allows exact replays; the bitterness and hatred, and the deep feelings of deception and cruelty, make the situation even worse than it was twenty years ago, since traditional animosities have now been confirmed by modern events. It is hard to judge whether the United States is better off with Somalia, its new associate—providing a base at Berbera, a voice in the Arab League, and support for the Mideast peace process, but on the other hand, with an irredentist cause unpopular in Africa and basic poverty—than it was with Ethiopia, the old one—holding a central position in the area, prestige in Africa, and chances of development, as well as having national and economic problems. The ongoing conflict in the Ogaden provides the USSR and Cuba with the excuse for continued military presence, prevents the opening up of Ethiopia to Western activity, and subjects the people of the Horn to misery. Perpetuation of the conflict seems to benefit no one except the Soviet Union—but even for the USSR, the conflict seems to have become an unwanted economic drain.

In the Sahara, the parties that benefit from the continuing conflict are the leaderships of the Polisario and of Libya. However, the leaderships of both Morocco and Algeria benefit from the political side effects of the conflict. The desert people themselves find no advantage in confinement to refugee camps or occasional attack on the cities. National budgets and energies are drained in Morocco and Mauritania, and to some extent in Algeria. Restraint on the part of the United States brings it no benefit in terms of relations with either Morocco or Algeria. Mediation may not satisfy the parties, but worried neutrality or careful verbal tilting is even worse. The longer the conflict continues, the greater is the Libyan penetration into the Polisario—another development that benefits neither the two African parties nor the United States. Although the Soviet Union has not appeared directly, its position in the conflict is not as uncomfortable as that of the United States.

Patterns of Conflict

The Iranian revolution brought on a spate of blame-throwing in Washington about the inadequacy of strategic intelligence and effective early warning systems. That exercise was completely misplaced.[7] There is no dearth of warning about crisis and conflicts. There is no ignorance about the general causes of conflict in Africa and the Middle East, or about the cases to which specific causes apply. And it does not take a specialized institute in the forecasting of political instability to indicate that Zimbabwe, Zaire, and Namibia will be problem cases in the coming two-year period.

The problem with intelligence on this level is the confusion between "better" and "more." Adding three more countries to the above list would not be much help in intelligence terms, since the causes of conflict are broadly applicable and the triggers of crisis potentially widespread. There was no lack of early warnings about the Iranian or Ethiopian revolutions or about either Shaba crisis or about the Ogaden or Saharan wars. What *was* absent was a sense of threshold or timing, an ability to determine whether a trigger event was a buildup to a larger crisis or merely a brief flareup of hostilities. Since we are unsure of when to act, the problem becomes one of overprediction, noise, and shouting wolf.

The most important lesson to be drawn from the study of African and Middle Eastern crises is that conflict resolution depends above all on the identification of the ripe moment in differing patterns of conflict and escalation. That moment can be identified along two basic dimensions: intensity and alternatives, "vertical" and "horizontal" characteristics of policymaking. ("We can either do more or we can do something else.") Since these are dimensions of perception, they are dimensions of manipulation, and they can be emphasized or even generated by the conciliator.

The moment of ripeness is associated with two vertical characteristics of intensity—*deadlock* and *deadline*.[8] The deadlock is of a peculiar sort: a perception of each side of its inability to achieve its aims, to resolve the problem, or to win the conflict by itself. Deadlock must be perceived by the parties involved not as a momentary pause but as a flat terrain stretching into the future, providing no later possibilities for decisive escalation.

Conflict resolution plays on perceptions of an intolerable situation, pointing out that things "can't go on like this"; and resolution depends on the conciliator's persuading the participants that escalation to break out of the deadlock is impossible—indeed, depends on his *making* it impossible, if necessary. Thus, the deadlock cannot be seen merely as a temporary stalemate, to be easily resolved in one's favor by a little effort, or even by a big offensive, a gamble, or foreign assistance. Rather, each party must recognize its opponents' strength and its own inability to overcome that strength, at least at acceptable cost. Shaba and the October War stalemate are good examples; so is Zimbabwe when the element of time costs is brought into the calculation.

For the conciliator, this factor means emphasizing the perils of deadlock when each party still recognizes the other as strong and before the parties' first-track or security position[9] (the outcome that can be obtained by the party without negotiation) becomes so well entrenched that it is more attractive than the second track. Deadlock is thus a matter as much of perception as of reality where the parties are concerned and as much a subject of persuasion as one of timing where the mediator is concerned. Successful conciliation produces a shift from a winning mentality to a composing mentality on the part of both parties. This dual shift is obviously a delicate matter. It occurred in Angola and Zaire and after the 1978 Shaba crisis and in Egypt and Israel after Sinai II (the second Sinai disengagement agreement of 1975) and may have occurred temporarily to SWAPO and South Africa during 1978 and again in 1980, but it had not happened by the end of 1980 in the Horn, the Sahara, or Chad.

Deadline is of course the conceptual opposite of deadlock; it represents a moment when things will swiftly get worse if they have not gotten better in ways that negotiation seeks to define. Here a catastrophe threatens the mutual checks the parties impose on each other. The catastrophe can be about to take place (if something is not done about it) or it can be a shocking moment that has just taken place or has just been narrowly missed. Yasser Arafat and Menachem Begin negotiated the 1981–1982 Lebanese cease-fire under the first condition, Augustinio Neto and Mobutu Sese Seko negotiated the 1978 post–Shaba crisis agreement under the second, and Anwar Sadat and Golda Meir might be seen to have negotiated the 1974–1975 Sinai disengagements under the third.

The striking fact, however, is that in Africa and the Middle East as well as elsewhere, conflict resolution—when it comes—comes most frequently after the crisis has just taken place, with losses on both sides that have not resolved the basic conflict. Yet this sort of event also poses problems for mediation. First, it leaves a memory of bitterness that is not helpful to conflict resolution. A stalemate crisis that has involved the army alone, for example, is likely to be shrugged off as a case of casualties for those whose business it is to inflict and to bear them. Reconciliation after a recent tragedy almost requires that the tragedy involve some innocent victims—a high price to pay indeed. The Europeans in Shaba, for example, contributed a shock effect that hurried resolution.

Second, a past catastrophe sets no deadline. Conflict resolution depends on a sense of urgency, but without a time by which the parties must agree, there is no pressure for agreement, and parties get used to living with the ever-receding sense of shock. In setting a deadline, the impending, rather than the recent, catastrophe is clearly a much more propitious definer of the ripe moment. Camp David negotiations in 1978, President Carter's visit to the Middle East in 1979, and Lord Carrington's chairing of Lancaster House talks in 1979 show the usefulness of deadlines in the hands of mediators. These events also show the need for mediators to create an artificial deadline in the absence of a real one when conflict resolution follows the close call or the catastrophe.

The horizontal dimension of conflict resolution concerns policy tracks or alternatives. In a sense, the conciliator's task is to get the situation off competing unilateral solutions (first tracks) and onto a bilateral solution (second track). The challenge is to present an alternative to the conflicting parties that attains some of the goals of their first tracks while eliminating or reconciling their more conflictual elements. Two separate actions are involved: the first tracks must be blocked, and the second track must be sold to the two parties. Conflict resolution therefore depends as much on rendering the conflict option unattractive as on conveying an attractive option of management and resolution, and the attractiveness of the second track is a function of the unattractiveness of the first.

First tracks can be rendered inoperative or unattractive at several times in their course: initially in prospect, during their exercise, and in retrospect. Mediators can convince the parties that their chances of effectively pursuing the conflict are slim. This strategy is obviously preferable, since it reduces cost in lives and losses, but it is hardest since no one can be sure the policy might not have been productive if the mediators had not meddled in the conflict. South Africa's Turnhalle plan was a first track that was deflected toward the second before it got very far because of the prospects of failure even before it began. The pursuit of conflict can also be stymied during its exercise, either by bogging down in its own tracks or by being blocked by the other party or even by the mediator. Zimbabwe is an African example of the latter two possibilities during 1979. Such a situation is difficult and costly, although if it brings a solution favorable to the probable eventual winner while saving some advantages for the other party, as in Zimbabwe, it maximizes its advantages. Finally, the first tracks can be used in retrospect to favor conflict resolution, if unilateral solutions have already failed. The repeated inability of Israel and Egypt to accomplish larger goals by warring over the Sinai meant that both parties' first tracks proved their own ineffectiveness and supported a search for a second-track alternative. But the first tracks had to be tried, rather than being used in prospect, since predictions of failure were not convincing.

Attempts at disestablishing first-track conflict strategies in order to sell a second-track mediated option are complicated by certain countereffects. Growing attachment to first-track strategies despite any inherent attractiveness of alternatives can come in three forms: the bargaining chip, the sidetrack, and the overcommitment. Bargaining chips are first tracks that were invented in order to enhance a party's position on a second track but that become so well rooted that they take on a life and attractiveness of their own. The paradox is that bargaining chips are of great importance as threats only because of their viability, but their viability makes them rivals to the second tracks they were designed to reinforce. South Africa's internal election plan, if it was intended as a threat alone, is an example of one that was kept alive and up to date until it finally overcame the other track. The Polisario in Algerian strategy may have had the same effect.

In the sidetrack effect, a party reacts to threats against its own threat position and loses sight of its goals, confusing means for ends. Parties can become so involved in secondary escalations that they are unable to respond to attempts at conflict resolution and yet are unable to pursue a successful first-track strategy. Moroccan King Hassan's refusal to attend meetings with Algerian President Chadli Benjedid on pretexts afforded by various Polisario attacks or Algerian President Houari Boumedienne's refusal to continue talks with Morocco because of differences over the Egyptian peace initiative are examples of sidetracked strategy that was not purposively oriented either toward winning on the first track or composing on the second track.

Third, a party can become procedurally or emotionally overcommitted to the first track, making it too late to follow the second track toward reconciliation, no matter how attractive the latter and no matter what substantive bridging of difference might be accomplished. Parties usually make—or are ready for—one last attempt at reconciliation before implementing a first track already prepared, but sometimes such attempts are too late for the party itself to be able to unhook from first-track commitments, particularly in regard to parts of its home establishment. Sadat was uninterested in mediation attempts in the summer of 1973 and Ethiopian leader Mengistu was uninterested in a call for negotiations by the Eritrean guerrillas in the summer of 1978, each just before the country's big offensives. Both would have lost credit in the eyes of their military had they decided to talk at that point. The moment was ripe for war, not for resolution.

Thus far in this discussion, a symmetry in the parties' positions has been implicitly assumed, with no consideration of the fact that the two parties' first tracks are likely to evolve at different rates with different ups and downs. Obviously, the mediator is out of a job when one party's first track becomes decisive in the conflict. But before that point, there still may be enough asymmetry between the two parties' positions that one party may entertain hopes of becoming successful. Since the parties may not be of equal strength or position in the conflict, and therefore one is likely to be stronger than the other, or one to be a challenger and the other a defender, the proper moment for mediation occurs when the combatant with the upper hand starts slipping and the underdog rises.

Decolonization situations are classic cases of this effect, with the conciliator playing a facilitating role. When the former ruling power feels its time has come and wants to come to terms before it loses everything, and the nationalist movement feels its strength growing and wants to win early and cheaply rather than face a protracted struggle (and possibly the replacement of current leaders by more radical rivals), the moment has come for a conciliator to step in. Settlements similar to the Lancaster House agreements in the history of Zimbabwe are the result.

Methods of Management

Effective preventive action requires diplomatic presence and diplomatic relations. U.S. sources of information and diplomatic leverage were badly hampered in two of the four cases previously discussed by the absence of an ambassador for extended periods: in Ethiopia for two years there was no chief of mission, and in Angola there never has been an embassy. The notion that U.S. recognition is a good that can be bought with suitable behavior makes about as much sense as the idea that a person should be allowed to register to vote only after his or her contribution to life has been properly demonstrated, or indeed, that the United States with its recognition of other countries is a licensing agency and not just another voter.

A particular problem in maintaining contacts in the current era comes from the contradiction between the need to deal with national liberation movements and the notion that official diplomats can only talk to recognized state representatives. Such proscriptions come from a bygone notion that meeting is recognizing and recognizing is approving, compounded by the special problems noted earlier about the nature of national liberation movements. Although there are tricky and only semieffective ways of getting around it, the long inhibition against Western diplomats' contacting Polisario representatives or the misrepresented commitment against negotiating with or recognizing (but not contacting) the Palestine Liberation Organization are senseless barriers against necessary information gathering and diplomatic leverage.

Effective preemptive action requires a sense of ideological blindness and forward commitment. Nostalgia for a friendly but dead emperor, antipathy to a Marxist but incumbent regime, righteous condemnation of revolutionaries and vicarious terrorists, and open-ended commitments to the changing goals of one of the parties in a conflict are all luxuries of true belief that lose sight of the real goal of policy. Policymakers are too frequently pressed by public interest groups to establish a foreign policy position through condemnation rather than through effective action. In a world of Marxists and monarchs, terrorists and colonialists, it may be hard to recognize "our own kind." In some cases, such as Namibia, U.S. negotiators have been remarkably deft in dealing with all kinds of parties, but in other cases the notion of reform first and conflict resolution after makes the fleeting ripe moment hard to grasp.

Conflict resolution is best carried out in concert. If a number of conciliators are available as a choice for the parties themselves, and if a number of friends of the conflicting parties can coordinate their good offices and pressure, the chances of success are improved. In arranging agreement on a proposal, it is best to start with allies who can then press principals, as was done in Namibia and Zimbabwe. By the same token, it is important that the conciliator bring its own allies along in the effort; an attempt to resolve conflict by a great power (like the United States) when a secondary power with close African ties (such as the United Kingdom or France) is sitting it out or quietly undermining the effort is a handicapped race, and the same is true in reverse in the Middle East, where the European initiative is doomed if Europe does not bring the United States along. The resolution of conflict in the Middle East and Africa demands extremely close coordination with both regional states and European powers. One might even include the Soviet Union in relevant cases, although the USSR has never operated very effectively in such a collaborative role. (Indeed, the Soviet Union has rarely mediated effectively to reduce conflict, even when it is operating alone, and has only sought to benefit from others' efforts.)

As the process of conciliation proceeds, the mediator must use its soundings of the parties to convince them that deadlock potentially lies at the end of their first tracks and that catastrophe impends or would be required to break that deadlock. Then, this perception must be reinforced with an objective referent that clearly indicates when things will become worse if something is not done—in other words, a deadline. Deadlines are best if they are independent of the conciliator, but they may need recalling, reinforcing, and even sanctioning in order to be effective and to be made to hold. Boxed in, the parties should begin looking about for some help out of their problem—including a conciliator with some good ideas.

In the Middle East, deadlines played an important role in the disengagement talks; they were provided by the fear of renewed hostilities and, with the mediation itself, by the threats of Secretary Kissinger to withdraw his good offices. The Shaban and Zimbabwean conciliations provide the best African examples of parties feeling the need for mediation. Neither the pair of combatants in the Saharan crisis nor those in the Horn of Africa have felt the need for a conciliator because they have not yet felt boxed in by their problem. The more numerous parties in Chad were called in to a series of mediated conferences in 1979 but came only reluctantly, as their defection from subsequent conferences has shown.

The conflict that is closest to building its own box is the Eritrean, where—uniquely among African disputes—the Soviet Union is best placed to offer good offices because of its ideological affinities for both sides.

Conflict resolution may mean using both carrots and sticks. Inducements to compromise may include economic and military aid, arms sales, supportive policy statements, and other instruments of diplomacy. Although positive inducements tend to be costly and habit-forming when they succeed, they also tend to create a more agreeable relationship and to be additionally useful as a basis for negative sanctions at another time. Negative inducements too can only be used lightly by a mediator. They most frequently take the form of contingent withdrawal of benefits, or threats, but they may also take the form of warnings or authoritative indications of unpleasant consequences outside the control of the parties, as for example in the comments of Secretary Kissinger during the Middle East shuttles.

Beyond these measures, however, the reinforcement of conflict is often required to force recognition of the deadlock and the deadline. This may mean reinforcing a faltering party, as the United States has done militarily for Israel in 1974 and for Morocco in 1980 or as France did with Mauritania in 1977 (albeit unsuccessfully) or as the West did twice with Zaire. A beaten Morocco or a beaten Somalia will never get an Algeria or an Ethiopia to recognize its grievance, but it will still be strong enough to cause trouble for friends and neighbors alike. The corollary is also not well recognized: that military aid to one side does not prevent the aiding party from also being an effective mediator.

In fact, the relationships of a well-placed conciliator can provide a ready supply of carrots and sticks, making the conciliator a distant balance-holder. By shifting weight from one party to the other in the conflict, a conciliator can reinforce deadlock and convey deadline, particularly if the mediator is able to reduce support for a client that is on top but not firmly enough to be able to win. The Kissinger-Sadat strategy in the Middle East is the best example, but the Shaba negotiations are also a case in point. This strategy has many real limitations, however. Two cannot play the game, lest a shifting of weight become a *renversement des alliances,* as in the Horn. Moreover, if the conciliator's own ally is not on top, shifting weight may merely serve to sink one side without buying concessions from the other, as in President Carter's policy toward Morocco during the Saharan dispute.

When the parties have been convinced of their need for a way out, the moment of the proposal has come, although sometimes a proposal is needed earlier than that, to bring out the insufficiencies of the first track. The characteristic of the successful second track is a formula, an overarching concept that frames the nature of the solution and either defines the terms of trade or establishes a principle to be applied to both parties. The formula must appear just and satisfactory to both parties, must therefore cover the major issues of the conflict (although not necessarily all of them), and must include important demands from both sides (not necessarily all of them but enough to ensure compliance with the agreement). The formula in the Middle East disengagements and in the Washington Treaty was territory for security; the formula in Shaba was the mutual restraint of hosted movements and the mutual return of refugees; the formula in Namibia was one-man-one-vote elections under paired UN-South African auspices. "Territory for security" is inadequate as a formula for the West Bank, so the post–Camp David autonomy talks were needed. Somalia cannot be expected to settle its problems with Ethiopia merely in return for a pat on the head from the world community. Resolution of the Saharan crisis cannot be accomplished without giving something to the Polisario, something to Algeria, and something to Morocco as well. A solution that provides balanced benefits for all Chadian parties is conceivable but had not yet occurred by 1982. Simple as this idea may be, it seems to be difficult for U.S. leaders in particular to remember in the heat of conflict, in part because policymakers are pressed to view conflicts in zero-sum terms as a matter of right and principle, and in part because adversary proceedings and debating contests are so much a part of the U.S. way of doing things. And yet, if a party is part of the problem and cannot be eliminated, it has gained a right to be part of the solution.

The conciliator should have an idea of a feasible and conceivable outcome before starting out on the venture. This outcome should not be imposed on the parties but should be made to grow out of contacts with them. Nor should it be held onto against all contrary movement and evidence from the discussion. It should be viewed flexibly. It is not clear that this condition was present in Kissinger's mediations, but it was in the Camp David, Lancaster House, and Namibian talks.

Projecting a solution ahead of time permits separation of the conflict into those aspects that can be included in the settlement and those that must be left to the healing effects of time. This distinction may refer to conflict-management outcomes as separate from conflict-resolution outcomes, e.g., a cease-fire to allow the parties to consider ways of reducing the substance of the disagreement, as in the 1963 wars in the Sahara and the Ogaden. (In both these cases, however, the process of substantive solution was upset by a new event—the decolonization of the Spanish Sahara and the Ethiopian revolution, respectively.) The distinction may also refer to knotty issues that can be resolved after the general settlement, such as Walvis Bay in Namibia or the composition of the army in Zimbabwe or Jerusalem.

Principles—such as self-determination, the inviolability of frontiers, or noninterference in internal affairs—are important legitimizers for political solutions and should be used as such but should not dictate the choice of the solution. Conflict resolution should need principles, but principles give no guidelines for choice among themselves. Indeed, the cause of conflict can usually be traced to the parties' interested adherence to *conflicting* principles. It is better to seek a balanced distribution of power than to search for a pure principle. A Saharan outcome that merely states that a specific referendum is the only correct translation of self-determination but that does not handle the problems of Algerian-Moroccan relations or the nature of the Mauritanian entity is no solution. A Chadian solution that calls for an election without specifying relations among the (already-known) winners, as did the Lagos plan, is no solution, as events showed. An agreement on one-man-one-vote in Namibia that does not deal with problems of structural relations in southern Africa would be ephemeral. An outcome in the Horn of Africa that merely reaffirms the sanctity of inherited boundaries perpetuates the conflict.

Procedural solutions are no substitute for substantive solutions, but they may be the best available. They are neutral in appearance, since the conciliator is not opting for one type of outcome but merely for one way in which an outcome can be reached—generally a peaceful rather than a violent means of conducting conflict. Procedural solutions have a further advantage of setting up new patterns and routines that can help the parties through the early phase of weak institutionalization.

But the limitations of procedural solutions are real. They are accepted by both sides because each thinks it will win, and after the results are in, disappointment can be violent. The only exception is those situations where a procedural solution effectively removes one of the parties, as in Zimbabwe; but even there the losers of the election were only removed from formal power. Where the parties remain to challenge the procedural results, procedural solutions are shaky. Referenda should be used to ratify, not to establish, terms of agreement.

Agreement in the formula stage should be signed and publicly agreed to before the search for implementing details begins to tear at the agreement. This may be a pious wish, and in the case where it could have been helpful—Namibia—it was hard enough to get a tentative agreement that later fell apart, let alone a signed one. In the Sahara, there was both general and specific agreement among the parties at a number of points, but the agreement still did not prevent a total collapse of understanding. In the Middle East series, even explicit agreement on a formula did not prevent disagreement both on its interpretation and on its implementation. Nonetheless, an agreement in stages, if possible, can be helpful in building assurance. If the agreement on a general level is accompanied by some gesture of de-escalation—exchange of prisoners, regrouping, etc.—momentum can often be increased.

But management is not enough. Any crisis stilled should be headed toward resolution, with incentive for the parties to get there. The conciliator cannot be expected to chaperon the parties until all their disputes are resolved, but the conciliator can be expected to include provisions whereby the parties are headed toward working out an agreement on their own, perhaps with the pressure or monitoring of the OAU or the UN.

Preventive diplomacy is not justifiable simply in its own terms or as an Olympian intervention to keep smaller states from hurting themselves. It is directly in the interest of a United States poised at the edge of an era that seems to promise a return of the cold war and increased great power hostilities through heightened chances of confrontation with a Soviet Union willing and capable of seizing targets of opportunity in the power vacuums of the Third World. Through their weakness—both inherent and in regard to their goals— Third World states are impelled to look for outside allies from whom they can borrow power in a fight, and their unstable relations with their neighbors continually throw them into conflict with their neighbors. The nine cases cited in this chapter are examples of such conflict, with very different sources at their origin. In every case, parties have looked abroad for the power to win when their domestic sources of power have proven to be insufficient. The escalation in the search for borrowed power is a familiar one: arms, technicians, advisers, and finally troops—in Ethiopia troops from the Soviet Union and in Shaba and Chad troops from France—enter the fray. The most effective way to keep African and Middle East conflicts from becoming East-West conflicts is through external efforts at conflict management and resolution.

Notes

1. See John Quitter, ed., *Intervention and World Politics,* a special issue of *Journal of International Affairs* 22, no. 2 (1968); Piero Gleijeses, *The Dominican Crisis: The 1965 Constitutionalist Revolt and American Intervention* (Baltimore: Johns Hopkins Press, 1978); Melvin Gurtov, *The U.S. against the Third World* (New York: Praeger, 1974); Townsend Hoopes, *The Limits of Intervention* (New York: McKay, 1969).

2. This chapter is a revised version of a paper presented at the meeting of the American Political Science Association, New York, September 1981. It is the product of a number of related projects: a study of Egyptian foreign policy conducted under a National Endowment for the Humanities senior fellowship at the American Research Center in Egypt, a study of conflict and intervention in Africa prepared for the Council on Foreign Relations, and several studies of conflict resolution in Africa conducted for the Africa Bureau of the Department of State. I am grateful for this experience and

support, but none of these supporters has any responsibility for my conclusions and recommendations.

3. See Jeffrey Rubin, ed., *The Dynamics of Third Party Intervention* (New York: Praeger, 1981), including I. William Zartman, "Explaining Disengagement"; Saadia Touval, *The Peace Brokers: Mediators in the Arab-Israeli Conflict 1948–79* (Princeton, N.J.: Princeton University Press, 1982); Saadia Touval and I. William Zartman, eds., *The Lessons of Mediation* (Princeton, N.J.: Princeton University Press, in press) (for background on Zimbabwe and Namibia inter alia); I. William Zartman, *Ripe for Resolution: Conflict and Intervention in Africa* (New Haven, Conn.: Yale University Press, 1982) (for background on Sahara, the Horn, Shaba, and Namibia); John Damis, *Conflict in Northwest Africa: The Western Sahara Dispute* (Stanford, Calif.: Hoover Institution, 1982); Tom J. Farer, *Warclouds on the Horn of Africa*, 2d ed. (Washington, D.C.: Carnegie Endowment for International Peace, 1979); Bereket Habte Selassie, *Conflict and Intervention on the Horn of Africa* (New York: Monthly Review Press, 1980); Oye Ogunbadejo, "Conflict in Africa: A Case Study of the Shaba Crisis, 1977," *World Affairs* (Winter 1979) 41, no. 3: 219–234; Robert Rotberg, *Suffer the Future* (Cambridge, Mass.: Harvard University Press, 1981); John Seiler, ed., *Southern Africa since the Portuguese Coup* (Boulder, Colo.: Westview Press, 1980); Robert Buijtenhuijse, *Le Frolinat et les revoltes populaires du Tchad* (Hague: Mouton, 1978).

Other cases that will need a good study include the Falkland Islands mediation attempts in 1982 and the Habib missions in the Middle East between Israel and Lebanon (and occupants) in 1981–1982. Source material is not repeated in the following discussion.

4. For more see Zartman, "Explaining Disengagement."

5. Brookings Institution, *Toward Peace in the Middle East* (Washington, D.C.: Brookings Institution, 1975).

6. See also I. William Zartman, "The Power of American Purpose," *Middle East Journal* 35, no. 2 (Spring 1981): 163–177.

7. See Richard Betts, "Why Intelligence Failures are Inevitable," *World Politics* 31, no. 1 (1978): 61–89.

8. For more on deadline, see I. William Zartman and Maureen Berman, *The Practical Negotiator* (New Haven, Conn.: Yale University Press, 1982).

9. Anatol Rapoport's "threat potentials," in *Two-Person Game Theory* (Ann Arbor: University of Michigan Press, 1966), p. 97.

15
Crisis Prevention Reexamined

Alexander L. George

We have reviewed the effort U.S. and Soviet leaders launched during the early seventies to develop a more constructive relationship to replace the dangerous confrontation-prone era of the cold war. The two sides agreed that whenever possible existing conflicts of interest should be negotiated in the spirit of mutual accommodation. At the same time, both sides understood that their global rivalry would continue and that they could be drawn into war-threatening confrontations. In response to Brezhnev's initiative Nixon joined in formulating general principles that committed the two superpowers to moderate the competitive thrust of their foreign policies and to cooperate with each other in order to head off dangerous confrontations. These general principles were regarded as providing the foundation for a crisis-prevention regime, but the enterprise proved to be abortive. At the Moscow Summit the two sides failed to thrash out their divergent conceptions of crisis prevention; in the months that followed they failed to pursue the necessary task of giving more concrete operational meaning to the general principles, however difficult that may have proved to be, or even to set up procedural arrangements for implementing their nascent crisis prevention regime. The delay in addressing these tasks proved highly damaging. As was noted in Chapter 7, within a few months of their June 1973 agreement to cooperate in crisis prevention that agreement was subjected to a severe test by the circumstances leading to the outbreak of the Egyptian-Syrian attack on Israel in October 1973. In the aftermath of this conflict the interests of the two superpowers collided even more sharply in the Middle East and Africa in ways that exposed the shallowness and ambiguities of their crisis-prevention agreement. Particularly damaging was the crisis that developed in Angola in 1975 when, as noted in Chapter 9, the initially low-level, covert competition between the two superpowers escalated into a major diplomatic confrontation. While the Soviet Union "won" the contest in Angola, its unexpectedly assertive behavior contributed importantly to a hardening image of the Soviets and to the erosion of public and congressional support in the United States for détente as a whole.

This final chapter analyzes the grave limitations and deficiencies of the "general principles" approach that the two sides employed in attempting to initiate cooperation in crisis prevention and provide a reconceptualization of the problem of moderating U.S.-Soviet rivalry.

Crisis Prevention as Part of the Détente Package

"Crisis prevention," differentiated from "crisis management," on which the two superpowers had managed to cooperate successfully even during the cold war, was placed on the agenda for high-level discussion and negotiation at the first summit meeting between Nixon and Brezhnev in Moscow in May 1972. An agreement to cooperate in crisis prevention became part of the Basic Principles Agreement (BPA) signed at the conclusion of the Moscow summit. The BPA has been referred to as the charter for détente, an appropriate designation insofar as it indicated those areas in which the two leaders planned to cooperate in order to construct the foundation for a more positive relation. In this respect the BPA outlined a skeletal framework for the development of a new U.S.-Soviet relationship, one that George W. Breslauer aptly refers to as "collaborative competition."

Crisis prevention was a significant component of the BPA, to be sure, but the mutual desire expressed in that document to forge ahead to reach meaningful agreements for strategic arms limitation and economic cooperation was even more important. No serious misunderstanding existed between Nixon and Brezhnev on this score. Quite a different matter was that part of the agreement that seemed to accord the Soviet Union political equality with the United States, a status to which Soviet leaders attributed far more significance than Nixon and Kissinger anticipated and, as noted in Chapter 5, that set into motion quite divergent interpretations as to what the two sides had agreed to.

In signing the BPA, a formal document that was only the most visible part of the richer texture of understandings, hopes, and expectations that had emerged in discussions between the two sides, Nixon and Brezhnev clearly viewed it as a package agreement. Its parts were interdependent; the two leaders were committing themselves to achieve meaningful progress on all fronts. Accordingly, the fact that the agreement to cooperate in crisis prevention was part of the total charter for détente left it hostage, in some vague sense, to substantial progress in the other important areas designated for cooperation. This is not to say that the linkage between the different components of the agenda for cooperation was specified or clearly understood. It took the form, rather, of a general agreement on the need for *reciprocity*. But, as Breslauer emphasizes in his account of the failure of détente, the *norms* of reciprocity were to remain inadequately developed, and the two sides also did not succeed in shaping *norms of restraint* for the competitive realm of their relationship.

As this brief summary suggests and previous chapters have detailed, both détente in general and the experiment in a cooperative approach to crisis prevention suffered from inadequate conceptualization, important ambiguities (some recognized, others not), latent disagreements, and unresolved issues that were to increasingly prejudice the effort to develop a more constructive and mutually satisfactory relationship between the two superpowers. So far as the task of managing U.S.-Soviet global rivalry more effectively is concerned, a number of lessons and new guidelines emerge from the present study.

Rules for Détente and Rules for Crisis Prevention

In recent years, even as the détente process ground to a halt and U.S.-Soviet relations began to assume an increasingly confrontational character once again, foreign policy specialists and indeed also Soviet and U.S. leaders have spoken from time to time of the need for a new code of conduct or rules to structure and regulate the U.S.-Soviet relationship. Proposals of this kind contain an important ambiguity insofar as they do not distinguish between (a) guidelines to define the type of collaborative-competitive relationship between the two superpowers that is considered to be desirable and (b) rules for regulating and moderating the continuing U.S.-Soviet global rivalry.

There is indeed a relationship between these two types of rules, but that relationship cannot be addressed effectively if the distinction between them remains blurred. Cooperation in crisis prevention and the development of norms, rules, and procedures for this purpose are possible *independently* of a collaborative overall relationship of the kind envisaged at the high point of détente and can play an important role even if the relationship remains strained and highly competitive. At the same time, if a charter for a more moderate form of competitive relationship can be agreed upon, the scope and procedures for cooperation in crisis prevention could be enlarged.

The first lesson drawn from this study, therefore, emphasizes the need to distinguish between two types of rules—first, guidelines for characterizing the nature of the overall U.S.-Soviet relationship aimed at, the agenda for achieving that relationship, and the reciprocal obligations it will entail; and, second, understandings that define norms of competition and procedures for cooperation in the interest of crisis prevention.

The Concept of Crisis Prevention

A second set of lessons concerns the concept of crisis prevention itself, which is laden with several ambiguities that need to be dealt with in turn. One of these, to which our study has called attention, concerns the distinction between crises that threaten to draw the two superpowers into war with each other and other crises that do not entail such a danger even though they do engage both powers' interests, attention, and involvement. This distinction was left ambiguous in the agreements for cooperation in crisis prevention signed by Nixon and Brezhnev. With the passage of time it became clear that Soviet leaders believed they had committed themselves to cooperate to prevent only those crises that threatened to result in a war with the United States. U.S. leaders, on the other hand, believed that their agreement with the Soviets was a broader one, extending as well to avoidance of crises that were not war-threatening. Lack of clarity and disagreement as to what types of crises were to be avoided was not merely a definitional problem but stemmed from the more fundamental, unresolved issue as to what limits should be observed on the global competition for influence between the two superpowers. Had Soviet leaders accepted a modification of their concept of peaceful coexistence by subscribing to vague language to the effect that the two superpowers should henceforth operate with "restraint" in their foreign policies? Had Nixon and Brezhnev agreed to avoid making gains in their global competition at each other's expense or only to avoid use of certain means in seeking such gains? Was competition to be confined to those parts of the globe where neither superpower already enjoyed a position of influence—and, if so, what degree of influence acquired in a certain area by one superpower should oblige the other superpower to forego efforts to reverse that situation? If one superpower's position of influence in a certain area were being undermined by local developments, should the other superpower desist from efforts to exacerbate the situation and to gain a position of influence there for itself?

Viewed from another standpoint, what limits can realistically be placed on the competition for global influence, given the forces of change that operate throughout the international system and complicate the search for order and stability? Further, granted that superpower competition for influence can be limited to some appreciable degree, to what extent can such limits be achieved through *cooperative* arrangements between the United States and the Soviet Union as against *unilateral* policies that each side undertakes on its own? We shall return to questions of this kind later in the discussion.

Another conclusion that emerges from this study is that crisis prevention needs to be conceptualized more precisely and then integrated into the framework of overall foreign policy. To begin with, *crisis prevention should be viewed as an objective, not as a strategy.* Clarity on this point is essential in order to discourage the tendency to assume that there is a single strategy for preventing U.S.-Soviet crises and that this strategy consists of a properly formulated set of rules that, if observed by the two sides, should significantly reduce the likelihood that the two powers' global competition would result in confrontations and crises. It confuses matters to think that the objective of crisis prevention can be achieved or even substantially promoted by devising a single, general-purpose strategy taking the form of rules of behavior or a code of conduct. Because the task of crisis prevention arises in many contexts and in strikingly different situations, the challenge to theorists and policymakers alike is to grasp the special characteristics of any given situation and to design an appropriate strategy or strategies for preventing a crisis or confrontation in that type of situation. What is needed, in other words, is a *repertoire of strategies,* coupled with skill in diagnosing emerging situations of potential crisis and in selecting an appropriate strategy and tailoring it to the special configuration of each case. In other words, crisis prevention is not a strategy but an objective in search of appropriate strategies. U.S.-Soviet cooperation based on rules for moderating and regulating competition for influence is only one such strategy. To say this is to restate important lessons that can be derived from the experience of the great powers in the nineteenth century. As Paul Gordon Lauren reminded us in Chapter 3, statesmen in that era understood that the task of crisis prevention could not be accomplished "by simply creating a single and all-purpose 'rule' of behavior designed to treat every contingency. For this reason the diplomats carefully designed many different types of regimes to meet many different kinds of problems."

A related finding is that the task of crisis prevention is an integral part of foreign policy as a whole; it is not a subfield or a functional task that can be separated from other foreign policy tasks and from other instruments of statecraft and diplomacy. There are, indeed, three ways in which U.S.-Soviet global rivalry can be moderated: first, by *unilateral U.S. policies* that do not require Soviet cooperation; second, by *third-party initiatives* undertaken with a view to moderating or resolving conflicts in third areas in which the two superpowers are already involved to some extent or may become involved; and, third, by *bilateral U.S.-Soviet cooperation,* which may be pursued via several different modalities. We shall deal briefly with the first two of these possibilities, even though they are of undoubted importance, reserving major attention to the various ways in which the two superpowers can cooperate and coordinate their behavior to moderate their global rivalry.

As for unilateral measures, the United States can continue to pursue the various familiar (though not always relevant or reliable) instruments of containment policy. Deterrence strategy, of course, is the foremost instrument of containment, and, insofar as it is relevant and effective in different kinds of situations and circumstances, it contributes significantly to inducing Soviet restraint and hence to moderating U.S.-Soviet competition. Even during the heyday of détente, deterrence was essential for avoiding certain types of crises and as a backup for efforts to induce Soviet caution and restraint. Deterrence operates continuously in certain areas of high U.S. interest, such as in western Europe, and it can be brought into play selectively in other areas and situations, often in conjunction with other policy instruments. At the same time, as was the case even during the cold war when the United States enjoyed strategic superiority and other assets that have since declined, deterrence does not provide a cheap and reliable way of protecting friendly regimes, of discouraging attempts to change the status quo in third areas, or of limiting Soviet influence. As will be noted later in this chapter, deterrence strategy has become even less effective in these respects as the Soviet Union has achieved strategic parity and has acquired military capabilities that give a global reach to its efforts to augment its influence and stature as a world power.

Even during the height of the cold war U.S. containment policy did not rely exclusively on deterrence strategy and the threat of a military response to encroachments on its allies. Military and economic assistance to allies with whom collective security arrangements of one kind or another had been made played an important, if not always a satisfactory role. In the contemporary era, the objective of moderating competition with the Soviet Union and reducing the likelihood of crises between the superpowers will be facilitated to the extent that the United States, acting alone or together with other states, can utilize its influence and resources to create "objective conditions" in third areas that eliminate or moderate local and regional instabilities that provide tempting opportunities for Soviet probing and involvement.

In many situations this objective will require U.S. policy to do what it can to facilitate and channel sociopolitical change in a particular country rather than opposing it. Crisis prevention should not be regarded as coterminous with maintaining a particular status quo. Before the United States takes sides in an internal conflict it should consider whether the assistance it can give will indeed make a critical difference—i.e., whether U.S. military supplies, advisers, and economic aid are, as Dean Acheson used to say, "the only missing ingredient" that, once provided, will stabilize the internal situation of the country in question and/or render it secure against the threats of its neighbors. If not, Acheson warned, the United States should not intervene. He might have added that what appears to be "the missing ingredient" sometimes proves to be the first step on the slippery slope to incremental involvement by the United States, a development all the more likely if policymakers exaggerate the decisive impact their limited aid will have or, as in the Angola case, neglect to anticipate that states supporting the other side in the local situation may also increase their assistance, thereby counterbalancing the aid the United States has given. This point highlights the problem of escalation dynamics and the difficulty of controlling and limiting one's involvement, which will be discussed later.

The United States—again, alone, together with friendly states, or merely in support of other actors—can make use of the strategy of *preventive diplomacy* to resolve or moderate third area conflicts before the Soviets become involved or entrenched. Success in this respect will reduce the number of situations into which the United States may be drawn in competition with the Soviet Union, its allies, or its proxies. The strategy of preventive diplomacy takes many forms, and, as I. William Zartman's chapter indicates, it can be adapted to a variety of situations and contexts. The United States itself has acquired useful experience—as in Rhodesia and Namibia—in efforts to make preventive diplomacy work. There is, as well, a considerable body of additional experience in mediating and resolving international conflicts from which to draw useful lessons and guidelines.

As both I. William Zartman in his discussion of preventive diplomacy and Larry C. Napper in his chapters emphasize, the goal of crisis prevention often requires U.S. policymakers to give special attention to understanding and working with the "political terrain" in the locale and region of concern. To do so, of course, requires reliable intelligence and competent analysis of the political currents in third areas. Not only are area specialists essential to provide such analyses and judgments of the local political terrain, they must be given timely opportunities to offer their advice, and they must be listened to more intelligently and taken more seriously than they are now by top-level policymakers who lack sufficient area competence themselves and who often tend to give, as Kissinger did in Angola, undue weight to the apparent requirements of the global or regional rivalry with the Soviet Union.

Initiatives by third parties can play an increasingly important role in avoiding, moderating, or eliminating involvement of the United States and the Soviet Union in third areas. Not only the United Nations but regional associations and blocs—such as the Organization of African Unity (OAU) and the Association of South East Asian Nations (ASEAN)—and individual states exercising regional influence (such as Mexico in the Caribbean) can mediate local conflicts and engage in preventive diplomacy. Regional associations such as the OAU and the Organization of American States (OAS) can establish ground rules that attempt to limit use of force in disputes among members and to regulate and limit superpower involvement. Regional actors can provide diplomatic pressure and assistance for reaching cease-fire agreements and military forces to supervise them. Regional associations can also attempt to limit and regulate the flow of certain types of weapons from external sources of supply.

Turning now to bilateral arrangements the two superpowers can undertake in the interest of moderating their rivalry and avoiding crises that, if not war-threatening, seriously damage their overall relationship, we address first the utility of general principles for crisis prevention such as those contained in the Basic Principles Agreement (BPA) and the Agreement on Prevention of Nuclear War (APNW). This question is of continuing relevance; despite the return to a more confrontational relationship, the leaders of both sides from time to time have spoken of the need for better rules or have argued that stricter adherence to existing principles by the other would make a significant contribution to crisis prevention. A minimal case indeed can be made on behalf of general rules or principles of this kind; they are useful insofar as they alert Soviet and U.S. leaders to the dangers of confrontation and motivate them to take timely action to adjust policies and restrain behavior that may lead to crises. General agreements to cooperate in crisis prevention can be useful also to the extent that they encourage the two sides to consult frequently with a view to finding ways of reducing the conflict potential inherent in their competition for influence in certain areas. It would be good practice for U.S. and Soviet leaders to hold well-prepared high-level meetings at which they discuss in detail those specific situations and areas in which their divergent interests are engaged. Such conversations should not only aim at clarifying their conflicting interests but explore common interests in seeking accommodations and solutions. Unfortunately, and particularly disappointing during the high point of détente, the two sides did not regularize the practice of engaging in diplomatic consultations on a timely basis to develop, if possible, *specific* crisis-prevention understandings and arrangements for a potential trouble spot in which their divergent interests threatened to escalate into a crisis.

If the history of the U.S.-Soviet relations in the past fifteen or twenty years could be thoroughly canvassed from this standpoint, that history would reveal many missed opportunities of this kind. We have presented two such cases in Chapter 9 to illustrate this point. In the Angolan case, for example, Kissinger has been fairly criticized for waiting too long before taking up the situation with the Soviets. During the earlier Egyptian-Israeli War of Attrition, Kissinger's fundamental and continuing misperception of the situation led him to take a complacent view of the possibility of Soviet military intervention. As a result he lost an opportunity to defuse the tense situation before the Soviets moved in powerful air defense forces.

The importance of timely diplomatic consultations to clarify an ambiguous situation or to resolve an emerging conflict is well illustrated also by Gloria Duffy's analysis in Chapter 12 of two incipient U.S.-Soviet crises over Cuba. In 1970 the United States took up with the Soviets on a timely basis through diplomatic channels evidence that pointed to the possible construction of a submarine base in Cuba. The matter was resolved amicably in a manner consistent with the quid pro quo by means of which Kennedy and Khrushchev had resolved the Cuban missile crisis. In sharp contrast, in 1979 the Carter administration failed to initiate diplomatic conversations with the Soviets to clarify evidence of the possible existence of a Soviet combat brigade in Cuba and to obtain appropriate assurance and/ or resolution of the dispute until the matter had become the source of a highly politicized public controversy.

All of these crises—the introduction of Soviet air defense forces into Egypt in 1970, the failure to control the escalation dynamics of superpower competition in Angola in 1975, Carter's mishandling of the Soviet combat brigade in Cuba in 1979—also emphasize the critical importance of timely, reliable intelligence and analysis if

policymakers are to take appropriate diplomatic action to head off
a crisis. In addition, Duffy's analysis of the Soviet combat brigade
crisis calls attention to the inadequate workings of the U.S. policymaking
system and the Carter administration's inept handling of public
opinion as factors that contributed to the failure to deal with the
issue before it became a public confrontation.

General principles for crisis prevention, therefore, are only a starting
point for developing procedures for consultation between the
superpowers to deal with specific situations before they get out of
hand. Implementation also requires appropriate policy planning,
intelligence processing, and keen analysis of emerging situations of
potential danger to alert top leaders on each side to the need for
initiating timely changes in their own country's policies that may
be necessary for avoiding a crisis.

General principles for crisis prevention that remain as vague,
ambiguous, and contradictory as those imbedded in the BPA not
only are of limited utility, but are also potentially harmful insofar
as they raise unwarranted expectations. That the Soviet Union's
objectionable behavior in third areas could be significantly moderated
if only the USSR could be induced to honor general principles for
mutual restraint was and continues to be a beguiling idea. If that
idea continues to be entertained by U.S. leaders and the public, it
will only serve to obscure the complexity of the problem and lead
to further frustration. The history of the BPA and the APNW,
reviewed earlier in this study, illustrates the severe limitations of
general principles as a strategy for crisis prevention. It is evident
that greater specificity and precision in arrangements designed to
avoid crises will be required, a lesson that is supported by Lauren's
observation that diplomats in the nineteenth century understood the
necessity "to reach agreement on specific conditions for specific
problems and, conversely, to avoid nebulous, abstract, and grandiose
schemes. . . . Experience demonstrated that those [crisis prevention]
regimes not containing precise conditions could provoke disputes."

As noted in Chapter 5, the BPA was in important respects a
pseudoagreement; the general principles stated therein concealed
important unresolved disagreements over the forms of permissible
competition in third areas. An important gap remained between the
Soviet definition of peaceful coexistence and the Nixon-Kissinger
view of mutual restraint. It is difficult to avoid the conclusion that
each side appeared to view the BPA as a vehicle for imposing more
constraints on the foreign policy of the other side than on its own.

Given the ambiguities and generalities of these crisis-preventive
principles and the fact that they are in no sense self-enforcing, such

agreements are likely eventually to provoke charges and counter-charges of nonfulfillment and thus to generate additional friction and disillusionment. Some high-ranking officials of the Nixon admin-istration interviewed for this book appeared to feel that crisis-prevention agreements of the kind made at the summits of 1972 and 1973 were the cause of more trouble than they were worth.

Quite clearly, a better understanding of the challenging task of crisis prevention and of the variety of modalities for cooperation available for achieving it is needed.

We have discussed the uses and limitations of one such modality, namely, general principles for crisis prevention. Two other modalities need attention: U.S.-Soviet agreements *not* to compete in certain areas and arrangements for some form of cooperation in managing the danger of escalation when competing in a given locale. The problem itself can be depicted quite simply: U.S.-Soviet competition, direct or through allies or proxies, carries with it the danger of escalation to higher, more dangerous levels. To be sure, escalation can be avoided if either side decides not to become engaged or withdraws from competition with the other in a particular locale.

The United States, for example, evidently decided after World War II not to compete with the Soviet Union for influence in Finland. It has continued to accept the "Finlandization" status of that country, which permits the Finns to retain political independence and au-tonomy in domestic affairs in return for avoiding foreign policies that might be considered unfriendly to the Soviet Union. Indeed, the United States might well be pleased to see a similar state of affairs develop in Poland or other East European states that have not thus far been allowed the same political and economic freedom enjoyed by the Finns. For its part, and for whatever reasons, the Soviet Union in the past has often foregone competing in parts of the Third World.

Apart from unilateral decisions taken by one side not to compete with the other in a particular locale, the two superpowers can also agree not to compete in a given region or country. They can accomplish this by adopting one or another of the practices often resorted to by the great powers in the era of classical diplomacy. These include but are not confined to some variant of spheres of influence. In addition, as Lauren has reminded us in Chapter 3, there is the possibility of creating buffer states and neutralized zones, neutralizing small states, or "localizing" a regional conflict by agreeing on a mutual hands-off policy by all outside powers. There have been few instances of such agreements between the superpowers thus far. Kennedy and Khrushchev agreed on the neutralization of Laos in

1962. Earlier, in 1955, the United States and the Soviet Union signed the Austrian State Treaty that ended the occupation and division of Austria, returned independence and sovereignty to that country, and established its formal neutralization. The neutralization of Afghanistan has been suggested as a way of resolving the crisis created by Soviet military intervention.

Problems of Avoiding Escalation of Competition

Even if traditional practices of this kind are employed more frequently by the superpowers in the future, there will surely remain many situations in which the United States and the Soviet Union will become engaged and either choose to compete or feel obliged to do so by constraints on their freedom of action. Then the danger arises of undesirable escalation leading to confrontation. The problem for each side becomes one of finding a way to compete that carries with it a reasonable prospect of success while at the same time avoiding escalation to undesirable levels of involvement and conflict. General principles for crisis prevention such as contained in the BPA are of little value for escalation control in these circumstances. The serious study and pursuit of crisis prevention must turn instead to the examination of three different models for cooperation in escalation control: norms, rules of engagement, and ad hoc ground rules.

Norms. Norms are tacit understandings, often of an uncertain or unstable character, regarding competitive behaviors that are and are not permissible in particular areas and under various conditions. Norms arise from previous experience or, rather, from interpretations and lessons drawn from earlier experience.[1] Sometimes experience yields a fairly explicit norm that may even take the form of a quasi-agreement, as in the case of the quid pro quo that ended the Cuban missile crisis. Kennedy agreed that the United States would not invade Cuba in the future in return for Khrushchev's withdrawal of the missiles and a pledge not to reintroduce offensive weapons. This case illustrates the interesting possibility that the terms on which the superpowers terminate a crisis may constitute, as it were, a tacit crisis-prevention agreement for the future. The quid pro quo ending the missile crisis in 1962 indeed provided the reference point for settling the disagreement that arose in 1970 over the construction of a submarine base in Cuba.

Twenty years of superpower competition in the Middle East, if examined closely, suggests that certain tacit norms or patterns of restraint *may* have emerged, though these are by no means as well defined or as explicitly formulated as in the Cuban case. If the United

States and the Soviet Union have not always wanted to cooperate or have not been able to cooperate effectively to prevent the resort to force by parties to the Arab-Israeli conflict, they have certainly come to recognize that it is in their mutual interest that each superpower should prevent its local allies from dragging the superpowers into war with each other. Part of the learning experience drawn by the superpowers from repeated outbreaks of warfare between the Arab states and Israel is that they must cooperate, if necessary, to bring about a timely cease-fire before either the Israelis or the Arab side is threatened with a devastating defeat. Of a piece with this is the shared expectation that each superpower will provide as much assistance to its side in Arab-Israeli conflicts as needed to enable it to avoid a military catastrophe.

This set of norms emerged most clearly from the War of Attrition of 1969–1970 and the October War of 1973. It seems to include acceptance of the possibility that under certain extreme conditions, when the survival of its local ally may be at stake, a superpower can threaten and, if necessary, introduce its own military forces into the Middle East. This occurred, as noted in Chapter 9, during the War of Attrition when Soviet air defense forces intervened to defend Egypt from deep penetration attacks of the Israeli air force that were threatening to topple Nasser's regime. Several years later during the October War the Soviet Union issued a threat of unilateral intervention in order to induce the United States to pressure Israel to observe the cease-fire and halt the Israeli destruction of the Egyptian Third Army. Brezhnev's threat was regarded as sufficiently credible in Washington to trigger pressure on the Israelis to halt their military operations and to agree to a new cease-fire. At the same time, it should be noted that the tacit norm that legitimizes military intervention by a superpower in Arab-Israeli conflicts is limited to certain extreme contingencies in which intervention is clearly needed to assure the survival of the regional ally.

During the course of a series of crises in the Middle East, therefore, what Robert Legvold calls "patterns of restraint"[2] have developed to regulate superpower involvement in the area's disputes. Such patterns of restraint, or norms, are tacit understandings at best. They rest on mutual U.S.-Soviet awareness that each power must somehow reconcile support for its allies in the Middle East with the types of restraint needed to avoid allowing itself to be drawn into dangerous confrontations and military clashes. Norms of this kind fall well short of formalized U.S.-Soviet agreements for cooperation in crisis prevention or crisis management in this region. Furthermore, tacit norms of this kind are subject to erosion over time with new developments and hence cannot be counted upon to work effectively in new situations that may arise. Thus, it may be noted that in recent times both the United States and the Soviet Union have stepped up noncrisis deployments and military exercises in the Middle East. Specifically, the deployment of U.S. ground forces to the Sinai in 1982 as part of the multinational force lowers a longstanding norm against stationing of superpower ground forces in the area during more or less normal periods. The possibility arises that the Soviets will not be far behind in seeking a way to position a limited contingent of Soviet troops in the area, possibly in Syria.

Erosion of the firmer norm concerning Cuba is also a possibility as the Soviets continue their arms build up there and the Reagan administration speaks of "going to the source" to oppose Cuban interventionism in the Caribbean and in Latin America.

Finally, not only are tacit norms for controlling the escalation potential of superpower competition often uncertain and subject to erosion over time, they tend to be area-specific in content and coverage. Norms of this kind have not emerged for all the areas in which the superpowers compete. For all these reasons the tacit norms and patterns of restraint derived from experience do not provide a firm or comprehensive basis for efforts to control escalation of superpower competition.

Rules of Engagement. It is useful to distinguish between norms of the kind we have discussed and explicit rules of engagement. Explicit rules hold out the promise of providing a stronger basis for cooperation in crisis prevention than tacit norms or implicit patterns of restraint. Explicit rules would provide the United States and the Soviet Union with a better shared understanding than would tacit norms of the various types of involvement and intervention that would be "permissible" to each superpower. Equally important, the two sides would have a common understanding of the conditions under which each type of intervention could be legitimately and safely resorted to. Further, if the rules of engagement accepted by the two sides were clear and sufficiently explicit, each side's behavior in a particular third-area competition would become more predictable to the other. This predictability would enhance the ability of the United States and the USSR to coordinate their actions in order to limit and control the dynamics of escalation inherent in any such competition. Some reasonably clear prior understanding would exist as to what each side is "entitled" to do in support of a local ally or client state under different circumstances. There would exist, as it were, a schedule of additional increments or types of involvement each side would be permitted in response to certain actions by the other superpower or its proxies. In brief, well-developed rules of engagement would assist the two sides in achieving "escalation control" as well as in setting an initial level of mutually acceptable involvement.

The general principles regarding cooperation in crisis prevention embodied in the Basic Principles Agreement and the Agreement on Prevention of Nuclear War, it should be recognized, are not rules of engagement. Rules of this kind would be much more specific in indicating types of involvement permitted and forbidden the two countries, for example, with reference to such questions as the following:

1. May Soviet and American military forces (or those of their proxies and allies) be used (a) to overthrow an existing government, (b) to defend an ally against external attack, (c) to defend a friendly government from internal opposition, etc.?
2. May the United States and the Soviet Union directly or indirectly sponsor or assist—and, if so, by what means—externally or internally based insurgents attempting to overthrow an existing regime?
3. May the United States and the Soviet Union support an expansionist or irredentist local power in its actions against another state?
4. May the superpowers give economic or military assistance—and, if so, what types—to either side in a civil war?

A proposal that the United States and the Soviet Union agree to abstain from some of these types of involvement in third areas has been made by the American Committee on East-West Accord. Taking note of the generality of the Basic Principles Agreement, the non-intervention articles of the UN Charter, and the Helsinki Accords, the American Committee proposes "negotiation of a much more precise set of ground rules having to do with specific geography and a specific ban on direct or indirect use of combat forces in those areas." The geographical areas in which such prohibitions would apply are designated as the Middle East, Southwest Asia, Africa, the Indian subcontinent, and Southeast Asia. Elaborating its proposal, the American Committee indicates that such a ban would include not only U.S. and Soviet forces but also "covert, paramilitary, or so-called 'volunteer' combat forces." Finally, the Committee states that such a U.S.-Soviet agreement should include the stipulation "that neither power would intervene with combat forces even if 'invited' to do so by one of the Third World countries."[3]

Several observations can be made about the feasibility and desirability of *general* legislation, embodied in rules of engagement, on questions of this kind. Such rules, clearly, would have to apply as restraints on the behavior of *both* the United States and the Soviet Union (and perhaps also on that of their allies attempting to act as their surrogates or proxies); they would be applicable with equal force to their competition in all third areas, not merely to those situations in which mutual observance of the rules would favor one superpower in the competition. Robert Legvold has cautioned those who argue for specific legislation of this kind that if the United States expects the Soviet Union to observe a certain rule or pattern of restraint it has to be prepared to do so also.[4]

What this means in practice is that each side must be prepared to accept the outcome of a competition in a particular area—even a quite unfavorable outcome—should both sides observe an agreed-upon set of constraints. For this reason and for others as well, the two superpowers are unlikely to accept general rules that are to apply equally in all contests. The consequences of observing such rules may be favorable or without serious cost in some cases but excessive in others. On the other hand, although across-the-board legislation of this kind is likely to be rejected or honored in the breach, rules of engagement designed for a *specific* area or type of situation might prove to be more acceptable and workable.

The complexity of the relationship between general rules that apply to all third areas and specific ones for a particular region or country is perhaps nowhere better illustrated than in the Carter administration's attempt to develop understandings with the Soviets that could lead to restraints on the transfer of conventional arms to third areas. The supply of weapons is a major instrument of the U.S.-Soviet competition in third areas, and it is therefore also highly relevant for devising cooperative strategies for crisis prevention. This paradox and the dilemma it poses for U.S. (and Soviet) policymakers was explored and demonstrated in Chapter 11 by Barry M. Blechman, Janne E. Nolan, and Alan Platt. Initial progress was made in the U.S.-Soviet conventional arms transfers talks leading to preliminary agreement on some general constraints that might be applied to all arms transfers. Difficulties arose and the talks foundered when the discussion turned to limitation of arms transfers to specific geographical regions. Part of the explanation for this outcome lies in the fact that the implications of restraints on arms transfers for U.S.-Soviet competition in third areas were not squarely faced within the Carter administration. Analysis of the lessons derived from this experience suggests strategies that might be more effective if such efforts are resumed in the future.

What, then, is the feasibility and future promise of the rules-of-engagement type of model for promoting cooperation in crisis prevention? In attempting to assess this difficult question, as has already been suggested, one must distinguish between *general* rules of engagement intended to be applicable to all third areas and *particular* rules agreed upon only for a single region or third area. The prospects for achieving rules limited to a specific area, however problematic and difficult even this objective might prove to be, are nonetheless more favorable than the possibility of getting agreement on or implementation of a single set of general rules intended to be applicable across the board for U.S.-Soviet competition in all third areas.

This is so because efforts to define specific rules of competition for a particular locale can take into account the *relative interests* of the two superpowers in that area. In constrast, efforts to devise general rules of engagement supposedly applicable to all third areas would encounter the difficulty that the balance of superpower interests varies considerably from one geographical area to another. Rules of engagement that may be acceptable and even quite attractive to a superpower for an area in which it has no important interests might be viewed as quite prejudicial if intended to apply equally to competition in locales in which its vital interests are at stake.

Given the fact that the relative interests of the United States and the Soviet Union vary from one area to another, we need to view their global rivalry as composed of a *variety of competitive "games" that have different structures and somewhat different logics* or implications for managing competition in the interest of crisis prevention. A more differentiated conception of superpower competition is needed that recognizes the different balance of interests that underlies the contest for influence in different parts of the world. By taking into account the magnitude and the symmetry or asymmetry of relative U.S.-Soviet interests in different areas we can identify six *game structures* of a distinctive kind that are imbedded in the overall competition. The first four are:

1. *High-interest symmetry:* locales in which both sides have very strong, if not vital, interests.
2. *Low-interest symmetry:* locales in which both sides have modest interests.
3. *Interest asymmetry favoring the Soviet Union:* locales in which Soviet interests are clearly and substantially more important than those of the United States.

4. *Interest asymmetry favoring the United States:* locales in which U.S. interests are clearly and substantially more important than those of the Soviet Union.

Each of these game structures rests on the important assumption that the two sides agree on that particular characterization of the balance of interests. This assumption, however, is not in fact always satisfied, and the four game structures thus far identified do not encompass the full range of competitive situations. Our typology must be extended to encompass at least two additional game structures:

5. *Disputed interest symmetry:* locales in which the United States and the Soviet Union do not agree on the relative balance of their interests.
6. *Uncertain interest symmetry:* locales of an ambiguous or fluid nature in which one or both superpowers are not certain of their own or the other's interests and find it difficult to assess how and to what extent their interests will become engaged in a developing, unstable situation.

Such a typology of game structures is useful as a reminder of the complexities of the global competition in which the superpowers are engaged. Implicit in the game structures, too, are different "logics" as regards the task of managing competition for influence and finding ways of cooperating to prevent dangerous, unwanted crises. All this, as already noted, complicates the task of devising a single set of general rules of engagement applicable to all game structures; at the same time, however, it points to an alternative approach of attempting to define somewhat different rules to regulate the competition in different game structures.

An analytical typology of this kind inevitably oversimplifies matters; it offers only a starting point for additional analysis that takes up other relevant variables which affect superpower competition, variables such as the *available capabilities* and the *viable strategies* available to the two sides for competing for influence in different game structures, and various *domestic and international constraints* on *defining* their interests in operational terms and in *pursuing* those interests. A superpower that labors under an asymmetry in any of these additional variables will operate at a disadvantage in its competitive contests with the other superpower. The disadvantaged superpower will have greater difficulty in securing outcomes consistent with the relative balance of interests. Another way of putting this is to note that outcomes of competition cannot be reliably predicted from game structures that take into account only the relative balance of interests. Accordingly, too, the "logics" of the different game structures that have been identified cannot be automatically or easily translated into different sets of rules for moderating superpower competition for each type of game. A superpower that enjoys advantages in capabilities and viable strategies, and in the ability to define and pursue interests without being unduly hampered by domestic and international constraints, will be reluctant to accept rules of engagement that dilute or cancel out these advantages. On the other hand, a superpower that suffers disadvantages in these respects may seek to impose rules on its competitor that compensate for those disadvantages.

How can the preceding analysis, once its complexities and limitations have been recognized, assist in policy planning directed at finding ways of moderating superpower rivalry? In the first place, the analytical framework that has been outlined thus far may be useful for studying and learning from the success or failure of past efforts to cooperate in controlling the escalation dynamics inherent in great-power competition. Our analytical model suggests that situations of high-interest symmetry ought to lend themselves more readily to development of rules and arrangements (and, for that matter, tacit norms) for crisis prevention. A situation of this kind emerged, for example, during World War II when Roosevelt, Stalin, and Churchill foresaw that competition for advantage in filling the vacuum of power in central Europe, once Hitler was defeated, might well result in severe conflict if not war. Accordingly, the Allied leaders mapped out zones of occupation for their respective armies and set up procedures and rules for collective decisionmaking and joint administration of occupied Germany. For this area of high-interest symmetry the Allies adopted what might be appropriately regarded as an explicit crisis-prevention regime. The arrangements they made for cooperation and for regulating their competition, to be sure, did not suffice to cope with the stresses occasioned by divergent interests later. But this historical case illustrates, nonetheless, the possibilities for developing explicit rules in situations of high-interest symmetry that serve to dampen possibilities for explosive conflict. Similarly one might regard the Four Power Agreement on the status of West Berlin in 1971 and the Helsinki Accord of 1975 (whatever its imperfections) as efforts to legislate rules of engagement (and accommodation) in a region, Europe, of high-interest symmetry.

At first glance it would appear that situations of low-interest symmetry should also lend themselves to rule making. The presumption is that since what is at stake for the two superpowers is so modest in these circumstances it should be relatively easy to agree on rules of engagement that strictly limit the levels of investment in their competition. As experience demonstrates, however, such a presumption is not always justified. Precisely because neither superpower has high stakes in an area, both powers may deem it unnecessary to develop explicit rules of engagement to limit the escalation potential of such competitive games. This was the case in Angola in 1975 when, after the Portuguese government's decision to grant independence to its colony, the two superpowers engaged in initially low-level competition that escalated into a major diplomatic crisis (see Chapter 9).

Our model also suggests that situations of pronounced interest asymmetry favoring one side or the other should lend themselves to development of norms, if not also rules of engagement, that reflect the disparity of interests. When one superpower perceives that the other side's interests are much more strongly engaged in a particular area than its own, the first power should moderate the *objectives* it will pursue in that area and/or the *means* it will employ on their behalf. Recognizing an existing asymmetry of interests in this way should facilitate crisis prevention. But, as history teaches us, the side with more modest interests at stake may still choose to compete either on behalf of less ambitious objectives or by using moderate, less risky means. For this reason, the shape that rules of engagement might take for situations of interest asymmetry is by no means self-evident or easily agreed upon. Thus, for example, since World War II the United States has recognized the important security interests of the Soviet Union in Eastern Europe, but it has also pressed the Soviets to settle for an "open" rather than a "closed" sphere of influence, one in which East European states would enjoy a greater measure of political freedom and access to the West. In this and other respects the United States has competed to some extent with Moscow for influence in that region. The objectives the United States has pursued in this part of the world have varied from time to time, being somewhat more ambitious during the height of the cold war; the means employed by Washington in pursuit of these objectives have also varied. Similar observations might be made about Soviet policy in areas in the Western Hemisphere that were traditionally placed off limits to European powers by the Monroe Doctrine.

One option open to the superpowers—which they do not appear to have utilized thus far—is the possibility of agreeing upon a single set of rules to apply reciprocally to both areas of interest asymmetry, Eastern Europe and the Western Hemisphere. Instead, to the extent that the United States and the Soviet Union have respected each other's arena of dominant interest, they have done so through reliance on tacit norms and ad hoc self-imposed restraints. On several occasions, for example, in Hungary in 1956 and in Czechoslovakia in 1968, the United States indirectly assured the Soviet Union that it would not seriously exploit difficulties Moscow was having in dealing with revolutionary upheavals in Eastern Europe. There may be comparable instances of Soviet restraint, for example vis-à-vis Chile in 1970–1973. The outstanding exception, of course, is the Soviet Union's relationship with Castro's Cuba and its abortive effort to place strategic missiles in that country. Other examples of efforts to cooperate in defining rules or norms for moderating competition in areas of high-interest asymmetry that bear closer analysis and evaluation than is possible here are the so-called Sonnenfeldt Doctrine of 1976, which seemed to suggest acceptance by the United States of an "organic" relationship between the Soviet Union and East European countries, and the Helsinki Accord of 1975, which attempted to introduce stability into relations between Eastern and Western Europe and, however imperfectly, to define some guidelines for limiting competition and promoting "confidence-building" even while encouraging freer communication, travel, and human rights.

Although neither rules nor unambiguous norms have been worked out to regulate competition in areas of interest asymmetry, nonetheless the two superpowers seem likely to act in the future with considerable prudence in each other's areas of prime interest. In contrast, one may assume that efforts to develop rules or norms will encounter greater difficulty for those parts of the globe characterized by uncertain and/ or disputed symmetry. The Middle East is a case in point. Here the Soviet Union, implementing its claim to equality with the United States, has tried unsuccessfully to get Washington to regard the area as one of high-interest symmetry that requires a joint U.S.-Soviet approach to peacemaking. Accordingly, as was noted earlier, crisis prevention in the Arab-Israeli conflict has been highly problematical and has come to rely on the emergence of tacit norms and patterns of restraint.

Development of norms and rules of engagement encounter even more difficulties in so-called gray areas, countries and regions where neither superpower has vital interests but where clarification of their interests and the balance of interests is laden with uncertainty. It is often said, with some justification, that the United States and the Soviet Union can reduce the risk of confrontations in such areas of disputed and uncertain symmetry by clarifying their intentions in a timely fashion in order to avoid being drawn into a low-level conflict in response to, or in anticipation of, what it thinks the other is or will be doing. However, in situations of this kind we find that diplomats often convey their own intentions or ask their opponents to clarify their interests in ways that lack clearness and credibility. There is no assurance that diplomatic signals of this kind will be recognized and taken with the degree of seriousness that they deserve. The danger of misperception and miscommunication is particularly serious when one superpower intervenes cautiously and on a low level in a local situation, probing to test the other superpower's reaction, and, receiving no response, decides to escalate its involvement. Failure to grasp that the opponent is conducting a carefully controlled probe and is engaged in the subtle asking of a question regarding one's own intentions can easily result in a miscalculation. As a result the opponent may step up its involvement, setting into motion developments that may lead to a superpower confrontation.

Specialists on Soviet foreign policy behavior believe that miscommunication of this kind has occurred repeatedly in the history of U.S.-Soviet relations. Testifying in the Senate hearings on Angola, Leon Goure, for example, stated that this case illustrated the chronic tendency of U.S. policymakers to discount initial Soviet probes and signals. As a result, "By the time the Russians have committed themselves to some course of action, have really become involved and are successful, we then begin to object. By that time it is late, they are in there. Retreat involves a matter of prestige, all kinds of political costs for them and they feel essentially that we have misled them."[5]

Digressing briefly, we note that diplomatic signaling to clarify intentions is also needed to control the danger that tense crises characterized by high asymmetry of interests may get out of hand. In such cases the superpower with lesser interests at stake may reassure its opponent that it does not intend seriously to contest the issue. An unusual example of this kind of unilateral cooperation in the interest of crisis prevention in a tense, potentially explosive situation occurred in October 1956 when President Eisenhower signalled Khrushchev that although the United States strongly opposed and condemned Soviet military intervention in Hungary it would not itself intervene militarily in support of the Nagy government. Another example of this kind was Stalin's subtle signal to Truman soon after the North Korean attack on South Korea to the effect that the Soviet Union regarded the conflict there as a civil war to be settled without outside intervention, thereby indirectly assuring Truman that the Soviets would not respond to U.S. military intervention on behalf of South Korea with military intervention of their own. Similar instances in which one great power clarified its interests and intentions in tense situations in the interest of crisis prevention occurred frequently in the nineteenth century and have additional counterparts in the history of U.S.-Soviet relations.

The willingness and ability of the superpowers to clarify their interests and intentions is, perhaps paradoxically, more problematic in their competition in gray areas of relatively low interest. In recent years Soviet and U.S. leaders seem to have become increasingly reluctant in many such situations to define and delimit their interests lest they "give away" such areas or encourage the other side to proceed in efforts to consolidate or increase its influence by allowing it to assume that such efforts will not risk a strong response.

This trend has been strengthened by several changes in Soviet and U.S. approaches to world politics. On the one hand, the Soviet leaders' conception of Soviet foreign policy interests has expanded with their country's emergence as a genuine global power, their claim to a superpower status of equality with the United States, and their interpretation of this new status as entitling them to have a say in shaping events and outcomes in all parts of the globe. In the United States, with the gradual erosion of détente and the return to a more confrontational relationship with the Soviet Union, the image of the Soviet adversary has not only hardened once again and raised concern over the scope of Moscow's foreign policy objectives and ambitions. In addition, there has been a return among United States leaders, at least in part, to the older image of a highly unstable international system that was prevalent during the cold war. According to this view, important components of the international system are tightly coupled so that a setback for the United States is not only a gain, sooner or later, for the Soviet Union but any such setback is also likely to have a "billiard ball" effect, destabilizing other parts of the system as well as leading to the likelihood of challenges to U.S. interests and setbacks elsewhere. The images of the Soviet Union and of the international system had been moderated somewhat during the era of détente, although not abandoned. Even while attempting to entice the Soviet Union into observing restraints in its foreign policy and into foregoing efforts to derive marginal gains at the expense of the United States, Kissinger felt it was important to threaten the stick as well as to react sharply to assertive Soviet foreign policy forays. Threats of punishment were more than just a part of the behavior modification techniques that Kissinger employed vis-à-vis the Soviets to encourage them to adopt new norms of international behavior and to moderate their foreign policy. He believed it was important to impress on Soviet leaders that efforts to make even marginal gains at the expense of the West would be resisted or would be made otherwise costly. Hence, even while pursuing détente Kissinger never abandoned the tendency of U.S. policymakers during the cold war to assess the value of remote outposts of seemingly secondary or trivial significance from the standpoint of U.S. security interests in global terms, which of course enhanced their importance. Members of the Carter administration attempted to set aside this global, geopolitical approach in favor of a regional perspective on problems of the Third World; the continued erosion of détente and assertive Soviet foreign policy forays made this approach increasingly controversial, even within the Carter administration, and it was finally abandoned after the Soviet invasion of Afghanistan.

Other factors also operate to make it very difficult for U.S. policymakers to clarify or delimit their interests in certain third areas. They are often constrained from doing so by domestic politics or by sensitive allies. As a result, Washington often finds it extremely difficult to discount the importance of gray areas from the standpoint of U.S. national interests except under the pressure of a crisis. There is the ever-present likelihood that someone in the foreign policy bureaucracy, members of Congress, or vocal interest groups will be quick to charge that the administration is insufficiently attentive to the need to protect U.S. interests abroad.

Clarification of U.S. interests and intentions in gray areas encounters another obstacle as well. Sometimes responsible policymakers simply are not able to define or anticipate the full extent of U.S. interests in a gray area before competition has escalated and approached a crisis stage. Often only when a situation has deteriorated to a certain point—for example, as a result of significant escalation, as with the Soviet-assisted Cuban intervention in Angola—do its broader ramifications for U.S. interests become evident in Washington, forcing consideration of a strong response. This dilemma cannot be avoided merely by enjoining U.S. policymakers to define their interests in advance, for in many situations what is at stake for the United States does increase substantially and somewhat unpredictably as a result of actions by the Soviet Union or its allies or proxies, or through internal developments within a third area.

In sum, it is very unlikely that the United States and the Soviet Union will find it easy to agree to general-purpose rules of engagement that are intended to apply across the board to all areas and situations in which the two superpowers may find themselves in competition. Specific rules contrived to limit or to regulate competition in a particular area, however, are much more feasible. Once again, the agreement ending the Cuban missile crisis comes to mind. This agreement, like all other-crisis prevention arrangements, is subject to erosion and obsolescence, but it has nevertheless been serviceable for over twenty years and has been invoked several times in dealing with troublesome developments. Specific rules or tacit norms appear to be promising also as a way of limiting the supply of arms into crisis-prone areas, such as the Korean peninsula, and controlling regional arms races. Even in situations as complex as Angola undoubtedly was in 1975, had Washington and Moscow consulted with each other as soon as the Alvor Agreement was signed and had they supported the efforts on its behalf by the Organization of African Unity, they might have agreed on rules severely restricting their own involvement as well as that of other states, such as South Africa, Cuba, and Zaire. Efforts to identify specific rules of engagement to limit or avoid competition in a third country should have priority in foreign policy planning and should be pursued in timely diplomatic consultations between the two superpowers.

Ad Hoc Ground Rules for Escalation Control. When norms and rules of engagement do not exist to regulate superpower involvement in a contested area, the task becomes one of improvising an ad hoc set of ground rules for managing that particular competition. This task is similar to the problem of keeping a limited war from expanding, a problem that the Korean War highlighted for U.S. policymakers and writers on strategy. When one or both sides in a conflict have unused military capabilities at their disposal, the danger exists that a low-level conflict will escalate to higher levels of violence. One must understand the peculiar dynamics of escalatory processes at least well enough to find ways of controlling unwanted escalation. And, as Thomas Schelling and Richard Smoke have emphasized,[6] the participants in such conflicts must identify various "saliencies" present in the configuration of the situation and attempt to utilize them in order to limit its escalatory potential.

Basically, a conflict can be kept limited in two ways—by limiting the objectives one pursues in a particular conflict and by limiting the means employed to achieve those objectives, however ambitious or limited they are. Limitation of means, in turn, can express itself in several different ways with reference, that is, to *weapons, targets, participants,* or *geographical boundaries.* Further, one may limit the number of weapons of a particular type that are employed—i.e., a quantitative limitation. Or one may also limit the *type* of weapons employed, the exclusion of certain types of weapons being referred to as a qualitative limitation. The distinction between number and type—quantitative and qualitative limitation—applies also to the targets brought under attack.

The quantitative and qualitative distinction applies also with regard to participants. Limitation of the conflict may be achieved in terms of types of personnel and the nature of their participation (e.g., whether personnel of an outside power are introduced into a local conflict and, if so, whether as military advisers or in different combat roles). Any particular type of participation can vary, of course, with regard to the number of persons involved in that type of activity. Finally, there is often an opportunity to limit a conflict by confining combat operations geographically; such a limitation is qualitative in nature.

Generally speaking, a pattern of limitations—or ground rules— can develop more easily with respect to qualitative than to quantitative dimensions of a conflict. This is so in that qualitative aspects—*types* of weapons used, *types* of targets attacked, *types* of personnel, *types* of participation, and geographical limits observed—are generally more easily recognized than variations in quantitative dimensions. Hence, violation of existing qualitative limitations is more easily monitored. Moreover, the introduction of a new weapon into combat, initiation of attacks against a type of target heretofore not under fire, intervention by external forces and/or a shift in their participation from an advisory or training role to a more important supporting or combat role—all such qualitative changes represent the crossing of a new threshold that alters the existing pattern of limitations and may trigger counterescalation by the opponent. Although escalation of the quantitative dimensions of a conflict by one side can also destabilize an existing pattern of limitations, the development of and adherence to qualitative limitations is usually more critical for achieving recognizable, stable ground rules for a local conflict.

All of these five types of limitations—on objectives, weapons, targets, geography, and participation—are relevant to great-power involvement in third-area conflicts. The problem of limiting a local conflict arises in the first instance, of course, for the local actors. It is complicated by the involvement of external actors, both regional actors and more distant powers. The task of limiting a conflict and controlling its escalatory potential can be considerably complicated, as in the Angola case, when many external actors with diverse interests are involved in some way. Control of escalation dynamics is likely to be more difficult also when, as is often the case, local actors pursue more ambitious objectives or are willing to take greater risks than their great power allies, as in the Middle East case.

The task of establishing a *stable* set of ground rules in a conflict is rendered much more difficult when each side attempts to establish a favorable pattern of limitations that will give it an advantage in the competition. Refusal to compete on grounds that seem to favor the opponent feeds the dynamics of escalation and draws the superpowers into increasing their intervention.

Escalation can be controlled, however, in a number of ways. One side may succeed in establishing escalation dominance—that is, it may convince its opponent that it has superior capabilities at just about every rung of the escalation ladder and, also, that it is willing to employ such capabilities if necessary. If the opponent is so persuaded and is rational, it will have no incentive under these circumstances to change the existing ground rules even though these foreshadow an unfavorable outcome. Escalation control can be achieved also if one or both sides feel that the costs and risks of stepping up their intervention are likely to be excessive in relation to the benefits to be attained thereby. The more important and valued the objectives pursued in the conflict, the greater the willingness to expend more resources and accept higher costs and risks. But conversely, the more limited the stakes in a particular conflict the more reluctant will the actor be to run the risks of escalation. Similarly, the fear of triggering an escalation spiral that will be difficult to bring under control will induce prudence and caution and create greater willingness to confine the competition within an established set of ground rules even though those rules appear to be somewhat disadvantageous to one side.

Reluctance to escalate in ways that would be highly advantageous is increased, of course, when it is known that the opponent, too, has unused intervention capabilities that would enable it to engage in effective counterescalation. However, if one side believes that its opponent will be constrained by domestic or diplomatic factors from engaging in counterescalation, as the Soviets came to believe the United States was in Angola, then that side will be less inhibited from stepping up its intervention.

Escalation control will be facilitated if one or both sides indicate that they are willing to moderate their objectives and settle for less. A willingness by one side to offer, or to negotiate for, a mutually acceptable outcome may remove the other side's incentive to escalate its intervention.

As these observations imply, the search for escalation control may involve bargaining, much of which may be tacit rather than explicit. There are dangers of misperception and miscalculation in this, as both the Middle East and Angolan cases demonstrate. Signaling may lack clarity and be beset with "noise"; or it may be poorly timed. Offers and threats may be lacking in credibility. As a result, the superpowers may be drawn further into a local conflict than they wanted or expected to be. And this possibility is much increased, of course, insofar as the local actors seek to manipulate the behavior of the superpowers to their own advantage.

In summary, we have identified three different models or modalities that the United States and the Soviet Union can employ to cooperate to prevent their global competition from escalating into crises of one kind or another. We believe that *a more exact and differentiated conceptualization of cooperation, such as is provided by these three models, is necessary as a corrective to the still current notion that U.S.-Soviet cooperation, if it is to be achieved, requires no more than agreement on general principles for behaving with restraint* and foregoing efforts to achieve unilateral advantages at each other's expense. In this connection, we have also emphasized that it is necessary for the two superpowers to move beyond agreement on general principles to construct *specific* crisis-prevention understandings and arrangements tailored to the special configuration of a given country or region in which they have conflicting interests. A variety of traditional diplomatic practices are available for this purpose, each of which deserves more detailed study and illustration than has been possible here.

It is important to recognize that cooperation in crisis prevention is possible even in the absence of formal rules to regulate competition. Indeed, tacit norms and patterns of restraint developed from past experience may be all that are available for this purpose in many situations. As for formal rules of engagement worked out and agreed to in advance, we believe that the possibilities for developing general rules of this kind that would apply to all types of situations and areas are far less promising than the likelihood of getting agreement on specific rules that are adapted to variations in the relative balance of U.S.-Soviet interests in different areas of the world. We have proposed as a useful starting point for moving in this direction a sixfold typology of relative U.S.-Soviet interests: high-interest symmetry; low-interest symmetry; high-interest asymmetry favoring the United States; high-interest asymmetry favoring the Soviet Union; disputed symmetry; and uncertain symmetry. Different rules of engagement are needed, in all likelihood, to facilitate cooperation in crisis prevention for each of these six variants of the balance of U.S.-Soviet interests. At the very least our sixfold typology, which is intended as an aid to policymaking and not as a blueprint, serves as a useful reminder that realistic efforts at crisis prevention must take into account the relative interests of the two sides in any particular situation, as the two sides perceive them.

This focus on the importance of relative interests also serves to highlight the need to clarify one's interests even while remaining aware that superpowers experience various difficulties in doing so. Sensitivity to this dimension of superpower competition in third areas should increase awareness of the ever-present danger that difficulties of signaling and inadequate policy analysis may lead to misperceptions and miscalculations that trigger unwanted, possibly avoidable crises. A more comprehensive review than was possible here is needed of crises that reflect missed opportunities for their prevention.

In many future situations, as in the past, neither tacit norms nor rules of engagement will be available or will be robust enough to provide a basis for possible cooperation in crisis prevention. One is left with a more problematic third modality, namely the improvisation by the two superpowers of ad hoc ground rules to control the escalation danger present in a low-level competition. An analytical framework derived from experience in conducting limited war in the past is available for conceptualizing the task of developing ad hoc ground rules in any specific situation.

Finally, as emphasized earlier in this chapter, unilateral policies and third-party initiatives can also contribute importantly to avoiding or managing superpower competition.

Prospects for Détente and Crisis Prevention

The prospects under the Reagan administration for an eventual reconstruction of détente on a more realistic basis and the possibility of developing cooperative arrangements with the Soviet Union in the interest of crisis prevention remain obscure at the present time. Continuing and deepening the drift toward a confrontational relationship that began in the latter part of the Carter administration, the Reagan administration has not yet developed a coherent view of the kind of longer-range relationship with the Soviet Union it regards as desirable and feasible. There are important disagreements within the administration on this fundamental question that have not been resolved; these disagreements, in turn, reflect the divergence of views and the images of the Soviet Union within the public and in Congress. At the same time, while undertaking a strengthening of U.S. military forces and adopting a tough posture and rhetoric in its foreign policy, the Reagan administration also conveys an interest in a more stable, less conflictual relationship with the Soviet Union.

On September 22, 1981, for example, President Reagan wrote to Chairman Brezhnev saying that the United States was interested in developing "a stable and constructive relationship with the Soviet

Union." Continuing, in language reminiscent of the rhetoric of détente, but without mentioning that word, Reagan added that such a relationship, however, must be built upon "restraint and reciprocity," elements that had been "missing from many Soviet actions in recent years." As examples of such Soviet behavior Reagan mentioned "the U.S.S.R.'s unremitting and comprehensive military buildup over the past 15 years . . ." and its "pursuit of unilateral advantage in various parts of the world—through direct and indirect use of force in regional conflicts." In this context, Reagan added that the role of Cuba in Africa and Latin America was particularly disturbing and also referred to developments in Poland, Afghanistan, and Kampuchea (Cambodia). He ended by expressing the hope that the two sides can succeed in establishing "a framework of mutual respect for each other's interest and a mutual restraint in the resolution of international crises. . . ."[7]

Although earlier in 1981 Secretary of State Alexander Haig had on several occasions spoken of the need for new "rules of conduct," the president's letter to Brezhnev evidently did not. Neither, apparently, did Reagan refer to the Basic Principles Agreement of 1972. Left ambiguous for the time being, therefore, is the administration's attitude towards the Basic Principles Agreement. In this respect, questions such as the following arise: Does the administration regard the Basic Principles Agreement as still operative? Is the administration's adherence to the provisions of the BPA conditional and, if so, with respect to what—a formal revision or clarification of parts of that agreement? New arms control agreements of the kind favored by the Reagan administration? Changes in Soviet policy in Afghanistan, Poland, Kampuchea, and elsewhere? Satisfactory assurances of a less assertive Soviet foreign policy generally? Etc.

Lacking in the Reagan administration's policy, also, is a more specific indication of the contributions it would be willing to make to the overall relationship with the Soviet Union under certain conditions, with respect to such matters as trade, credits, scientific and cultural exchanges, etc. In other words, while urging the Soviet Union to adhere to the norm of "reciprocity," the Reagan administration has not put forward a definition of this norm; nor has it indicated what obligations "reciprocity" would impose on the United States as well as the Soviet Union. Similarly, while enjoining the Soviet Union to behave in the world in accord with the norm of "restraint" and while giving concrete examples of Soviet actions regarded as inconsistent with such a norm, the Reagan administration has not given a very clear indication of what "restraint" would imply for its own foreign policy behavior.

One of the major lessons that emerges from Breslauer's analysis in Chapter 13 of why détente failed is that the two superpowers operated with divergent interpretations of the norms of reciprocity and restraint, so it is all the more important to address this problem explicitly in considering what kind of new "stable and constructive relationship" with the Soviet Union the United States is trying to achieve.

It may well be that the Reagan administration has not evolved a clear or fixed view on these matters and that its day-to-day actions are not guided by any well-defined or predetermined conception of what kind of U.S.-Soviet relationship it should strive for. If so, this lack of an objective is likely to constrain somewhat the prospects as well as the modalities for inducing the Soviets to cooperate in some way in the interest of crisis prevention. Such cooperation is possible, however, even in the context of a relationship that is heavily infused with confrontation, such as was the cold war, or a somewhat more moderate relationship that strives for containment without dangerous confrontations. If the risk of serious confrontations increases in the future, incentives for cooperation in preventing or managing them will increase. In fact, it is always possible that steps towards a new collaborative-competitive relationship, similar in some respects to the Nixon-Brezhnev détente model, will be undertaken only after the superpowers experience dangerous confrontations. A new crisis that takes the two superpowers once again to the brink of thermonuclear war may have a catalytic function in this respect similar to that provided by the Cuban missile crisis.

In the meanwhile the Reagan administration is likely to rely more on unilateral policies and measures than on cooperative strategies to achieve the objective of crisis prevention. We have discussed several of these—U.S. economic and military assistance, the construction and strengthening of collective security alliances, preventive diplomacy, deterrence. Given the greater prominence deterrence strategy is assuming once again as the major backup for the administration's effort to develop a new containment policy, it behooves us to take stock of its uses and limitations.

A strengthening of the U.S. military posture is essential given the failure of détente and the continued buildup of Soviet forces. Under present and foreseeable world conditions there is no substitute for a strong, clear, articulate deterrence posture. But at the same time it is incumbent on U.S. policymakers, Congress, and the public to understand that *strengthening military capabilities cannot substitute for a well-conceived, realistically grounded foreign policy.* Creating a position of strength or a more favorable balance of forces is only a means to an end. The end itself—i.e., the kind of relationship with the Soviet Union that the strengthening of the U.S. military posture is designed to help achieve—must be clarified, and, as was noted in Chapter 2, a comprehensive strategy for developing that kind of relationship must be formulated.

Beginning with President Ford and continuing with his successors in the White House, U.S. leaders have gradually given greater emphasis to containment alone as the basis for policy toward the Soviet Union. Yet many of the conditions that made containment possible during the cold war are lacking in the contemporary era. Collective security arrangements with allies in Europe and elsewhere are much more difficult to arrange or to bring into play as instruments for containment today than in the late forties, the fifties, and the sixties. Even heavy military expenditures will not create a position of strength that can be converted into appreciable diplomatic dividends. Strengthening of the U.S. military posture may be a necessary condition, but it is certainly not a sufficient condition for achieving the limited objective of "containment without confrontation" in U.S. relations with the Soviet Union. The other conditions and strategies needed for this purpose will require equal emphasis and equal priority in policy planning.

More to the point, a substantial strengthening of U.S. military capabilities will not provide much assurance that rivalry with the Soviet Union in third areas can be moderated and controlled to avoid further extension of Soviet influence, additional crises, and confrontations. We must not forget the hard-earned lessons regarding the limited utility of deterrence for preventing encroachments on U.S. interests in third areas that were given during the cold war. Although deterrence was an essential and useful part of containment during that period, it became increasingly evident that deterrence was an unreliable, imperfect strategy at middle and lower levels of conflict. There were several reasons for this unreliability. A state that is dissatisfied with a given situation or sees an opportunity to advance its interests can usually find some way of challenging the status quo, even in the face of a commitment by the United States that is backed by a deterrence posture of some kind. As was evident during the cold war, it was difficult for the United States to devise a comprehensive strategy that deterred all of the options available to an opponent. *This gap in deterrence is even greater in today's world, and it is evident particularly in situations characterized by low-level conflict, internal instability, national liberation struggles, indirect and limited involvement by outside powers, use of proxies, etc.*

Even when U.S. deterrence strategy has been successful, it can often best be regarded as no more than a *time-buying* strategy. Successful deterrence seldom removes the underlying conflict of interest or the causes of instability. The motivation of other actors to change the status quo in a third area usually persists in the face of deterrence and may become even stronger. The dissatisfied actors may simply create or await more favorable circumstances to renew their challenge. But successful deterrence does at least provide time for the two sides to use, if they will, to work out ways of reducing the conflict-escalation potential of the situation.[8] It is often the better part of wisdom to regard deterrence, therefore, as an aid to other conflict-resolution methods to be achieved via diplomacy. Another lesson learned from misapplications of deterrence strategy by the United States during the Cold War is that deterrence, which is only an instrument of policy, cannot reliably compensate for a foreign policy that is confused or mistaken, or one that enjoys inadequate or unstable support from Congress and the public.

Finally, one must ask whether it is realistic to expect of U.S. foreign policy that it prevent any further extension of Soviet influence or that it induce Soviet leaders to forego this aim altogether. Rather, the United States must expect that the Soviet Union will continue to seek to enhance its global position, winning on some occasions and losing on others. What U.S. policy can hope to do is to compete more effectively itself where it can, to act to limit the expansion of Soviet influence, particularly in areas of high interest to the United States, and to induce, by a variety of means, however imperfectly, Soviet leaders to moderate their behavior.

Notes

1. This definition of norms is similar to the concept of "tacit rules of the game" employed by Joanne Gowa and Nils H. Wessell, *Ground Rules: Soviet and American Involvement in Regional Conflicts,* Philadelphia Policy Papers (Philadelphia: Foreign Policy Research Institute, 1982). This monograph provides a useful discussion of some aspects of the problem of managing U.S.-Soviet rivalry. Particularly suggestive of the kind of policy planning germane to the problem is the authors' discussion of the ways in which various measures of restraint and consultation might be applied in three regions: the Horn of Africa, South Africa, and Yugoslavia.

2. Robert Legvold, "The Super Rivals: Conflict in the Third World," *Foreign Affairs* 57 (Spring 1979):755–778.

3. The proposal, said to be under study, is briefly described in a newsletter, *Basic Positions,* issued by the American Committee on East-West Accord (Washington, D.C., 1982). In this particular statement Latin America and the Caribbean are not listed among the geographical areas to which the

proposed agreement would apply. A number of other questions concerning the desirability and feasibility of the proposal also come to mind, which the American Committee study will presumably address: (1) How would such an agreement be reconciled with existing U.S. and Soviet commitments and involvements in third areas? (2) Would the United States and the Soviet Union be permitted under such an agreement to help defend an ally or friendly government from external attack or from an internal coup or armed insurrection? (3) Would the two superpowers be permitted to transfer weapons and send military advisers to countries in these geographical areas? (4) Could such an agreement remain a bilateral one between the United States and the Soviet Union or would it have to include other countries that could intervene in third areas either as covert proxies of the superpowers or on their own? (5) What arrangements would be made for monitoring compliance with the agreement and for resolving disagreements as to whether violations of its provisions have occurred?

4. Legvold, "The Super Rivals."

5. U.S. Congress, Senate, Committee on Foreign Relations, Subcommittee on African Affairs, *Hearings on Angola* (Washington, D.C.: Government Printing Office, 1976), p. 113.

6. Thomas C. Schelling, *The Strategy of Conflict* (Cambridge, Mass.: Harvard University Press, 1960); and Richard Smoke, *War: Controlling Escalation* (Cambridge, Mass.: Harvard University Press, 1977).

7. *New York Times,* September 23, 1981. Reagan's letter was sent a day before the initial meeting of Secretary of State Haig and Foreign Minister Gromyko at the United Nations. The verbatim text of President Reagan's letter was not released. The quoted material is from the summary statement issued by the State Department. The letter was said to be one of several exchanged by Reagan and Brezhnev in 1981. Reagan repeated his hopes for "a more constructive relationship" with the Soviet Union in his commencement address at Eureka College on May 9, 1982.

8. Alexander L. George and Richard Smoke, *Deterrence in American Foreign Policy: Theory and Practice* (New York: Columbia University Press, 1974).

The Contributors

Coit D. Blacker is the associate director of the Arms Control and Disarmament Program at Stanford University and a lecturer in the Department of Political Science. In 1982, under the auspices of the International Affairs Fellowship Program of the Council on Foreign Relations, Dr. Blacker served as special assistant to Senator Gary Hart (D.-Colo.) on arms control and U.S.-Soviet relations.

Barry M. Blechman is vice president of the Roosevelt Center for American Policy Studies in Washington, D.C. He served as assistant director of the U.S. Arms Control and Disarmament Agency during the Carter administration, at which time he was the deputy chairman of the U.S. delegation for conventional arms transfer negotiations.

George W. Breslauer is associate professor of Political Science at the University of California at Berkeley. He is the author of *Five Images of the Soviet Future* and of *Khrushchev and Brezhnev as Leaders*. He has coauthored two books and contributed numerous articles to journals and collected volumes.

Gloria Duffy is executive director of The Ploughshares Fund, a San Francisco–based foundation. Educated at Occidental College and Columbia University, she was a Fellow of the Arms Control and Disarmament Program at Stanford University when this essay was written. She has been a resident consultant at The Rand Corporation and communications director of the Arms Control Association in Washington, D.C.

Alexander L. George is Graham H. Stuart Professor of International Relations at Stanford University. He is the author of *Deterrence in*

American Foreign Policy (with Richard Smoke); *Woodrow Wilson and Colonel House* (with Juliette L. George); *Presidential Decision-making in Foreign Policy* (Westview, 1980), and *Limits of Coercive Diplomacy* (with David K. Hall and William E. Simons).

Paul Gordon Lauren is professor of the Ambassador Mansfield Course on International Relations at the University of Montana, where he teaches diplomatic history. He is a former Rockefeller Foundation Humanities Fellow. He has published two books, *Diplomats and Bureaucrats* and *Diplomacy: New Approaches in History, Theory, and Policy,* in addition to articles in *Diplomatic History, International Studies Quarterly, Journal of Conflict Resolution,* and *International History Review.*

Larry C. Napper is a career Foreign Service officer currently assigned to the Office of Soviet Union Affairs, Department of State. Prior to this assignment, he served on the staffs of the U.S. embassies in Moscow and Gaborone, Botswana. Mr. Napper spent the 1979–1980 academic year at Stanford University, where the research for the case studies included in this volume was completed.

Janne E. Nolan is currently a visiting scholar at the Georgetown Center for Strategic and International Studies and was formerly a Research Fellow at the Stanford University Arms Control Program. From 1977 to 1980, Ms. Nolan was an official of the U.S. Arms Control and Disarmament Agency and served as a delegate to the U.S.-Soviet Arms Transfer Negotiations.

Alan Platt, senior associate at the Rand Corporation, completed most of the work on this chapter while he was a National Fellow at the Hoover Institution, Stanford University. He has previously served as chief foreign policy assistant to former Senator Edmund Muskie and as chief of the Arms Transfer Division of the U.S. Arms Control and Disarmament Agency.

I. William Zartman is professor of international politics and director of African studies at the Johns Hopkins School of Advanced International Studies in Washington, D.C., and president of the Middle East Studies Association. He is coauthor with Maureen Berman of *The Practical Negotiator* and coauthor and editor of *The Negotiation Process* and *The 50% Solution,* and he has helped establish the international negotiating seminar for the International Peace Academy. Dr. Zartman is a consultant for the State Department and has written a number of works on the Middle East and African politics.

Index

Aaron, David, 237
Accommodation, 35, 177–178, 256, 365
ACDA. *See* Arms Control and Disarmament Agency
Acheson, Dean, 371
Ad hoc ground rules, 389–393
Adjudication, 48
Administrative Reforms Mission (MRA), 347
Afghanistan, 43, 45, 46. *See also* Soviet Union, and Afghanistan
Africa, 5, 36, 42, 44, 45, 51, 156, 269, 352, 394
   sub-Saharan, 267, 268
   See also individual countries
African Frontline Presidents, 165–166, 167, 168, 169, 171, 175, 177, 345, 346
African political terrain variables, 156, 169–176
Agreement on Prevention of Nuclear War (APNW) (1973), 8, 110–111, 112–113, 114–115, 116, 128, 129, 139, 151(n1), 261, 372, 374, 379
Aircraft, 264, 276. *See also* Soviet Union, MiG-23s; Soviet Union, transport aircraft
Air defense systems, 264, 277
Air Force Intelligence (U.S.), 299
Alabama claims arbitration (1871–1872), 49
Åland Islands, 40, 42
Algeria, 85, 228, 348, 349, 351, 355, 360

and Soviet Union, 90, 93, 281, 296
Ali, Salem Robaye, 230
Allende, Salvador, 326
Alvor Agreement (1975), 157, 158, 159, 173, 174, 199, 202, 203, 205, 206, 213, 215, 389
American Committee on East-West Accord, 379
Angola-Dutch treaty (1824), 45
Angola, 156–158, 159, 165, 346, 353. *See also* Angolan crisis
Angolan crisis (1975), 8–9, 27, 133–134, 156, 158–164, 170(table), 171–172, 173, 365. *See also* U.S.-Soviet relations, and Angola
Antisatellite weapons, 10
APNW. *See* Agreement on Prevention of Nuclear War
Arab-Israeli conflict, 24, 66. *See also* October War; Six-Day War; Soviet Union, and Arab-Israeli conflict; United States, and Arab-Israeli conflict; War of Attrition
Arab League, 228, 351
Arafat, Yasser, 353
Arbatov, Georgi, 126, 127, 303
Arbitration, 48, 49
Argentina, 275
Armed Forces Movement. *See* Lisbon coup
Armed Forces of the North (FAN), 347
Arms control, 3, 6, 10, 88, 319, 330,

Soviet Union
and Afghanistan, 2, 12, 238, 307,
308, 309, 333, 376, 388, 394
and Africa, 133–134, 269, 292, 350
and Angola, 157, 159, 160, 162,
164, 172, 173–174, 187, 199,
204, 209, 212, 241, 242, 328
and Arab-Israeli conflict, 65–67,
70–76, 85, 86–88, 89, 90–91,
96–97, 140, 187, 325. *See also*
Egypt, and Soviet Union
and arms control, 88
arms transfers, 255–256, 281,
282(table), 296, 298, 325. *See
also* Conventional arms
transfers
Communist Party of the (CPSU),
119, 125
and conflict resolution, 358
and Cuba, 11–12, 163, 187, 200,
229, 338, 385. *See also* Cuban
missile crisis
decision-making elite, 66,
105(n110), 308–309, 333, 387
and Ethiopia, 229, 230, 231, 232,
235, 238, 239, 240, 241–242,
243–244, 245, 246, 247–248,
281, 328
and international communist
movement, 20, 333
Jews, 205, 327, 328, 337
and Latin America, 326
and Middle East, 65–70, 80, 88,
90–95, 96, 257, 326
MiG-23s, 296–298, 306, 309
military capabilities, 121, 122, 128,
131–132, 133, 321–322, 333,
337, 338, 395. *See also*
Strategic forces parity
naval forces, 133, 288, 289–290,
291, 292–295, 309, 321
and North Korea, 258–259
and Ogaden War, 225, 231–232,
234–235, 236, 242, 351
Peace Program, 119
and PRC, 161. *See also* Sino-
Soviet split
and Rhodesia, 167, 175–176
and Sino-American relations, 25,
325, 329
and Somalia, 229–230, 232,

242–243, 244
third area foreign policy, 3, 7, 28,
121, 127–128, 131–132, 204,
242, 243, 247–248, 255, 269,
322, 323, 326–327, 328, 375,
388
transport aircraft, 133, 251(n46)
and West Germany, 88
See also Détente; North Vietnam;
Russia; U.S.-Soviet relations;
individual countries, and Soviet
Union
Spain, 36, 356
Spanish Sahara, 360
Spheres of influence, 6, 43–46, 52,
163, 331, 375, 384
SS-20, 333
Stalin, Joseph, 383, 386
"Standstill Diplomacy: 1971–1973,"
142
Stevenson, Adlai, 303
Stevenson amendment, 217, 328
Stone, Richard, 300–301, 303, 312
Strategic Arms Limitation Talks
(SALT), 327
I (1972), 22, 107, 122, 128, 132,
332
II, 2, 5, 10, 11, 12, 150, 163, 205,
216, 239, 264, 292, 297, 300,
302, 303, 304, 305, 306,
307–308, 309, 313, 329, 332,
337
Strategic forces parity, 122, 123–125,
127, 128, 129–130, 131, 132,
336
Strategic studies, 4
Submarines. *See* Cuban missile crisis,
1970
Sudan, 92, 231, 228, 245
Suez Canal, 44, 142, 145, 190
Sumatra, 45
Summits. *See* Moscow summits;
Vienna summit; Vladivostok
meeting
Surface-to-surface missiles, 259, 264,
276, 277
SWAPO. *See* South West African
Peoples Organization
Sweden, 37, 157
Switzerland, 38
Syria, 85, 91, 351